Conversations with Nostradamus

His Prophecies Explained

(Revised and Updated)

Volume Two

BY

DOLORES CANNON

Reprinted by permission of The Putnam Publishing Group from *The Prophecies of Nostradamus* by Erika Cheetham. © Copyright 1975, Erika Cheetham. Extracted from *The Prophecies of Nostradamus*, published by Corgi Books, a division of Transworld Publishers Ltd. © Copyright 1973 by Erika Cheetham.
All rights reserved.
Reprinted by permission of David Higham Associates, London, from *Nostradamus* by James Laver. © Copyright 1942, James Laver.
Reprinted by permission of William Morrow & Co. from *My Life and Prophecies* by Jean Dixon. © Copyright 1969, Jeane Dixon.

For permission, or serialization, condensation, adaptions, or for our catalog of other publications, write to Ozark Mountain Publishers, P.O. Box 754, Huntsville, AR 72740-0754, Attn.: Permission Department.

Library of Congress Cataloging-in-Publication Data
Cannon, Dolores, 1931 - 2014
Conversations with Nostradamus by Dolores Cannon
Communications from Nostradamus via several mediums through hypnosis, supervised by D. Cannon. Includes the Prophecies of Nostradamus, in Middle French with English translation. Includes index. Contents: v. I-II-III (Revised editions)
1. Nostradamus, 1503-1566. 2. Prophecies. 3. Hypnosis. 4. Reincarnation therapy.
    5. Astrology.
I. Cannon, Dolores, 1931-2014   II. Nostradamus, 1503-1566. Prophecies. English
    & French.   III. Title.
Library of Congress Catalog Card Number: 92-60547
ISBN 0-9632776-1-8 (v. II)

First Edition Printed by America West Publishers, 1990
Revised Edition published 1992 1994 1997 2001 2011 2012 2015 2016 2018 x2 2019 2020 x2, 2021
Cover Design: Joe Alexander; Computer Enhancement: Jenelle Johannes
Book set in Old Style 7, San Marco & Eurostile typefaces.
Book Design: Kris Kleeberg
Published by:

OZARK
MOUNTAIN
PUBLISHERS
P.O. Box 754
Huntsville, AR 72740

WWW.OZARKMT.COM
Printed in the United States of America

Dedication

To John Feeley,
who had the courage and curiosity to cross the boundaries
of time and space, to wander into the realm of the unknown
to bring back this information.
He also had a great adventure while doing it.
Thanks, John, for taking me along with you.

Since Volume One and Two were first published, I have received many requests from readers to be put in touch with John Feeley for astrological purposes. I wish to report that John died in the summer of 1990 of AIDS at the age of 38. He had a copy of this dedication taped to the wall by his bed. He was very proud to have been a part of this research project. Thanks, John, for a job well done. Good luck in your work on the other side.

Books by Dolores Cannon

Conversations With Nostradamus, Volume I
Conversations With Nostradamus, Volume II
Conversations With Nostradamus, Volume III
Jesus and the Essenes
They Walked With Jesus
Between Death & Life
(Formerly titled Conversations With A Spirit)
A Soul Remembers Hiroshima
Keepers of the Garden
The Legend of Starcrash
Legacy from the Stars
The Custodians
The Convoluted Universe, Book One

For more information about any of the above titles or other titles in our catalog, please write or visit our website.

OZARK MOUNTAIN PUBLISHERS

P.O. Box 754
Huntsville, AR 72740

WWW.OZARKMT.COM

Wholesale Inquiries Welcome

Table of Contents

Section Three: Work in the Aftermath

Section One

The New Contact

Chapter 1

The Adventure Continues

THE IDEA OF WRITING A SEQUEL never even occurred to me when I took on the assignment of translating Nostradamus' quatrains. I thought that by selecting a few hundred at random I would have enough to make an interesting book but the more we translated, the more involved the story became. The book just kept growing and growing. I began to wonder how big a book could be and still be salable. I had to start discarding and selecting which quatrains to include. I had to decide which ones were more relevant to the story and which ones Nostradamus wished me to relate to the world. Finally it became apparent that this could go on for quite a while. As the story evolved and more pieces of the puzzle came to light, I continued adding to the book, but at this rate it might be years before the project would be finished. It was then I decided that I had to call a halt to this and tie up the loose ends of the first volume.

Reluctantly, I put the other information aside to form into a sequel. When I did this several things happened that caused the story to take some more strange twists and turns. Since these new events were leading away from the story of Elena and Brenda, I then knew for certain that there would have to be another book. The story of my adventures with Nostradamus continued but in a different direction. As always, life gets in the way and has a habit of altering circumstances. But the determination of either Nostradamus, the powers that be, or whoever it was that was directing this project, was strong enough to find ways around any obstacle that was put in its path. What more obvious proof did I need that this project was indeed destined to be completed? How much evidence did I need that I was merely a pawn or instrument in revealing to the world something which was begun and hidden 400 years ago?

This was a project that was assigned to me without my conscious knowledge or agreement. If I had realized the scope of it, I don't know that I would have taken it on. It all began so inconspicuously and innocently that I had no feeling of being overwhelmed until I was months into the task. By then, it was too late to back out. Maybe this was the wisdom behind it. "They" apparently counted upon my insatiable curiosity to lead me on and not allow me to drop the assignment when the going got tough. They knew of my fascination with puzzles and my desire to bring unknown knowledge to light. Whatever their motives behind the strange workings of this project, they knew I would not give up until the job was finished. Nostradamus had already astounded me with his wisdom, his wonderful use of symbolism, the pure art behind his work which has never truly been revealed to the world. I can appreciate the time and mental effort the interpreters and translators have put into their work over the years, but they have never quite been able to grasp the true greatness of the man and the trials he went through to disguise his words in order to preserve them for posterity. Maybe through my efforts we can at last see him for what he was in order to take heed of his warnings.

As explained in the first volume of this work, Elena was the key, the bridge to the great man Nostradamus. Through my work with hypnotic regression and reincarnation, I discovered that she had been one of Nostradamus' students in a past life in the 1500's in France. Or maybe it would be more accurate to say that Nostradamus discovered me. By some unknown power, he was able to sense that I was in communication with his student, and he was also aware that I was living in a future time. In his desire to reveal the true meanings of his prophecies to our generation, he gave me the assignment of translation. In a sense he *ordered* me to take on the job. He impressed upon me the urgency of the task and the importance of it being completed *now* in our time period.

Had there really been a way of getting out of this? I honestly don't know. I could have walked away from it. When the information first began to come through, I wrestled within myself over whether I really wanted to know what the future held. I had a perfect way out. Elena moved to Alaska immediately after the project was initiated. It could have ended there because there wasn't enough information for a book. I could have put the tapes in a box and labeled them for use as a possible chapter in a book of miscellaneous regressions to be written sometime down the road. But the urgency, the tone of pleading in Nostradamus' voice stayed with me. His last words to me were that he would come through anyone else that I chose to work with, he was that determined. Elena had been the bridge between our world and his; the key to this Pandora's box. And as with that proverbial box, all the troubles of the world could now be released to public view.

The idea intrigued me enough as a psychic investigator to want to attempt it as an experiment. I had to see if he really meant what he said, that he would truly be able to speak to me through someone else. I knew there was no way out; my curiosity was too great. The only possibility for escape would be if the contact through Elena was a one-time fluke. In that case, Nostradamus could be relegated and returned to his proper niche in time, because there would be no possible way to complete the assignment.

This is where Brenda entered the scenario. Brenda was a quiet, unassuming and extremely sensitive music student whose I.Q. level had been tested at the genius level. Whether this had any connection or not, she had proven to be an excellent somnambulistic subject and I had been working with her for over a year on other projects. She had decided to direct her talents toward a career in classical music, preferably composing, and her whole world revolved around that. Working and going to college took up all of her time. The story of my experiment with her and the breakthrough once again to Nostradamus was told in the first book. Then the floodgate opened and the translations of the quatrains inundated us. During that time over 300 were interpreted. But they came forth in a hodgepodge of disconnected pieces. I had the unenviable task of putting them into some continuity. Only then did we see that the story that unfolded was awe-inspiring and horrible. Was this truly the world that Nostradamus foresaw? Were these the inescapable events in our future? He said he was telling us these things so we could do something to change the future; to stop these things from coming to pass.

What Nostradamus revealed to me is not the future I want for myself, my children and my grandchildren. The translation and interpretation of his quatrains is remarkable and clear when he explains them piece by piece and symbol by symbol. I do believe they have finally been interpreted correctly, but this does not mean I want them to occur. The story told in my first book and in this sequel is *his* vision, *his* prophecy, *his* picture of the world to come. Even if none of it ever happens it still makes an interesting tale, and this is my philosophy. This is the only way I can deal with this and not become caught up in it and overwhelmed. My subjects feel the same way. They feel the work is important but their private lives come first. They think it is fascinating work, but they have no intention of allowing it to consume them. Thus, while working on this project, we live in two separate worlds simultaneously while trying to convey the knowledge of this great sage to humanity.

Another one of the characters in my first book was John Feeley. He came into the picture quite by "accident," and by "coincidence," just when Nostradamus told me I would need a "drawer of horoscopes," since many of his quatrains contained astrological information. Since John was a professional astrologer, and also interested in psychic phenomena, he was the perfect one to help on this project. John was born in Massachusetts and while still a teenager studied with Isabelle Hickey, the foremost astrologer in Boston at that time. Afterwards, he went on to study with the Rosicrucians in San Jose, California. Although he received the basics from these people, he was mostly self-taught after that. He researched and developed his talents and skills in the direction of esoteric astrology. He became a member of the American Federation of Astrologers in 1971. He was brought up as a Catholic, but he describes himself as a deist, one who believes in God. He says, "I've come more to universalist understanding. I'm interested in all religions and all faiths because there's a golden thread of authority running through all of them. I see God alive and aware in everybody and everything. So that's my personal philosophy. Spiritually, I try to do the best I can. I believe in all cultures and all beliefs. They all have a validity to them." John has traveled widely and lived in other countries.

He began sitting in on some of the sessions to clarify and date some of the quatrains through his astrological ephemeris. His help was invaluable. It was to become even more valuable in the future as fate was to take over and mold this story into yet another strange direction.

After a year of working on this, it became obvious it was no accident that all of us came together as players in this strange scenario. Could all of this have been ordained and plotted on the other side so that our paths would cross? Was this really our true destiny in this life? As I look back on it now I cannot believe that it was mere coincidence we all came together in this project. It was orchestrated too well. By whom? Coincidence? Fate? The entire set of circumstances was really so fragile. By one single event being out of place we might have missed each other entirely and this story might never have been told. But the energy behind this project was so great that it had taken on a life of its own. And like a snowball rolling downhill, it slowly gathered momentum, size and power. There was no stopping it. The final impact must be felt.

In this experiment I used Erika Cheetham's book, *The Prophecies of Nostradamus,* because it was the latest translation of Nostradamus' quatrains. The quatrains were in both the original French and English. It was easy and convenient to read, and it contained her explanation of obscure and foreign words used in the quatrains. Beneath many of them she gave her interpretation based on her studies. There were also many quatrains which contained no explanations. These had never been satisfactorily interpreted by anyone. Many were so vague they could have applied to many different events, or the symbolism was so convoluted it was impossible to interpret. Neither I nor anyone else involved in this experiment had read or studied these quatrains beforehand. It would have done us no good anyway. If, for 400 years, dedicated people had been spending large portions of their lives trying to understand them, how could we hope to by scanning through the book? Besides, when the interpretations began to come through they were like nothing anyone had ever imagined, yet they were so clear and concise when explained by the master himself.

At the beginning of each session, after she was in a deep trance, I would instruct Brenda to contact Nostradamus through the magic mirror which he utilized to see his visions. This was the same mirror that

Elena had seen Nostradamus use during her past life as his student Dyonisus. When Brenda also saw this mirror in his study, it became a focal point in our communication with him. It became our magic doorway between his world and ours, the connecting link in the joining of our spirits. When Brenda contacted Nostradamus, he was asked to meet us in a special meeting place. This was done according to his explicit instructions given through both Elena and Brenda. It appeared that this special meeting place was in some other dimension. It was gray and formless with no more substance than drifting clouds. Here Nostradamus would show Brenda scenes and explain the meanings of the quatrains to her. When our allotted time was up he would simply leave, often offering no explanation but merely departing quickly. When this occurred the visions were also cut off. The only time she had a visual observation of where he lived was during our first contact. All other meetings were held in this strange otherworldly place after he had first been contacted through the magic mirror.

After working with Nostradamus on the translation of his quatrains for many months, a pattern began to develop. But something was disturbing me. At first it was only like a vague shadow, it would drift over my mind for just the fraction of a second. It was there only long enough to cause a rippling in the calm surface, just a hint that all was not as it appeared to be. It was a whisper that there was more going on than appeared on the surface. Over the months it remained vague but became stronger. It was a persistent nagging in the back of my mind that I was a mere pawn, but for *what*?

In the beginning, I was so intent on the project that I was not aware of the creeping uneasiness. Since everything about the project was weird and strange, what was one more unusual feeling? At the onset, we were only able to interpret about five or six quatrains at a session. This gradually increased until we were dealing with as many as 30. Quatrains concerning the far past were passed over in favor of more immediate ones. He promised we would return to these but he felt the quatrains concerning present and future events were of more importance to us.

As the number of quatrains we had translated increased, the uneasy feeling became more obvious. Often when I read the quatrain to him he would immediately give me the interpretation. At other times he would ask me to repeat it, emphasizing certain phrases and wanting the spelling of certain words. At these times it was almost as though he didn't recognize his own work. At first I thought it was because the translators had changed the wording so much when putting it into English that it was unrecognizable to him. I could almost see him scratching his head and wondering which quatrain I were reading. As we continued, I wondered if he *did* recognize it.

One day I made the offhand remark to Brenda, "Wouldn't it be funny if we were helping him write these?" These words were hardly out of my mouth when I felt cold chills run through my body.

"Yes," she answered, "and he's saying, 'Please repeat that. I'm writing these down and I didn't get that part. Would you please spell that.'" She laughed at her joke, but suddenly it was not funny to me. I was cold all over. The vague nagging thoughts which had haunted me were now given form and substance. For some reason the idea frightened me, because it was unfathomable. Then I remembered what he had said about not being able to finish the seventh century of quatrains because the time lines had not been clear. I then got the full impact of his explanation of how he received his quatrains. He had said that while in trance he would write, but it was as though the forces from beyond the mirror would be guiding his hand. When he returned to consciousness, he would be aware of what he had seen but was often surprised at what he had written. While in trance he would see several things, one scene right after another. Then he would see that only one quatrain had been written, but the complex meaning applied to all he had seen. He was often amazed at the complexity of the puzzle and confessed that he felt there was some other element, other than his conscious mind, that was better at manipulating the words into these puzzles.

Of course! At the time I thought it had sounded like automatic writing. Could it be possible? We knew that through some strange mechanism we did not understand, we were in communication with him while he was still alive in his time period in France. He had been most emphatic that we were not in touch with the dead. If he was alive at the same time we are alive, that brings up the theory of simultaneous time which is something I do not understand and do not wish to understand. Every time I try to think of this concept of everything occurring at once: past, present and future, I do not feel enlightened, I just get dizzy. So I have tried to leave that idea well enough alone.

Later, when I was speaking to someone who had read about Nostradamus, he said, "Do you know that Nostradamus said in one of his biographies that he was helped in the writing of the quatrains? He was helped by what he called the 'spirits of the future.'"

If I hadn't been sitting down I think I would have fallen down. I was stunned. Is that what we were, the spirits of the future? I made a mental note to try to find that book when I began my research and see what else it had to say.

But the whole idea was preposterous. Nostradamus wrote his quatrains in the 1500's in French. They had been published, translated, interpreted, and pondered over for 400 years. I had bought the latest translation in 1986 and I was reading from that. To my rational mind the idea was impossible. But if it were impossible, why did the idea persist? Why did it make me so uncomfortable? Because somehow, in some inconceivable way, it held the whisper of truth?

So on the faint chance there might be something to it, I became very careful in working with Nostradamus. I only read the quatrain, deliberately not giving him any more information, however unwittingly, about our time period or anything that might relate to the quatrains. I was not going to consciously influence him in any way. I don't know if this did any good. If he were somehow tapping into our subconscious (as he said he did), he would still have access to our minds to explain the visions he was seeing. But the only way I felt I could handle this was to become more cautious, and I felt it gave me more control anyway. At least I didn't feel as uncomfortable. The vague feelings had retreated. I just wouldn't think about simultaneous time and things that gave me headaches.

Chapter 2

𝕸ore Quatrains
𝕴nterpreted by 𝕭renda

THESE ARE SOME OF THE QUATRAINS that were not included in the first book. Many of those pertaining to the past have been excluded because of their lack of pertinence to this project. I have included only those that had interesting twists to their interpretation or those that have never been satisfactorily explained by other interpreters.

THE PAST

D: *The interpreters can't understand this next quatrain. They said it has to be absolutely wrong.*

B: That was the wrong thing to say. He's getting very upset.

D: *Well, tell him not to get upset with me. He gave a date in this one, and they said it has to be wrong because they can't understand it.*

B: He says he seems to remember their saying that before and he was able to prove *them* wrong.

CENTURY VI-54

Au poinct du jour au second chant du coq,	At daybreak at second cock-crow,
Ceulx de Tunes, de Fez, & de Bugie,	those of Tunis, Fez and of Bougie; the Arabs captured by the king
Par les Arabes captif le Roi Maroq,	of Morocco in the year sixteen
L'an mil six cens & sept, de Liturgie.	hundred and seven by the Liturgy.

D: *They don't understand why he put the word "liturgy" in there.*

B: He says he's not sure how they mean he was wrong. This quatrain does not refer to an actual confrontation or battle. What it refers to is the break of day, at second cock-crow. It represents the dawning of a new era. He says the history of mankind can be divided into general eras (ancient and present history, medieval times and the Middle Ages) according to the philosophical thought that was prevalent during that period of time. At this time a new era will become apparent. He specified second cock-crow, meaning that people are becoming aware that things are changing and perhaps becoming better. Until this time, North Africa in general had been strictly Islamic. At this time the leader of a kingdom will convert to Christianity and try to spread the influence of Christianity in this bastion of Muslim. He says that is why he put the word "liturgy," to try to give them the clue that this referred to religious and philosophical thought and not physical warfare. Up to this time, Islam had been very strong and had strongholds scattered across wide tracts of land. Now the tide was turning and it was time for Islam to retreat somewhat with Christianity filling in the gap for the time being.

D: *What about that date, 1607?*

B: He says this is when it will start. That *was* when it started taking place. He says he's getting confused because from his point of view it *will* be, and from our point of view it *was*. (*Laugh*) Whenever something new happens in philosophical thought, that particular branch of philosophy has a tendency to grow, and strongly affect areas that are under the influence of older philosophies that might be becoming tired, so to speak.

D: *Yes, you told me before that Nostradamus taught philosophy during his time and that's why he's interested in these philosophical events. I want to read to you what the translators said. I hope he doesn't get angry.*

B: He says he's not really sure he wants to hear it. But if you wish to read it, that is fine. He's already upset, so it's no big deal.

D: *They say, "This quatrain seems to be one of Nostradamus' total failures. He appears to see the fall of the Ottoman Empire through a new European king in 1607. But the only point in Nostradamus' favor is that no commentary can agree upon what is meant by the 'Liturgy.'"*

B: He says he doesn't recall mentioning anything about Europe in the entire quatrain. He was talking totally of North Africa. He's jumping up and down at this point. (*We laughed.*) He says it just emphasizes the importance of this communication, because he does not want his quatrains interpreted wrongly for all time to come. He's really getting excited. I suggest we continue to the next quatrain.

CENTURY IX-92

Le roi vouldra dans cité neuf entrer	The king will want to enter the new city, they come to subdue it
Par ennemis expugner lon viendra	through its enemies; a captive
Captif libere faulx dire & perpetrer	falsely freed to speak and act; the
Roi dehors estre, loin d'ennemis tiendra.	king to be outside, he will stay far from the enemy.

D: *I have said before that every time he refers to the new city they think he means New York.*

B: He says he'll admit that often he does, but it doesn't always hold true. It is easy to see why they relate that if you concentrate on the phrase "the new city." But he says this quatrain has already come to pass. This event took place during the French Revolution. The phrase "the new city" refers to Paris after the lower classes overthrew the upper classes taking over and changing everything from the way it was before. Because it was a totally different social order, he referred to it as a new city. He says the king wanted to make peace with the peasants and continue to be king. He released a spokesman from the Bastille who had been falsely imprisoned and then falsely released, because this spokesman was one of the peasants. The king was thinking that if he showed mercy he would sway the populace to his viewpoint. As soon as this prisoner's purpose was accomplished, he would have been guillotined.

D: *That's what is meant by "the captive falsely freed to speak and act. The king will be outside. He will stay far from the enemy."*

B: Yes. The king kept himself safe while keeping an eye on things. He does not say which king, he simply says "the king."

D: *Did he mean the King of France?*

B: Yes, but there is more than one king involved with the French Revolution. It might be safe to assume he's speaking of Louis XVI.

D: *There was more than one king? I don't know French history that well.*

B: Neither does this vehicle. Anyway, he says he doesn't want to discuss this quatrain much, for now that he has given the clues, one could study the history texts and find the event.

D: *Okay. That's one thing I have discovered. He's not telling us everything. He's still leaving some things for us to find out by ourselves.*

B: He says one must exercise the mind for it to grow or one would turn into a dullard.

D: *(Laugh) You can't have all the answers handed to you, can you?*

B: He says he has had too much practice with being mysterious. It's hard to open up all the way.

D: *I can believe that. This way we'll still have some mysteries in these puzzles allowing other people to see what they can get from them.*

CENTURY IV-44

*Deux gros de Mende, de Rondés
& Milhau,
Cahours, Limoges, Castres malo
sepmano
De nuech l'intrado de Bourdeaux
un cailhau,
Par Perigort au toc de la campano.*

The two large ones of Mende, of Rodez and Milhau, Cahors and Limoges, Castres a bad week: by night the entry; from Bordeaux an insult, through Perigord at the peal of the bell.

D: *Oh, that has so many names. I know I murdered them.* (Laugh)
B: He says, yes, he sees them limping off the battlefield now, dripping blood all over. (*I laughed.*) But he says not to worry, this quatrain has to do with the French Revolution.
D: *Then I don't have to worry about those names anyway.*
B: Not now. But later you will.
D: *I'm seeing them for the first time, and that's what makes it hard. I see all those names and I think, "Oh my gosh, I know I'm going to really make a mess of them."*
B: He says you could always take a course in French.
D: (Laugh) *Like he said, though, the French now is different than the French he speaks.*
B: This is true. But he says there would be less murdering involved. The accent you speak is misplaced in time due to the centuries between your time and his time. And he'd rather hear a misplaced French accent than a misplaced British accent.
D: *But I try the best I can.*
B: He realizes this.

CENTURY IV-57

*Ignare envie au grand Roi
supportee,
Tiendra propos deffendre les
escripitz:
Sa femme non femme par
un autre tentee,
Plus double deux ne fort ne criz.*

Ignorant envy supported by the great king, he will propose forbidding the writings. His wife, not his wife, tempted by another, no longer will the double dealing couple protest against it.

B: He says this quatrain has to do with Louis XVI and the French Revolution.
D: *The translators thought it had to do with Nostradamus' writings being forbidden by the king.*
B: No. He says that during the French Revolution many things were put under martial law, including the publication of flyers and pamphlets and such. People who published so-called inflammatory material were apt to be beheaded or get into trouble. He asks that you compare it with the American Revolution. Since that took place in the New

World instead of on the island of Great Britain, they had a lot more leeway and freedom in what they did. They were able to print a lot of pamphlets and flyers to stir up the blood. But he says in the French Revolution the king was *right there.*

CENTURY IV-47

Le noir farouche quand
    aura essayé
Sa main sanguine par feu,
fer, arcs tendus:
Trestout le peuple sera tant effrayé,
Voir les plus grans par col &
    pieds pendus.
	When the ferocious king will have exercised his bloody hand through fire, the sword and the bended bow. All the nation will be so terrified to see the great ones hanging by their neck and feet.

B: He says this quatrain refers to Robespierre and the time of the terror. It could have some indirect bearing on the events that are to come, but other quatrains have explained that in greater detail. The main thing he saw was all the nobility being hung and killed during the French Revolution and afterwards through the Reign of Terror with Robespierre.

D: *The translators said the quatrain is about the mad King Charles IX who killed for he sake of blood, and that it also refers to the French Huguenots.*

B: He says that indirectly, yes, it could refer to this. It was clever of them to figure that out for it was a bloody time also, but during the time of the French Revolution so much more blood was spilt. The Revolution was an important event in French history, and loomed very large in his vision.

CENTURY III-49

Regne Gaulois tu seras bien changé,
En lieu estrange est translaté
    l'empire:
En autres moeurs & lois seras rangé,
Roan & Chartres te feront bien
    du pire.
	Kingdom of France you will be greatly changed, the Empire expands to foreign places. You will be set up with other laws and customs; Rouen and Chartres will do their worst towards you.

Again I had great difficulty with the pronunciation of these names. Brenda corrected me with a definite French accent. It is interesting to note that a man who was familiar with French was present during this session. He said later that she was pronouncing these names with an Old French accent.

B: He says this quatrain refers to the French Revolution. It refers to the king and the royal family of France being ousted, and a Republic set up instead thereby changing the laws and the rules. But France's Empirical power will spread throughout the new world for a period of time. As well as continuing, it also will spread in the Far East. He says this quatrain mainly refers to the great changes that took place in France in 1789 (the date of the French Revolution).

D: *The translators said this relates to the future. They said it has not happened yet because France has never been an Empire.*

This was a mistake on my part. Trying to conduct a regression session and also read from a book at the same time can be difficult. I misread the quote from the book. But before I could correct myself, Nostradamus figuratively jumped on me with both feet. He became very angry. Thus, it was obvious I was not interacting with Brenda's mind, because such a slip would not have upset her.

B: He's getting excited at this point. (*Speaking very fast.*) He says France *was* an Empire. France had Canada. France had Louisiana and its attached land, later ceded as the Louisiana Purchase. France had French Guiana. France had Indo-China. France—and he keeps naming all of these places. He's saying if that's not an empire, what is? Great Britain had a strip of seaboard on the American coast until it revolted. The British had an island here and an island there, and a port here and a port there. If that was called an empire, why wasn't France called an empire? (*She calmed down.*) He is very patriotic.

D: (Laugh) *I think he is. And he has good reason to be.*

I tried to soothe his ruffled feathers by reading it correctly, but he found fault with that as well.

D: *The translator says, "This is important because Nostradamus here calls France an Empire rather than a kingdom and clearly sees a change in the future."*

B: He says the British were called an empire rather than a kingdom, even though they were led by a king and not an emperor. And France was led by an emperor (Napoleon) for a while, but then it became a democracy. He says even though it's in the future from his point of view, from our point of view it should be history long past. People should go back and read history books once more.

CENTURY III-97

Nouvelle loi terre neufve occuper,
Vers la Syrie, Judee & Palestine:
Le grand empire barbare corruer,
Avant que Phœbus son siecle
*   determine.*

A new law will occupy a new land around Syria, Judea and Palestine. The great barbarian Empire will crumble before the century of the sun is finished.

B: He says this quatrain refers to the forays and conquests of Napoleon. He will relate this in the past tense since it's in our past. Napoleon traveled far and wide, and established occupation rule in many countries in the Middle East in the process of tracking down cultural heritage and cultural artifacts. He says the century of the sun refers to Louis XIV, the Sun King. Michel de Notredame was predicting that Napoleon would not be successful, and his quest for world conquest would fail within a hundred years of Louis XIV's time.

Nostradamus is amazingly accurate with this prediction. King Louis XIV died in 1715, and Napoleon was jailed in exile on St. Helena in 1815. His empire did crumble within a hundred years of the time of the Sun King.

B: He says you should be able to go to your history books and correlate the quatrain with the African and Middle Eastern campaigns of Napoleon. The phrase, the barbaric empires will fail, represents that the javelins and curved swords the Arab soldiers and horsemen had were not comparable to the muskets and guns that Napoleon's troops had.

D: *The translators say this quatrain refers to the creation of the state of Israel.*

B: He says this is incorrect.

D: *And they think the 20th century is the century of the sun.*

B: He says that is a *very* egocentric attitude. The century of the sun is the century of Louis XIV, the Sun King. He says this is the purpose of this project, to clear up the misconceptions that have occurred.

CENTURY VIII-59

Par deux fois hault, par deux fois mis à bas	Twice put up and twice cast down, the East will also weaken the
L'orient aussi l' occident faiblira	West. Its adversary after several
Son adversaire apres plusieurs combats,	battles chased by sea will fail at time of need.
Par mer chassé au besoin faillira.	

B: He says this quatrain refers to Napoleon. Napoleon came to power once and then was exiled. He escaped and came to power again. He was once more defeated and once more exiled. A critical point when the tide turned was that Napoleon had diverted some of his forces into a sort of navy, but they failed to come through at the crucial time.

D: *"The East will also weaken the West."*

B: That line refers to his disastrous attempt to conquer Russia by marching to Moscow. He was caught by the winter and his men were freezing to death. That's why he said "the East will conquer the West," since Napoleon was from a western nation and Russia is a part of the East. That event turned Napoleon's tides of fortune.

D: *The translators are interpreting the East as meaning Asia and say the quatrain refers to an attack on the Western Powers.*

CENTURY IV-42

Geneve & Langres par ceux
de Chartres & Dole,
Et par Grenoble captif au
Montlimard:
Seysett, Losanne par
fraudulente dole
Les trahiront par or soixante marc.

Geneva and Langres through the people of Chartres and Dôle, and Grenoble, captive at Montelimar: Seysel, Lausanne, through a fradulent trick will betray them for sixty gold marks.

He corrected me on each name as I fumbled through the pronunciation.

B: He says for the most part the city names are straightforward. Actually, what he's wanting to explain is the symbolism involved to give people a clue to his thought processes, so they can figure out where he's coming from with his quatrains. This quatrain deals with World War I. He says in this situation there are factions that want to try to work things out and balance the inadequacies before it is too late. One faction is represented by the name Geneva, meaning a city in a country that has always been neutral. He says this faction is bucking against factions that are very nationalistic. Also, there is another faction of people who were turncoats and who would, for the 60 gold marks, have betrayed France to Germany from within. The gold marks represent Germany. He says it seemed that all was lost, at first, to both the neutral faction and the nationalistic faction. It seemed for a while that the turncoat faction had gained ascendancy since, as you will know by looking back at your history, when the war first began things seemed pretty grim for the allied side. Another thing that didn't help, and this he represented by naming so many different cities, was the confusing tangle of diplomatic agreements between the various European countries at the time. He says if you will recall, what is in the past for you and the future for him, the ruling royal families of all the heads of state were related to each other. It was one big, not exactly happy, family of cousins, aunts, uncles, brothers, and sisters. So things were pretty decadent. He says this quatrain also applies to events during World War II, and in this case the 60 gold marks particularly refer to the events in that war where the higher echelon of German government were bought and sold like commodities. People could be bought, and everyone had their price, so they sold out.

D: *They are again translating it literally.*

B: (*With sarcasm.*) Yes, of course. Some of it could be applied to what will be happening with the Anti-Christ, but he says that particular situation is so broad and complex that almost anything could be applied to it.

CENTURY IV-46

Bien defendu le faict
par excellence,
Garde toy Tours de ta
proche ruine:
Londres & Nantes par
Reims fera defense
Ne passe outre au temps
de la bruine.

The deed, through its excellence, strongly forbidden, Tours, beware of your approaching ruin. London and Nantes will make a defense through Reims. Do not go further afield at the time of the fog.

B: He says this quatrain refers to the events of World War I particularly because of the line, "Don't go further in the field at the time of the fog." He was warning about mustard gas. He says "London claiming defense through the Reims" applies to the different nations banding together to fight on French soil to win the war.

CENTURY I-24

A cité neufue pensif pour
condemner,
L' oisel de proye au ciel se
vient offrir:
Apres victoire à captifs pardonner,
Cremone & Mantoue grands
maux aura souffert.

At the New City he is thoughtful to condemn; the bird of prey offers himself to the gods. After victory he pardons his captives. At Cremona and Mantua great hardships will be suffered.

B: He says this quatrain refers to the United States and World War I. Americans have a reputation for being generous and various nationalities who are not would be apt to take advantage of this. He says the end of the refrain pertains to the economic difficulties and the social upheaval that came between the World Wars.
D: *I thought the new city might refer to the United States.*
B: That and the vulture offering itself up to the gods. He says if you look on one of your coins, he sees an eagle and the phrase, "In God we trust."
D: *That's obvious then. "The bird of prey." But an eagle is not a vulture.*
B: He says an eagle is a vulture and so is a buzzard.
D: *Okay. I won't argue with him.* (Laugh)

It was a good thing I didn't dispute him. I should have known by this time that Nostradamus is more knowledgeable than I am about many things, and I should take his word for it. When I began my research I found that the Old World vultures are grouped with hawks and eagles. The New World species form two groups: one consisting of condors, vultures, and buzzards, and another that includes the eagle. I have always thought of vultures and buzzards as strictly scavengers but I found that they are listed as birds of prey along with the eagles. It's obvious he was quoting information he was familiar with in his land.

D: *The translators said this quatrain dealt with Napoleon and the siege of Mantua because of the names he mentioned.*

B: He says if you remember, the United States' troops were very prominent in Italy during World War I since Italy was on the same side as the United States during that war.

This was one of many examples where Nostradamus used the names of cities to indicate a country. The quatrains have been consistently misinterpreted because the translators often thought he was referring to an event that would happen in a certain city, when actually he was using those names as symbols for countries.

CENTURY I-36

*Tard la monarque se
    viendra repentir
De n'avoir mis à mort
    son adversaire:
Mais viendra bien à plus
    hault consentir,
Que tout son song par mort
    fera deffaire.*

Too late the king will repent that he did not put his adversary to death. But he will soon come to agree to far greater things which will cause all his line to die.

B: He says this refers to Germany and the fact that Hitler could have been stopped when he was young. The Chancellor and the ones who were in power did not do so, and they lived to regret the decision.

CENTURY I-88

*Le divin mal surprendra le
    grand prince,
Un peu devant aura femme
    espousee.
Son appuy & credit à un coup
    viendra mince,
Conseil mourra pour la teste rasee.*

The divine wrath overtakes the great Prince, a short while before he will marry. Both supporters and credit will suddenly diminish. Counsel, he will die because of the shaven heads.

B: He says this quatrain has multiple meanings, all of which have taken place. The most recent of which refers to the event of King Edward giving up the throne to marry a divorcée without offending the people. The other things it refers to happened earlier, and that's the most recent event to which that quatrain applies.

D: *I remember that event.*

CENTURY III-82

Friens, Antibor, villes autour
   de Nice,
Seront vastees fort par mer
   & par terre:
Les saturelles terre & mer
   vent propice,
Prins, morts, troussez, pillés,
   sans loi de guerre.

Frejus, Antibes, the towns around
Nice will be greatly devastated by
land and sea; the locusts, by land
and sea, the wind being favorable,
captured, dead, trussed up,
plundered without law of war.

B: He says this quatrain refers to events in World War II. He mentions
two towns, but in general all of France was raped by Germany. It was
then rescued and the Germans were devoured by the locusts on D-Day
when the great fleet crossed over the water and landed on the shores
of France. He says the weather that day was ideal for the operation.
Alternate meanings for those two anagrams also refer to some of the
major Allied victories in the Pacific and that region of the world.

D: *It doesn't necessarily have to be France.*

B: Correct.

D: *The interpreters have figured this out fairly well. They thought it was
the invasion of France.*

B: Yes. He says he understands that some of them have been interpreted
correctly or nearly so, and he is glad for that. But not all of them have
been, so he's trying to make things as clear as he can to be of the
greatest benefit.

D: *I'm finding out that they didn't even come close on many of them. They
couldn't even* imagine *some of the things he saw.*

CENTURY IV-58

Soleil ardent dans le gosier coller,
De sang humain arrouser terre
   Etrusque:
Chef seille d'eaue, mener
   son fils filer,
Captive dame conduicte
   en terre Turque.

To swallow the burning sun in the
throat, the Tuscan land sprinkled
with human blood, the leader
leads his son away, the pail of
water, a captive lady led into
Turkish lands.

B: He says this quatrain has to do with the career of Mussolini and Italy's
situation during World War II.

D: *I thought because he mentioned "Turkish" that it might refer to the
Anti-Christ.*

B: No, not in this case. "The captive lady led into Turkish lands" refers
to the Jewish refugees trying to sneak through Turkey to get to the
British potentate which ended up being Israel later on. The British
had it at that time.

D: That shows I am often wrong, too. Every time he mentions Turkey, I automatically think of the Anti-Christ.

B: He says in that part of the world there are just layers upon layers of history. So many events have happened it's easy to make the wrong historical connection.

CENTURY IX-99

Vent Aquilon fera partir le siege,	The north wind will cause the
Par murs gerer cendres, chauls	siege to be raised, to throw over
& pousiere,	the walls cinders, lime and dust;
Par pluie apres qui leur fera	afterwards through rain which
bien piege,	does them much harm, the last
Dernier secours encontre	help is met at their frontier.
leur frontiere.	

B: He says the bulk of this quatrain has already taken place. It refers to Hitler's attempt to invade Russia. He went as far as he could but the Russian winter caused him to turn back before he was able to reach his objective of destroying Moscow. He says the dust, cinders and lime refer to the scorched earth policy where the Russians burned all of their crops as they retreated so the Germans would not have anything to eat. As they got into more moderate climes where the winter wasn't quite as harsh, the tanks—he calls them "metal beasts," but the picture he gives here is of tanks—and other machines churned the roads into such mud that they got stuck and couldn't go any farther. They were barely able to cross over the frontier back into their own territory with the very last of their men.

The translators said this refers to Napoleon's retreat from Moscow. They might be correct also because Nostradamus said his quatrains have several meanings.

CENTURY II-70

Le dard du ciel fera son estendre,	The dart from heaven will make its
Mors en parlant: grande execution:	journey; Death while speaking; a
Le pierre en l' arbre la fiere gent	great execution. The stone in the
rendue,	tree, the proud nation brought
Bruit humain monstre purge	down; rumor of a human monster,
expiation.	purge and expiation.

B: He says this quatrain refers to the dropping of the atomic bomb on Hiroshima and Nagasaki. The dart speeding its way through the heavens was the plane that carried the bomb which is represented by the stone in the tree. He says the great nation brought low was Japan as the empire was knocked totally flat. Because of this, they considered President Truman of the United States to be a monster and felt his representative, General MacArthur, would be a monster as well. But when they realized that he respected them and their traditions, they decided he wasn't such a monster after all.

D: *It says, "after a dart from heaven made its journey, death while speaking, a great execution." "Death while speaking" is the phrase I question. Does that still deal with the atomic bomb?*

B: Yes, because it came so suddenly out of nowhere. Just "boom," and the whole city fell flat.

D: *"The stone in the tree." The tree is the...*

B: The reason he used the imagery of the tree is because the Japanese symbol for their empire—and also coincidentally one of the symbols used for Tokyo—is the sun rising behind a tree.

D: *I know their symbol is the rising sun.*

B: He's not talking about the flag. The symbol for Tokyo—and the empire in general—in Japanese language, writing in their ideograms, is the sun rising behind a tree. So the stone in the tree is a symbol for the bomb dropping on Japan which refers to the symbolism in their language.

D: *Their translation refers to Napoleon.*

B: He says he has devoted enough quatrains to Napoleon, and other quatrains will refer to him, but this particular quatrain does not.

To me, the mention of the symbol of the tree in connection with the atomic bomb brought forth the image of the mushroom cloud so often associated with the explosion. An atomic explosion could also be compared to the shape of a tree by someone seeing it for the first time.

CENTURY II-92

Feu couleur d' or du ciel en terre veu,	Fire the color of gold from the sky seen on Earth, struck by the high
Frappé du haut nay, faict cas merveilleux:	born one, a marvellous happening. Great slaughter of humanity; a
Grand meutre humain: prinse du grand nepveu.	nephew taken from the great one; the death of the spectator, the
Morte d' expectacles eschappe l' orgueilleux.	proud one escapes.

B: He says this quatrain also refers to the atomic bombing of Japan.

D: *"The nephew taken from the great one."*

B: He says that is a member of the Imperial house, a young relative to the Emperor.

D: *"The proud one escapes."*

B: This corresponds to the Imperial house. The United States had the foresight not to drop any atomic bombs on Tokyo, and therefore the Emperor was not killed by an atomic blast.

D: *As soon as I said it I could see what it meant. He must have been very*

impressed by the atomic explosion. He has so many quatrains refer-
ring to it.

B: He said if you only knew what it did to the landscape of time. He is surprised he didn't write a thousand quatrains on that alone.

D: *What* did *it do to the landscape of time?*

B: He says he can show this vessel the imagery, but neither he nor the vessel will be able to put it in spoken language.

D: *I'd like her to attempt it.*

B: He says he will show this vessel the imagery, and since her command of English is better than his, she will attempt to put it into words for him.

D: (After a pause) *He will do it whenever she awakens?*

B: He's already done it.

After Brenda had regained consciousness, without knowing why she began to describe the scene Nostradamus had left in her mind about the atomic explosions and what it had done to the time lines.

B: First of all, let me describe to you what the landscape of time, in general, looks like. Imagine if you will a gigantic plane that is the purest, blackest velvet you can ever imagine. Across this plane there are lines of neon bright light. It looks like a gigantic emission-line spectrum in astronomy. You see, there are two different types of spectrum that they can take of light. You can take an absorption-line spectrum which shows the rainbow color of light, and there are black lines in it because those particular wavelengths of light are not emitted by the sun. And you can take an emission-line spectrum, where the spectrum is black and all you see are colored lines where it would be absorbed in the other spectrum. I know I'm talking Greek to you, but the readers will be able to make sense out of it. The time lines look like a gigantic emission-line spectrum which is a very small portion of the entire timescape in general. This is just a *section* of the timescape he's looking at. In this landscape each one of these lines represent a time line, a possible reality, or a possible future. There are many possible futures. These lines go along neatly, nicely, and orderly, and suddenly they all run together into a central point.

D: *That's what he calls a nexus?*

B: Right. They all run together, and at the point where they all meet it looks like a gigantic explosion—a big blast of light frozen at its most expanded point. And instead of being able to see the nexus, you see this explosion that has been frozen instead. This was the effect on the time lines of the inventing of atomic power. In so many of the various realities the world did not survive the inventing of the atomic bomb. In this world, the scientists did not know whether or not it would set off a chain reaction and make every atom in the world explode, thus destroying the world. That was one of their fears. Well, in alternate realities that did indeed happen because of the way these alternate realities were structured. As you know, when it comes to a point where a problem can go one way or the other, it actually goes both ways, but only one way is expressed in your reality. The other way is expressed in another reality.

D: *Yes, we covered that in another session about alternate universes.*

B: This is another aspect of that. So all of these time lines run together into a gigantic nexus because this was such a crucial point of technological development. It was a very dangerous road to take, because there are other technologies that could be developed for the same effect or for the same type of technological advancement—alternate energies and powers. Some realities survived the inventing of atomic power and some did not. Even the ones that did were still drastically affected, either politically, historically or economically. So atomic power had a humongous effect on the timescape in general.

She was touching upon a theory we had discussed in another session: the idea that there are several alternate universes or realities that exist side-by-side, and each is not aware of the other. It is a complicated theory, but the gist of it is that there is energy created behind every decision and action in the world. When one path is chosen, the energy of the other decision must go somewhere. Thus, another reality comes into existence to accommodate that alternate reality. This also explains the idea of several possible futures depending on the action chosen by the participants, and Nostradamus' concern that we choose the correct path, the one with the least possible disastrous effects. This will be explained in further detail in my book, *The Convoluted Universe*.

I told Brenda why Nostradamus put the illustration in her mind and why he wanted her to explain it to us.

D: *He has described time in a lot of ways, and he talks about different time lines, nexuses and central nexuses. For instance, he said the Anti-Christ is at a main nexus, and no matter which time line you go down, he's going to be involved. The Great Genius is at another nexus. He's like a bright light on the horizon. These two are so involved in our future that there's no way to get around them, but we can lessen the possible disastrous effects.*

Chapter 3

The Present Time

*Les fleurs passés diminue
le monde,
Long temps la paix terres
inhabitées:
Seur marchera par ciel, serre,
mer & onde:
Puis de nouveau les guerres
suscitées*

Pestilences extinguished, the world becomes smaller, for a long time the lands will be inhabited peacefully. People will travel safely through the sky (over) land and seas: then wars will start up again.

B: He says this quatrain refers to what you consider to be the present and the near future. He was looking into a time where the art of medicine would be much advanced and many plagues would be eliminated. He's naming off some plagues, such as the Black Plague, smallpox and various diseases which in his time spread very quickly killing far and wide. He says in your time, in the 20th century, such diseases are under control.

D: *That's true.*

B: He says the part about traveling through the air refers to when he saw people traveling all over in flying machines. Due to the advances in technology, in both traveling and communication, the world is much smaller by contrast because it doesn't take nearly so long to travel or to communicate around the world. It's so quick that it's like talking to your next door neighbor, so in that respect the world is smaller. He says for the most part people are living in a state of peace. Even though since World War II there have been continuous minor scrimmages, there have not been any wars that have taken major amounts of the world's manpower. He says later on that will change, particularly when the Anti-Christ rises up and starts causing trouble. He will embroil the whole world in a big battle.

D: *The translators said this quatrain is very clear in its meaning.*

B: Yes. He says in this particular case he was enumerating some commonplace things to help fill out the picture. Since they seemed so fantastic and impossible, the Inquisition felt he was just putting that in to throw them off the scent. Thus, he did not have to do much to disguise it.

CENTURY I-15

Mars nous menace par la force bellique, Septante fois fera le sang espandre: Auge & ruine de l' Ecclesiastique, Et plus ceux qui d' eux rien voudront entendre.	Mars threatens us with the force of war and will cause blood to be spilt 70 times. The clergy will be both exalted and reviled moreover, by those who wish to learn nothing of them.

B: He says this quatrain refers to the fact that there is always some kind of armed conflict taking place, particularly in the 20th century. Also various offices and positions that formerly held respect—established orthodox-type religions, for example—will no longer command the power and respect they once did due to their own misuse of power.

D: *"Mars threatens us with the force of war and will cause blood to be spilt 70 times"? What is the significance of that number?*

B: He says he has already explained that it refers to the armed conflicts that are always taking place.

D: *It doesn't mean a specific number of conflicts then.*

B: He says you could possibly link it up with a specific number of certain types of armed conflicts, but only after the century has occurred.

CENTURY IV-56

Apres victoire du babieuse langue L'esprit tempte en tranquil & repos: Victeur sanguin par conflict faict harangue, Roustir la langue & la chair & les os.	After the victory of the raging tongue, the spirit tempted in tranquil rest. Throughout the battle the bloody victor makes speeches, roasting the tongue, the flesh and the bones.

B: He says this quatrain predicted the events of Watergate. The roasting tongue refers to the biting accusations that were thrown back and forth in that situation. He says at another time he will go into greater detail on that for you. If you remember the situation from Watergate, a lot of applications should be at least partially apparent—how wild accusations were thrown back and forth, and things such as that.

CENTURY II-28

Le penultiesme du surnom du prophete, *Prendra Diane pour son jour & repos:* *Loing vaguera par frenetique teste,* *Et delivrant un grand peuple d' impos.*	The last but one of the prophets' name, will take Monday for his day of rest. He will wander far in his frenzy delivering a great nation from subjection.

B: He says this quatrain refers to events that have taken place in the recent past that are still having repercussions, because they are events that leave the Middle East vulnerable to the Anti-Christ and the time of troubles. The events are the downfall of the Shah of Iran and the uprising of the Ayatollahs of the Muslim religion which make Iran a very strong, conservative, fundamentalist Muslim state. He says one of the main leaders of this movement, due to his religious duties on their religious holiday of Friday and his duties of state on the other days, will make a point of taking off Monday to rest and recuperate for handling all of this.

D: *According to this, does he think the Ayatollah has delivered Iran from subjection?*

B: From their point of view.

D: *What does it mean, "the last but one of the prophet's name"?*

B: He says the prophet refers to the Muslim prophet, Mohammed. As is the custom of that part of the world, he has a whole string of names. He says if you were to find a source that has his complete names and all of his surnames, then take the next to the last one of the names that are not the familial name, that will give you a clue as to who he's talking about.

D: *Is he talking about the Shah of Iran?*

B: No, he's talking about the Ayatollahs.

D: *Then if I look up the names, I will find the name of the Ayatollah.*

B: Yes. He says there are several Ayatollahs. When you look up the prophet's name, mentally block out the family name and look at the other names, then take the next to the last one.

D: *I wonder if it might be an anagram.*

B: He says that is for you to figure out. He's not going to tell you everything. Now that he has given the clues, one should be able to find it.

When I tried to locate the entire name of Mohammed, all I could find was that his father was Abdullah and his mother was Aminah. His father belonged to the family of Hashim, which was the noblest tribe of the Quraish section of the Arabian race, and he was said to be directly descended from Ishmael. His grandfather was Abdul-Muttalib. All this may mean something to someone who is familiar with the names in that part of the world, but I am unable to isolate anything significant. (Information found in *A Dictionary of Islam,* by Thomas Patrick Hughes.)

CENTURY II-10

Avant long temps le tout	Before long everything will be
sera rangé,	organized; we await a very evil
Nous esperons un siecle bien	century. The state of the masked
senestre	and the solitary ones greatly
L' estat des masques & des	changed, few will find that they
seuls bien changé,	wish to retain their rank.
Peu trouverant qu' á son	
rang vueille estre.	

B: He says this quatrain refers to a series of events, some of which have taken place and some of which are still taking place. Generally, it refers to the various revolutions and social reforms that have taken place on the Asian continent during the 20th century. He says the state changing from the masked and the solitary ones refers to the abolishing of the caste system in India. The quatrain also refers to the various revolutions taking place in the Middle East, particularly the Iranian revolution. The phrase "few wanting to retain their rank" pertains to the new regime which took over Iran after the Shah. Those who were in power under the Shah were trying to disguise their positions and disclaim any connection with him, so they could retain what they could. The very evil century is the time that's coming and includes the time leading up to it. The 20th century starting from ... well, the whole century in particular but especially since World War II, has not been particularly peaceful. So he is referring to it as evil. Since World War II until the end of the time of troubles will almost encompass a century itself.

CENTURY I-70

Plui, faim, guerre en Perse	Rain, famine and war will not
non cessée,	cease in Persia; too great a faith
La foi trop grand trahira	will betray the monarch. Those
le monarque:	(actions) started in France will end
Par la finie en Gaule commencee,	there, a secret sign for one to be
Secret augure pour à un estre	sparing.
parque.	

B: He says part of this quatrain has already taken place in the recent past, and part of it is yet to come. He says "too great a faith will cause the downfall of the monarch" refers to the downfall of the Shah of Iran, and that the rise of the fundamentalist sect of Islam in Iran was the basic cause of these troubles. He says from our point of view the events have not all worked themselves out yet. So this quatrain is in the process of coming to pass now. He says the "sign for one to be sparing" refers to the many political upsets still happening in that part of the world. One of the men who will help the Anti-Christ come to power will realize that instead of indiscriminately executing people, some of them, due to their connections, will be useful to him and the Anti-Christ. So he gives them a hard time instead. "Those actions started in France," refers to the present Ayatollah because he was in exile in France. He says it means the Ayatollah developed many of his notions about coming to power and ruling a fundamentalist state while in exile. He started out with a distorted view of the world and it was reinforced while he was in France. It was there that he crystallized some of his ideas and they warped slightly. Eventually he did indeed come to power.

CENTURY I-13

Les exilez par ire, haine intestine,
Feront au Roy grand conjuration:
Secret mettront ennemis par
  la mine,
Et ses vieux siens contre
  aux sedition.

Through anger and internal hatreds, the exiles will hatch a great plot against the king. Secretly they will place enemies as a threat, and his own old (adherents) will find sedition against them.

B: He says this quatrain refers to the problem of terrorism that has arisen in the 20th century. He says the exiles refers to the Palestinians. He was trying to forewarn us of some of the atrocities that would be committed in acts of terrorism.

Chapter 4

Near Future

Coq, chiens & chats de sang seront repeus	The cock, cats and dogs will be replete with blood when
Et de la playe du tyran trouvé mort	the tyrant is found dead of a
Au lict d' un autre jambes & bras rompus	wound in the bed of another, both arms and legs broken,
Qui n' aviat peur de mourir de cruelle mort.	he who was not afraid dies a cruel death.

B: He says this quatrain refers to several different situations. On one hand, it refers to the situation now in Nicaragua. The "cocks, cats and dogs that are replete with blood" refers to how the various forces will be fighting and bickering back and forth. This quatrain points out that foreign powers are supplying the guerrillan (Spanish pronunciation) troops. It also shows that these troops are fighting in the hills. He says the cocks represent foreign powers, and in particular it refers to France. The cats refer to the guerrillas and how they hide and sneak around the bush. They sneak out and fight and then sneak back again. And the dogs represent the soldiers and how they kind of plow forward trying to keep everything under control by force.

D: *Does this mean France is involved in this?*

B: Yes. It's not generally known, but France is having some underhanded dealings in this matter. He asks that you read the rest of the quatrain again. (*I repeated it.*) He says it refers to a leader who will start out being popular in Nicaragua and will then be assassinated. It will be thought that the leader is pro-democracy, pro-West and pro-American. After he is assassinated and some documents come to light he will actually be found to be pro-Soviet instead, in other words, he is in the bed of another.

D: *Then it says, "Both arms and legs broken. He who was not afraid dies a cruel death."*

B: Yes. That's a warning to the leaders involved with the situation, particularly the leaders in Nicaragua and the surrounding countries. If they're not careful they can be overthrown by military coups. In other words, their arms and legs will be broken and they will be powerless to resist. They won't be able to do anything. Also, it's a warning to the leaders of the *higher* powers like the larger countries, he means. If they get too involved with what's going on and let it distort their overall viewpoint, it can have negative repercussions for them as well.

This interpretation was given in 1987 when there were no obvious problems in that area. Since the eruption of trouble in Panama and South America in late 1989, I believe this quatrain could have many meanings referring to that area of the world.

D: *Is the United States involved there also?*

B: Yes. There are quite a few nations involved. The United States is the most open about their involvement, simply due to the nature of their government. The Soviet Union is involved and their satellites are trying to draw pressure into that area of the world, particularly Cuba. There are others but he's being unclear on the names of some of the smaller countries involved. He's saying that Japan is also involved, because of the pressure on Japan concerning international trade in this and other situations in the modern world.

D: *Are the Soviets using their satellite countries?*

B: Yes. Bulgaria, Albania, and other countries are involved. To put it into modern slang, "The Soviets are running a laundering operation." You hear of criminals who get money by unjust means and they launder it by running it through another company to make it "clean" money. The Soviets are doing something similar with arms and illegal assistance by running it through another country. It's the type of assistance that's not entirely above board.

D: *So everyone's involved but no one's really broadcasting it ... except us.*

B: Yes, exactly.

CENTURY I-51

Chef d' Aries, Jupiter & Saturne,	The head of Aries, Jupiter and
Dieu eternel quelles mutations?	Saturn. Eternal God, what
Puis par long siecle son maling	changes! Then the bad times
temps retourne	will return again after a long
Gaule, & Italie quelles	century; what turmoil
emotions?	in France and Italy.

D: *The translators thought this quatrain might have an error in the typesetting.*

B: He says such a thing is possible. That is one of the hazards in dealing with the printing profession.

D: *In the book he has a question mark after "Eternal God, what changes!" They think this is an error, that it's supposed to be an exclamation mark, and they changed it.*

B: He says it should be an exclamation point, because he was exclaiming what changes have been wrought. He was not asking what changes, because the changes were very evident to him in his vision. He's trying to pin the quatrain down for me. He says the turmoil in France and Italy refers to ... well, the 20th century term for it is "worker's strikes." Since they didn't have that phenomenon in his time he's allowing me to use a 20th century term for it. Three major world leaders represented by Aries, Jupiter, and Saturn confer together making an agreement to improve the lot of the world in general. And things will appear to be good for a long while. He says some of the changes made are communistic-type changes. Then the workers will realize that once again they have gotten the short end of the stick. And so they will start trouble to try to institute some changes. He's not able to communicate very well with this quatrain. The main picture that keeps coming across (he uses a lot of images) is the color green. I don't know what the color has to do with this, but he keeps showing me images of a field of green grass, as if I were floating above it looking down. But he's not able to make the connection clear between that and this quatrain.

D: *Is this something that has not happened yet?*

B: He says it is in the process of happening. He gives me the image of Aries, Jupiter and Saturn in association with Roosevelt, Churchill and Stalin. It is something they started that will not be completed until after the beginning of the next century.

D: *The translator thought he was talking about a conjunction of Aries, Jupiter, and Saturn.*

B: That is a very natural thing for them to think because he wrote it like that, he says, to throw the hounds off the scent. And I see that he's referring to priests when he says that.

D: *In French it says, "Chef de Aries," and they have translated it as the "Head of Aries."*

B: He says Chief, or leader or head would be close enough. He says in all appearances the efforts to translate have been sincere, just misguided in some cases.

CENTURY V-53

La loi du Sol, & Venus contendens,	The law of the Sun contending with Venus, appropriating the
Appropiant l'esprit de prophetie:	spirit of prophecy. Neither
Ne l' un ne l' autre ne seront entendus,	the one nor the other will be understood; the law of the
Par Sol tiendra la loy du grand Messie.	great Messiah retained through the Sun.

D: *There are astrological signs in here.*

B: He says to quit making assumptions.

D: *Well, you know I'm trying to do this, too.* (Laugh)

B: He says not to try to do it, but just to communicate what you learn. He seems to be a bit feisty today.

D: *Okay, I might be coming to the wrong conclusions.*

B: He says although it is astrological and allegorical, this quatrain refers to the development of Christianity. It shows how Christianity lost its spirit. He says people's minds and intentions did not agree with what the Catholic church allowed to be printed in the Bible. And people's spirit and emotions were not comfortable with the church. But they still followed it with the mind because that is what their parents had done. The teachings as presented in the Bible were followed on the surface but without true conviction behind them. He says as a result, the structure of the church will be like a building with dry rot in the time of troubles. It will appear to be sound and complete, but it will actually be about to crumble into dust. He says the Catholic church won't be the only one crumbling at that time. It seems the vibrations are altered in a way that is not good, and they grow out of control. The way in which they develop is not in keeping with the spirit of God.

D: *Are you talking about the counterbalance of energy? One group of positive people against a negative group?*

B: He says he's not speaking of a balance of forces here, for unfortunately one of the contributing factors to the time of troubles is the balance being altered temporarily where the so-called "evil" forces seem to have the upper hand. But the forces will swing back the other way and things will balance again after the time of troubles. He says at this time the balance is tilted so it is very easy for negative influences to flourish. With the balance leaning somewhat in their favor, they are able to flourish with the appearance of good. This is what is meant in the Scriptures as knowing them by the fruit of their tree.

D: *Referring to this quatrain, John wants to know if this will happen when the sun conjuncts with Venus?*

J: *In December of 1990 Venus will be in close aspect to the sun in the sign of Sagittarius. Does this mean this will be when the so-called "Christians" are on the wane and more spiritual people are taking over their position?*

B: He says it will be a time of upheaval. The change will begin to take place deep down but will not become apparent at that time. The so-called "Christians" will still have their day in the sun, but they will accidentally do themselves in. The ones who are truly spiritual won't have to do anything themselves, but simply step into the gap that is left.

J: Can we have a date for that?

B: He says these events will be taking place like the flow of a river within the next decade, but he does not give any particular dates.

D: Maybe it will be a gradual thing.

CENTURY II-64

Seicher de faim, de soif,
gent Genevoise,
Espoir prochain viendra
au defaillir:
Sur point tremblant sera
loi Gebenoise.
Classe au grand port ne se
peut acuillir.

The people of Geneva will dry up with thirst and hunger, hope at hand will come to failure; the law of the Cevennes will be at breaking point, the fleet cannot be received at the great port.

B: He says this quatrain refers to the fact that, in the world in general, as the political situation becomes more confusing, the less effective diplomats will be at their Geneva conventions. Switzerland is known to be a neutral country, and he also realizes it is the financial and banking center. Through these world tribulations and conflicts, the diplomats' resources will keep drying up on them, so they cannot progress towards constructive discussions between the world leaders. Also, due to the world troubles, the world economy is going to be somewhat shaky. The bankers in Geneva are going to feel that their resources and power are drying up on them because they're not able to be as effective as they had been before.

D: Is that what it means by "the law of Cevennes will be at the breaking point"?

B: Yes, he says that Cevennes is an anagram for the name of the man who developed the basic economic structure that your economy is currently based upon. And as with all such constructs, it has its faults. This situation will reach the breaking point, so that the entire thing breaks down and a new economic and banking system will have to be constructed. But he says, even at that, it will be only a temporary solution. After the Anti-Christ is subdued and the great genius comes, that problem will be solved and will no longer apply because the way of doing things in the world will be so much different than they are now.

The only person I could find that might possibly be the one referred to by the anagram of Cevennes was John Maynard Keynes. He was an economist who is credited with influencing our modern way of life.

CENTURY IV-99

L' aisné vaillant de la fille du Roy,	The brave eldest son of a
Repoussera si profond les	king's daughter will drive the
Celtiques:	Celts back very far. He will
Qu'il mettra foudres, combien	use thunderbolts, so many in
en tel arroi	such an array, few and
Peu & loing puis profond és	distant, then deep into
Hesperiques.	the West.

B: He says this has not yet taken place. This quatrain refers to the manner in which the Irish problem will be resolved. He says the island of Eire, the Irish nation, is deeply divided and has been for centuries. The problem will be resolved through a prince. He's not able to make it clear whether he is referring to Prince Charles or to one of his sons, but one of them will have a major part to play in bringing peace to Ireland. This man will find some leverage with which to deal with the problem, in order to bring it to a head, so that the Irish will have to choose between total destruction and peace. At first the threat of total destruction will be very imminent, very real, and very close. But as they are forced into working out their problems and they come up with workable solutions, the threat of destruction will recede. It's just like the rumbling of a thunderstorm on the horizon. The Irish nation will be united once more and not divided as the British Empire currently has it.

D: *They think by saying thunderbolts that he means missiles or rockets.*

B: That is one of the threats the prince will use. He won't carry through with the threat, but he will use it to give him more leverage.

D: *The translators say the Celts represent the French.*

B: *(Angrily)* Bullshit! The Celts were originally on the British Isle in Scotland, Wales and England. The Romans and the Anglo-Saxons drove them westward across the sea to Ireland where they became part of the Irish people.

D: *Through my work I have had communication with Celts living in Ireland in that time period. But the translator says, "The Celts referred to are the French who are driven back by an unidentified leader."*

B: I would suggest we move along. Michel de Notredame is getting most upset. He's not handling it very well this time. His mustache is doing strange things.

CENTURY IV-84

Un grand d' Auxerre mourra bien miserable,	An important man from Auxerre will die very wretch-
Chassé de ceux qui soubs lui ont esté:	edly, driven out by the people who were under him. Bound
Serré de chaines, apres d'un rude cable,	in chains, then with a strong rope, the year that Mars,
En l' an que Mars, Venus & Sol, mis en esté.	Venus and the Sun are in conjunction in the summer.

B: He says this event should take place within this decade (1980's). When he uses the phrase "in the summer," he is thinking of high summer when Sirius is high in the sky. The man that will be driven out was a good leader and a good man, but there was a campaign against him to besmirch his name. He says he will be driven out of power in chains, and that eventually, during a riot of some sort, he will be hung. He says this is one of those small events that one does not realize how they connect with a larger picture until years after. He says this incident is one of those small things that in later years will be seen to be connected to the time leading into the time of troubles.

D: *What is the connection of that name "Auxerre"?*

B: He says that name refers to the region this man is from. He's not able to give me a specific place, but he is giving me a feeling for southern Europe not too far from the coast.

J: *Will this conjunction take place in the fire sign of Leo?* (She nodded and John hurriedly leafed through his book.) *Then I have the date. Those planets will be in conjunction on July 23, 1989.*

John came up with this date very quickly by glancing through the ephemeris while the session was being conducted. Later, on closer examination he found that it was not a true conjunction, but all three of the planets were in Leo. It is a rare occurrence for these three planets to be in exact conjunction. When we examined the quatrain we discovered that it may have been translated incorrectly. The French does not say "conjunct," it is *"mis en esté,"* which I conclude can be literally translated as *"placed* in summer." If this is how Nostradamus intended for the quatrain to read, then it does not have to be a true conjunction; all the planets can be together in the same sign. In modern astrology the planets must be no more than ten degrees or so apart to be considered a true conjunction. When the translators interpreted this quatrain they may not have been aware that a true conjunction requires a certain number of degrees. If my assumptions are accurate, then the date John gave so hastily for this prediction would be correct. All three planets are in Leo beginning July 23, 1989 and remain within that sign for about a week.

At the time this prediction was made in 1987 I thought it was absurd and not likely to be fulfilled. I presumed that Nostradamus was seeing the death of a leader of a country. It seemed absurd to me because nowadays leaders are not hung, and when they're assassinated they're usually shot. But strangely, it has seemed to come true in a way I would not have expected. Almost to the day, on July 31, 1989, it was announced that Lt. Colonel William Higgins was hung in Beirut, Lebanon by pro-Iranian Shiite Moslems in retaliation for the capture of an influential Moslem cleric. Higgins was serving as the head of an observer group attached to the U.N. peacekeeping force in south Lebanon when he was kidnapped in February 1988.

Nostradamus' symbolism seems to fit all too well. The quatrain reads "Driven out by the people who were under him." The word "chassé" in French can also be translated as "hunted or chased." This would fit if it referred to the people who kidnapped him, or to those troops under him who certainly did hunt for him. "Bound in chains" certainly could refer to his year's imprisonment by his captors before he was hung "with a strong rope." "Auxerre" still may hold one of the keys as an unsolved anagram. The date was a few days off, but it has been surmised by some experts that Lt. Col. Higgins may have been already dead when the videotape of his hanging was taken. Thus an important man *did* "die very wretchedly," and I believe the repercussions have yet to be felt. U.S. ships were sent to that area in the anticipation of more hostages being slain, and open hostilities could have broken out. But after a few weeks, things calmed down again into an uneasy atmosphere of tense waiting for the unexpected.

CENTURY IV-55

Quant la corneille sur tout de brique joincte, Durant sept heures ne fera que crier: Mort presagee de sang statue taincte, Tyran meutri, aux Dieux peuple prier.

When the crow on a tower made of brick will do nothing but croak for seven hours; it foretells death, a statue stained with blood, a tyrant murdered, people praying to their Gods.

B: He says this quatrain takes place during the time of troubles and is almost entirely symbolic. The crow sitting on the tower croaking represents the news media and their communication satellites high over the world croaking out news of doom. He is also using the tower as a symbol of sudden and perhaps painful change.

D: *Oh, like the Tarot card.*

B: Yes, he's using the symbolism of the Tarot card. The news media croaking nothing but doom for seven hours represents that the news commentators who sit around making speculations on these world events will have been doing this for seven years during this conflict. And they'll be predicting the absolute worst. He says "a statue stained with blood" represents the United States (by the Statue of Liberty) initiating an act that will figuratively put blood on her hands. So he represented this by saying "a statue stained with blood." He says there will be a trigger-happy general, or someone of high rank, who will call out for a special strike force that the general public doesn't know about. This strike force was originally designed to protect the President, a Vice-President, or someone like that. Regardless of where they are in the world, if something happens to them or they get into trouble, this strike force can rescue them and pay back the offending parties. Through a misunderstanding, someone will think the President is in danger, although he really won't be, and the strike force will be sent out causing a big brouhaha and a lot of repercussions. The crows croaking doom will have been commenting on the negativity of the world situation in general but when this event happens they're really going to have a heyday. First, they're going to be able to comment about it ahead of time because someone will accidentally have his plane headed where the President is, and the newsmen will start speculating on what's going on. Then after the event happens, they'll chew it to death. But meanwhile, everyone will be hoping the repercussions will not be too serious. The part about the people praying to their gods mean everyone will be using whatever methods they are familiar with to calm themselves such as having faith and letting the higher powers see everything through.

D: *But it says, "a tyrant murdered." Is that part of this?*

B: Yes, it is. The strike force goes in to rescue the President because they think he's in trouble of being kidnapped or something like that. Nostradamus gives a strong impression that France is going to be involved with this, too, somehow. The strike force, thinking that the situation is different than it is, will end up killing an official that's with the President. The representative of the country where this will happen will be a cabinet member, prime minister, or someone fairly high up in that country's government. But he will end up being murdered by this strike force while they're in the process of "rescuing" the President. This will occur during the 1990's.

D: *Is there any significance to the tower being made out of brick?*

B: It indicates that the event will be a man-made situation rather than a natural disaster, since brick is manufactured by man. He said that if he had wanted to symbolize a natural disaster, he would have called it a tower made of stone, since stones are formed by nature.

D: *I'm beginning to see that everything he uses has a reason.*

CENTURY II-78

Le grand Neptune du profond de la mer,	Great Neptune from the depths of the sea, of mixed
De gent Punique & sang Gaulois meslé:	African race and French blood, the islands remain
Les isles à sang pour le tardif ramer,	bloody because of the slow one; it will harm him more
Plus lui nuira que l' occult mal celé.	than a badly concealed secret.

B: He says this quatrain refers to events in the Caribbean Islands that will be taking place during the time of troubles. He says that due to the nature of the society there, crooked politics are normal, and during the time of the Anti-Christ they will become even more blatantly crooked. At one point they will dig their own grave with this, and some badly concealed secrets will come to light getting some important people into trouble.

It suddenly dawned on me that "Of mixed African race and French blood" might refer to Haiti.

B: Yes. He says Haiti is one of the Caribbean Islands. He says "the slow one" refers to the American President who will be slow to react to outside aggression. "The islands remaining bloody" refers to the sea battles that will be going on around the islands. Meanwhile the islands are asking for protection from the United States, and the president is slow to react. So in desperation some of the leaders of the islands reveal some of the goings-on that involve the American president, in a way that will get him into trouble as Watergate did Nixon. He says every leader has secrets that could get them into that kind of trouble. It's just a matter of keeping the secrets hidden.

D: *I didn't realize they were going to come that close to our continent.*
B: He says it won't be forces directly under the Anti-Christ but other aggressive countries taking advantage of the upset of the balance of world powers.

When I was preparing this book for printing, I was amazed at the similarity between this prediction and what was then (in 1989) occurring in Panama and Central America. I believe the American President referred to as "the slow one" could rightfully describe George Bush. The news media have continually made reference to his hesitancy to react to aggressive situations. Also during the Panama invasion there was rumors that secrets might be revealed about him. This quatrain could mean that we are not finished with troubles in our own back yard involving the countries and islands in the Caribbean.

Chapter 5

The Anti-Christ Emerges

THESE ARE SOME MORE BITS AND PIECES of the puzzle of the Anti-Christ and his ambitions to take over the world. They may help us to understand Nostradamus' lengthy predictions of the coming time of troubles.

CENTURY V-25

Le prince Arabe Mars, Sol,
Venus, Lyon,
Regne d' Eglise par mer
succombera:
Devers la Perse bien pres
d' un million.
Bisance, Egypte, ver. serp.
invadera.

The Arab Prince, Mars, the Sun, Venus and Leo, the rule of the Church will succumb to the sea. Towards Persia very nearly a million men will invade Egypt and Byzantium, the true serpent.

B: He says we should not find it surprising that this refers to trouble in the Middle East. The leaders will have different motivations in how they're involved with this conflict. One leader is egotistical and wants to be in the limelight. The other leader has mixed feelings about it. He is a fanatic, so he's fanatical about his country, but the fanaticism borders on love and hate. Sometimes when this leader comes to his senses, he realizes that he's obsessed but there's nothing he can do about it. These two leaders will be conspiring together to upset the balance of world power. He says they will break forth from the boundaries of their countries and overtake other parts of the territory in a very quick and brilliant maneuver. That's why he mentions Egypt and the Byzantium, because each leader will expand in a separate direction, yet they will be allied together.

When he mentions Byzantium he refers to Turkey. Istanbul (Constantinople) was built on the site of this ancient city. It became increasingly apparent that when he mentioned a place name in his quatrains, he was often not referring to that city, *per se,* but to the country in which it was located.

D: *They have translated Mars, Sun, Venus, and Leo as astrological conjunctions and they have tried to pinpoint a date by doing that.*

B: He used those astrological signs to be able to give thumbnail personality sketches of the leaders involved in just one or two words. If one knows the horological and astrological associations and traits of these various planets and signs, then it gives you an idea as to the personality types of the various leaders.

The other portion of this quatrain is interpreted in Chapter 16, "The Ravage of the Church," Volume One.

CENTURY I-47

Du lac Leman les sermons
fascheront,
Les Jours seront reduicts
par les sepmaines:
Puis mois, puis an, puis
tous deffailliront,
Les magistrats damneront
leurs loix vaines.

The speeches of Lake Leman will become angered, the days will drag out into weeks, then months, then years, then all will fail. The authorities will condemn their useless powers.

B: He says this quatrain refers to one of the reasons behind the breakdown in diplomatic relations and communications that will be taking place throughout Europe during the time of troubles. Leaders will get together to meet about important things and make decisions. They won't be able to begin because they will be arguing over minor things like what shape of table they should meet around, who should sit at the head of the table, and things such as this, until the whole scheme falls through. They end up not being able to discuss any of the major things they met to discuss because of all the quibbling over minor details.

D: *They think Lake Leman refers to the League of Nations or Geneva.*

B: He says Lake Leman refers to a major lake in Switzerland near where they will meet.

CENTURY III-34

Quand le deffaut du Soleil lors sera.	Then when the eclipse of the sun will be in broad daylight the
Sur le plain jour le monstre sera veu:	monster will be seen. It will be interpreted quite differently; they
Tout autrement on l'interpretera,	will not care about expense, none
Cherté n'a garde mil n'y aura pourveu.	will have provided for it.

B: He says this quatrain refers to the appearance of the Anti-Christ in the international arena. For many years the Anti-Christ will be working silently behind the scenes, consolidating his power. But the structure he has built, will not be visible until an event takes place that temporarily dims the apparent power of the major nations. It is believed to be a temporary setback in the image these nations have projected for many years. People will see that something else has taken place as well. The Anti-Christ and his organization will be sparing no expense to help the organization grow and gain more power. The people they will be moving against will not be prepared for this, for they won't know about this particular threat.

D: *The translators interpreted this to mean that something will happen during an eclipse of the sun.*

B: He says he was using that metaphorically. It appears there will be an eclipse of the sun at a crucial moment, but he was not specifically referring to that.

CENTURY I-18

Par la discorde negligence Gauloise,	Because of French discord and negligence an opening shall be
Sera passaige à Mahommet ouvert:	given to the Mohammedans.
De sang trempé la terre & mer Senoise,	The land and sea of Siena will be soaked in blood, and the port of
Le port phocen de voiles & nefs convert.	Marseilles covered with ships and sails.

He corrected my pronunciation of the names.

B: He says this quatrain refers to events that for the most part have taken place in the past including the occupation of France and the North African campaign of the Axis powers during World War II. He says a similar pattern of events will also take place during the time of the Anti-Christ. The negligence of the NATO powers will be one of the things that will help the Anti-Christ to take over Europe.

D: *I think you said before that they wouldn't realize what's going on until too late.*

CENTURY VIII-30

*Dedans Tholoze non loing
de Beluzer
Faisant un puis long, palais
d'espectacle,
Tresor trouvé un chacun ira vexer,
Et en deux locz & pres del vasacle.*

In Toulouse, not far from Beluzer making a deep pit a palace of spectacle, the treasure found will come to vex everyone in two places and near the Basacle.

B: He says this quatrain refers to events that will happen during the time of the Anti-Christ. The place names give the location in France near Beluzer and Toulouse. The great pit will be caused by the accidental detonation of some buried weapons or some concealed weapons. The event will cause the people in charge to be ridiculed. The palace of spectacle is an analogy to their positions no longer being held in respect. They are a source of ridicule for they made a very poor decision in bad judgment. Some information will come to light concerning some corruption in high places, this will cause consternation, not only in France but in another nation as well, for it will be information concerning some diplomatic goings-on. The information is symbolized by the treasure found. This will come to light at a bad time and will alarm the parties involved.

D: *That's what is meant by "the treasure found will come to vex everyone in two places and near the Basacle."*

The dictionary defines a basacle as a seesaw or similarly balanced apparatus. A basacle bridge is a drawbridge. Nostradamus must be insinuating something with this symbolism.

B: The ones in France are those who will make a poor judgment concerning the weapons being concealed there. It will cause vexation in the capital.

D: *The translators say they can't identify the word "Beluzer." They think it's an anagram.*

B: He says it was a village in his time, a rather rural spot. He named that spot although he knew the name would change or perhaps the village would no longer be there. The weapons involved would be concealed in a rural area where there would be less chances of someone discovering them.

D: *Did he give the name of a rural village to symbolize the weapons being buried in a rural location?*

B: No, it's not a symbol. It's the location. The weapons will be buried near that rural village (Beluzer), but its name will have changed through the centuries or perhaps most of the people will have moved away so it might not be called a village.

D: *Then that would explain why the translators couldn't identify it as a place in our time.*

CENTURY II-59

Classe Gauloise par appuy de grande garde,
Du grand Neptune, & ses tridens souldars:
Rongée Provence pour soustenir grand bande,
Plus Mars Narbon, par javelots & dards.

The French fleet with the support of the main guard of great Neptune and his trident warriors; Provence scrounged to sustain this great band, moreover, fighting at Narbonne with javelins and arrows.

B: He says this refers to the Anti-Christ's European campaign. Ships will land and the forces will begin going inland taking the land under their power. He says it will be like a horde of locusts going across the land because they will be stripping it of food to support the army and make it difficult for the local people.

D: *When he talks about javelins and arrows, he doesn't really mean those does he?*

B: No. He was just referring to the fighting. He says instead of javelins and arrows, it will be bullets and spear-like devices shot by guns, but he could be referring to mortar shells. Plus, he says there will be new weapons that have been developed behind the scenes that this vehicle and you would not yet know about, because they still have not yet been exposed to the public.

CENTURY I-73

France à cinq pars par neglect assaillie,
Tunis, Argel esmuez par Persiens:
Leon, Seville, Barcelonne faillie
N'aura la classe par les Venetiens.

France shall be accused of neglect by her five partners. Tunis, Algiers stirred up by the Persians. Leon, Seville and Barcelona having failed, they will not have the fleet because of the Venetians.

B: He says this quatrain has a double meaning. The first of which refers to the Maginot Line during World War II. France poured all of her defenses into building a defense line between her and Germany, from one end of her border up to the Belgian border, not dreaming that the Germans would be audacious enough just to go around the line and plow through Belgium to get to France. In that way they were short-sighted and they failed. He also says this quatrain refers to some of the Mediterranean campaigns during World War II, but it also refers to the time when the Anti-Christ will be campaigning to take over Europe. The southern European countries will feel the effects of his campaign first because he will be coming up through the south across the Mediterranean. Those countries are: Greece, Turkey, Italy, France, and Spain.

D: *Then who are these five partners?*

B: He says at the beginning of World War II the allies were doing a fair amount of backstabbing. They were telling France how stupid she was to pour all her defenses into this useless wall that the Germans circumvented.

D: *The translators say it means France was attacked on five sides.*

B: No, he says this refers to dissension in the ranks, so to speak. He says this will also take place somewhat during the conflict to come, but not to the same degree. At the beginning of World War II such audacious conduct as the Germans displayed was totally unknown in modern history, but this time the world will be more prepared. When the Anti-Christ starts making his moves and displaying audacious conduct, the world will not be surprised—or *as* surprised—and they will know what moves to take to help counterbalance this.

D: *I figured Seville and Barcelona dealt with Spain, but in another quatrain I believed he said the Iberian Peninsula would not be taken by the Anti-Christ.*

B: This is correct. But this will not prevent the Anti-Christ from *trying*. He will not be successful, partially because his fleet will be concentrated in the central and eastern part of the Mediterranean in an attempt to take over that part of Europe. And partially because the British naval station at Gibraltar will have a bearing upon what happens to the Iberian Peninsula. It is true they will not be taken, but they will be involved with the conflict.

CENTURY II-47

*L' ennemi grand vieil dueil
  meurt de poison,*
Les souverains par infiniz subjugez
Pierres plouvoir, cachez soubz
  la foison,
Par mort articles en vain
  sont alleguez.
	The enemy watches with grief the old man dead from poison; the kings are overcome by an immeasurable (number). It rains stones, hidden under the fleece; vainly articles are asserted by the dead man.

B: He says this quatrain refers to some of the victories obtained by the Chinese army during the time of troubles. The fleece refers to the quilted jackets they wear as part of their uniform. A rain of stones refers to the hail of bullets that will rain down upon anyone facing this army.

D: *"The enemy watches with grief, the old man dead from poison"?*

B: There'll be a beloved leader who will have been poisoned. They will all stand around watching him die and not be able to do anything about it.

When I was putting this book together, I assumed that this quatrain referred to the coming war with the Anti-Christ, especially since the army and bullets are mentioned. But when the internal trouble erupted in China in May and June of 1989, I wondered if it could refer to that. This would have been an inconceivable event in 1987 when this quatrain was translated. Who would have thought that the Chinese army would fire upon its own people? Although the reference to "a rain of stones hidden under the fleece" could also be translated literally since the students did throw rocks at the advancing soldiers and tanks. This quatrain could refer to the eventual outcome of the problems in that country. "The kings are overcome by an immeasurable number," could certainly refer to the enormous population in China. Brenda said that "the enemy watches with grief the old man dead from poison," meant that a leader would be poisoned and they would watch him die and not be able to do anything about it. I wonder if this could be symbolic poison and refer to the death of the type of government that the Chinese people exist under at the present time? I get the feeling that if this is one of the interpretations of this quatrain, that it won't be a sudden revolution, but a gradual one.

CENTURY I-90

Bourdeaux, Poitiers au son de la campane,	Bordeaux and Poitiers at the sound of the bell will go with a
A grand classe ira jusques à l'Angon:	great fleet as far as Langon. A great rage will surge up against
Contre Gaulois sera leur tramontane,	the French, when a hideous monster is born near Orgon.
Quand monstre hideux naistra pres de Orgon.	

B: He says this quatrain refers to events that will take place during the time of the Anti-Christ. He says the "great rage that will rise up against the French when a hideous monster is born near Orgon" refers to the French Pope who will be a tool of the Anti-Christ.

D: *They have interpreted this quite literally as the birth of a monster, saying "This is probably like the two-headed child that Nostradamus saw and described in another book."*

B: He says he does not see why this ... how would they think this would cause a rage to rise up against all of France? I would suggest that we move to the next quatrain. Michel de Notredame is getting upset again.

D: *Well, from time to time I like to tell him what they have said.*

CENTURY III-17

Mont Aventine brusler *nuict sera veu,* *Le ciel obscur tout à un* *coup en Flandres:* *Quand le monarque chassera* *son nepveu,* *Leurs gens à Eglise commettront* *les esclandres.*	Mount Aventine will be seen burning at night, the sky in Flanders will be suddenly obscured. When the King drives out his nephew their churchmen will commit scandals.

B: He says this has a couple of different meanings, one of which has already taken place in the past. The other meanings have to do with events in the future. He says Mount Aventine being seen in flames refers to the Anti-Christ's destruction of Rome, because that is one of the seven hills of Rome. He says the sky in Flanders becoming suddenly clouded over refers to, in part, how the weather systems will be messed up due to the earth changes. It also refers to the smoke and dust raised by land armies on the march and from armies fighting. He says you will notice whenever there is a battle and a din is raised from violence, there's always a storm afterwards. Fighting men have observed this. It's because the central energy source knows battle is contrary to what the entire universe is trying to accomplish. And so the wisdom of the earth has seen that the quickest way to stop a battle is to start dumping rain on it and no one will have the heart to fight. He says the king kicking out the nephew and the churchmen committing scandals means that in the process of his taking over the Catholic church, the Anti-Christ will have the pope disinherit and excommunicate some of the cardinals which will cause a big scandal in the church, exposing other scandalous things that have been going on.

D: *I thought the king might refer to the pope.*

B: The nephew refers to the cardinals that will be excommunicated.

CENTURY IV-64

Le deffaillant en habit *de bourgeois,* *Viendra le Roi tempter* *de son offence:* *Quinze souldartz la plupart* *Ustagois,* *Vie derniere & chef de* *sa chevance.*	The defaulter, dressed as a citizen will come to try the king with his offense; Fifteen soldiers, for the most part outlaws, the end of his life and the greater part of his estate.

B: He says this quatrain predicts the collapse of various monetary systems as a part of the world troubles. Countries will be defaulting on their colonies and individuals will be defaulting on their property to try to get everything in balance again. He says there are some other things involved here, too. Different world leaders will be disgraced in the process, and it will be a very confused time.

D: *What does it mean by "fifteen soldiers, for the most part outlaws"?*

B: In the process of all this, some people will be ousted or kicked out of their position, and others will rise up to power. And one of the generals that is ousted will be able to gather fifteen companies of soldiers to follow him, to try to take the place by storm and change the situation.

D: *Then it mostly has to do with money problems.*

B: Yes, definitely, definitely, definitely!

D: *The translators had no explanation for it.*

CENTURY II-33

Par le torrent qui descent
  de Veronne,
Par lors qu' au Pau guidera
  son entrée:
Un grand naufrage, & non moins
  en Garonne
Quand ceux de Gennes marcheront
  leur contree.

Through the torrent which pours down from Verona there where the entry is guided to the Po, a great wreck, and not less so in Garonne when the people of Genoa will march against their country.

B: He says during the time of troubles there will be breakdowns in communication and transportation systems. One of the results will be a horrible train wreck in the Alps where the trains must go through tunnels to get through the mountains. He says there will be several accidents like this, but this one will be particularly horrible. Two trains will collide in one of the tunnels close to the entrance. The train entering won't have time to stop before the other one coming out of the tunnel collides with it. The train will jump the tracks and some of the cars will collide with the mountainside around the tunnel mouth. The other cars will topple end over end down the mountain. It will be a horrible accident. He says "where the torrent enters the mouth" refers to streams which run very fast up in the mountains sometimes cutting tunnels through the rocks.

D: *What about the last part? "And not less so in Garonne, when the people of Genoa will march against their country."*

B: He says that refers to the general situation in that part of Europe during the time of troubles. Since the Anti-Christ will be coming up through southern Europe, there will be various insurrections and revolutions going on. Some people will think, "Well, this is our chance to break free of this country and start our own country or what-have-you."

D: *They will make use of the confusion and the upheavals to do this.*

Chapter 6

The Deeds of the Monster

CENTURY IV-41

Gymnique sexe captive par
hostage,
Viendra de nuit custodes decevoir:
Le chef du camp deceu par
son langage:
Lairra à la gente, sera piteux
à voir.

A female (sex) captive as a hostage will come by night to deceive the guards. The leader of the camp deceived by her language will leave her to the people, it will be pitiful to see.

B: He says this quatrain contains a great deal of symbolism. One aspect of the Anti-Christ will be the perversion of philosophy, represented by the sex captive coming by night. With this perversion of philosophy he will try to weaken his opponents from within. This particular campaign of his will be very effective because his perversion of philosophy will deceive those (the guards) who are on the lookout for it. And after "she" has deceived the guards, "she" is able to get to the *leader* of the guards. The leader is also deceived by soft words flowing like honey. The leader feels there is no harm, leaving this particular bit of propaganda free to work its havoc on the general populace. Nostradamus says this philosophy makes use of the perversion of that which is well and good. There are already good examples of this in existence in this time, in the form of some of the television preachers.

D: *What does he mean by that?*

B: The Anti-Christ will observe them to see what they do to be so effective, and he will use their methods of wheedling people to convince them that their ideas are wrong and they need to change to his new set of ideas.

D: *He's going to use this philosophy as part of his own?*

B: He's going to use some of these methods to spread *his* philosophy.

47

D: *Yes, that's a very symbolic quatrain. Of course, the translators are translating it literally.*

B: They *always* seem to. (*I laughed.*)

D: *They think it means a real woman being abandoned to a mob after tricking the guards.*

B: He's just shaking his head.

CENTURY IV-36

Les jeux nouveau en Gaule redressés,	New games are set up in Gaul, after the victory of the Insubrian
Après victoire de l'Insubre champaigne:	campaign. The mountains of Hesperia the great ones tied and
Monts d'Esperie, les grands liés, troussés:	bound. Romania and Spain will tremble with fear.
De peur trembler la Romaigne l'Espaigne.	

B: He says this quatrain has several references. The one we're concerned with refers to the Anti-Christ's southern European campaign. His influence will begin spreading to where it will be threatening Spain on the western side and threatening Romania on the eastern side.

D: *Gaul is France?*

B: Yes. Because at this point in the campaign the Anti-Christ will have already taken over much of France and will be preparing to take over Spain.

D: *What are the Insubrians?*

B: He says that is a historical connotation. He's not really saying much about Insubrians. He says you'll be able to find information on it in the encyclopedia.

D: *It says "after the victory of the Insubrian campaign."*

B: Yes. He says there is specific symbolism there. You will find some parallels in Roman history when the Roman empire was trying to expand northward into central Europe. The Romans were only able to go so far before they ran into problems. But the Anti-Christ will learn from history to overcome these problems. It refers to the campaign the Anti-Christ has for that part of the world. If you look up the history, you will find some interesting parallels.

D: *He's talking about the mountains of Hesperia. What is Hesperia?*

B: The "mountains of Hesperia" refer to the mountains of eastern Europe, particularly the Alps and the Caucasians. That area is mountainous and difficult to maneuver in.

When I did my research I found some interesting parallels, as Nostradamus said I would, that could apply to the Anti-Christ's campaign in that area.

The Insubres were one of several Gallic peoples of the continent, known as Celtæ, who crossed the Alps and settled in what is now known as Milan and the Po valley in the 5th century B.C.E. These people were fierce warriors. Undaunted by the prospect of death they fell upon their enemies with an ardor and impetuosity that swept away an army in an instant. They destroyed, but they did not create. Within a few centuries they were conquered by the Romans due to the Roman's staying power and their ability to endure and persevere.

I think this refers to what happens after the Anti-Christ's victory in Italy. Is Nostradamus comparing the Anti-Christ's forces to the fierce Insubrian warriors or to the more enduring Romans?

CENTURY IV-43

Seront ouis au ciel les armes battre:	Weapons will be heard fighting in the skies: in the same year the
Celui an mesme les divins ennemis:	divine are enemies: they will want unjustly to query the holy laws,
Voudrant loix sainctes injustement debatre,	through lightning and war many believers put to death.
Par foudre & guerre bien croyans à mort mis.	

B: He says this quatrain refers to the time of troubles. Specifically, it describes some aspects concerning the sacking of the Vatican Library. He says "questioning the holy law" is the Anti-Christ saying these printed materials that have been put under edict, should not be. As a consequence, many people will be trying to defend the church and will die fighting. And many others' faith will either change radically or die due to the new material that is revealed.

In Volume One it was revealed that one of the tactics of the Anti-Christ's special brand of psychological warfare would be the destruction of cultural relics and monuments in Rome and other cities. Through the help of the Last Pope, who will be a tool of the Anti-Christ, he will gain access to the secret archives of the Vatican Library. Instead of destroying this material he will reveal it to the world, estimating that this will do more damage to the church than getting rid of the material.

D: *The translators have correctly identified aerial warfare because of the third line, but they couldn't figure out what he meant by divine enemies.*

B: The enemies involved will not know all there is to know. They will be fighting for the Anti-Christ, but they believe they'll be doing it for the good of the Prophet, Mohammed. Plus, the phrase "divine enemies" corresponds to the fact that this situation has been referred to in some of the prophetic books of the Bible.

D: *The same situation or what?*

B: The time of troubles in general. The Bible describes various visions of calamities that are to come.

D: *Is it in the book of Revelation?*

B: He says not specifically in Revelation. He hesitates to identify Revelation because the vision of that prophet was so *final*. And Nostradamus' vision is not as final because he sees life continuing afterwards. So he says even though he understands the symbolism, he's not sure if he's seeing the same era of time as the other prophet.

D: *This quatrain contains some strange words and a Latin phrase the translators don't understand.*

CENTURY VIII-48

Saturne en Cancer, Jupiter avec Mars,	Saturn in Cancer, Jupiter with Mars in February 'Chaldondon'
Dedans Feurier Chaldondon salva terre.	salva tierra. Sierra Morena
Sault Castalon affailli de trois pars.	besieged on three sides near Verbiesque, war and mortal conflict.
Pres de Verbiesque conflit mortelle guerre.	

I had trouble with the pronunciation of these names and he asked me to spell Verbiesque.

D: *That is a place name the translators don't understand.*

B: He says he wrote it down the way it sounded to him because it's not French, even though it is a French spelling. It is not a French place name, but rather a place in Russia. He asks you to repeat the unknown phrase and spell Chaldondon. (*I did so.*) He says this quatrain refers to the fact that the roots of some of the events in the conflict to come (during the time of troubles) were laid in the previous World Wars. He says there will be much destruction. Some of the events that take place will cause past heinous events to look like child's play in comparison. He says to remember that the Anti-Christ will make a very close study of Hitler. He will have access to books not generally available or known to the general public, and it will be possible for him to obtain secret Nazi documents on Hitler. He says the Latin words ... rather than trying to bash the meaning through the vessel's mind which has no knowledge of Latin, he will urge the scholars to consult their Latin text. He says to look for anagrams and a metaphorical meaning drawn from Latin sources as well as literal meanings.

D: *I know "tierra" means "earth." They have a possible translation for Chaldondon. The book says it might be the Latin word Chaldens, which means soothsayer. That's as close as they can come in Latin.*

B: He says that's close enough. It's good the scholars have been able to translate these words. He says now they must remain aware of the part of your knowledge referred to as "metaphysical" or "psychic"—

or whatever phrase you wish to use. It must be relied upon and developed to bring the earth through this time of troubles. They needed this motivation centuries ago when the traditional church became separated from the Gnostic branch of religion.

J: *I'm thinking of the Balkan areas. The Balkans have been the scene of many, many battles through both World War I and II. Could the phrase also mean that the Greek church compared to the Roman church is much simpler? This separation of religion took place in the 1400's. Would this mean that the Greek church and the Balkans will be important in this quatrain?*

B: He says, no. A connection with that geographical area of the world is correct, but you persist in trying to emphasize Christianity. He says, I'm trying to tell you that Christianity has entered its sunset. When the early councils started persecuting those Christians who believed in spiritual enlightenment and psychic development—and he says he's speaking about long before the split of the Roman and Greek churches—they became separated from their source. That's when the Gnostic branch was cut off and burned.

D: *Are we on the right track relating that phrase to a soothsayer or a predictor?*

B: Yes. And John's connection with that area of Europe is on track because there will be many crucial battles fought there. He says they will be fought there partially because Ogmios' roots will not be far from there.

D: *So this is where he will come from. I think he once said central Europe, but he didn't say where. Is that what he means by "Sault Castalon" which they translated as "Sierra Morena"? Besieged on three sides near Verbiesque. War and mortal conflict."*

B: He says this indicates that there will be much fighting in eastern Europe, where Europe and Asia blend together. It's that part of Europe where you're not sure if you're still on the European continent or the Asian continent.

Ogmios was the mythological name given by Nostradamus to the nemesis, or the leader of the underground forces against the Anti-Christ. He was introduced in Volume One.

CENTURY II-41

La grand estoille par sept jours brulera,	The great star will burn for seven days and the cloud will make the
Nuée fera deux soleils apparoir:	sun appear double. The large
Le gros mastin fera toute nuict hurlera,	mastiff will howl all night when the great pontiff changes his abode.
Quand grand pontife changera de terroir.	

B: He says this quatrain refers to the time of troubles. The great pontiff changing his abode refers to the last pope who changes his loyalties from the church to the Anti-Christ. He says the great star burning for seven days refers to the explosion of a fantastic, very advanced, satellite which has its ancestry in the present day star wars programs. The satellite will explode and burn for seven days. It will burn so brightly that through the clouds caused by the explosion it will appear to be a second sun. The mastiff that will howl all night refers to a secret branch of the priesthood in the Catholic Church that no one knows about except a few high priest members. This secret branch of the priesthood is like a private army, and the commander-in-chief is the pope. Their job is to fight for the church if the need should arise, similar to the way the Jesuits used to be the soldiers of Christ. The members of this particular order of priesthood will be very finely educated, trained in all of the martial arts and all ways of committing violence. But when the pope sells out and allies himself with the Anti-Christ, it in effect leaves this army leaderless. What can they do but howl all night and try to figure out a solution?

D: *I thought maybe the great star and the double star might have referred to UFOs or to the Others.*

B: Not in this case, because it's at the time of war. Whenever a war of this scale takes place—a planetary-wide war like World War II or this one coming up—the Others stay clear until the situation is resolved one way or the other.

D: *The translators think the double sun might mean a comet. That's how they're translating it.*

B: He's making a rude noise with his lips.

D: *They're thinking it might be an atomic explosion but they're mostly thinking of a comet. They said the seven days could also mean seven years. They didn't know how to explain it.*

B: He says that's apparent.

CENTURY VI-35

Pres de Rion & proche à la blanche laine,	Near the Bear and close to the white wool, Aries, Taurus, Cancer,
Aries, Taurus, Cancer, Leo, la Vierge,	Leo, Virgo, Mars, Jupiter, the
Mars, Jupiter, le sol ardra grand plaine,	Sun will burn the great plain, woods and cities; letters hidden
Bois & citez, lettres cachez au cierge.	in the candle.

B: He says this quatrain refers to some of the events that will take place during the time of troubles. The line "the sun will burn the plain" refers to a certain amount of nuclear confrontation that will exist during the time of troubles. He says the great bear refers to Russia. The phrase "the white wool" refers to the snow and also the white robes the enemy will wear because they are woven from the hair of sheep. He says you must get the horoscope of the Anti-Christ and look up these signs and the way they relate to each other and their various aspects. Compare it to the planets' positions and their influences on the Anti-Christ's horoscope to get a picture of the conflict. He says this will give you a feeling for how some of the time of troubles will be, particularly around 1997.

D: *What does that last line mean? "Letters hidden in the candle."*

B: He says that refers to the fact that clandestine organizations will be very plentiful and pervasive causing everyone to be careful about what they say. Many people will be members of various underground organizations as well as organizations for espionage. And one will have to guard one's words carefully and figure out novel ways of communicating in order to not be betrayed.

John was busy looking in his ephemeris and asked, "Are transiting Mars and Jupiter conjunct?" Nostradamus said they were. "Okay, that gives us a time period, sometime in 1997."

D: *It seems like a lot of these quatrains deal with the Anti-Christ.*

B: He says this man causes some of the most terrible events in the history of humanity. He says it's a very crucial and unstable time. You will notice he also saw a lot of events which occurred during the French Revolution because it was another crucial and unstable time as far as his country was concerned. These events concern the whole world and not just his country, so naturally he would see many visions about them.

D: *When we go through the entire book we will probably find more on the French Revolution.*

B: He says there are plenty there.

D: *It seems to me that a lot of these predictions pertain to many different events. I wonder if he was seeing many different possibilities that could happen and that they might not all come true.*

B: He says the main reason why he wanted this communication was to avoid the worst of what he's seen, some of the so-called "worse-case scenarios." He says these things could very easily take place and with great determination and resolve they could be altered for the better. He says, unfortunately, at this time, the worst things he has seen are the most possible. But he knows he must try his best to help lessen the destruction.

D: *He has said before that sometimes he saw a nexus in time and that there are many different paths and therefore many possibilities.*

B: This is correct. He says at this point, since it is such a major nexus, no matter which path we choose it seems to contain most of these visions. But he says there are other paths where various events could be avoided.

J: *In this quatrain Mars conjuncts with Jupiter in Virgo in September 1992. Is this when the Anti-Christ comes to power by using nuclear force?*

B: It's a good date. He says at that time he will come to power using conventional warfare but with a very strong threat of nuclear force. He will not actually have the material on hand for a nuclear confrontation, but the people he's confronting don't know this. He acts so aggressively they're convinced he can carry through with his threat of nuclear force. It will be a successful bluff; the same method Hitler used.

D: *There were some quatrains that referred to the enemies of the Anti-Christ using nuclear weapons.*

B: He says some people in other countries will have nuclear weapons. Some of them will use small-scale atomic weapons, but most of them will hold back because they wish to avoid a nuclear confrontation. He says it will be a very touchy situation.

D: *In this quatrain he said the "sun will burn the great plain."*

B: The Anti-Christ will indeed end up using nuclear weapons in his grand strategy and he will use them more than he first thought. But at the very beginning when he first comes to power, he won't have those kind of weapons.

D: *There was one quatrain that referred to a bomb which exploded in the Mediterranean poisoning the fish. (Century II-3, Chapter 15, "The Coming of the Anti-Christ," Volume One.)*

B: Yes, but that's much later in his campaign when he has achieved a great deal of power.

D: *You also said he would use other weapons that haven't been developed yet.*

B: He says they are already developed, you just don't know about them.

CENTURY IV-48

Planure Ausonne fertile, spacieuse, Produira taons si tant de sauterelles: Clarté solaire deviendra nubileuse, Rouger le tout, grand peste venir d'elles.	The plains of Ausonia, rich and wide, will produce so many gadflies and grasshoppers, that the light of the sun will be clouded over. They will devour everything and a great pestilence will come from them.

D: *The translators said that one word could be translated "locusts" instead of grasshoppers, but it's the same idea.*

B: Yes. (*He asked for the spelling of Ausonia.*) He says this event occurs during the time of troubles. The name Ausonia is used symbolically to represent an underground movement of guerrilla fighters from the rural areas. At first, and for quite a while they won't have any decisive victories against the enemy, but they will be annoying like a lot of mosquitoes or gnats buzzing around. They manage to keep the enemy distracted just enough to give the fighting men a chance to win some victories.

D: *It says, "the light of the sun will be clouded over."*

B: Yes. That line refers to the local crop duster-type planes they will use to help accomplish some of their mischief.

D: *"They will devour everything and a great pestilence will come from them."*

B: Whenever they think the enemy forces are coming in their direction they will harvest and hide all of the food. Thus, the enemy cannot live off the land as they would like. If they can't harvest and hide the food they burn it, depending upon what kind of facilities they have. It's the scorched earth policy.

D: *The translators think Ausonia means Naples.*

B: No. It refers to the extensive plains of Ausonia. He's using it to symbolize the rural areas one must go through when traveling from town to town.

D: *They think he means an actual plague of locusts or grasshoppers.*

B: No, it's just a symbol for the underground movement mischief.

CENTURY IV-49

Devant le peuple, sang sera respandu,	Blood will be spilt in front of the people, which will not go far from the high heavens. But for a long time it will not be heard, the spirit of a single man will bear witness to it.
Que de haut ciel ne viendra esloigner:	
Mais d'un long temps ne sera entendu.	
L'esprit d'un seul le viendra tesmoigner.	

B: He says the symbolism here is very complex. The quatrain refers to some of the events in World War II, but the main thrust of its prediction refers to the time of troubles. When it says the blood will be spilt in front of the people, that refers to leaders being assassinated. "But for a long time it will not be heard," refers to the fact that some of the deposed leaders' struggles for power will occur from within. It will be a long time before the whole story is revealed.

D: *Who is the single man? It says, "the spirit of a single man will bear witness to it."*

B: He says while these horrible events are happening the man represented by Ogmios will put things together and realize the full impact of it all. That will fire his determination to be more than just an underground group leader. He will decide to do something to overthrow the Anti-Christ.

D: *It says, "which will not go far from the high heavens." Does that refer to blood being spilt?*

B: Wrong. "The blood being spilt in front of the people, that will not go far from the high heavens," represents the leaders. He says you must remember that in his time kings are ordained by God, and therefore are considered to be just one step away from God. Plus the karmic relationships and the karmic symbolism of this situation are very important. This event will be closer to the heavens than the everyday things that happen to people.

CENTURY IV-54

Du nom qui onques ne fut
   au Roy Gaulois,
Jamais ne fut un fouldre
   si craintif:
Tremblant l'Italie, l'Espaigne
   & les Anglois,
De femme estrangiers
   grandement attentif.
	Of a name which never held by a French king, never was there so fearful a thunderbolt. Italy, Spain and the English tremble; he will be greatly attentive to foreign women.

B: He says the fearful thunderbolt refers to nuclear weapons. He says "of a name never held by a French king" refers to the underground leader who will rise to a position of leadership over all of France during the time of troubles. Since one of his grandparents is from a different country it causes him to have a different name than most Frenchmen, and therefore it's not a French name. That's why he represented it by saying "not held by a French king." And he says "being attentive to foreign women" means that when he deals with leaders and people of other countries, he's willing to listen to their point of view as long as the people express it gently rather than trying to force it. He says it's one of those quatrains that describe the situation during the time of troubles.

D: *The translators think it describes Napoleon.*

B: No. It is not Napoleon, it is Ogmios.

D: *But they said Napoleon was not the name of a French king either.*

B: He says Ogmios' extraction is from eastern Europe. His name will sound very strange to French ears.

CENTURY IV-60

Les sept enfans en hostaige
   laissés,
Le tiers viendra son enfant
   trucider:
Deux par son filz seront
   d'estoc percés,
Gennes, Florence, los
   viendra encunder.
	The seven children left in hostage, the third will come to slaughter his child. Two will be pierced by a hook because of his son, he will come to strike against Genoa and Florence.

B: He says this quatrain describes the downfall of the United Nations during the time of troubles. Someone coming to kill someone else represents the backstabbing that will occur as a result of the collapse of the central form of debate.

D: *It says, "two will be pierced by a hook because of his son."*

B: When things return to order and people begin figuring out who did what, there will be a lot of political assassinations taking place. But instead of killing the leaders, some of the countries will occasionally choose to do something to one of the followers or their children, to get the results they desire.

D: *That sounds kind of drastic, too.*

B: It will be a very unreasonable time. It will happen toward the end of the time of troubles.

D: *Then it says, "he will come to strike against Genoa and Florence."*

B: That describes the destruction of cultural centers. He'll be striking against places like that or trying to reduce them to rubble.

D: *We've covered that before. The translators thought this dealt with the seven children of Catherine de' Medici.*

B: (*Slowly and affected*) Ha! Ha! Ha!

D: *They said it didn't make sense, but it was the only way they could put seven children into a quatrain.*

B: He's ranting and raving a bit. He's saying, "Fools! I am surrounded by fools!" (*Laugh*) And he's not calling you a fool or this vessel a fool. He's speaking of the foolishness of other unenlightened people.

D: (Laugh) *We didn't write these interpretations.*

B: He said, "Of course not. That's what you need me for."

D: *And that's why we have you here. You're doing a terrific job.*

CENTURY IX-69

Sur le mont de Bailly & la Bresle	On the mountain of Sain Bel and
Seront caichez de Grenoble	l'Arbresle will be hidden the proud
les fiers,	people of Grenoble. Beyond
Oultre Lyon, Vien, eulx si	Lyons, at Vienne there will be such
grande gresle,	great hail, locust on the land, not
Langoult en terre n' en restera	a third of it will remain.
un tiers.	

I had a terrible time with the pronunciations of these names. I had to spell both the English and the French versions before he could understand me.

B: He says this quatrain describes the side effects of the war the Anti-Christ wages on the European continent. The people will hide in underground chambers or in tunnels in the mountains for protection from destruction that will rain down from the skies. There will be great destruction and plagues upon the land as is portrayed in the quatrain. He says it's at this time that men will turn cannibalistic because they will not be able to get the wheat that will still be growing copiously on the American continent.

D: *We covered quatrains dealing with that before.*

B: Yes, that's why he brought it up.

This aspect of the Third War was covered in detail in Volume One.

D: *They say that one of the words, "langoult," means "locust" in Old French, but in modern French it means "lobster."*

B: (*Smiling*) He says that "locust" is the correct interpretation.

D: (Laugh) *I thought so. I didn't think he meant "lobsters on the land."*

B: He says it is natural for things to change through the centuries.

Chapter 7

The Far Future

CENTURY I-59

Les exilez deportez dans les isles,	The exiles deported to the islands
Au changement d'un plus cruel	at the advent of an even more
monarque	cruel king will be murdered.
Seront meurtis: & mis deux	Two will be burnt who were not
les scintiles,	sparing in their speech.
Qui de parler ne seront	
estez parques.	

B: He says this quatrain has multiple meanings, one of which has already come to pass. He will refer to another meaning of it. It's difficult to say what he means by this quatrain because some of the islands the exiles will be deported to do not exist yet. He says a lot of these islands will be created during the Earth changes by the rising and falling of the ocean floor, Earthquakes, and volcanoes. There will be several new islands and in one particular country they will be used as penal colonies. Later on, when the Anti-Christ becomes more powerful, the men there will be tortured to death. What he is saying here is that the hostages on the island will be murdered when a more cruel king comes to power.

D: *Will this be far in the future?*

B: No, he says it will be just before the end of this millennium because it will be during the time of the Anti-Christ.

CENTURY II-45

Trop le ciel pleure l'Androgyn procrée,	The heavens weep too much for the birth of Androgeus, near the heavens human blood is spilt. It is too late for the great nation to be revived because of the death, soon, yet too late, comes the awaited help.
Pres de ciel sang humain respondu:	
Par mort trop tard grand peuple recrée,	
Tard & tost vient le secours attendu.	

D: *The word is Androgyn in the French and they have translated it as Androgeus.*

B: He says to use the word "Androgyn" instead. This concerns some sociological changes that will be sparked by the establishment of space colonies. He says the only way these space colonies will be able to function is for men and women to work together harmoniously, and be rid of their narrow minded, bigoted, and chauvinistic attitudes about sex roles. He says the birth of Androgyn symbolizes that men and women will be able to do what is best suited for them without worrying whether or not it's suitable for someone of their sex. This type of change will also affect the people left on Earth. This sociological upheaval causes great dissent among some of the nations, like in the Middle East. He says these countries will have to resolve their beliefs in order to accommodate these new concepts. He says there will be a lot of bloodshed, particularly among the space forces. This will be due to space accidents, not war, as people adjust to a new way of living. He says many pilots will die.

D: *I can see the connection now with Androgenus.*

B: He says he believes those lines are fairly clear.

The legend of Androgenus is one of the creation myths which claim that in the beginning there were three types of sexual creatures. There were male, female, and a hermaphrodite that had the characteristics of both. In our time the word "androgynous" refers to the quality of having both sexes in one plant or body. It's interesting that he chose to use the word "androgyn" which applies more accurately to this quatrain. The dictionary defines it as "a male sex hormone or similar substance that can give rise to masculine characteristics." Thus, in the future, the lines that separate our stereotyped views of male and female will blur, and although the people will maintain their physical qualities, their functioning roles in society will not be the same as they are today. Men and women will finally attain equality. No wonder this vision was important to Nostradamus. Later in this book we see that his views of male-female roles were chauvinistic and greatly influenced by the time he lived in.

CENTURY IV-53

Les fugitifs & bannis revoquez,	The fugitives and the banished are
Peres & fils grand garnissant	recalled, fathers and sons
les hauts puits:	strengthening the deep wells.
Le cruel pere & les siens suffoquez,	The cruel father and his followers
Son fils plus pire submergé dans	suffocated; His most wicked son
le puits.	drowned in the well.

B: He says this refers to the far future when space colonies and space flight will be very common. Space colonies will be created within the solar system but away from the Earth by those who could not fit in on the Earth. Because the Earth will be slightly overcrowded, these people will decide to start their own colony in space, rather than give up cherished beliefs and ideas or try to fit in with the general crowd. But then trouble will begin on Earth. Someone will economically manipulate the Earth causing the Earth's leaders to call on the colonies for help. The colonies will be able to supply the Earth with things they manufacture in space that cannot be produced on Earth. In the phrase "strengthening the deep well," the word "wells" refers to the phrase "gravity wells."

D: *Gravity wells?*

B: Yes. Gravity wells are found around each planet. That is, you must pull against the influence of gravity to get away from the planet and you must account for it whenever you're maneuvering near that planet. To strengthen these wells they send materials and supplies down to the Earth powers who need it. In the process of this exchange a man who reenters the atmosphere makes a miscalculation and burns up. This describes the son drowned in the well. "The cruel father and his followers suffocated" describes those who attempted to ruin the lives of many and bring back the time of troubles but who did not succeed. The people of the colonies are the ones that finally capture the cruel father because he tries to escape from Earth by spaceship. Since they are already in space, the people of the colonies are able to intercept him. They decide a suitable fate for him is to send him out the air lock without a spacesuit.

D: *Before when he mentioned people being suffocated, it meant they were silenced and not allowed to speak.*

B: This is a different meaning and a different situation.

D: *I see. What one quatrain means, another one might not mean. This is a very complex explanation.*

B: He says it will take place in the far future. It has no immediate concern or effect on you. The quatrains he is primarily worried about now are the ones concerning the time of troubles since it is so close. But he knows that it would be nice to satisfy your curiosity about the far future.

D: *Yes. We like to know about those things too because we are curious.*

B: He thought so. He said humans don't change through the centuries.

Chapter 8

The Hadrian Quatrains

I HAD PURPOSELY NOT INCLUDED these quatrains in the first book because I felt they contained an error on the part of Nostradamus. I should have known this could not be true, but until I was able to do more research (as he suggested) I didn't feel comfortable including them. The notion that he could be wrong gave me a queasy feeling in the pit of my stomach. After all, I had accepted all of his other explanations without any question. If this was a glaring error, then it would put all of the other translations in doubt.

CENTURY I-8

Combien de fois prinse cité solaire	How often will you be captured, O city of the sun? Changing laws
Seras changeant les loix barbares & vaines:	that are barbaric and vain. Bad times approach you. No longer
Ton mal s'approche. Plus sera tributaire,	will you be enslaved. Great Hadrie will revive your veins.
La grand Hadrie recourira des veines.	

B: He says this quatrain describes events in World War I and II as well as events caused by the Anti-Christ. When he says "city of the Sun" he's referring to Paris because he had foreseen the presence of the Sun King in Paris making it the City of the Sun. He says during the 20th century the city has been overrun, conquered and reconquered many times. But he says it will come through in the end. It won't be totally demolished like some of these cities will be.

D: *Who does he mean by the great Hadrie?*

B: He says he's referring to Hadrian, the law-giver.

D: *(I was unfamiliar with the name.) Is he a mythological or historical figure?*

B: He lived in ancient history. He says he was the first great lawgiver who codified a very just and workable system of law. By using the name as an anagram, he's symbolically referring to one who will help the world recover after the Anti-Christ; one who will be a great giver of law.

D: *They translate Hadrie as meaning King Henry IV of France.*

B: He says it's obvious the people of your day are not educated in ancient history and cannot draw parallels between past and present.

D: *I realize he works a lot with mythology and ancient history, subjects we no longer study.*

B: He says the opportunity to study it is there, but the people are lazy.

D: *(Laugh) True.*

CENTURY I-9

*De l'Orient viendra la cœur
    Punique
Facher Hadrie & les hoirs
    Romulides
Accompagné de la classe Libyque
Temples Mellites & proches
    isles vuides.*

From the Orient will come the African heart to trouble Hadrie and the heirs of Romulus. Accompanied by the Libyan fleet the temples of Malta and nearby islands shall be deserted.

B: He says this quatrain refers to the various shifts of power that will occur as the world recovers from the Anti-Christ and settles down to its new order of things. One change will reestablish the Ethiopian royalty from a hidden line further east in the Middle East. He says in addition to this, the Chinese nation will show the nations of Africa how to be conservative with their land and how to raise food for millions of people in small areas of land, as it is done in China. This will help them stay away from the patterns of repeated plagues and droughts that they currently suffer from. He says various shifts of power back and forth will trouble the law-giver, Hadrian, until he finds a way to accommodate for this in the law he's drawing up to help the world recover from the Anti-Christ.

D: *It says "the heirs of Romulus." I think of Romulus as being associated with Italy.*

B: Yes. He says the quatrain predicts that the shifts will trouble Hadrian and the heirs of Romulus. The people of Europe will also be troubled by these shifts of power.

D: *Then it says, "accompanied by the Libyan fleet, the temples of Malta and nearby islands will be deserted." I want to clarify that part.*

B: He says he's already adequately explained it.

D: *The Libyan, I know that has to do with ...*

B: With North Africa. *(Impatiently)* He says the power shifts of North Africa, of Africa in general, and of Asia will be disturbing Europe. This explains why they abandon some of the harder-to-defend islands in the Mediterranean. He says to open your psychic eyes.

D: *Be patient. Sometimes when I go over the quatrains later I can see more clearly what he is trying to say to me, but it's difficult to understand them all at once. Again the translators have interpreted Hadrie as King Henry.*

B: He says he's not interested in their interpretations. He wants to get as many quatrains done as he can.

After interpreting these quatrains, I tried to find out who Hadrian was and my first attempts always begin with my encyclopedia. I must admit that my research at this point was not as thorough as it should have been. The only law-giver I could find who lived in ancient times was Hammurabi. I did find an emperor of Rome named Hadrian, but I didn't think he was the one referred to because I couldn't see what he had to do with law. I wondered if this could have been a mistake on the part of Nostradamus. Could he actually have been referring to Hammurabi? I couldn't see how that name could be anagrammatized from Hadrie; only the first syllables were the same. This bothered me so I put them aside until the next quatrain mentioning Hadrie came up. When it did, I decided to ask him about it.

CENTURY II-55

Dans le conflict le grand qui peu valloit,	In the conflict the great man who is of little worth will perform an
A son dernier fera cas merveilleux:	astonishing deed at his end. While Hadrie sees what is
Pendant qu' Hadrie verra ce qu'il falloit,	needed, during a banquet he stabs the proud.
Dans le banquet pongnale l'orgueilleux.	

D: *We've got that word "Hadrie" again.*

B: He says the great man of little worth refers to a man in a governmental position who should be holding a higher position, and he feels very bitter about this. So he's plotting for the downfall of those who are above him in the echelons of government. "He stabs the proud," so to speak. He asks for you to repeat the line about Hadrian.

D: *"While Hadrie sees what is needed, during a banquet he stabs the proud."*

B: He says this man will be acting behind the scenes in a very sneaky manner. And during a time of plenty, represented by the banquet, he will drag down the others who have bypassed him. But Hadrian, who is wise enough to protect himself from the man as well as being wise in the law, will clearly see the situation and correct it.

D: *I had trouble with the word "Hadrian." There were a couple of other quatrains where he mentioned him, and I believe he said the word had* something to do with ancient history, that Hadrian was a great law-giver. I was trying to do some research, but I couldn't find Hadrian. I did find Hammurabi and that's why I was confused.

B: He says there is a Hadrian. He says you are not familiar with research techniques, and that you have not researched thoroughly. He says there is one called "Hadrian, the Law-giver." He suggests you go to the place for the learning of law and pursue their library.

D: *They list Hammurabi as a giver of law in ancient times.*

B: He's jumping up and down. He says you're being obstinate and stubborn. He doesn't like dealing with Aries for this reason. He says, of course there's a Hammurabi, but there's also a Hadrian. (*I had to laugh; I was really getting chewed-out.*)

D: *Okay, I thought he might have gotten the two confused. But I was afraid I would make him mad if I said anything.*

B: He says you're being stupid and obstinate again. He's jumping up and down. He says he knows what he's talking about. If he meant Hammurabi, he would have said Hammurabi. He says he said Hadrian, and by God, he meant Hadrian. He's stomping his foot with every word.

D: (*This was the angriest I had ever heard him.*) *Okay. If I do more research I will find Hadrian. That's what confused me. I thought I would ask him as long as the word came up again.*

B: He says, how could there be any confusion or resemblance between Hammurabi and Hadrian? Just because they both start with an "Ha" sound doesn't mean they're alike. He says to go on to the next quatrain or he's going away.

D: (*Loud laugh*) *I'm sorry. I didn't want him to get angry, but I wanted to clarify that for myself.*

B: He's already made it clear, he thought, but he says you persist in asking dumb questions. He's saying, "Look for Hadrian." And you keep saying, "Well, how about Hammurabi, what about Hammurabi?" He's saying, "Forget about Hammurabi, go find Hadrian."

D: *Okay. That's what I'll do. I just wanted some reassurance that I was on the right track. I should know by now that he knows what he's talking about.* (Laugh)

CENTURY III-11

Les armes battre an ciel
  longue saison
L'arbre au milieu de la
  cité tombé:
Verbine, rongne, glaive
  en face, Tison
Lors le monarque d'Hadrie
  succombé.

The weapons fight in the sky for a long period; the tree fell in the middle of the city. The sacred branch cut, a sword opposite Tison, then the King Hadrie falls.

D: *This quatrain contains the word "Hadrie" and the translators always interpret it the same. They say in their definition, "Hadrie is one of Nostradamus' most popular anagrams for King Henry the Fourth."*

B: He says just because he uses an anagram more than once doesn't mean he's using it to refer to the same person. There are several names that could be anagrammatized by Hadrie. He says there's Hadrian, Henry, and a whole host of names. It's difficult to come up with original anagrams for some people without making it so obscure that no one can figure out who he's talking about.

D: *Every time the translators have said it means King Henry.*

B: He says perhaps that explains why they can't interpret some of his quatrains. This may be a quatrain that has nothing to do with King Henry IV, but he says that's the way it goes. This quatrain has several meanings. The first two lines describe, in a nutshell, the effects of World War II and how it finally ended. He says World War II was the first war to make extensive use of the air raids over cities that the Germans called *blitzkrieg* or "lightning war." This was the first time in history this happened, and so it appeared very prominent in his vision. The tree that fell in the middle of the city symbolizes the bomb that was dropped on Hiroshima and Nagasaki. It was just a slender, silver cylinder that dropped down, like the trunk of a tree.

D: *(I suddenly had an inspiration.) We call it a mushroom cloud, but when the cloud rose it did resemble the top of a tree.*

B: Yes. And he says "the sacred branch cut" symbolizes how atomic power disrupts the tree of life. He's using psychic symbolism, as well as literal chemical and physical symbolism. He says the after effects of such a weapon, in regards to the mutations of cells and cancer, cause another type of cutting away from the tree of life. Afterwards, people in general also become cut off from their spiritual source through the power of the industrial might backed by nuclear power. He asks that you read the last line again.

D: *"A sword opposite Tison. Then the King Hadrie falls."*

(He corrected my pronunciation.)

B: He says this last line refers to an event in our future. It refers to the fall of the English royal house. This will take place during the time of the Anti-Christ. He says it will be through the so-called "fortunes of war" that this will happen.

D: *Does he want to elaborate? Does he mean that the family will die?*

B: He says the quatrain predicts a combination of the male descendants of the family either being killed in battle or dying from a disease released from biological bombs designed to affect only men. The enemy will have biological bombs that release viruses killing all of the soldiers. Slashing the fighting forces so they'll have less soldiers to confront on the battlefield. But the bomb doesn't discriminate. It also affects men who are not fighting, such as older men at home and young boys. So in this way the male members of the English ruling family will be killed. And he says the women of the royal family will be either too old to bear children or through the side-effects of this bomb and other horrible weapons will be rendered sterile. So in this way the English royal family will die out. He says that if England chooses to continue as a monarchy she will have to search the more distant branches of the royal family to find someone to bear the crown. He says they can choose either way and history will run smoothly in either direction, but if they choose tradition, the bearer of the crown will be found from a very unexpected source.

D: *I thought it was interesting that they could invent something that would be able to discriminate between male and female.*

B: He says such diseases have already been invented in your time but they're top military secrets. The virus that attacks has different effects on men and women. They're in the process of refining it, so it will primarily kill men and render women incapable of bearing children. He says he is pulling this vocabulary from the vessel's mind since he is familiar with the concepts, but the words do not exist in his time. When the virus invades the cell, it will be able to discriminate between the X chromosome and the Y chromosome. The presence of the extra X chromosome or the presence of the Y chromosome will affect the virus, determining how it will affect that cell and the entire body.

D: *But I think using a weapon of this sort would be like cutting your own throat, because it's going to hurt the population in general.*

B: He says people who are rabid for war do not think of this.

Maybe this is another reason why he put this in the same quatrain that refers to the atom bomb. Neither did we think of the consequences on the population in general when we used the bomb. He may be drawing another parallel here.

B: These weapons will be dropped on England. But they don't realize the risks they're taking because the weather patterns could cause some of the virus to spread to the mainland mass, thereby destroying part of that population as well.

D: *That's what I thought. It's going to hurt the future population of the world if people can't procreate or reproduce.*

B: He says you're throwing it too far in scope. It's only going to be dropped on England, not the whole world so primarily the English will be affected. But he says the doctors in England, being the good medical men that they are, will be able to create a vaccine or a serum that will counteract the effects of the virus and help make people immune to it. But he says it will take time.

D: *That really sounds drastic, but then everything the Anti-Christ does is extreme.*

B: He says it's difficult for people to take the Anti-Christ seriously
because he goes to the limit with everything.

D: *Then in the case of this quatrain, King Hadrie doesn't refer to
Hadrian.*

B: King Hadrie represents the royal family.

D: *The translators haven't even come close in their interpretations.*

B: He says he's not surprised.

By following Nostradamus' instructions I finally was able to locate
Hadrian in books about the history of law. He was an emperor of Rome
in 117 C.E. (common era, or A.D.). This was the man I had skimmed over
before. This incident taught me a lesson about jumping to conclusions
and doing hasty research. I should also have realized that Nostradamus
had been extremely accurate in giving his interpretations to us, and he
would not be apt to make a mistake of this magnitude.

In Hadrian's time, Rome was filled with people from many different
countries and of many different religions. They all insisted that in the
matter of law they should be judged by the rules and customs of their own
countries instead of the laws that applied to the citizens of Rome. It was
a jumbled and complicated mess. Hadrian was the first to codify and
arrange laws that treated everyone fairly and equally; a huge undertaking.
In our time this is called "equity." So again Nostradamus was correct.
Hadrian was a great law-giver, and he used his name as a symbol of the
law or a law-giver in his quatrains. This was another example of Nostradamus' incredibly complex mind.

Chapter 9

The Horoscopes

I HAD TAKEN SOME OF THE QUATRAINS to John's apartment for clarification of the astrological data. John had been working on one quatrain in particular.

CENTURY I-50

De l'aquatique triplicité naistra.	From the three water signs will be
D'un qui fera le jeudi pour	born a man who will celebrate
sa feste:	Thursday as his holiday. His
Son bruit, loz, regne, sa	renown, praise, rule and power
puissance croistra,	will grow on land and sea, bringing
Par terre & mer aux	trouble to the East.
Oriens tempeste.	

John said the three water signs could refer to a grand trine and would have considerable influence if they were located in a horoscope. We had already been told that the water signs also referred to three bodies of water near the Anti-Christ's location. John asked if he could attend a session and ask Nostradamus for more astrological information. The daring idea of drawing up a horoscope for the Anti-Christ had occurred to him, and I thought it would be fantastic and exciting. I also thought it was impossible because Nostradamus was having such difficulty seeing anything pertaining to the Anti-Christ. His deeds were clearly visible but the man himself was very cloudy. I agreed that John should try, at least it would be an interesting experiment.

After Brenda entered her deep trance, we attempted to get the astrological information.

D: *When we asked about the Anti-Christ before, you said one of the clues to his identity was that part of his horoscope involved three water signs which we think may be a grand trine. The astrologer would like to ask some questions to help clarify that.*

J: (He read the quatrain.) *If this is referring to a grand trine we would like to know which planets will be in trine with each other in the water signs. This would help us find his natal horoscope.*

B: He says he will convey what he can. He will try to tell the communicator which planets will be in what sign, allowing the astrologer to calculate what time this refers to. He says if a piece of information comes across that seems contradictory or does not seem to make sense, it may be a mistake in the interpretation of the concepts between his mind and the mind of the communicator. And feel free to question or clarify the information he's trying to give. He asks if this seems fair and reasonable? (*John agreed.*) (*Smiling*) He has just gently admonished me. He said, "Not everything can be described in music, my dear." (*We laughed.*)

D: *In the Anti-Christ's horoscope, can you see where the sun would be?*

B: He says the sun will be in a place of fire giving him a magnetic personality. He says the three water signs are ... he's showing me a picture of the night sky with a triangle drawn upon it, with circles on each of the points of the triangle. Mercury is on the balance of the scales and Neptune is in his seat of power of the sea. He says what he's going to say next will have the critics baying like a pack of hounds, but he says that old man Pluto will be in the place of mystery. Unfortunately, the information he's giving is a combination of the Anti-Christ's natal horoscope and its interaction with the positions of the planets at the time he rises to power. He says he may not be able to make clear which he's referring to, but he's confident that John can work it out. If John has problems he's free to ask questions.

J: *I would like to know where Saturn and Jupiter are located.*

B: Jupiter will have a very prominent placement. Jupiter is the same as Thor, and Thor is the Anti-Christ's day. (*This refers to Thursday, which is mentioned many times in the quatrains.*) He says Jupiter is the reigning head of the planets, and is the leader of powers. Saturn is in the place of intellect. I'm just repeating what he's saying. I'm describing what I see and what he's trying to show me. I don't know if what I say makes sense or not. It makes no sense to me, but then it's not my field of knowledge. He says he's being deliberately vague and mysterious so the vessel will not become panicked about trying to accurately communicate information of an unknown nature.

D: *You're doing fine.*

B: He says this is another place where the critics can start baying like a pack of hounds. He says the power of Uranus is also in his horoscope, and this influence relates to the water as well. Uranus has the power of water and lightning combined. His horoscope is one of extremes contributing to the magnetism he will have over people. It also contributes to his swift rise to power and his sudden fall. His life is a life of extremes.

D: *He said the critics will start howling like a pack of hounds. Is that because these planets were supposedly not known in his time?*

B: This is correct. He says if you read the classics correctly, you will know about these planets. There is a lot of ancient knowledge that was forgotten at the fall of the Atlantean civilization which must be gradually reattained.

D: *Do you mean they were aware of these planets?*

B: Definitely. He says they were much more advanced than you are in your time. Twentieth-century people tend to be very egocentric, believing they have the highest attainment of science, knowledge, and technology. But this is not true. He says there are many records that are available to him. They are old and moldering in libraries and hidden places, and have probably been destroyed since his time. He says, for example, he has the availability of old copies of Scriptures that have since been banned and changed, giving clues to some of the ancient knowledge.

J: *I have a couple of questions on this because I believe I can draw up his horoscope in my head. The position of Pluto in the sign of mystery would be when Pluto was in the sign of Virgo. Is this correct?*

B: I get a feeling he's very pleased. He says you and he think along the same lines, and he's glad you can do this. It makes it easier for him to communicate.

J: *I want to go through this again and get the entire horoscope before we move on. He mentioned that Pluto was in the sign of mystery. Uranus will probably be in the sign of Aquarius because of the lightning and thunder. And Saturn will probably be in the sign of either Gemini or Aquarius.*

B: He says that Saturn is in Gemini.

J: *Mars will be in Capricorn and Venus in Pisces. Mercury will be in Libra and the moon must be in a water sign.*

B: He says this is true.

J: *Would the moon be in Scorpio? And would the sun be in the sign of Sagittarius?*

B: He says, yes.

J: *Then we have all of them except for his rising sign so we can plot it. What would be the ascendant of this horoscope?*

B: He keeps saying two things for the ascendant, and I'm not sure which one he is emphasizing. I am seeing Aries and Taurus.

J: *That could be true if Aries were rising and Taurus were intercepted in the first house.*

B: But he keeps giving me a picture of both a ram and a bull. I, as communicator, apologize for being dense about this.

J: *No, don't worry about it. I understand what you're trying to say. What about the north node or the part of fortune?*

B: *(She seemed confused.)* What?

D: *Does Nostradamus know the word "node"?*

J: *The north node or the dragon's head?*

B: He says he has run across the term "dragon's head" and it is familiar to him, but the concept is not in the brain of the communicator. The major disadvantage to this mode of communication is a great block where astrological concepts are concerned. This makes it difficult to communicate information he wants to give. He realizes there will be skeptics who will not understand.

J: *How old is the Anti-Christ now?*

B: He says he's in his late teens. I keep hearing 17 or 19. Seventeen is coming in stronger.

D: *Earlier he said he was in his adolescence.*

J: *One more question. (He had been looking up the signs in his book.) Does December 16, 1968 sound like the birthdate of the Anti-Christ?*

B: One moment please. (*Pause*) He says it feels right. It is late in that year.

J: *I'm looking at the ephemeris and that date looks like it could be the time.*

D: *Does he know what an ephemeris is?*

B: He said it's a chart of the stars.

J: *On that date the planets line up to where it would be advantageous for a very spiritual or very demonic person to be born.*

B: Unfortunately he chooses the demonic rather than the spiritual path due to the influence of his traumatic adolescence.

J: *I want to communicate to Nostradamus that this information is very valuable and I am grateful for it. Now through a transit map I can understand how he will come to power.*

B: He says he is grateful to you for being here at this time to receive the information because the time of troubles will be very serious. And he says the forces of good need all the help they can get because they will be overshadowed. He feels anything he can do to help with this will be good for him as well because he feels a karmic debt in this matter.

D: *Then I'm glad we are also helping him.*

B: He says anything he can get communicated clearly and accurately is a plus for all of us, except for the Anti-Christ, that is. He said that with a chuckle.

D: *Well, that's what we're trying to do; outwit the Anti-Christ.*

B: He says he would like to communicate more about his natal horoscope. Perhaps in another session he can sneak some more information past my subconscious to you. He says it's difficult battering through a brick wall. Michel de Notredame is excited and delighted with being able to talk to a fellow spirit and communicate detailed information in a compact form. But at the same time he realizes, it's somewhat diffi-cult because the communicator, myself, does not understand the con-cepts he's trying to convey. He says it's easier now that he has discovered this method of communicating astrological information. This is almost as easy as communicating regular information. He will be glad to go more in depth with this if you have more questions or you're curious.

D: We can come back and check with him. I figured there had to be a way to get around her block.

John was very obviously excited by this confirmation. It was a tremendous breakthrough to obtain the birthdate of the Anti-Christ. I felt he could hardly wait for the session to be over so he could begin drawing up his chart.

We thought Nostradamus had done very well under the circumstances, since neither Brenda nor I knew very much about astrology. This was one of the most difficult sessions we had. It was very tedious because the answers did not flow with the rapidity that was characteristic of the other sessions. But then they had not contained such difficult and foreign concepts.

When Brenda awakened she said her head felt very strange. Not exactly a headache, but there was a feeling of pressure, like her skull was too small for her brain.

I said, "He tried to put too much into it."

Since it was not an uncomfortable feeling, she laughed about it and said, "Oh, my poor brain!"

LATER, AS JOHN STUDIED THE INFORMATION, it was quite obvious that all the signs were not present, especially the grand trine of water signs. This was not surprising. Nostradamus said he was giving signs that would be prominent in the Anti-Christ's horoscope *and* at the time of his rise to power. John had been given the unenviable task of trying to sort them out.

When he found that there would be several grand trines of water signs during the summer of 1994, he felt that might be when the Anti-Christ would come to full power. But could this be accurate? The Anti-Christ would be about 25 years old at that time, which is incredibly young for such an accomplishment.

During another session John decided to use the same method to obtain information about other characters in our scenario. An important participant is the last pope. According to Nostradamus' predictions that were translated in Volume One, there will be three more popes before the collapse of the Catholic Church. He said the present pope will be assassinated in the very near future. The second one will also be assassinated to allow the third pope to take the seat of the papacy. This last pope will be under the Anti-Christ's control and will be his tool. During this time the burning of Rome and the sacking of the Vatican Library occurs.

J: Will the last pope be French?

B: He says he has a strong feeling he will be. The man will be of swarthy complexion, and his character can be likened to the Tarot card "inverted Hierophant." He says trying to use astrological symbols is very difficult with this vessel. It's due to ignorance and not fear on the vessel's part. But he says that using symbols this vessel is familiar with, such as the Tarot, makes it very easy to communicate the concepts efficiently. Thus he may use Tarot symbolism more often than astrological symbols.

J: *Can you give us the last pope's birthdate and birthyear?*

B: He says this is difficult. He's going to have to use vague wording again. He says my subconscious is raising its horrible head. Those were the words he used and he gave me this picture of a Chinese New Year dragonhead with streamers all around, blocking the view.

D: (Laugh) *Well, we have been able to suppress that dragon.*

B: He says this man is a man of mystery; a man of dark waters. He says this man is Cancer, and that the signs of mystery and darkness are very prominent in his horoscope. He's having difficulty with the numbers and the birthdate. He says he'll get back to that in a moment. This man has a physical deformity of some sort. He's not sure if it is a shoulder that is slightly crooked or hunched, or a clubfoot, but it is a deformity of that nature. It will be a congenital defect in the bone. It won't be caused by injury; he was born that way. Consequently, his mind has been scarred by the cruelty and callousness of people towards others who are different. He says this man of swarthy complexion and blue eyes entered the church at a young age out of bitterness and desperation, because he felt he would never find a girl to love him and marry him. He entered the church so he wouldn't have to deal with this. This man was a young man ... (he slipped the date in quickly past her subconscious) born in 1932, and his parents were involved with the Nazi movement in France. Consequently, he is scarred by this as well. He says he had to bear the taunts of his schoolmates in later years after World War II. They called him "Nazi-lover" and things such as this. He says had it not been for the cruelty and callousness of the people he was exposed to in his environment, he could have been a good man, perhaps even kindly. But as it turned out, he was warped into cruelty from pain. He wants to get back at the world because of what happened when he was young.

D: Is this why it's easier for him to become a tool of the Anti-Christ?

B: Yes. This makes him very susceptible to that. (*Quickly*) His birthdate is April 4, 1932.

D: *What is his ascendant?*

B: Sagittarius.

John gestured that that was all he needed to know to do a birth chart.

B: He says he's always happy to give you dates. He's noticed that if he slips them out quickly before anyone has a chance to think about it, then the awful subconscious of this vessel will not get in the way.

The following is a brief summary of what John found when he drew up the horoscope for the birthdate, April 4, 1932.

In this horoscope we see a stellium of planets (three or more planets in the same sign) in the sign of the Ram, Aries. The Sun, Mercury, Mars, and Uranus all take place in the 5th house of creativity, pleasures and speculation. With an emphasis on the sign of Aries, the individual will be strong minded and will "butt" his way to the "top." The Sun combines with erratic Uranus and vacillating Mercury, signifying a magnetic personality, a keen mind and a strong desire to have his way. The Moon in Pisces indicates a sense of compassion for others that leads him into the priesthood. The Moon in conjunction with the South Node predicts a need for him to go through an emotional purification. There will be a strong tie to the mother figure, as well. Mercury conjunct Uranus shows originality of thought and self-reliance, but at times he is subject to chaotic thinking. Venus in Taurus in the house of service indicates he will work well with his colleagues and they can help him attain his ambitions. Mars in good relation to Saturn portends a strong sense of discipline and the ability to accomplish goals and projects with great determination. The tendency to hold in his frustrations could result in bitterness and the inclination for revenge. Uranus in negative aspect to Pluto predicts a life full of changes and upheavals that will test the caliber of his spirit.

 A NOTHER IMPORTANT PARTICIPANT referred to by Nostradamus is Ogmios. None of us were familiar with this strange name when it first came through, but it was again a symbolic reference to mythology. Ogmios was the Celtic equivalent of the legendary Hercules. He is supposed to represent the nemesis of the Anti-Christ. It's through his efforts as a leader of the underground movement that the people rise to resist the Anti-Christ.

J: Could you give us a birthdate for Ogmios?

I didn't think it would be possible to do this, but Nostradamus responded with no hesitation.

B: He's giving me the month and date, and he's trying to get the year to me now. (*Pause*) October 17, 1952.

It was an unexpected and thrilling surprise to be able to get such concise information so quickly.

D: John wants to try to draw up his horoscope so we will know about his personality.

B: Yes. He says he will make an effort to get birthdates through when they are requested. This leader will originally come from somewhere in central Europe. He provides this information in case John needs a geographical location of his birth for the horoscope.

John wasted no time. He was already looking up the date in his ephemeris.

J: *In Ogmios' horoscope it shows he was born under the new moon of Libra, taking place in 1952, with Saturn close to this planetary alignment. To me, this shows he is an old soul. He's done battle with negative forces in his previous lifetimes.*

B: Yes. This man is well prepared spiritually to take on this task, for his opponent will be very powerful and have negative spiritual forces around him. He will need to be well girded for battle on all planes. He will be of the people, as he is a man who will have worked his way up through the ranks, so to speak. He came from a simple background, and what he has attained he did by working for it honestly. He has some technical training, but the primary skill he relies upon is his practicality. He is able to see to the root of matters. This man is an old soul, and he has his priorities straight. He knows what is and what is not important for the final outcome. He is one of those people who will help pave the way for the Great Genius who comes after the Anti-Christ, for this man realizes that he is not the one to lead the world to ultimate peace. But he is the one to help bring down those who would destroy the world, leaving room for the one who will guide the world to ultimate peace.

J: *What is his ascendant?*

B: He keeps saying Taurus.

John nodded. That was all he needed to draw up a horoscope on this man identified as Ogmios.

The following is a brief summary he compiled for the birthdate, October 17, 1952.

In Ogmios' horoscope chart, we see a stellium of planets in the sign of balance, Libra. The Sun, the Moon, Saturn, and Neptune are all found in the 6th house of health, work, and service to others. This indicates he will be sensitive to the needs of others. There is a strong sense of humility, and as he grows in life he will become patient, persistent, and unassuming. The Moon here signifies that a balance of personality will be achieved through spiritual growth. Part of his "destiny" in life is service to others. Mercury in good aspect to Mars pertains to the use of one's reason and logic in difficult situations. Venus in the sign of Scorpio shows deep-felt emotions often not apparent on the surface. There will be many tests concerning his emotional development. Jupiter in Taurus in the 1st house of personality shows a warm, earthy sense of humor and in general a jovial character. The formation of a Grand Cross composed of his Venus, Jupiter, Pluto, and the Nodes predicts he has a "special mission" to accomplish, even though he may be reluctant to be involved in such an undertaking. There's great strength and balance here prophesying an admirable adversary for the Anti-Christ.

The following are some remarks that Nostradamus made about Ogmios while working through Brenda.

B: He says that Ogmios is a man of great stature. He will be a gruff person and very direct. This man makes a good friend but he says you would not want him as your enemy. That's why he makes such a good adversary for the Anti-Christ.

J: *Will Ogmios be part of a religious organization or will that have anything to do with the underground?*

B: He will have been exposed to religious training. He will be an upstanding man of principles and morals. The principles are his own and not influenced by ecclesiastica, he says.

J: *This is implied in his horoscope by Saturn square Uranus, which indicates that the person will buck under any type of organization or restraint.*

B: This is true. That's why he's the one to bring about the downfall of the Anti-Christ. This man is a leader and he will have an organization under him to help him with his quest, but he says he won't want a ring in his nose. (*We laughed.*)

J: *What sun sign was Nostradamus? What was his birthdate?*

D: *I think John wants to look up your horoscope.* (Laugh)

B: He says to be honest he's not really sure. His parents were lax about recording the births of their children. He doesn't bother celebrating his birthday because it could be the day he feels he was born on, the day that his mother thinks he was born on, or the day that he was registered for being baptized or christened.

D: *Are these dates all different?*

B: He says, yes, so he doesn't worry about it. What the young astrologer might want to do—and he says it will help him also—is to take what he knows about his life, the dates in his life, the year and place of his birth, and then pick the date that is the most logical and fitting in accordance with what you know. He shrugs his shoulders at this point. He says, "I know that doesn't help much but that's the way it is."

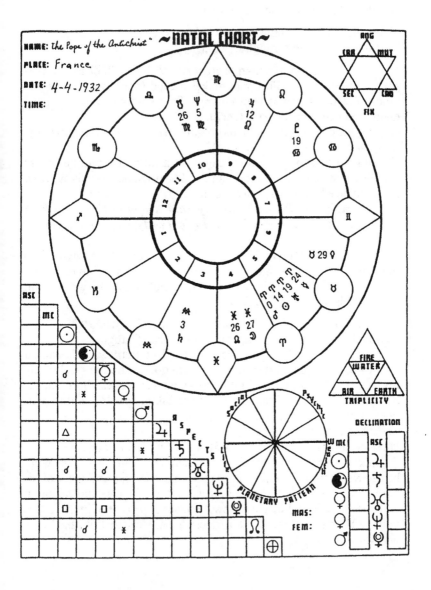

This is the horoscope for the birthdate of the Pope of the Anti-Christ: April 4, 1932.

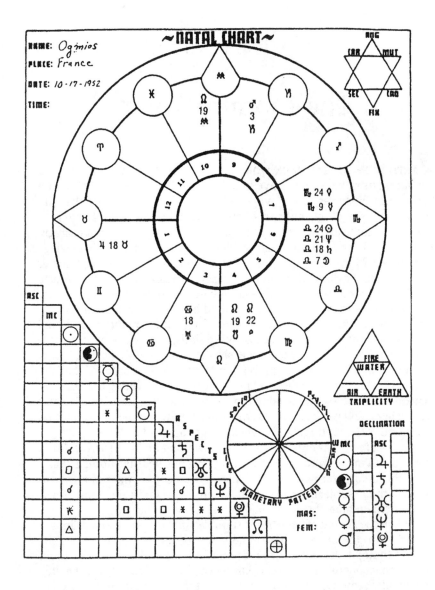

This is the horoscope for the birthdate of Ogmios, October 17, 1952.

Chapter 10

The Tapestry Room

ALTHOUGH WE HAD BEEN WORKING SUCCESSFULLY through Brenda for six months, we should have known it would not be long before life would put obstacles in our way again. It's an accepted fact that life doesn't run smoothly, and part of our lesson while living on Earth is to learn to adapt to and work around problems. It had become increasingly difficult for Brenda to continue working part-time and attending college part-time. Monetary problems, in particular, were becoming critical. Reluctantly, she decided to put her treasured dream of a career in music on the shelf for a while. She desperately needed to work full time to get her money affairs in order. She promised herself she would not give up on her dream, but she would postpone it for a while. Finding a full time job was difficult. Although she had office skills, there was nothing available in our area. Out of desperation, she took an assembly-line job working nights in a local chicken processing plant. She still believed that she would be able to work with me once a week. I was willing to adapt my schedule to fit hers so we wouldn't lose contact with Nostradamus. After giving her a few weeks break to adjust to her new routine, she suggested that we meet around midnight when she got off work.

As I sat in my car outside of her house waiting for her to arrive, I was not anticipating any problem except my being up later than normal. I had done this before in my work. If I believe the story is important, I try to work with my subjects when it is most convenient for them. Again, I had not anticipated the obstacles that life can throw in the way.

When she got out of her car, she stumbled into the house and collapsed wearily into the nearest chair. She moaned that she was so tired she hadn't thought she could make it home. She said she knew she could handle the monotonous assembly line work (she could merely use the time to mentally compose music) and she thought she was adapting to the complete reversal of days and nights. What she had not counted on was the rigors her body would be put through. Physically, she was not used to this kind of work. She showed me her hands that were so important to her as a pianist. The joints were swollen from the prolonged contact with the ice-cold chickens. Her arm and shoulder muscles were aching from the repetitious motions she made as the chickens went by on the conveyor belts. She was almost in tears as she announced, "All I want to do is collapse in bed. I'm not even going to eat anything." She looked at me sadly, "I really don't see any way that we'll be able to work together as long as I have this job. I'm just too tired all the time." Although I was disappointed, I have always agreed that the welfare of my subjects comes first. I left so she could get some rest.

I kept in touch with her and her life turned into a kind of robot nightmare. Working until midnight and then coming home to collapse into a stupor that she would awaken from around noon the next day, then eating and starting the whole routine over again. She never seemed to get enough sleep or rest and was tired all the time. Her hands and arms didn't get better, they progressively worsened until she was in almost constant pain. There was no way we could meet on the weekends because they became precious to her and she jealously guarded them. She needed the time to herself to prepare for the onslaught of the next week. To make matters worse her boyfriend got a job traveling out of state. Her only solution was to sleep more. I saw it as a form of retreating from life, retreating into the comfort of sleep which was a temporary escape. Her friends were trying to help her find a regular job with normal hours, so she could escape the nightmare she was going through.

During this time I also became depressed. I had created a sort of time-table for myself. I had hoped to complete all 1000 of the quatrains by the summer of 1987. Now that seemed impossible, as everything had come to a standstill. I had no idea of how to proceed. I felt as though I had failed in my commitment, or that in some way I had let Nostradamus down. But there was nothing I could do. I couldn't force Brenda to work if she didn't want to. That's not the way I operate anyway. Force has never been a part of my technique. I have always gotten better results by building rapport and trust with my subjects. They feel safe knowing I would never do anything to harm them or put them in jeopardy. Even if she would consent to have a session to please me, in her state of perpetual exhaustion I couldn't be sure if any of the information that came through was reliable. The information might have a hard time filtering through the physical and mental torment she was going through.

I discussed this during one of my visits with John. I thought she might also be suffering from some kind of psychic burnout. After all, we had been working steadily on this project for six months, and maybe she needed a rest. Even though I was depressed at not being able to continue with the story, I thought it best to give her some breathing room. I felt she would let me know when she was ready to work again.

John did not react the same way. He was feeling a pressure that I didn't know about. He said he was not satisfied with the information we had received about the Anti-Christ's horoscope. It didn't sound right, and he didn't feel comfortable with it. In the first place he didn't think the Anti-Christ could really be that young at the present time. The horoscopes for the last pope and the nemesis, Ogmios, seemed to be accurate, but he felt the need to question Nostradamus again for more details to clarify the Anti-Christ's horoscope. He was anxious to get more information. I understood his problem and appreciated his desire to be as accurate as possible, but I could only repeat that we wouldn't be able to work with Brenda until she found another job. We had no idea when that would be, and this irritated John. Then, he dropped another bombshell. He had been seriously considering moving out of the state, and had finally decided to go to Florida by the end of May, which was less than two months away. This was why he was so desperate to complete his end of the project.

I left his house feeling more depressed than ever. I exclaimed aloud as I gripped the steering wheel of my car, "People are always coming and going, always moving in and out of my life! What am I to do?" I felt as though I was up against a brick wall with no way over or around it. Then, almost as quickly as the frustration had taken over, another thought entered like a fresh, cool breeze sweeping across my mind and allowing the fragrance of common sense to enter. What was the matter with me? I was reacting as though it was totally my responsibility to find an answer to this. This was *not* my problem. I didn't have control over this. I *never* had control over it from the very beginning. I didn't start this. *They* did. They had already worked around obstacles bigger than this to bring it all together, so let *them* work it out if they really intended for this project to be completed. *I* was the one who had set a time-table, not them. I had no idea of what kind of schedule they had in mind. I silently thanked them for the opportunity to work on this and for the information that had already come through, and then I mentally placed it in their hands. It was their responsibility, it always had been. I was merely a puppet maneuvered according to some unseen plan. It was a good plan, and it felt right, so they must know what they were doing.

I almost laughed out loud. It felt as though a huge weight had been lifted from my shoulders. The feeling of freedom was exhilarating. Somehow, I knew it would all work out.

I went over the material I had accumulated for the Nostradamus manuscript and decided, that although there were still several unanswered questions, there was enough of a story to make a book. Maybe this was the wisdom behind the delay; it made me complete the manuscript instead of holding onto it for more information. The first book would contain enough relevant material to at least start people thinking. I didn't know if I would ever be able to translate the remaining quatrains, but it didn't matter. I was at peace with myself. I was no longer up against a brick wall but high on a mountain top overlooking a beautiful landscape stretching as far as the eye could see. I instinctively knew that whatever was meant to happen would happen, and nothing I did or didn't do would make the slightest difference. This was all part of a master plan, and I was learning to rely on faith alone. I discovered that faith means believing in something totally, without any physical evidence to back up that belief. So I returned to my life with calm assurance.

ONCE I MADE THE DECISION to let "them" handle it, the answer came quickly. I was at John's apartment tying up the loose ends on the quatrains to be included in the first book. I decided to omit the horoscope material if he did not feel comfortable with it. He leaned back in his chair and stroked his blond beard. "I've been thinking about it and I've come up with a solution. Put *me* under and see if I can contact Nostradamus."

"Oh, sure," I laughed, "I've already done the impossible twice. You want me to do it *three* times?"

"No, I'm serious," he said. "Brenda had so much difficulty with the astrological information because it was foreign to her. She did the best she could but it was a strain on her. Just imagine what might happen if I could talk to him myself and get the information firsthand. I could understand it because I already have the concepts in my mind." He was getting excited about the idea.

I shook my head, "I don't even know if it would work. And can't you hear the skeptics? I thought if astrological information came through Brenda it would have more validity because she doesn't know about such things. If you receive any information they would really think this is a hoax because you're an expert. They would surely think we set it all up."

He slammed his fist on the table, "I don't care what they think. They're going to think what they want anyway. This project has become important to me, too. I want to get the clearest information we can. And I feel that time is running out on me."

I could see he was serious about it and that it was important to him. "Well, I don't know if it would work, but ... I suppose it would do no harm to try."

He grinned broadly, "That's right! What harm would it do to try." Then he added, with a faraway look in his eye, "Besides, I've always wanted to meet Nostradamus."

Although I was full of doubts, the idea was intriguing. I am always open to a challenge. I agreed to try, and we set up the appointment.

ON THE DAY OF THE SESSION I was back in the same position I had been in with Brenda. We were again experimenting in an attempt to reach Nostradamus with no guarantee of what the results would be. The only difference in this case was that John was aware of what was going on, and he was a willing participant. I had no idea of how to contact Nostradamus before, and it had worked, so I decided to try the same procedure I used with Brenda. The most likely place to begin would be to get

John in a spirit state between lives and then feel our way from there. Since he was in the habit of regular meditation and went into a trance state every day, he was a very easy subject. He required almost no induction at all and reached a very deep level quite easily. I counted him to a spirit state where he would not be directly involved with a life and asked him what he was doing.

J: I'm walking down a hall. It looks like there are precious stones in the walls, like emeralds, rubies, peridot and crystal. It's so beautiful. It's very radiant and very hallowed. You feel … it's a very hushed feeling. Ahead of me is a library. I'm walking into it now. It looks like precious stones are on all the mantels and doors, and they shine with their own light. I'm in a huge study. There are books and scrolls on everything, and all types of manuscripts on the shelves. There is a beautiful light streaming in illuminating the whole place. It's made of gold, silver and precious stones, but they all reflect light so you can read. The whole building seems to be made of this wondrous material.

This library in the spirit realm was not a strange place to me. I have journeyed there many times with the aid of my subjects. Several have mentioned it and their descriptions vary only slightly. The guardian of the library has always been eager to help me in my quest for knowledge, and I have used this place to gain information about many various topics. Would it be the key to finding Nostradamus?

D: *This is one of my favorite places. Are there other people here?*
J: Oh, there are people in the other part. It's a big area; almost cathedral size. There's a man there—he's a spirit, and he is just luminous. He's talking about preparing for the Earth school, and there are only a few people listening to him right now. Other people are in groups or walking around silently carrying manuscripts and books to different places. It's the air of … (he had difficulty finding the word) like scholars. They're studying. Everybody has a sense of purpose, and there's a sense of serenity. There's music that seems to fill the whole place. It's just barely audible but it tinkles. It's pretty music.
D: *It sounds like a very beautiful place.*
J: Yeah, it's really nice. Everything glimmers and everybody is in beautiful robes. The clothing looks like it's transparent but electric colors shine through them. They're the people's auras.
D: *Is there anyone in charge? How do you find anything?*
J: Yes, there is a spirit guide who is the guardian of the library. He is at a desk there and he is writing at the present time. And I am asked, "What is your request?"
D: *Is he very busy at this moment?*
J: Oh, no. He says, "No, no, no, no. This is wonderful. To be of service is very important."

D: *All right. Would he be able to help me with an experiment?*

J: (*Enthusiastically*) Okay. That would be fine.

D: *Ask him if there is a place you can go to see the happenings on Earth back through time?*

J: He says it can be done here in the library either by studying the books or by stepping into the viewing rooms. But he says they are well aware of your purpose, and they suggest I go to the Tapestry Room. It would be better suited to your needs.

D: *What is that?*

J: He says you will find what you need in the Tapestry Room. So I'm walking down this beautiful corridor with walls that look like lapis lazuli and marble. At the end of the corridor is a big doorway. I'm opening the door, and there is a *dazzling* bright light.

D: *What is causing the bright light?*

J: It is a man, or a spirit form. He says he's the guardian of the Tapestry Room and is allowing me to enter. This is a very honored place. There is a wonderful aroma in the air. It smells like a combination of a fresh breeze tinged with salt and perfumes from a garden. It's almost like incense. It's a beautiful room and it's very, very tall. It goes up for maybe two or three hundred feet. No, maybe a hundred feet would be more accurate. The ceiling has a rounded point like a church nave. There are windows at the top of it and on either side of the walls. They're up high and they light up the room. And there are chandeliers that hang down from the ceiling that look like Aladdin lamps. But there are a lot of them, maybe 15 or 20. The walls and the floor seem to be made of marble. And there is some heavy furniture at different intervals, like groups of chairs and tables opposite the tapestry. They're not contemporary and they're not antique, but they're very functional, comfortable and inviting. The guardian says sometimes teachers bring their students here to explain the wonders and the intricacies of the tapestry to them. It feels like I'm in a special museum where people can come to examine and study this. I'm going to look at the tapestry. It's so beautiful. It's metallic; made of metal threads and they're just gorgeous. They glimmer and shine. (*A sudden intake of breath.*) And it looks like it *breathes*. It's like ... it *is* alive. I mean it just undulates and sparkles. Some of the strands glisten, and others are kind of dull. It's really hard to describe. It actually is like a living thing, but it's not frightening; it's beautiful. There are all different types of threads. And, oh! It's just *glorious*. Nothing on Earth could ever be compared to it. There is just no way to describe how glorious this is, because it's so vibrant it's almost electric. And the guardian says that each thread represents a life.

D: *It sounds very complicated.*

J: Oh, some of it is complicated, but it makes a beautiful design. An eternal design. And ... I can see the world beyond that. By looking at this tapestry, I can see any event that has taken place.

D: *What do you mean?*

J: It's like looking through the tapestry, and I can see people's daily lives. Now the guardian is explaining that every life that has ever been lived is represented as a thread in this tapestry. This is where all the threads of human life, the souls that incarnate, are connected. It illustrates perfectly how each life is interwoven, crossing and touching all other lives until eventually all of humanity is affected. The absolute oneness of humanity is represented by the tapestry. It is one but composed of all these many parts. Each cannot exist without the other and they all intertwine and influence each other.

D: *Well, if it's composed of everyone's life, then it would be alive. Does the guard care if we look at it?*

J: Oh, he doesn't care; he knows we have a purpose. He says, "Go ahead, please look at it, but don't look any deeper. I *don't* want you looking at other people's lives because spreading that knowledge can be detrimental to their development." (*John went back to the description.*) The tapestry is huge. It seems to be about, oh, I would say at least 20 to 25 feet tall. And it seems to go on *forever.* It would take me hours just to walk the length of it. It must go on for a mile or more. It runs along the left-hand wall, and the light coming in from the windows shines on it. But there's a point that I cannot go beyond.

D: *Do you know why?*

J: The guardian of the tapestry says that is part of the spiritual evolvement of all souls. Only spiritually evolved people have access to that part of the tapestry. It's like a little sign that says, "Do not go beyond this point." (*Laugh*) But it's not so much a sign as a feeling that this is as far as I can walk. It's like looking at the most beautiful creation of art. It's made up of strands that range from a tiny piece of string all the way up to cable size; as thick as your wrist.

D: *I had pictured them as threads.*

J: No, they're not as small as threads. I called them that because they're interwoven, but it goes from a tiny string in some places to larger sizes. Most of them are kind of rope size and then they get thicker and thicker as they go along. There are greens, blues, reds, yellows, oranges and blacks. Yeah, there are even a few black ones in there. The black ones stand out because they don't seem to go as far as the other colors do. Hmm. That's strange.

D: *Do these colors have any significance?*

J: I'll ask the guardian. He says, "Yes, they represent the spiritual energy of all souls."

D: *Well, what would be the significance of the darker colors as opposed to the brighter ones?*

J: "The darker colors," he says, "really have no significance. The black ones are special for they have chosen a very unusual path."

D: *I thought the darker colors might mean they were more ... well, I'm thinking of negative lives.*

J: No. He says there is no negativity in this tapestry. The black ones have just chosen an unusual way of manifesting. But he says, "Do not question that. That's not for you to know at this moment. You have come here for another purpose."

D: *Yes, but first I want to ask a few questions. You said there are teachers teaching their pupils about this tapestry. Is this a way they can look at the pattern of their past lives?*

J: Yes. I'm looking at one group right now. The teacher is dressed in nice robes, and he has a very benevolent look on his face. He is pointing out to different souls what is happening and what has happened. He's teaching them about this tapestry and what the different intricacies of the patterns mean. He has something like a shimmery pointer. It's golden-colored with something at the tip of it that looks like a crystal, but it's actually a diamond that lights up with its own light. He points to a thread in the tapestry and that thread, cable, rope or whatever you want to call it, will seem to light up on its own. He points out different characteristics about lifetimes, about how people have evolved and where they have to grow. They're all taking notes, not so much with pen and paper but with their own heads.

D: *Is he explaining to these pupils about their own lives so they can make decisions in future lives?*

J: Yes, I get the impression they're there to study their past lifetimes and how their thread has woven itself into this tapestry of life. This is what the ancients call the "Akashic Records." (*I was surprised.*) These are the Akashic records that advanced souls understand. He says some of the records are kept in book form, but those are for souls who are not as highly advanced.

D: (I didn't understand.) *Then everyone wouldn't have a thread in this tapestry?*

J: No, all life has a thread in this tapestry, but only advanced souls are able to understand the concept of the tapestry, and to have access to it. Lesser developed souls have Akashic record books they can look through. It would be like a child going into a college library. They should go to the children's section of a local library instead.

D: *Then they wouldn't understand what they were seeing even if they came here?*

J: Right. They wouldn't understand this because the tapestry has a purpose. It goes into the higher dimensions, even above here, and this is a very complex place. This tapestry eventually ends in Godhood where it's all brightness. It all leads to this beautiful light.

D: *Can you ask the guardian if very many people who are alive ever come to see this tapestry? Or is it unusual for us to be here?*

J: He says you'd be surprised how many people have come to this room who are still in the body. Many come to view it as a work of art. He says this has sometimes been an inspiration for artists who are skilled in painting, sculpture and the textile arts. They sometimes come here because this is one of the most glorious works of art in all creation. It has many different designs, such as wild contemporary patterns, Oriental designs or Native American arrangements.

D: *How do they get there?*

J: He says some come in the astral state when they dream. Others come while they are traveling within the soul worlds when they use meditation, astral projection or hypnosis like you are using now.

D: *I wondered if it was unusual to come while you were still in body.*

J: He says, "No, not as unusual as you might think. You'd be surprised at the numbers that *do* come here, but not all of humanity is ready to come to this place just yet."

D: *Can he tell we aren't dead?*

J: Yes, he's walking along with me and he says he knows I am still in the body. He sees the silver thread that lies behind me.

D: *Oh, he knows you're still connected to a body. And that we are doing this as a kind of experiment.*

J: Yes, he understands that. Most of the other people don't have silver threads coming out of their bodies.

D: *Well, has anyone who came here while still in the body ever been refused entry into that room?*

J: He said, "You'd be surprised. We have had to ask people to leave this area. One soul came and tried to tear his thread out of the tapestry. He thought it would be the best way he could end his existence. The man was suffering from some type of dementia in the Earth plane, and he didn't realize he was really in the spiritual plane. He was very confused. We had to guide him back. He is now in an institution and being heavily sedated so he doesn't go into these trance states that he was able to do so easily. But he came to try to destroy the tapestry, or to destroy what he thought was his thread. In actuality, it wasn't even his thread."

D: *But there aren't very many people who try to do things like that, are there?*

J: No, that was a very rare case. That man was given great spiritual strength in his physical incarnation, but he thought it was delusion and that has left him unbalanced in the mental body. As a result he is being physically restrained as well as being given chemicals to keep him from astral traveling. He would have been a great world server if he had allowed himself to find his pattern. But he allowed the intellectual side of his nature to gain too much on him.

D: *I suppose that's one reason why they have a guardian there.*

J: Well, you have to have a guardian. Sometimes strange things happen here because this is a portrait of time, and things have to be kept in balance. There are checks and balances along this tapestry.

D: *You said sometimes there are other people that are asked to leave? Do they try to see things they shouldn't or what?*

J: He says, "You *can* see things, because behind the tapestry is your sense of time, and you can follow a cord and go through time. Most people do not need to know about their future while they are still in the body, unless they are going to use the knowledge for a spiritual course."

D: *Are these the type of people who are asked to leave?*

J: He says, "No, this is the place of love and no one is ever asked to leave here unless he tries to deface the tapestry or is abusive. We just have to watch the tapestry, because sometimes in rare cases things do happen. In the past great forces have come *through* the tapestry itself. One time you had nuclear explosions and there were a lot of people leaving the planet so quickly they came *through* the tapestry. So we have to be here to be of service to them."

D: *I guess all kinds of strange things happen there. I appreciate you telling me these things. We were curious.*

J: "Yes," he says, "that's understandable. Don't worry. We are well aware of your mission and your soul's growth. I'm here to be of service to all of you."

D: *We're trying to use this information in a very positive way if we can. Would I be allowed to come if I was going to use it in a negative way?*

J: No. Nothing can be disguised or hidden here. We know your motives better than you know them yourself.

I was beginning to understand why we were led to the Tapestry Room to further our mission.

D: *If I asked you to look at one person, would you be able to find them for me in the tapestry?*

J: (*Positively*) Yes!

D: *We could try anyway, couldn't we? Ask the guardian if he has ever heard of a man who lived in the 1500s whose name was Nostradamus or Michel de Notredame.*

J: The guardian says that normally you aren't allowed to look at other people's lives. This is too disruptive. But he says they are well aware of your purpose and goal, so I will be allowed to enter the tapestry. I'm picking out Nostradamus' thread right now. It's a bright luminous gold. I'm following it through the tapestry, and it's like flying. The guardian says, "I will be watching. I will call you back if need be."

Chapter 11

The Golden Thread
of Nostradamus

J LITERALLY HELD MY BREATH as John flew through a black void lit only by the glowing golden thread of Nostradamus. Would he succeed in finding him?

J: I'm following the tapestry thread, and it comes into a room.
D: *Tell me what you see.*
J: I see a man who is bent over and writing with a quill.

I let my breath out. Apparently we had found him. We had again accomplished the impossible. My mind was racing ahead trying to think of a way to get Nostradamus' attention. At other times we had contacted him while he was in a state of meditation.

While I pondered the situation, I asked for a description of the room.

J: Oh, it's kind of small, but it's full of books—not books but rolled-up pieces of ... not paper ... it's parchment. There are one or two books there that are like ours in the 20th century. (This is an example of the need for accuracy by the hypnotized subject.) There's something like a globe but it's like an astrolabe. That's what it is. It's made of metal. It's round and spherical but it's open. It's like spokes make up the sphere. And that's on the table. He is sipping out of a cup that has some type of herbal tea in it. It's an infusion. The brewed herbs smell wonderful. He's dressed in a hat that comes over his ears, and he's got on something white, like church robes except he has on a very heavy over-robe made of a furrish-type material. It looks almost like a thick velvet, but it's made from ... (*surprised*) like rabbits!

Often during hypnotic regressions people can get hung up on describing extremely minute details if they aren't moved along.

D: *What does the man look like? Can you describe his features?*

J: He's a distinguished-looking man. He's got grayish hair and a long thin nose. Uh-oh! His eyes! They light up. They're deep-set and full of sparkle. But he's elderly for his time.

Both Elena and Brenda mentioned Nostradamus' wonderful eyes as a predominant feature.

J: (*Surprised*) Oh! He just turned to smile at me.

D: *Does he know you're there?*

J: Yes, he knows I'm here, and he feels really good. He's put down his writing pen, he's smiling and motioning me to come closer. ... He's bending over an oval that looks like polished obsidian, or polished volcanic glass. (*Surprised*) And my face is in it! He's looking at my face in the glass and he's saying, "I have never seen you but I know who you are. You're the young astrologer!" And I said, "Yes, I am."

John said later that he could see himself as a glowing energy spirit clothed in a robe that was rainbow colored and iridescent but not gaudy. He couldn't see his features because of the bright aura. They were only visible in the mirror.

D: *How did he know you were there?*

J: He sensed my presence.

No wonder we didn't startle him. He was probably quite used to having spirits pop in on him.

J: He says that I am a spirit of the future.

D: *Does he know what this is all about?*

J: He says, "Yes. You come from the group in the 20th century that is trying to clear up my quatrains." He's really happy, and he says, "It's delightful to meet you. Now maybe I can show you the things the others were not able to understand." He's very excited. He's old but he's ... spry, that's the word, he's very spry. Now he's taking a sip of his infusion, and I ask him what's in it. He says he's got hyssop, a bit of licorice root, and a bit of cinnamon. He says he keeps the cinnamon in a little silver box because it's a very rare spice.

D: *Can you tell him why you came? The young lady was not familiar with astrology so not all of the information was clear.*

J: I'll tell him that now. (*Pause*) He says he will be delighted to clarify anything. He says sometimes it's hard for him to communicate through women. He has a sense of what we would call "chauvinism" toward women, and sometimes he feels very uncomfortable talking through what he perceives as a woman spirit. He says often the woman vehicle has her aches and pains and her emotions that color the communication. He knows that all spirits can be either male or female, but in this role he's alive in women don't have the same place that they have in our century. You know, men in his time period didn't talk much with women. It's like, "Oh, woman's complaints. They're always complaining." (*I laughed.*) Women weren't treated as equals like we treat women in the 20th century. They were looked on as domestic help or as the bearer of children. Just someone who takes care of the house, cooks the meals, and has their role of that nature. He sometimes finds it difficult to discuss intellectual ideas with a woman, because he doesn't think they have the brain capacity to understand everything he wants to speak about. (*We both laughed.*)

D: *Does it bother him that he communicates to me, and I'm a woman?*

J: Oh, no, he doesn't mind that in the least. He says, "Because I'm not working *through* Dolores." He says from his knowledge he sees that you've been a masculine entity many times. Because your energy is of that nature he feels he can relate very well to you.

Nostradamus has displayed his chauvinism many times in the past, and I have been the target of his barbed criticism when I did not understand, or I failed to follow his instructions. This could have been his teacher/pupil role rather than a man relating to a woman he considered inferior. But I have also been witness to his delightful sense of humor and his impatience with the translators. I felt his remarks referred to women in general and were not aimed specifically at Brenda.

D: *Well, we did have some questions about the Anti-Christ's horoscope. Will he be able to help with that?*

J: (*Long pause*) Yes, he pulled out a piece of parchment and he's got a horoscope before me. (*Pause, as he appeared to study it.*) It's a square horoscope. It's a different type of horoscope than I'm used to seeing.

D: *Tell me what you see.*

I was afraid if we didn't get it on tape, he might not be able to remember the details when he awakened. It would depend on the depth of the trance.

J: He points to the date at the top. It's 1962.

D: *Just the year? Does it have a month or anything?*

J: (*Pause*) He's pointed to February. February, 1962. He doesn't give a date. And it's in Gothic letters. I see February, 1962, and the number one has a dash through it. It's almost like a cuneiform or some type of writing the ancients had. The lines are really thick.

D: *You said the horoscope is in a square?*

J: It's in a square and it has diamond patterns within it. It appears that this was how horoscopes were drawn up in that period.

D: *Can you understand what he's showing you?*

J: Yes. He's got the symbol for the sun in the first house. (*Pause*) Aquarius. He's got Aquarius on the ascendant, or as he says, the "rising." And in there he has the Sun and the Moon, Mercury, Venus, Mars, Jupiter and Saturn.

D: *All in the first house?*

J: (*His voice was full of surprise.*) Yes! And he's saying, "This is a very important person. He will use this energy for all the wrong reasons when it could be used for positive reasons. He will have great psychic powers."

D: *What else is he showing you?*

J: (*Long pause*) I see an image now in the mirror. I see a man with a dark mustache. He's in his mid-twenties. He's a *very* handsome man, with strong features. He's dressed in a business suit right now and he's talking with people at a power base in the Middle East.

D: *What do you mean by "power base"?*

J: It's a mansion. There are other men with Arabic headdresses on and they seem to be discussing things. They're sitting on low cushions around a huge brass table or brass tray. There are all types of coffee, a silver and gold coffee service, and they're eating finger foods. I see a *big* park out the window. It's got palm trees running in rows and a swimming pool in the center. But it isn't a swimming pool, it's a fountain pool. This is in Egypt because in the distance I can see memorials. Not the pyramids, but some kind of a temple. Nostradamus is showing me this in his dark mirror.

D: *Does he tell you what this represents?*

J: He says this is taking place right now. (The beginning of April 1987.) There's a very big fat Arab man there, and he's very jovial. He's laughing and he says, "Oh, we'll have them Americans eating out of our hands soon enough."

D: *Hmm. Do you know what he means?*

J: (*Pause*) I can't get that ... that's just what he said.

D: *Well, does Nostradamus tell you who this young dark man is?*

J: The man is probably one of the most handsome man I've ever seen. His beauty is almost ethereal. If he walked into a room, people's eyes would automatically be drawn to him. His beauty is almost transcendental, in a sense. It doesn't look human. His skin and his features are flawless. He's kind of tall but well proportioned. He's impeccably dressed and he carries himself very well. His suit looks like one of the finest suits ever seen on the Earth. And on his finger he has a magnificent stone. It's interesting because it's a big diamond but it's set in a black stone which is set in a gold ring. And he wears it on his *middle* finger which is a strange place to wear a ring. Nostradamus says this is the man the horoscope represents.

D: *Is he the Anti-Christ?*

J: He will eventually be known as the Anti-Christ, Nostradamus says. But for now do not use that term.

D: *Could he give me a clue as to how he would be known now?*

J: Nostradamus says this is not to be given. Later you will know who he is. It would not be good to reveal his identity because he has to fulfill his destiny.

D: *And this scene is taking place in Egypt?*

J: Yes. Nostradamus took the horoscope away and is showing me the image in this ... it's like a black glass mirror. But it's not glass, it's obsidian. It's like a volcanic stone, but it's so shiny it's almost like glass.

This sounded like the same mirror seen by both Elena and Brenda.

J: And yes, they're sitting around having a conference.

D: *Is this the man he wants you to see?*

J: Oh yes. He's got an aura of light around him. But it's not a spiritual light, it's like a magnet in light. Your eyes are automatically drawn to him. He's very affectionate and loving to all the men around the table. There's camaraderie and good cheer. They're not drinking alcohol but they smoke hashish. There's one man with a water pipe, and there's a man that's like a priest, but he's not a western priest. He's got on white robes and a white hat. It's like a fez but it isn't a fez. They're all getting up now and they're bowing down to Mecca. They're doing absolutions to Allah. There are seven of these men and they're discussing the future of this man.

D: *What are they saying?*

J: They're giving him support and money. They're telling him to go to Switzerland to draw money from a bank account there. And he will use this money ... it will take him into Syria, Iraq, and Iran. It looks like they're talking about making him a religious leader for the Moslem people. It's similar to how our politicians create candidates for office, but they're going to make him a religious leader. A woman has come in and she bows at his feet, replenishes the food and pours more coffee in the cups and then leaves.

D: *Is this the young man's house?*

J: No, it belongs to the man who is the laughing Arab. The big jolly fat man. It's his estate. It's beautiful. This man is very rich.

D: *They're going to be backers of this young man, and they want him to go to Switzerland, draw money out of this account and then go to Syria and these other countries.*

J: Syria and Iraq first, and then into Iran. But they cannot go into Iran yet, because he will run into difficulties with the ruler of that country. (This was before Ayatollah Khomeni died.) They're planning a counter-revolution in the Islamic world. That is the purpose of this meeting. And it's taking place ... *now.*

D: *Then they are planning to have him* appear *to be a religious leader.*

J: Well, he will be like a religious leader, but have a more moderate religious stance. It's not that he's going to be a religious leader like the Ayatollah Khomeni. He's progressive because he's college educated and knows a lot about computers and finance as well. He's in the world of business, but he has a charisma that is strong. Everyone is basking in his light. They get good feelings just being around him.

D: *Why did they choose him to do this?*

J: The priest has pointed him out to them. The priest has brought him up and has been very influential in his life. (*John's voice dropped low.*) And this man is scary looking.

D: *Who is?*

J: The priest is scary looking. I've never seen such a hateful visage. His eyes are like daggers and they burn with fire. Ohh, he just has so much hate. He is truly evil incarnate.

D: *Hmm, you wouldn't think that of a priest, would you?*

J: But he is. He is just ...

John clenched his hands against the couch he was lying on. You could see him visibly shrink or pull away from whatever he was seeing. Even his voice displayed revulsion.

J: Ohh! My spirit shrinks back, and Nostradamus pulls the vision away. Nostradamus says, "There it is. There is the Anti-Christ's power."

D: *Does it come from the priest?*

J: Yes. Looking into his face was like looking into an abyss. It was similar to a black hole in space that sucks up all the light energy. The visage of this person's face is trying to pull at your soul. Nostradamus is saying, "I feel it also, even across time he tries to pull."

D: *It's not so much the young man who will be doing these things, but the priest will be the man behind him. Am I understanding this correctly?*

J: The young man will inherit this power from the evil man when the evil man leaves. He has instructed and groomed him for an important role. And when his mission is fulfilled, the young man will inherit that evil. Oh! He's just horrible. (*John made sounds of revulsion and his whole body quivered.*)

D: *It seems hard to believe that such a young, beautiful person could have this evilness within him.*

J: No. He will inherit it when the teacher-priest leaves this life. I see it like a benediction descending into him, a mantle of evil covering him and impregnating his very soul at that time.

D: *Will this nature show itself before that time?*

J: No. The teacher possesses such hatred. He is evil personified. When he leaves the planet this young man will inherit his power.

D: *Do you think the priest has groomed this young man because he knows this?*

J: Oh, yes. Psychically he is very powerful.

D: *Then this is what the priest intended from the beginning. Of course, the other people in the room don't know this, do they?*

J: No. They mistrust the priest though. It's very hard for them to like him. His aura is one of negativity and they have a hard time dealing with him, but he has made them so rich.

D: *Ah, he has done things for them.*

J: He has helped to make them very rich. And he has manipulated things. He has been stirring up trouble all over the place. (*Surprised*) He is the one behind the killing of the President of Egypt.

Anwar Sadat, the Egyptian President and winner of the 1978 Nobel Peace Prize, was assassinated in October, 1981, while watching a military parade. A small group of men in military uniforms leaped from a truck in the parade hurling grenades and spraying the reviewing stand with submachine gunfire. The assassins were said to have been linked to a group of conspirators described as a violent Muslim fundamentalist sect which had sought to set up an Islamic republic in Egypt. Before the investigation was over several hundred militants were arrested, some after grenade and machine-gun battles with the police. The government said there were "indications that the conspirators received financial assistance from outside sources, but did not elaborate." (*Collier's Encyclopedia 1981 Yearbook.*)

This type of grooming and backing of a person to give him such power seemed hard to believe. Americans are used to planning things and having them come to fruition quickly. Can it be that people in that part of the world have the patience to plot and plan for something that may not take form for several decades, or even within their lifetime?

D: *Then they don't know the influence this priest will have on this young man in the future.*

J: Well, they know the young man is the priest's *protégé*. Nostradamus is saying that's enough now on the Anti-Christ. He's saying that it's not good to use the word "*Anti*-Christ," that is such a Christian term. He says Hitler was not a Christian, and Napoleon was not a Christian even though he professed to be one, yet they are considered to be the other two Anti-Christs. He says those people had inherited this same evil energy.

D: *"Anti-Christ" is the word people have used, and they said Nostradamus himself used it in his quatrains. That's the reason we use it.*

J: He says not to worry about the semantics of words. Now he says this man will be known as the Anti-Christ in the far away future of the 20th century, but at this point in his life he won't be known as that. He will be known as a world savior or someone who brings peace, until the teacher expires, giving him the power of evil. Oooh, (*John shivered*) he's so scary looking. That man ... his face ... it was just like following down a hole.

D: *Well, I don't want you to feel uncomfortable.*

J: No, he's gone now. Nostradamus is back and he's saying, "You have now seen the complete face of evil." Even Nostradamus is shuttered.

He says, "It is the complete negative force of the universe that you were just looking at. Some people call it the Devil." But he says the Devil is limited in his power by our picture of him as a little man with red horns and a tail. He says *this* force is much more powerful than you can believe for it is the culmination of all the negativity the Earth has collected since its beginning.

D: *Now I can see more clearly how his predictions might come to pass, with this type of a force behind them. I'm curious, was there a reason why he wouldn't allow the woman vehicle to see that image? Did he think it might be too awful for her to look at, or what?*

J: *(Laughing)* He says, "You can't show women *everything*." He is saying that she was sort of a transcurrent—is that the word? Transcurrent vehicle?

There is no such word as transcurrent. But I believe he was trying to say that Brenda was only passing through, and was just a temporary channel.

D: *Yes, but we must tell him that you are a temporary vehicle, too, because you will be moving away.*

J: He says, don't worry, you will *always* be able to contact him. There will always be a vehicle for him to come through. But he says to try to contact him through male entities for they seem to respond better to his information and knowledge. He's saying, "I'll be happy to work with the female entity again, but I hope Dolores can find another male entity to work with. It seems I respond easier with men than I do with women." I have the feeling that Nostradamus is a bit of a chauvinist. *(Laugh)* He doesn't trust women or take easily to them. And he had a slight smile on his face when I said that. He asks you again to try to find another male vehicle. He's looking at the dark mirror now and is saying, "Oh, don't worry. You will attract what you will need. This is all part of your spirit guide's master plan." He says you will come in contact with a male person who will be of tremendous value and assistance to you.

D: *Can he give me an idea of what the person looks like so I will know when I meet him?*

J: He says your spirit guide will present the opportunity soon enough.

D: *Okay. But it seems that in our time women are more intuitive and therefore can more easily do this type of work. He said the work is important enough that he would try to come through anyone I worked with.*

I didn't want to give up working with Brenda. We had obtained such excellent results. I was trying to convince him of this. I certainly didn't want to have to search for yet *another* subject for this experiment.

J: He repeats that he would prefer to work with a male, because male energies and his energies get along very well. *(Laugh)* He says, "You know, John, one of the reasons I have discord with women is because of the constant aggravation caused by my servant girl. My maid gives me a lot of problems. She's constantly bothering me. She's always knocking on my door and disturbing me or interrupting me with minor, insignificant things." He just gave me an example. She will come to the door, knock, and say something like, "One of the sheep has gotten out." He would yell at her to go and catch it because it's her job, not his. He's paying her three sous a month to take care of these things so he won't be bothered. That must be a good salary for the time.

D: *Maybe the girl is curious about what goes on in that room.* (Laugh)

J: He's showing me a picture of his horoscope, and there is Moon square Mars. He says, "See, John. Yes, you understand now why I have difficulties with women." This is an astrological aspect that shows combativeness, with the moon representing the female entity—it could be females in general—and Mars representing temper, drive and things of this nature. A square is an inharmonious aspect. He's showing me the sun trine Jupiter which means he relates better to men than he does to women. It also means it's easy for him to receive and give information.

D: *Is there a date on that horoscope?*

J: He doesn't want me to see that. He says, "I'd be happy to show you this horoscope, but I don't want you to draw it up and use it. You know a little knowledge can be dangerous. John, you wouldn't want your horoscope published and neither do I." *(Laugh)*

D: *Are the symbols he uses different than yours?*

J: They're very similar, except they're a little more embellished. They have curlicues here and there which are just extra. I'm showing him the symbols of Pluto, Uranus and Neptune. And I'm telling him that Uranus is the unexpected, the changer. Neptune is the mystic, but also the dissolver. And Pluto is the challenger and the generation. I'm showing them to him. *(Surprised)* I've got an ephemeris with me. I must have picked it up in the library.

He said later that it was not a book. It was more like a large scroll. He just suddenly realized he must have been carrying it since he left the library.

D: *Does he have these symbols?*

J: No, he doesn't. Oh, he's delighted. He says this will help him in his work. He's really excited. I'm showing him the ephemerides and he's smiling. He's writing them down and placing them in his own horoscope. Now he's reading my mind and taking information from it. And he says, "Ah! I see why my wife died. Pluto in the seventh house."

D: *What did he mean by that? How did she die?*

J: She died of the plague.

D: *How did he connect that with Pluto in the seventh house?*

J: He read from my mind that Pluto represents mass consciousness. With Pluto being destructive and the seventh house ruling relationships, that could be how he came to that conclusion. I showed him the three symbols of these planets, and he said this will help him in his centuries. He says other astrologers of his time only know of the planets through Saturn. I'm telling him the dates of the discoveries of these other planets, and he's writing them down. He's very excited about this.

D: *He did say in one of our sessions that he knew of the existence of some of these planets because of ancient legends.*

J: I asked him that, and he says, yes, he's known of the existence of the other planets, but he didn't have names for them. He didn't understand their qualities and what they represented. Now that he has the information and the ephemeris—an astrological book of data—this will help him immensely. He's just writing up a storm.

D: *Well, is it possible to leave the book there for him?*

J: No, I have to take it with me when I leave, but he's writing the cycles down. He says, "You can talk to me while I'm writing."

D: *That way you really are helping him by showing him these things.*

J: Yes, he's very happy. He's saying, "I always wanted to know more about these things. And I knew it would come to me." He feels like a kid who has found a treasure. But he says, "We know there's only a brevity of time, so you can talk to me. One half of my mind can do calculations while the other half converses. So, if you have a question ..."

D: *All right. Do you think we need any more information on Ogmios? You have his horoscope. Do you want to know more?*

J: He's saying, "John, go over to the mirror there." And I'm going over to the mirror. Oh, he showed me Ogmios! (*Pause*) I suppose he's a priest now, because he has priest's vestments on, but he's quite dissatisfied with the church. It doesn't look like he's going to be with the church much longer. And it looks like he's in the city of Prague, Czechoslovakia. It's beautiful and medieval but still modern with cars and things like that.

D: *Do you think this is where he is at the present time?*

J: Yes, that's what he's showing me. It's the present time.

D: *What does the man look like, physically?*

J: He's kind of short and stocky, but he has a kind face. He reminds me of Pope John XXIII. He's built like him but much nicer looking, and he has much kinder eyes. I mean, Pope John XXIII had kind eyes as well, but Ogmios has good full features. They're thick, Slavic features but they're kind. He has a smiling, happy-go-lucky type of face, but he's very serious and determined to help. He's a very intelligent man, and he knows a lot about many different subjects. He even has books that have been forbidden to him, but he has gotten access to them because he knows how to worm his way around things. (*Laugh*) He's a charmer, and he means well. He doesn't have one negative thought or attitude toward others. In fact, he'd sacrifice anything for other people. He's a very kind, loving person. Right now he's moving down a corridor, and he seems to be doing secretarial work for someone in a high position in the church. Now I see him in Rome, walking in the Vatican gardens. Other people make fun of him a bit because it seems he's so precocious. The way they talk about him. He's so happy-go-lucky and full of good cheer while the other men are just so dour-faced.

D: *It seems strange to me that a man who is a priest could end up being the nemesis of the Anti-Christ.*

J: I don't think he's going to be a priest forever. He has the faith and good intentions, but he doesn't have the negativity that most religions carry. He's a devoted world server. That is what Nostradamus just said.

D: *Does Nostradamus want to show you his horoscope, or do you have enough information already?*

J: He says, in time. He says your other guides will give you more information about this.

D: *Okay. We also have a horoscope on the last pope who will be a tool for the Anti-Christ. Ogmios, the Anti-Christ and this last pope are the three main characters in our scenario for the future. Can he tell you any more about the last pope?*

J: He's showing me this anteroom where there is a man at a desk. (*Surprised*) We're at the Vatican again. The man is behind a desk and he's very intense on what he's writing. I'm walking across the room now, and I can look over his shoulder to see what he's writing. (*Pause*) It's about finances, and how to recoup their losses. He's very concerned about the money the church has, but is losing. He's trying to stem the flow of it. He's thinking of making investments in different areas so the church will become wealthy again, because the church is now losing money.

D: *Is the mirror showing us what these men are doing now?*

J: Yes. He says this is happening at our present time.

D: *As you look at this man—I know he's sitting down—can you see if he has some kind of a deformity?*

J: He's sitting down, but he's going to walk with a limp. It's a slight limp and not very noticeable. I mean, it will be noticeable, but he's not going to stumble.

D: *We weren't sure about the exact nature of the deformity.*

J: Right now this man is really upset and angry. People have been taking money from the church that they shouldn't have. He's even thinking they might have to sell some church property in different areas of the world, but they don't want to do that because they'll lose their financial base. He's thinking of going to Switzerland to get loans and make other financial arrangements. At the present time he has something to do with the finances of the church.

D: *Is he in a position of some authority?*

J: Yes, he has three or four people beneath him who are secretaries and gofers. He's a bishop and is dressed in a white robe. He's now going upstairs to meet with the pope about the church's finances. He's preparing a statement for a council meeting about this. That's why he was writing.

Over a year later, in October, 1988, the Vatican announced they had a $64 million deficit, confirming what John had seen while looking over the last pope's shoulder.

D: *I think it's important that you have seen all three of these people. You might be able to recognize them later.*

J: Oh, yes. This man has a dour look. He has a long, skinny nose, and he carries himself like he is smelling something awful. (*Laugh*) You know. He has his nose in the air.

D: (Laugh) *Does Nostradamus have any other astrological information to give you at this time?*

J: Nostradamus is saying it's time for him to get back to his own work on that level, and not to communicate with spirits. "Oh, it's good to have met you, John. And please come back again because I will share more information with you." He has to go now because someone is bringing a sick child for him to see.

I wanted instructions before we left.

D: *When we return will he know you are there if you come to his room?*

J: Yes, he says he will recognize me. He says to come to the back study because his front study is where he performs some of his medical treatments. At this time his servant girl is knocking on the door for him to come and see the sick child. He would like to leave now.

D: *All right. We really appreciate what he's done.*

J: He's saying, "Thank *you* very much. I didn't know about these other planets. I knew of them from the ancients, that beyond Saturn there were other planets, but I didn't know what they were called or what their cycles were. This will be very helpful for me in the future in my work on the centuries."

D: *Then we will try to come a few more times before this vehicle has to move.*

J: He says he would be delighted, and to please come back again. ... He's gone. ... The horoscope looked interesting: square and diamond shapes each representing the 12 houses. And the writing was very thick. ... Now I'm back in the Tapestry Room.

D: *I think you've done very well and I appreciate what you've been doing for me. Would you like to attempt this again?*

J: Oh, yes, it's wonderful. Being with Nostradamus is like being with an old friend.

D: *Is there anything else you would like to see in the tapestry before we leave it?*

J: I see my own thread now. It's silver and copper in color, as it weaves through the tapestry. The guardian of the tapestry is saying it's time for me to leave. He says, "You don't need this knowledge. In time you can look but not at the present time." (*Pause*) He's discussing my soul's growth. And he's sort of calling me to task on it. (*John laughed.*) He says I was such a bright ray of light, and I had allowed myself to grow dim. That's why I had to go back to the Earth school.

D: *So you can make amends?*

J: Well, by understanding universal laws and love, I could gain my light back. It's easier to go through the Earth school than to incarnate on other dimensions. It's quicker.

D: *How do you feel about him telling you that?*

J: Well, I don't like it. I'm embarrassed, actually. I feel very chastised. I mean, he's perfectly right that it's my fault. I've sidestepped my responsibility, so I had to incarnate. But it's not like he's pointing his finger and saying, "No, no, no, no, no." He doing it lovingly. He's embraced me now, and he says, "Good luck on your mission."

I could not resist the temptation, so I asked, "I wonder if my thread is in there anywhere?"

J: *Yes,* your thread's there. Your thread is a bright shiny copper color that gets stronger. It starts out kind of small and then it gets bigger and bigger, influencing a lot of other threads. This tapestry is very magical. (*Abruptly*) He's asking us to leave. "You were looking at your own life, and that's not good to do at this point."

D: *It's just human curiosity, but I suppose we shouldn't get too nosy.*

J: Yes. I think the guardian of the tapestry was implying that we shouldn't look too much into our own future. He's saying, "You've had enough to look at for now."

D: *That makes sense. Because if we know what's going to happen to us, would we still do the things we are planning to do?*

Then it was time to leave this incredible adventure and return to the land of the living and our every-day human world. Since John had proved to be such an excellent subject, I definitely wanted to continue working with him in the short time we had left. So I conditioned him to respond to a keyword before he was awakened. The keyword can be anything but I usually allow the subject's subconscious to choose the word. Using this shortcut makes the sessions easier because a long induction is not required, and the subject will go immediately into trance. We can then proceed with our work instead of wasting time with induction and deepening techniques.

John remembered quite a bit of the session. Upon awakening he laughed and said, "That was *quite* an experience!"

I asked, "I wonder how he knew you were there?"

He answered, "Well, I saw myself, and I was wearing this luminous-like robe. And he said, 'Oh, it's you!' It was as if he were surprised. And he was just like that picture. (He was referring to the drawing in Volume One that Elena had made from her memories of Nostradamus.) Except I'm taller than he is." He chuckled at the memory. John is about 6'4" and he said Nostradamus didn't even come up to his shoulder. He noticed this difference while walking around the room with him. "He appears quite short when I stand next to him, and he's very friendly."

I remarked that I had read that people in those days were shorter than modern men. I thought it was curious that the picture Elena had drawn did resemble him. This would appear to be proof that they were indeed seeing the same person. Brenda had also thought the portrait was a good likeness of him.

"I saw him at a point in his life when he was a bit more gray. He looked a little older and he had sharper features than in the picture. He was really excited and happy to meet me."

D: *When you saw your face in the mirror, did you look like yourself?*

J: My face looked very similar. My body didn't. I wasn't as overweight, I was skinnier. And I had on this luminous robe. It had rainbow patterns woven into it, but they weren't like gaudy rainbows, they were sparkly. It was nice.

D: *I guess he's used to seeing spirits, and that's why it didn't bother him.*

J: No, it didn't bother him at all. He felt my presence, but I had to go to the mirror so he could see me, and that's when he recognized me. Then he said, "Oh, come on in" and he welcomed me into his study. He knew I was from the future, and that I was a part of the group from the 20th century. He allowed me to walk around and see the different things in his study. He showed me things in the magic mirror which was like a sheet of obsidian glass.

D: *Elena and Brenda both said it was dark-looking. Maybe they had a hard time describing it because it's not really a mirror as we know it.*

J: No, it looks like obsidian or a black crystal or a volcanic stone. He was very excited that I had the ephemeris from the library. It was apparently meant for him. He went through it ... (*making motions*) writing like crazy. (*Laugh*) And he said, "You can talk to me at the same time, but this is important information I need." It gave other positions of the planets he didn't know about. He said he will use them when he works on his quatrains.

D: *This makes me wonder. Which comes first, the cart or the horse? Are we speaking to him before he's writing his quatrains? (Laugh) Because he does mention Neptune and these other planets in them. I had this idea before and it bothered me. Are we helping him?*

J: (*Seriously*) I think we are.

D: *Several people have said that. Maybe we're writing them for him when*

I read them to him. Who knows? It's a strange feeling. (I laughed
nervously.)

J: Yes. It makes you wonder where's the sense of time? I did have a
feeling that somehow we *are* helping him. When he mentioned your
spirit guide, I saw this luminous being. I didn't see a face, but it was
as if someone was directing this whole thing.

D: (Laugh) *Somebody's up there writing this.*

J: So don't worry about it. Your spirit guide is putting the situations
together.

John remarked about the scene he was shown of the future Anti-
Christ. The mansion was located on the Nile, and the ruins he could see
in the background were tall pillars, like some ancient Egyptian monuments. He also sensed that the dark evil man was very psychic. He
seemed to be aware we were in the room because he kept looking around
as though he sensed our presence. The men were also suspicious of being
overheard because they stopped talking when the servant girl entered the room.

John heard them call the evil man "Imam," which he said means
"priest" in Arabic or whatever language they were speaking. The name
was used as a title of respect. This man is supposed to be a religious figure,
but it was apparently a front.

John said he got the feeling the young man's parents were dead, and
that they had been killed in the Egyptian war. Also, the priest was a relative who had taken care of him since that time.

It was incredible that we had been able to get so much corroborating
information on our first attempt. I wasn't even sure we would be able to
reach Nostradamus through a new vehicle. But John had succeeded far
beyond any expectations I might have had, and far beyond any element
of chance. It was apparent we had a clear connection with the great man,
and that he was sincere when he said I would always be able to contact
him, no matter what channel I used. I would have to get as much information as I could before John departed. He was excited about this and
was willing to work as many times a week as we could arrange.

Chapter 12

Nostradamus and Astrology

$\mathcal{D}$URING THESE SESSIONS there were often other people present as observers. Sometimes they asked permission to ask questions, but oftentimes they passed me notes. At this session, John's friend Don, a fellow astrologer from Houston, was present. He and John had prepared a list of questions that dealt mostly with aspects of astrology which meant nothing to me.

I used the keyword and John went into a deep trance immediately. I then counted him to a spirit state where he would not be directly involved with a life. He described the scene, "I'm walking in a beautiful garden where there are fountains and conduits of water. The birds are singing. The smells of the flowers are just wonderful. I'm going up the steps to the temple and into the Tapestry Room."

This time he needed no prompting. He went directly to the tapestry and found the golden thread of Nostradamus' life. Following the glowing strand, he emerged in Nostradamus' back study where we had been instructed to come.

J: I'm peering in the obsidian glass mirror. He smiles and says, "Welcome. Good to see you."
D: *Is he in trance at this time?*
J: He can communicate with me because he is sort of meditating. He's not in a trance state, *per se,* but he's in contemplation.
D: *Does he mind speaking with us for a while?*
J: Oh, no, no. He's elated. He knows who we are.
D: *As long as he's not busy or preoccupied with anything at this time.*
J: No, he's not preoccupied right now, he says. He feels good. He's at peace with himself. He thanks me for showing him the ephemeris of the planets that weren't discovered in his time. He now uses some of them for his predictions. I wasn't allowed to leave the book there. But he says he was able to write his own version of it in a special code so other people couldn't use it. He says some of this information could cause trouble, especially in the time period he lives in.

D: *Of course, most people wouldn't understand it, would they?*

J: Some people would understand because they have a classical education. Many of the ancient Roman and Greek philosophers had mentioned other planets besides the known ones. You see, there are other
astrologers in this country who would only use the information for
their own means. Not all of them use their knowledge scrupulously or
to be of service, but to line their own purses.

D: *Is this one reason why he put it into code?*

J: Yes, he hasn't even discussed this with his best students. He was able
to continue his work with this information and he appreciates our
help. He's elated about the fact that we give him information about
the future as well.

D: *I wondered if we were giving him the answers or if he was giving us the
answers. Which comes first? Who's helping who? (Laugh) Or is it a
cooperative effort?*

J: It's cooperative. We give him information. We are the spirits of
the future.

It has been suggested by other astrologers that I ask Nostradamus
about the calendar he used in his time period. The Julian calendar was
in effect then. The Gregorian calendar, which we use in our time, went
into effect in 1582 in France (after the death of Nostradamus). The rest
of the world was slow to follow. England did not adopt it until 1752, and
Russia began using it after the Bolshevist Revolution in 1917. There are
discrepancies between the two calendars and much confusion concerning
historical dates. The astrologers thought if he were making astrological
predictions based on his calendar, then naturally they would not be accurate in our time. So I followed their suggestions and asked him if he used
a calendar in his calculations.

J: He uses books of astrological data called "ephemerides." He's saying
things like, "It's not a totally accurate calendar they use right now."
He uses it for the seasons and day-to-day life, but he mostly uses his
books of astrological data when he writes his horoscopes.

D: Are they the same?

J: No, there's some discrepancy there. The calendar isn't the same as the
books of astrological data. This is data that has been used from the
time of the Egyptians and the Babylonians, that goes all the way to the
year 6000.

D: *Is he aware that the calendar was changed in the future?*

J: Yes, he's very aware of the changes.

D: *This is what I wanted to clarify. If he were drawing up astrological
data based on the calendar of his day, would it have to be adjusted
according to our calendar? For instance, if in one of his quatrains he
were to say that the sun was in Pisces, would Pisces be a different
month or length of time in his day than it would be in our day?*

J: When he predicts the future he only uses astrological data because he knows that different calendars will mean different effects in the future. For instance, he sees Pisces as a time before the vernal equinox and not as a specific date on the traditional calendars. It's all done by the stars and they haven't changed that much.

D: *Then his calendar has no influence on his predictions?*

J: He only uses the calendar of his time to look up when he has to go to church. He must go to church because he's very well respected in his community, and church is very important in his time. He would be called a heretic if he didn't go. The church people know he's quite a learned man.

D: *Well, if he's using an astrological calendar, does that make it more difficult to predict the years?*

J: I have that thought in mind and he shakes his head, "no." He's showing me a huge leather-bound book. It's like a portfolio. And he's opening it. It lists the planetary positions. (*Surprised*) And they go all the way back to 4000 B.C.E.! Now he's showing me how it goes on into the future, even beyond the 21st century into the 22nd, the 23rd, the 24th, and on and on. Finally, I see the last calculations show the year 6000 A.D.

D: *Is that as far as the book goes?*

J: It's as far as this ephemeris goes. It's almost as if each page in it represents a hundred-year span of astrological positions.

D: *And this book is very old?*

J: No, he says it's information that is part of himself.

D: *I thought maybe he obtained the book somewhere.*

J: No, he has gleaned this information from other books and ephemerides. He knows about the procession of ages. For instance, he knows he lives in the Age of Pisces and that we are in the dawn of the Age of Aquarius. He knew about the Age of Aries, Taurus, Gemini, Leo, and Cancer. And he knows that the Pole Star has changed. But he's made these astrological calculations to go with the time period concerning the procession of ages.

I wondered if this is what his student, Dyonisus, meant when he said Nostradamus looked at the sky at the time he was seeing an event happen because Nostradamus would see the stars the way they appeared at the time of an event.

D: *When he sees an event, how does he relate it to the data?*

J: He looks through the astrological book of data, and concentrates on different time periods. This is one of the bases of how he composes his quatrains. He can zero in on the different dates and years.

Although my next few questions had nothing to do with this project, I could not resist the temptation to find out more when the opportunity presented itself.

D: While he has the book open, they say on the day Christ was born there was a bright star in the heavens, and there has always been a lot of controversy about what it was. I'm curious if he has any data on that? Was it a conjunction?

J: Yes. He says it was a conjunction of Jupiter and Saturn affected by the Sun. The light of Jupiter and Saturn combined to create a great light in the sky and it stayed there for months. Christ's Sun, Jupiter, and Saturn were in the sign of Pisces. He was born in ... March.

D: There have always been discrepancies concerning this event, such as when to start the year A.D., and as long as he had the book open, I thought it would be a good time to ask about it. Would a conjunction such as this predict a very important event?

J: Yes, knowing Jupiter and Saturn were coming to a conjunction and that this would be especially bright over the near Middle East, the three Magi saw that this was a star signifying the birth of a great world server, and that's why they traveled to see His birth.

D: Then they were astrologers also.

J: Yes, the Magi were astrologers. They weren't kings. They were wealthy men who were highly regarded for their knowledge in their respective countries.

D: I've often suspected that. Thank you for answering my question. John wanted to clarify a few more points concerning the Anti-Christ's horoscope. I know Nostradamus is not comfortable with that word.

J: He says that's okay, but he's not the Anti-Christ yet. He's going over to his shelf now and taking out a scroll. He's opening it up, and there's the horoscope. We see February, 1962 at the top of it and Aquarius in the first house. I'm asking, "Is it intercepted anywhere?" And he says, "No, it's straight in Aquarius." The sun, the moon, Mercury, Venus, Mars, Jupiter, and Saturn are all in the first house.

D: Are any of those conjunctions?

J: No, there are no conjunctions. Wait a minute. There is a conjunction between ... I think it's Venus and Mars. They're close enough but they're all different degrees.

D: Then it's not a real conjunction?

J: Yes, they're all conjuncting by sign, but not by the same degree. Some of them are in conjunction with each other. Then, I see the planet Pluto in what would be the eighth house on this chart, in Virgo. This is where his occult energy comes from. It's a very uneven-looking chart because all the other planets are in the first house. He must have been born about sunrise. Then, I see—I'm trying to see it a little clearer—what looks like a yod.

D: (I didn't understand.) A what?

J: A yod between them. He says it's not a true yod, but it's similar.

Dn: (The other astrologer.) Between what planets?

D: Can you hear the other person in the room when he speaks?

J: Yes, I hear another person. Nostradamus says there's a semi-sextile between Uranus and Pluto, but Uranus opposes all these Aquarian planets. Uranus is in the sign of Leo in the seventh house. He says Pluto will be very important in his life. When Pluto moves into the sign of Sagittarius we'll see a lot of changes. This will be an influential time in his life.

Later, we found that Pluto will move into Sagittarius in November 1995, which fits into the timetable of events.

D: *Are there any other signs in the other houses that you need to know about?*
J: I'm asking him where Neptune is? (*Laugh*) He says, "I didn't put Neptune in there."
D: *I'm surprised he put in Pluto and Uranus.*
J: The reason he didn't put Neptune in is because this man will not have any compassion. But he says, "For you, I'll put it in." Where will you put it? (*Pause*) I think it's in Virgo. No, not Virgo, it's in Scorpio. The symbols he uses for Virgo and Scorpio are very different. In our time these symbols are very similar. He's saying, "Yes, Neptune is in the sign of Scorpio." And it takes place in the tenth house. He says this is the planet of mystery.

It was obvious that although he was not familiar with these planets and their astrological meanings before, he was now using them since John had shown him the scroll from the library.

D: *Are there any other symbols in the other houses, besides the astrological symbols?*
J: (*Mumbling, hard to understand, as though he is speaking to Nostradamus.*) Do you use the Arabian part system? He says, "No. I'm a straight astrologer, and I use only the planets."
D: *Okay. I thought there might be some other symbols he used that you were not familiar with. Can you see this horoscope clearly enough to reproduce it for me later?*
J: Yes. It's just a little different from the last chart.

I then gave John post-hypnotic suggestions that all the signs and their arrangement in this unfamiliar pattern would remain very clear in his mind, and that he would be able to draw it for me when he awakened.

Since John had finished scrutinizing the chart, he continued by giving an explanation for the discrepancy between the date given to Brenda and the horoscope shown to him.

J: He says the other horoscope, drawn for Sagittarius 1968, is when the Anti-Christ lost his family. They were killed in the Egyptian war by the Israelis.
D: *I was going to ask about the two different dates. We couldn't understand how he could gain so much power by the time he's in his twenties.*

J: He says the date the other channel picked up on was not his birthdate but the day that he lost his parents. She had that confused.

D: *Well, she had a difficult time receiving astrological data.*

J: Yes, she did. He was a young boy of five or six when that took place. And his uncle, the evil priest, has been grooming him and is the real power behind the throne. Nostradamus is letting me look in the mirror now. I'm seeing a picture of university buildings, and the man we know as the Anti-Christ is coming out of one of them. He is a very intelligent and beautiful man with a magnetic aura about him that draws people to him. He's studying and doing research on a project at this university at this time. He's incorporating the philosophies of Voltaire, Hegel, Marx, Engels, and other famous philosophers into one philosophy.

Brenda also had said that the young Anti-Christ was presently a college student in Egypt. This was one of the few insights that she was given about his present location.

D: *Nostradamus once told us we would never know very much about the Anti-Christ's background because it would remain a mystery.*

J: There is mystery in the sense that his parents were killed, and Imam, the priest, will also keep things mysterious. Imam is the personification of what you would call the Devil. He has a venomous hatred for the Israelis and wants to see Israel stomped and destroyed. He will stir up trouble and work to that aim. He's not a bad looking man, but his eyes hold you and draw into you until you feel like your soul is being sucked out. His eyes are like black holes.

D: *It's a wonder the young man wouldn't feel this.*

J: The young man loves him because he has been nourished and loved by him. This evil being's true weakness is this young man. He's done everything possible to make his life comfortable and happy. So great love exists between them. When this evil *being*—it's not a man— finishes with the shell of his body, he will transfer his essence and his energy to him. This is when the young man will become the Anti-Christ. But this will happen in the 1990s.

D: *Is this when Pluto will cause the change and he will start his rise to power?*

J: Right. He will become more influential than he is now. The evil being is currently dealing with money matters, creating a base for the Anti-Christ to rise on. He is getting money from Arabs of all nationalities throughout the Islamic world to help support him in his efforts. He's also going to help foster some revolutionary changes in Syria, Iraq, and Iran. And he's going to do that soon enough.

D: *When he gave us astrological signs through Brenda, he said some of those signs did not pertain to his natal horoscope but to the horoscope of his coming to power.*

J: The channel got what she thought was his birthdate, but it was actually the death of his parents which was traumatic for him because he was very young at the time. Then he was cared for by his uncle; the evil being. The Anti-Christ doesn't know it, but his father and mother were murdered. It appeared that they died because of the war, but actually, the uncle had hired assassins because he wanted the boy for himself.

D: *Was he plotting even then?*

J: Yes, he plotted then to take the parents, and the young man doesn't know this. Nostradamus says that's the mystery surrounding his beginnings. The evil being was born in the 1930s. He saw the rise of Israel into Palestine, his country, and saw his life taken away. He dedicated himself to the black forces of the universe and allowed them to take over his life. It's the same situation we know of as walk-ins that come to be of service. He allowed a negative walk-in to take his place in his life. His whole purpose is to groom the Anti-Christ to take his powerful place in the world's destiny.

D: *Maybe that's why he had to start with a child.*

J: Right.

D: *Do you think the other horoscopes are accurate?*

J: He feels that most of the other things she channeled were basically accurate. He says she specifically had a difficult time with the Anti-Christ's horoscope.

D: *We were also confused about the mention of a grand trine.*

J: The grand trine takes place in the Anti-Christ's ascendancy. Saturn is in Pisces. I can't see the rest of it. He says, "Look that up; it will be in the mid-1990s."

D: *He also said the three water signs related to three bodies of water.*

J: Yes, Nostradamus says he was referring to the near East. When he comes to power, Saturn will be in the water sign of Pisces. He says he will make his rise in power in the early to mid-1990s.

I asked John, "Do you think this will clarify what you were looking for?"

J: Yes, now I can draw up the horoscope the way I see it.

Later, when John had time to look in his ephemeris, he found that a grand trine of water signs will occur several times during the summer of 1994. Two of these occurrences were considered to be the most likely. In July 1994, there will be a conjunction of the Sun and Mercury in grand trine with Jupiter and Saturn. This was believed to be the most important occurrence because of the presence of the Sun. The second grand trine occurs in September of 1994, involving Mars, Jupiter and Saturn. These are all powerful planets with important influences, and we believe the Anti-Christ will emerge sometime during that period. It's interesting that no grand trines (involving major planets in water signs) occur throughout the remainder of the 1990s.

Don wanted to ask some questions he and John had agreed upon before the session.

D: *We have another astrologer here who would like to ask some questions.*

Dn: *In Nostradamus' time which planets rule which signs? In our time there's a question about which planets rule the signs of Virgo and Libra.*

J: He says the sign of the Ram is ruled by Mars, the red planet which appears in the evening skies. He says the sign of Taurus is ruled by Venus, the beautiful star; Gemini is ruled by Mercury; Cancer by the sign of the moon; and Leo has the sun. Scorpio is ruled by your planet Pluto; one of the most destructive planets there is. Sagittarius is ruled by Jove ... Jupiter. Capricorn is Saturn's taskmaster; Uranus, the planet of change, rules the sign of Aquarius; and Neptune will rule the sign of the fish. Virgo, he says, will be ruled by another planet that hasn't been discovered yet in your time. Libra will be ruled by a newly-discovered planet also. He says, "Just as in our time, we can only see up to Saturn, but we know there are other planets beyond it. It is similar in your age; you'll discover planets that will rule Virgo and then Libra."

D: *Then he has no rulership for Virgo and Libra in his time?*

J: He says, "In my time there's no ruler for Libra, Virgo, Aquarius, or Pisces, but we assigned Jupiter to Pisces and Saturn to Aquarius. We also assigned Mars to Scorpio." He says as the centuries go on we will discover two more planets, and they will cause tremendous excitement. The first planet will rule Virgo, and the second planet will bring in the true Aquarian Age of wisdom. He calls the Aquarian age the Golden age. He says this planet will be sighted in the ... (*hesitation*) 22nd century. Nostradamus says, "You've got that wrong, John. (*Laugh*) It will be about 2040 that this discovery will take place." The two planets are a part of another solar system. He's giving me a picture of this other solar system that has a binary star. That means it has two stars.

D: *Is that close to Earth?*

J: Yes, he says it's close to Earth, but our scientists are overlooking it. He says they'll be able to sight this star with stronger telescopes.

D: *Do you mean the two solar systems, ours and that one, will overlap?*

J: Our solar system and that solar system are overlapping (*surprised*) now. At this present time.

Dn: *Could Pluto have been a part of that solar system?*

J: He is saying that Uranus, Neptune, and Pluto have all been part of that solar system.

D: *Then what happened?*

J: Oh, I see what he means now. He says that there were two stars which exploded, and these planets were thrown into our orbit. Uranus, Neptune, Pluto, and the two other planets were previously part of this other solar system. He says he received this information when he went into trance and traveled. Nostradamus astral travels.

D: *Are they orbiting our sun at this present time?*

J: They're not in an exact orbit but they're drawn to the sun, like Pluto.

D: *What do you mean, they're not in an exact orbit?*

J: They have a wider degree of arc, he says.

D: *Is this one reason why the scientists haven't seen them yet?*

J: Yes. He says that binary star was an older system and it exploded and burnt itself out.

We referred again to Don's questions.

D: *We were also wondering if something happened in Nostradamus' life that made him want to start predicting the future?*

J: He says, yes, there was.

D: *Would he like to share it with us?*

J: (*Sadly*) He says, "It's painful ... but I lost my family. I went through a very deep depression at that time, and I felt very useless. Because I was able to see a vision of things to come in the future, I applied myself to my astrological abilities. This is how I began predicting the future." He's very sad. He says, "I loved my wife and my children dearly. They died from the plague, and I could do nothing to help them." (*This was all said with emotion.*)

D: *He was a doctor at that time, wasn't he?*

J: Yes, and he couldn't do anything to help them. (*Still sadly.*) "I had my business to take care of," he said. "I lost my faith in life when my wife died, but I've regained it. I'm married again now, and I've got a good woman who really helps me."

D: *Does he have children now?*

J: Yes, he does. And he says, "It's as if ... I'm released. I'm training my children in the right ways."

D: *That's good. Was he interested in astrology before his first family died?*

J: Oh, yes. He says, "I was well versed in astrology, for I did horoscopes for my illustrious patrons."

D: *When did he start writing down the things he sees?*

J: He's been writing for quite a while, he says. He felt a need to write things down. He had visions of the future and felt it would be important to discuss them and leave them as a legacy.

D: *The problem is that he made them too obscure and many people can't understand them.*

J: The people who need to understand them will.

D: *That is our part in all this.*

J: (*Suddenly*) There's a knock at the door. (*I looked around. I thought he meant a knock at the door of his apartment.*) He's going to the door. (*Very softly.*) It's his wife. She's very pretty. We could call her a bit chubby, but she has a kindly face and she's smiling at him. He kisses her and she says, (*gently*) "Well, come on dear. We've got to eat now. You've been in your study all afternoon. Now it's time for you to eat. I've prepared some lamb. Come on." And he's saying, "Well, I have to go now."

D: *What about us? Can't he talk to us anymore?*

J: No. He says, "I'm sorry. Contact me again soon. I'm looking forward to it, but now I need to go."

I was trying to think of some way to keep communicating with him because we still had a lot of time left.

D: *Can we talk to him after he eats his meal?*

J: I'm asking. I told him we could come back. And he says, "No, I have to go." We can't speak to him anymore today.

D: *All right then. We do appreciate him speaking to us for the length of time he has.*

J: He's getting impatient. He's saying, "I have to go. I told my wife that I was doing something important, but she said it is time to eat." I get the feeling she thinks he spends too much time in here. And if she doesn't insist, he will miss his meal. He says, "Please come back and contact me again." He's gone. The room is empty now. It's a very nice room. I thought the furniture was rustic, but actually it's been smoothed and polished. It shows that a lot of loving care has gone into it.

D: *Would you be allowed to have access to the rest of the house, to see what it looks like?*

J: We should stay only in this room. It has a beautiful bronze brazier that he lights sometimes and ... he sees into the fire. He keeps things very neat. There are rushes on the floor, and a special carpet underneath his chair to keep his feet warm. (*Abruptly*) There's someone saying, "Come on, John, you have to leave here now." I have to go. The guardian of the tapestry is saying, "You can't force yourself on other people. Please don't do that." He's giving me a warning. "Do not try to disturb another's free will." ... (*Aggravated*) Okay! Yeah, I understand. And he says, "Just be careful. Now you can leave." He's very stern.

D: *Tell him we were not really forcing ourselves. We've never tried to stay if the person didn't want us to.*

J: Oh, the guardian is very stern today. He understands, but because he thought we were trying to force Nostradamus against his will, he called me on it. He says, "One of the laws of the universe is not to coerce or inflict your will on other people. So don't do that or you will create bad karma for yourself."

D: *Does he understand we had no intention of doing that?*

J: (*Laugh*) He says, "You tried to."

D: *Well, we just wanted to know if we could see him after he got through eating.* (Laugh)

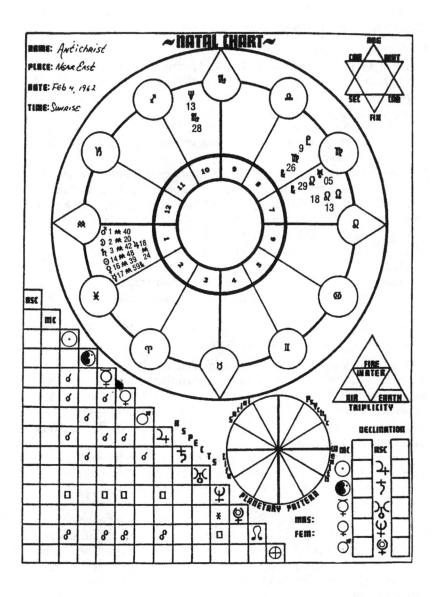

Horoscope for the Anti-Christ with birth date of February 4, 1962.

J: Yeah. I'm telling him. I said we weren't really trying to coerce him, and he's not mad.

I wanted to smooth out the guardian's feelings. If we did anything to offend him, he might not allow us to return through the tapestry.

D: *You were just looking at the room, that's all.*
J: He says it's best only to be there when Nostradamus is there. Because I appear as a spirit or a ghost-like apparition, other people might feel my presence. He says when Nostradamus is eating, that's usually when the servant girl comes in to clean the room. This could have frightened her, and she has enough hard times in her life. (*Laugh*)
D: *I didn't know if anyone else could pick up on our presence when they were in the house.*
J: Well, Nostradamus has told his wife that he communicates and she understands. She's a real helpmate to him because she loves and cares for him. The guardian has pulled me back into the Tapestry Room, and he said, "It's now time for you to go. We'll see you later." (*Laughter*) He isn't mad. He's just very stern.
D: *Tell him we didn't have any idea anyone else could sense our presence.*
J: He says, "Yes, I understand. But you must not break any rules of the universe; otherwise you can be severely reprimanded."
D: *Well, we're trying very hard to do what we're supposed to do. We don't want to break any rules.*
J: He knows that. He's saying, "Bye!" (*Surprised*) Everything's gone! It's all gray. I'm not there any more.

It was as though a switch had been pulled, and he was suddenly not in contact with the Tapestry Room. It seemed there was definitely someone on the other side who had control of our access to the room and also the length of time we could stay. There was no choice but to bring John back to full consciousness. He then asked Don curiously, "What did he talk about astrologically?"

Don then explained about the rulerships of the signs, and about a future discovery of two new planets which cannot be seen at the present time. It seemed Nostradamus was aware of these things by going out of his body and traveling by astral projection.

When John looked for the Anti-Christ's birthdate in his ephemeris he found that February 4, 1962 had to be the date. The data completely and accurately corresponded to the diamond-shaped horoscope that Nostradamus had shown him on the parchment scroll. I'm sure he felt the same surge of excitement that I did when I heard about it. The odds of this happening by chance, even to a professional astrologer, must be too tremendous to calculate. Even with all of the astrological data John has in his subconscious mind, he could hardly have come up with all these correct placements out of the thousands available in the ephemeris. It was important for him to be there to interpret the astrological information because to the rest of us, it was literally like trying to understand Greek. We may be familiar with the signs of the zodiac, but it took a professional to comprehend quickly what he was being shown. In addition, the writing was peculiar and for Brenda or myself, it would have added only more confusion. This was the logic behind showing this information to John.

John now felt he had enough information about the Anti-Christ's horoscope from Nostradamus that he could proceed with the birth chart and interpretation. He had gotten his wish.

The following is a brief summary of what John found:

This is a very unusual and intense chart. All of the traditional planets: The Sun, the Moon, Mercury, Venus, Mars, Jupiter, Saturn, and the South Node are aligned in the First House of Personality. The Sun, here, promises an excellent constitution and a desire to "be someone" in this life. The Moon, here, indicates a very inquisitive mind, scientifically and intellectually, with a keen awareness of technology. Mercury emphasizes these traits to a considerable degree. Venus represents emotions that are cool, calm, and detached. It's easier to be loving to all than just one. Mars, the planet of action, foretells a drive that functions on pure intellectual energy. A good grasp of mechanics also goes with this position. Jupiter points to a somewhat charming and humanitarian personality. The planet Saturn in the First House portends to obstacles in early life followed by a great discipline to achieve one's goals. It's interesting that his Aquarian stellium makes an adverse aspect to Neptune, the planet of compassion in the Tenth House. This foretells that he will rise to power in a swift but clandestine fashion. Once in power, he could abuse the privilege. Pluto in the sign of Virgo in the Eighth House stresses great psychic ability but also a strong manipulative tendency. Uranus in the sign of Leo in the Seventh House of partnerships represents open "enemies" as well as disruptions in personal relationships. There is great power in this horoscope, indicating a very advanced soul who has had the "test of power" in previous lives and is again being tested.

In an earlier session with Brenda, we dealt with the following quatrain. Nostradamus gave us specific instructions at that time. He said for us to relate this quatrain to the horoscopes, but we didn't have them at the time.

CENTURY V-24

Le regne & lois souz Venus eslevé,	The kingdom and law raised under Venus, Saturn will dominate
Saturne aura sus Jupiter empire:	Jupiter. Law and empire raised
La loi & regne par le Soleil levé,	by the Sun, will endure the worst
Par Saturnins endurera le pire.	through those of Saturn.

B: He says this quatrain refers to the organization run by the one he has referred to as "Ogmios." This organization will survive through the worst of the troubled times and serve as a basis for future governments

after the Anti-Christ has been brought down. He says to read the line
with the sun in it.

D: *"The law and empire raised by the sun."*

B: Yes. He says the glory and the positive nature of the sun will be
behind Ogmios and help him endure the worst.

D: *I'm trying to understand the significance of this line. "Will endure the
worst through those of Saturn."*

B: He says in order to obtain specific shades of meaning and to be able to
translate the depths of this quatrain, consult the horoscopes of Ogmios
and the Anti-Christ, paying close attention to the relative positions of
the various celestial bodies in them. Also, use the comparisons given
in this quatrain to get an idea of the development of this underground
organization.

D: *Compare the placement of three planets, Venus, Saturn and Jupiter?*

B: Dolores, he says for you not to try to interpret astrological information
because you will come to the wrong conclusions. Let the astrologer
work with his knowledge and his tools.

D: *I'm sure he can understand it a lot better than I can. It's Greek to me.*
(Laugh)

B: He says, to let the Greeks speak Greek and for you to worry about
communication. *(We laughed.)*

D: *We're giving John a lot of work to do on these quatrains.*

B: He says he assumed this would be the case, that John was to add to the
available information.

Now that John had the two horoscopes, he could follow Nostradamus'
instructions. After he had a chance to compare them, we met again and
he gave the following information:

J: What's really interesting is that "Saturn will dominate Jupiter" is in
both of their horoscopes. Saturn, the co-ruler of the sign of Aquarius,
shows up in the Anti-Christ's horoscope. He has Saturn in the first
house in Aquarius, along with Jupiter in Aquarius. Saturn dominates
Jupiter in this horoscope, because Saturn is in its co-ruling position.
It's interesting that in Ogmios' horoscope Saturn is also in a dominating position. It's in Libra, the sign of its exaltation. And it dominates
Ogmios' Jupiter because his Jupiter takes place in Taurus, which is
not really the best place for Jupiter. It's a comfortable position for
Jupiter, but it's not really in its ruling position. So it's true that for this
quatrain, Saturn is dominating Jupiter in both horoscopes.

D: *Nostradamus also wanted you to compare those planets mentioned in
the quatrain.*

J: Yes. Venus is in Aquarius in the Anti-Christ's horoscope and in
Scorpio in Ogmios'. The Venus aspects between these two are square
each other which means they have a sense of conflict of purpose.
Venus in Scorpio is much more emotional and sensitive than Venus in

the sign of Aquarius, which is cool and detached. The Anti-Christ will lack compassion and an understanding of other people, whereas Venus in the seventh house in Ogmios' chart shows that he's a much more loving person, even though he might not have personal relationships. He has become spiritually loving to all people. Anytime we have Venus in Scorpio, it goes through a transformation process. Let's see. "The kingdom and law raised under Venus. Saturn will dominate Jupiter. Law and empire raised by the sun will endure the worst through those of Saturn." Saturn is in its fall position in the sign of Aquarius and in the sign of its detriment in the sign of Libra in the Anti-Christ's horoscope. "The sun will endure the worst" indicates that these are not the best placements for the sun in traditional astrology. The sun is in fall in the sign of Aquarius means—I usually compare it to the time of the year—it's like the cool, snowy days of January and February. This is when the sun is making its return from the southern latitudes, and that's why it was considered the Fall. When the sun is in Libra we have equal days and nights again. Because the night gets stronger during the month of Libra, and Ogmios' sun is in the sign of Libra, this means the night is descending. In the Anti-Christ's horoscope the sun is in Aquarius, which is in Fall. This means the sun has moved away and is slowly returning again. These are the darkest times of the year for the sun energy.

D: *"The kingdom and law raised under Venus." Do you think this refers to the Anti-Christ's kingdom coming to power?*

J: Well, Venus in Aquarius shows he's going to come across as a very strong humanitarian as he helps the world. He might even use something similar to the World Peace Movement. He's going to use humanitarian impulses to his advantage.

D: *Let's see, he said, "Use the comparisons given in this quatrain to get an idea of the development of the underground organization."*

J: The Libra planets that show up in Ogmios' chart are in good aspect to the Anti-Christ's which shows they are compatible. So Ogmios might start out as a follower of the Anti-Christ, but when he sees the Anti-Christ's inhumanity, he will separate from him. In other words, Ogmios will believe that this man is trying to make humanity more prosperous, but he will be disillusioned when he sees him in his true light. His aspects show that in the beginning Ogmios doesn't want to see himself as a leader.

D: *Is he being led into something he's unsure of?*

J: Right. He has strong humanitarian principles with his north node in the sign of Aquarius. His spiritual destiny is represented by the north node, showing that he has grown as a soul in previous lifetimes, and now it's time for him to help mankind. It's time for him to come before the world. His underground organization is ruled by Scorpio in the seventh house, so he will have a network of partners, friends, and key contacts who will be hidden. Pluto in the fourth house shows that his base of operations will be close to where he was born.

D: *I'm not sure but I think he was born somewhere in France.*

J: Ogmios will make a good adversary because he will understand the Anti-Christ. He probably will have worked for him in the beginning.

In Chapter 6, "The Deeds of the Monster," we were instructed to compare a date in the quatrain to the Anti-Christ's horoscope to obtain a clearer picture of events around 1997 when he would begin using nuclear weapons. We could not follow Nostradamus' instructions at that time because we did not have the horoscope. When we were able to do this we discovered something completely unexpected hidden within its obscure wording.

CENTURY VI-35

Pres de Rion & proche à la blanche laine,	Near the Bear and close to the white wool, Aries, Taurus, Cancer,
Aries, Taurus, Cancer, Leo, la Vierge,	Leo, Virgo, Mars, Jupiter, the Sun will burn the great plain, woods and
Mars, Jupiter, le sol ardra grand plaine,	cities; letters hidden in the candle.
Bois & citez, lettres cachez au cierge.	

John worked with Nostradamus on the astrological signs, and came to the conclusion that the Anti-Christ would first come to power in 1992 in a very subtle way by using conventional warfare in minor wars. He would use the threat of nuclear confrontation but would not have the weapons. On January 23, 1998 he would use nuclear weapons for the first time. Nostradamus then gave us specific instructions.

B: He says you must get the horoscope of the Anti-Christ and look up these signs and the way they relate to each other and their various aspects. Compare it to the planets' positions and their influences on the Anti-Christ's horoscope to get a picture of the conflict. He says this will give you a feeling for how some of the time of troubles will be, particularly around 1997.

Now that we had the all-important missing piece we could follow his instructions and make the comparisons. A chart was drawn for the date and the following are the conclusions:

On January 23, 1998 transiting Mars and Jupiter will be exactly conjunct at 27 degrees Aquarius, and will be conjuncting the Anti-Christ's Aquarian stellium (three or more planets in the same sign). There are many significant aspects found by comparing this date with his chart. The Mars/Jupiter conjunction is in opposition to his natal north node and his Uranus. Uranus is the planet of sudden destructive events, and the north node represents the person's accomplishments in life. Also on that date

Pluto is square his natal Pluto. Pluto is the planet of death of the old, so that the new may be born. The Anti-Christ's Pluto is in the eighth house, which is known as the "house of death," and is ruled by Pluto. This fits in with the beginning of the use of major nuclear weapons. The Anti-Christ's Mars, Moon, and Saturn are all conjunct the Sun in the chart of that date (January 23, 1998). Any time the Sun in a chart is involved with major events in another chart (particularly when Saturn and Mars are together), this is very significant because the Sun is the life force. There are also other significant aspects between the charts.

There was a stumbling block when the signs in the quatrain were compared to the Anti-Christ's horoscope. There were no planets in Aries, Taurus, or Cancer. Pluto was in Virgo, and the north node and Uranus were in Leo, but none of the other signs appeared to have a connection. The next step was to check out the rulers of these signs. That was when the intriguing discovery was made. The rulers are Aries/Mars, Taurus/Venus, Cancer/Moon, Leo/Sun, Virgo/Mercury. When the quatrain was examined in this manner it became obvious that in his own sly way Nostradamus had hidden the major part of the stellium of the Anti-Christ's horoscope within this quatrain. It also was showing his relationship to an important event pattern. The clues were there for anyone to find, but only someone educated in astrology would know what to look for. We felt the exhilaration that you feel when you have successfully solved a complicated puzzle. Of course, we would never have made the connection without Nostradamus' instructions. When he said to get the Anti-Christ's horoscope, he was really telling us that the clues were in the quatrain. He expected astrologers to see the connections, which no one had done until now. We had an advantage over other investigators because John had been shown the horoscope by Nostradamus, and we now had his birthdate. I should have known that Nostradamus would not have completely hidden the identity of such an important personage. He felt the future of our world rested upon this man's actions, he would have to plant clues. But his quatrains are composed of so many layers that the clues are too cleverly disguised. I consider it a remarkable discovery to find the planets listed that would identify this "world destroyer." I can only marvel at the complex genius of our friend who lived 400 years ago.

The astrologer wanted to emphasize that these two dates (1992 and 1998) are *probability* dates. The possibilities are very high for the advance of the Anti-Christ's takeover through the use of nuclear power at that time. But it doesn't *have* to happen if enough will is used to channel the energy in more positive directions. Nostradamus may have been showing us possibilities, probabilities, because he knew that history repeats itself.

I realize these chapters dealing with astrology may be difficult reading, but I think they are important to people who understand astrological terms. They also give us more insight into the personalities of the main characters shaping our future.

Chapter 13

The Force of the Evil Priest

WHEN I CONDUCT MY REGRESSION WORK I always mentally place white light around the subject to protect them against any negative influence while they are in trance or on these astral journeys. Although I was being very careful for my subjects, my guides have chastised me because I was neglecting to protect myself. I have always put the welfare of my subjects first, and it had not occurred to me to worry about myself. My guides then taught me a procedure for effective protection and I have used it ever since.

While working with John I neglected to include myself within the protective aura. I discovered, much to my dismay, that my guides were justified in being concerned for my safety. During this strange session I found there are indeed forces out there of which we are not aware; forces beyond our comprehension to understand or even anticipate.

I again used the keyword and directed John to go to the spirit state where he easily found the Tapestry Room and focused in on the golden thread of Nostradamus. In a matter of seconds we were again transported to the great man's study.

J: I see Nostradamus. He's been at his desk writing and copying things. He's smiling at me. And he says, "Oh, it's you again! One of my spirit friends. I knew you people would be showing up soon." He's in a very delightful mood today. He just told me, "A debt that has been long awaited has been paid." He feels good about things and says, "Now I can travel." I asked him, "Are you going on a trip?" He says he has to go to Avignon.

D: *Will we still be able to contact him whenever we need to?*

J: Yes, he says he'll still be available. But at this time he's thinking of going to Avignon.

D: *Would we be prying to ask why?*

J: I asked him, "Why are you going to Avignon?" And he said, "Well, it's really none of your business." (*Laugh*)

D: (Laugh) *Just tell him we're curious.*

J: He says, "Well, I understand. People are curious about everything I do, and you are curious about my personal life."

D: *It's our nature to ask a lot of questions.*

J: (*Abruptly*) He just showed me a closet.

D: *A closet?*

J: And it's a ... (*surprised*) *toilet.* (*Loud laugh.*) It's as if he wants us to know, "Hey, I'm a *person.* I have to excrete, too."

D: *(*Laughter from the group.*) What does it look like?*

J: He says this is a very special room he has made like a closet. It has a wooden seat with a hole in it. There's a bucket of ashes which he pours in the toilet. There's also a water bucket where he washes.

D: *Oh? Was it common in his day to have this?*

J: He says, "*NO.* I've had this especially put into my house. My servants and my wife use outdoors." They use a privy that he has outside. But he says, "This is for my own personal use. Sometimes I do my best thinking in here." (*Laughter from the group.*)

D: *Oh boy! That does make him human.*

J: He just wants to say that, yes, he's human. He's as real as you are. He's had a glass of wine, so he's in a real frisky, frolicking mood.

D: *Well, tell him I would never have asked him such a personal question if he hadn't shown it to us. (*Laugh*)*

J: (*Laugh*) Yeah. He's just in a delightful mood.

D: *Then does he mind speaking with us for a little while?*

J: He says, "I'll be happy to speak with you. Would you be interested in looking into the life of the young Anti-Christ again?"

D: *All right, we might see that.*

J: He's motioning for me to look into the mirror. It's clearing and an image is forming in it.

There was a pause, then a sharp intake of breath. John's jovial mood suddenly changed.

J: It's very spooky.

D: *What do you mean?*

J: (*His voice was very quiet.*) Because the Imam knows that we are in the room with him.

D: *He does?*

J: Yes, and he does *not* like it.

D: *He can't do anything about it, can he?*

Later, I wished I hadn't said that because I found out very quickly that there was indeed something he could do about it.

J: Now he's generating a whole force field of negativity and evil, and he's trying to block us.

At that moment the strangest thing happened. I literally felt something; an energy, a field or whatever it was. It hit me so hard I almost fell off my chair. For a moment the room blurred and went black. I felt a definite impact from something invisible. On the tape recording you could hear the chair I was sitting in creak, as though from a sudden movement. I couldn't have imagined it. The others in the room were also aware that something had happened when I lunged backward against the chair, but they were as unaware as I was of what was going on. I gasped, and my vision cleared. My whole body tingled and I felt a sensation in my third eye chakra area that lasted for several seconds. It did not seem to affect John since he continued to talk, but I was dizzy and I had difficulty concentrating on the conversation. The others in the room were seated further away and it did not seem to affect them. One of the observers said later that he saw what appeared to be a black cloud suddenly obscure the sleeping figure on the couch and begin to spread into the room. Immediately, he mentally projected a white light force field to counteract whatever was happening.

John continued, apparently unaware that anything had occurred on our end of the connection.

J: He's instructing the young man in mind techniques. He says, "We're being influenced right now by other forces that we need to drive out. Think *hate*, think *hate*, think *hate* ..."

This was repeated several times as a chant with tremendous force behind it. Then, it apparently began to affect John.

J: We have to leave. We cannot go on with this.
D: *I know you have to leave. I'm feeling it and I don't like it. It's all right. We don't have to be there. Let's leave.*
J: Yes. The mirror is black now. Nostradamus' mood has changed. He says, "You don't understand the importance of how evil this man can be. He will be *extremely* evil. You just don't realize what he's able to do, and he *will* do it."

Now that we were removed from the scene, my head was returning to normal and I was able to think clearly again. I had to admit it had shaken me.

D: *How did he know we were there?*
J: Nostradamus is saying that the Imam is one of the most talented psychics that has ever existed. He's evil incarnated. He's descended from evil that has been around the Earth for centuries. He's one of the leaders of spirits who rebel against their destiny, their evolvement or spiritual growth. He says western men have called this the Devil. He has come to Earth and incarnated through the Imam—he *is* the Imam—and knows what he has to do. It is indescribable how evil this man is. Nostradamus is saying, "Oh, John, you don't understand. It's horrible. You don't know what I have seen."
D: *I think if what I just felt was a bit of it, then I imagine we can begin to understand it.*

J: Nostradamus says it's important to deal with this problem beforehand so we can lessen it. He says it's just like astrology—forewarned is forearmed.

D: *Well, apparently the Imam sensed us when we came into the room.*

J: Yes, that's what Nostradamus is saying. This evil mentalist sensed our presence and knows we are spying on him.

D: *Then it's better if we don't look at him at this time.*

J: No. It's gone. I mean, we're out of that. He says they are going to try to prevent us from looking at them and seeing what they're doing.

D: *Do they know we're doing it now?*

J: Yes, he says they are aware of us.

D: *They weren't aware of us before, were they?*

J: This mentalist was aware of something, but now he's seen us.

D: *(Surprised) He has seen us?*

J: He's seen *me* ... in spirit form.

D: *In spirit form. Well, maybe that won't be so bad then, because he might not be able to recognize you.*

J: Nostradamus says we have to stop him because he's really evil. He's like a vampire that could suck your soul from your body. He lives on generated energy. He lives on other souls.

D: *Wasn't our protection powerful enough?*

J: Yes, our protection is very powerful. But what Nostradamus is telling me about this entity is that his energy will later go into the Anti-Christ.

D: *Do you think his seeing us will cause any problems?*

J: *(Quietly and seriously)* Well, Nostradamus says, "Be careful."

D: *After all, we are half a world away. (I laughed nervously.)*

J: Yes. He says, "Don't worry about it; you'll be protected. But ... be careful in your dreams. Protect your dreams. Protect yourself in the astral state before you sleep, John, because he might come then."

D: *(This was all very unsettling.) All right. Does he see any harm in what we're doing if we have adequate protection?*

J: Nostradamus is just shaking his head and saying, "Be careful. That's all."

D: *Well, I think it's better that we don't see the Anti-Christ again. We don't have to look in on their lives. It should be sufficient that you've seen them and know what they look like. That's all we need. From now on we will just talk with Nostradamus. Will that be all right?*

J: *(Seriously)* Hmmm, his mood has changed a bit. He was so happy and jovial; but now he seems a little depressed.

D: *Maybe he didn't expect that to happen. Maybe it took him by surprise, too.*

J: Yes, it's like ... *(He frowned.)* He's very morose.

D: *Would Nostradamus have the ability to protect you?*

J: *(Seriously)* No, he says it's a whole different situation. You don't realize that this is like a raging inferno. This man's spirit will consume anything that it can. Nostradamus says, "Don't worry, I won't show him to you again."

Nostradamus also seemed to be upset about what had happened. I believe he didn't really expect the Imam to sense our presence. He quite innocently showed us what they were doing at the time, just as he had done twice before. I don't think he would have deliberately put us into any kind of danger, and he was probably as surprised as we were when the force came from the mirror. He had been in a very delightful mood before this happened, and we were anticipating trying to interpret some of the quatrains through John. But this incident caused such a change in his mood that Nostradamus suggested we leave and he abruptly ended the session.

After John was brought back to consciousness, he discussed what he saw when the negative force came through as he was viewing the Anti-Christ.

D: *You didn't tell us what you were seeing before that force knocked us out of the scene.*

J: Well, they were in this room. The shades were drawn and it was dark. It seemed as if they were practicing mental mastery because it was like they were in trance. The Imam and the man that is to be the Anti-Christ were practicing mind techniques.

D: *They were both in trance?*

J: It was as if they were in trance, yes. And that's how he was able to see me.

D: *Maybe they had to be in more of a psychic state to know we were peeking in on them. Before, when we saw them in the mansion, he suspected we were there and he had a feeling that someone was watching him. This time you said he knew we were there, and he put up the force field to throw us back.*

J: Well, he threw me back. I mean, that mirror just went "whaap."

D: *That's what it felt like to me.* (Nervous laugh.) *It was definitely a physical feeling, and one I wouldn't want to repeat.*

J: I felt protected, but this person who is the Imam is very powerful. It was like the spirit of the Devil. I mean, I don't believe in the Devil, but it was like the Devil.

I tried to reassure him and also myself.

D: *Well, he's on the other side of the world, in Egypt.*

J: Apparently that doesn't make any difference.

D: *Common sense tells us that they're over there and we're here. But how could we feel something from that far?*

J: None of it really makes sense. Nostradamus was showing him to me from the 1500s as he looked forward to our present time, yet the Imam was aware of me and could affect you physically from half way around the world. It is all very complicated.

D: *I really don't think you could be in danger. The Imam may just have seen you as some type of glowing spirit form and thought you were some kind of ghost.* (Laugh) *I don't see how he could assume you were a human person spying on him.*

This is what I desperately wanted to believe.

J: (*Seriously*) I don't know. I don't have any idea how I appeared to him.

John didn't seem to be worried about the situation. Although this whole experience was very unsettling, I felt no danger because I thought John was the only one the Imam had been aware of. I knew that I would never again forget to include myself within the circle of protection, or anyone else in the room who was interested. I believe, after being put into a predicament like this, the average person would have decided not to pursue this project any further and would have backed out of any further sessions. But John's curiosity apparently was as strong as my own. He remembered that Nostradamus had warned him to protect himself especially at night before he went to sleep. He said this was his normal habit, as he always asked for the protection of God during the night. He wasn't worried and felt he could mentally handle this unusual situation. I couldn't possibly conceive of any way a priest in faraway Egypt could harm us half a world away. But there was always that eerie and nagging impression that Nostradamus knew more about this sinister force than we did. John was soon to discover that there are many strange things in this universe that our mortal minds cannot comprehend.

John had his first strange experience a few days after our unexpected encounter with the Imam's energy force field. It occurred when he was trying to go to sleep. I recorded his description of the event.

J: I was drifting off to sleep, but I was still half awake. I felt that I was in a room covered by a glass dome, and that I was looking up at a man above me who was trying to get into the room. This man couldn't see me. I could see him, but he couldn't see me. He was looking for a way to get into the room, but he couldn't come in. It was not my room *here,* but it seemed to be in the other world. He was the same man that I've seen before, the Imam. He has Arab-looking features and a hawk nose. He was determined to get into this room, but he couldn't.

John said he could see the man feeling along the glass with his hands and peering into it, looking for a way to get in.

D: *Was it a glass wall of some kind?*

J: Yes, it was like glass. He couldn't see in though, so it must have been dark. I believe that the wall was the protective energy surrounding me. I had the feeling he was trying to find me and see what I looked like. I had no sense of fear or anything like that because I felt I was protected. I feel this evil entity knows something is going on, but he can't find out because we've got protection. I woke up right after this experience and I said, "I have to remember this so I can tell Dolores." It didn't frighten me, but it was unusual. I don't have dreams like that.

$\mathcal{D}$URING THE NEXT WEEK I didn't work with John because he had friends visiting him. On one of those nights he forgot to put his customary protection around himself before going to sleep, mostly because of the disruption of his routine. During the night he awoke suddenly as a large black indistinct form lunged out of the closet toward his bed. The only thing he could distinguish was a large Arabian knife. It wasn't quite big enough for a sword, but it was large for a knife. It was a scimitar, the curved knife normally associated with that part of the world. The dark figure lunged toward him with the knife poised ready to strike him. John frantically rolled on his side just as the knife plunged into the bed next to him. He immediately invoked protection and the figure with the knife evaporated. He knew it was no dream, but he could find no explanation for it. Later he wondered if it might have some connection to the evil Imam, and maybe the priest was still trying to locate him. I didn't know what to think. Even if it were the Imam, why use a knife against John? Such a thing couldn't physically harm him if it was a spiritual manifestation—or could it? Maybe the purpose was not to harm him but to frighten him. Whatever the reason, I don't think John will forget to protect himself again, especially at night when we are in our most vulnerable state.

Chapter 14

666, The Secret of the Number of the Beast

WE ONCE AGAIN JOURNEYED through the tapestry to locate Nostradamus.

J: (*Sadly*) He looks unhappy today.
D: *Do you know why?*
J: (*With much compassion.*) He's been crying.
D: *Does he know you're there?*
J: (*Pause*) Not at this moment. I'm letting him feel his grief.
D: *Do you know what's the matter?*
J: (*Sadly*) Someone close to him has died. He looks a lot older.
D: *You know we don't like to intrude, but we would like to speak with him. What do you think?*
J: (*Pause*) He's felt my presence in the room and looked up from his grief. (*Pause*) I've given my complete love and compassion to him, and I am filling the room with love to let him know that he is loved and cared for.
D: *Does this help?*

I really felt that we were intruding and that we should leave, but maybe we could help Nostradamus in some small way.

J: Yes, it's helping him. He's ... he's drying his eyes for a bit.
D: *Does he want to tell you what has happened?*
J: He says a favorite god-nephew of his has just passed away and while he tried to help him medically, he couldn't really do anything. He tried everything possible to save this little boy, and he feels a sense of futility. He says his wife has a sister and their families are very close. He also held the baby at baptism; this is why he called him a god-nephew. The family has just left and they are preparing for the burial of the body.
D: *What was wrong with the child?*

J: He doesn't have the word "genetic" like we do, but he says there was something between the parents. (*Nostradamus apparently was having difficulty communicating what he meant.*) Their child inherited something and it was very difficult for him to figure out the cure. It was similar to a bronchial respiratory problem and the child had increasing difficulty breathing. He says it was as if the child didn't have completely developed lungs. It was three or four years old when it passed on. He was very amazed that it lived that long. But at least he knew his name and his parents' name. "He was like a little angel," Nostradamus is saying. It was very hard for him because he was such a delight. He says, "My children are now grown and living their lives. My wife and I love to look at the little ones; they are so refreshing and curious about life. He was a bit of sparkle to me."

D: *Well, with that type of illness there was nothing he could have done about it, and so he really can't blame himself.*

J: No, he knew that. He doesn't blame himself. It's just that ... he does grieve.

D: *Yes, but we know Nostradamus is only human. There are limitations to what he can do.*

J: This is what he feels by his sense of futility.

D: *What do you think? Is he willing to work with us for a little while to get his mind off of it? Or does he feel we're intruding?*

J: (*Pause*) He seems to be collecting himself a bit. (*Pause*) He's got a bowl of water now, and he's washing his face and his hands. Now he's drying them with a towel and this has awakened him a bit. And he says, (*resolutely*) "I will be here to assist you." He's drying his face and his hands now. He takes the bowl of water and opens the window and dumps it outside. Then he puts the bowl back onto the tripod. And he's sitting down at the table and taking the black obsidian mirror out of a velvet bag.

I could only think, "What wonderful dedication!" To be willing to work even though he was overcome with grief emphasized that he must truly feel an obligation to this project.

D: *He keeps the mirror covered?*

J: Yes, he keeps it covered. And he says, "We'll talk about visions of the future today, John. I will show you how I see the future." He sits in meditative repose and it looks like he does some breathing exercises, then he concentrates and imagines a candleflame in his mind. All of a sudden the mirror explodes with light, and this is how he sees the future.

D: *Can you see anything in the mirror?*

J: It's very cloudy. With all the clouds, it looks like an approaching thunderhead. He's still in meditative thought.

D: *I want to impress upon him that we appreciate his doing this, even though he's not in the best frame of mind. This shows his dedication to the project.*

J: He says, "Well, let's get on with talking a bit."

D: *Would he care if I read some quatrains and asked him for the translations?*

J: He says he will talk about the mirror. Do you have questions about what you would like to see in the future? He will show me the answers in the mirror. At another time we can go over quatrains because now it's more important to see *through* the mirror.

D: *With the other vehicle I read quatrains and he told me what they meant.*

J: He knows that, and he understands. But he doesn't want to do that now because he's feeling such grief. It's easier to work with the mirror. He says you'll have lots of questions for the mirror.

D: *All right. I respect his mental state, and I wouldn't want to do anything to upset him.*

J: He says this is a wonderful way of meditating on human life and its fulfillment. I have a feeling that Nostradamus doesn't believe in reincarnation. As a result, he felt bad about the child's death. It's his own personal belief. There seems to be a wall around the possibility of us talking about that area with him, so I better not even speak about it. But he's happy to talk with the mirror. He says, "I could show you things I see in my meditations."

I looked at the others in the room. This was so unexpected, it was difficult to think of anything to ask. I had planned on working with the quatrains. The others only shook their heads. I shrugged and continued.

D: *Okay. Can he see the upcoming elections of the late 1980s in the United States?*

J: Well, ... I'm picking up that election. (*Pause*)

D: *Tell me what you see.*

J: He's showing me a picture of a victory speech at an election. (*Pause*) And he's saying that this man won't live his term of office. He will die in office.

D: *Can you see what he looks like?*

J: He has dark hair with some gray, and he appears to be in his late 50s. I don't think it's George Bush. I think it's someone else. He can't give me a name, but he says that's not important. Elections and people, they're constantly changing. He says, "Don't trivialize what information I have in my mirror."

At this time in April of 1987 no one had any idea who would be running for President. Later, so many candidates entered the race that it could have gone in any direction. There were no clear-cut favorites. After the 1988 primaries, Michael Dukakis had been nominated. John didn't recognize the man Nostradamus showed him except to acknowledge that he didn't think it was George Bush. This would make sense since few people would have recognized Dukakis before the primaries. After the election, George Bush was elected President. I don't know if this counts as an error on Nostradamus' part or not. He could have been showing John one of the candidates giving a speech, and it didn't necessarily have to be the winner. In the final count with this type of work it comes down to individual interpretation of what is being shown, or how one relates to concepts being presented. Since we are all human we are not infallible. We were put into the same position in Chapter 21 when Nostradamus asked us who would be the next king of France.

J: He's showing me more pictures.

D: *Okay. Maybe he can show us something and then we can come up with questions.*

J: Yes, he's showing me how the Anti-Christ comes to power.

We learned our lesson when we were zapped by the force of the evil priest. And while we were no longer interested in looking into the present life of the developing Anti-Christ, it could be intriguing to look further into his future.

J: He's saying that the Anti-Christ will have great communication systems at his disposal because I see him talking into computers, and it's his voice that's activating the computer. There are big computer banks all over the place. (*Pause*) He's saying there's a coalition of other men that will be of service to him, and that he will mesmerize them. He means religious leaders ... like the Ayatollah Khomeni. He tries to unite people like Jerry Falwell and the religious right in the United States with the spirit of ecumenism and projects like helping the poor countries of the world. But he will really be duping them.

D: *Is this how he's going to begin?*

J: Yes. But Nostradamus says, "Don't worry."

D: *It seems we will have a lot to worry about if this war occurs.*

J: He says that's still a bit in the future. In the beginning, the Anti-Christ will be looked up to as a world savior. He will have wondrous inventions that he will market and use to help people. In other words, he comes across as a world savior to help humanity.

D: *Are these inventions that his country will produce?*

J: No, he himself will invent them.

D: *What type of inventions?*

J: He will make advances in computers, hydroponic gardening, and in farming intensively to help alleviate hunger in the starving nations. He will appear with these helpful inventions, and people will look up to him because he will make a lot of money from them. He will be quite innovative, and this is how he will rise to power.

D: *At that time will he proclaim to be a savior for the world, like a religious savior?*

J: No, he won't say he's a savior for the world, but he will try to influence people with rational thought. He will tell them that *they* are thinking, when he is actively manipulating.

D: *Then he won't appear to be a religious leader?*

J: He'll appear to be a *spiritual* leader, but not in the conventional religious sense.

D: *Will these other religious leaders unite behind him because they think he's on the right track? I mean, how is a Moslem going to influence fundamental Christian leaders?*

J: Money will answer a lot of people's problems, and this is one way he'll gain their respect. He will try to unite the world by helping the poorer nations. It doesn't matter what their religions are. He will be seen as a strong humanitarian who is trying to help the afflicted, the poor, and the sick. He will really help a lot, but he has his other plans. This is just a part of his manipulation plot.

D: *What will he finally do to show his true nature?*

J: Up until this point he is functioning from his true humanitarian self, but after the death of the Imam the mantle of evil descends upon him. This is when he *seemingly* will scheme to bring the world under his control.

D: *What do you mean by "seemingly"?*

J: He will be asking the richer nations of the Earth for money supposedly to give to the poorer nations, but he'll be funneling some of that money into his own private resources. He will also start huge communication networks. And he *will* be successful at helping other countries. In that way he will win the total respect of all religious leaders as well as all governments.

D: *And they will think that because of all the good things he is doing that everything is all right. Up until this time even he will believe he's doing the right thing?*

J: He has a very strong humanitarian streak which will turn against itself after the death of the Imam. Then he will be jaded and corrupt.

Someone in the room wondered: if we're being given all this information on the Anti-Christ so we'll be aware of the situation, were there any steps we might take to prevent this, or if we had any choice in the matter of stopping him?

J: He says this is his own fate that has been foretold for centuries. To become the Anti-Christ is his destiny in his life. *But* others will know who he is. They will not fall into the trap of his false glamor. When all the world acclaims him as a humanitarian or as a peace-server within the world, there will be a vocal minority that will say, "Hey, this is him. This *is* the Anti-Christ." They will recognize him and finally mushroom into an underground network that will help advance the cause of truth, rather than the man of deception and lies. Thus, information of this nature will be of service, because it will help in the resistance.

D: *Do you think he will be taking over countries before they realize what he is doing?*

J: No. He will try to reunite the world by being of help to it. He first unites the world by being a true humanitarian. This is very difficult because at the time he comes to power, we will have gone through an economic and financial loss, and famine. He will then try to unite all the nations of the world to help *all* people. He uses a banner of humanitarianism. We *must* remember that! Please remember that! That is what this man will use.

D: *It will be very hard to convince anyone because they will say he is only doing good things. People aren't going to believe that he is evil, and the resistance movement won't be very popular.*

J: That's right. When we see all the signs of this leader coming to power, many people will almost bow down and worship him because he has helped the world so much. He will be looked up to and admired and he will win all types of prizes and acclaim. (John said later he even saw him winning the Nobel Peace Prize.) Everyone will think he is wondrous because he's helped bring a sense of prosperity to all the countries that have been suffering economic loss. But you see, by helping all these other countries and through his communication networks he will have access to the files of all people: birth data, financial information, and things of this nature. So it will be doubly hard to oppose him when he controls the world banking industry and the world economic credit. Eventually, he will try to starve the underground and crush the resistance. But he will do this clandestinely, not overtly.

D: *Someone in the room would like to know the significance of the 666 in Revelation. Does it have something to do with this or not?*

J: He's showing me columns and columns of numbers and more numbers. It looks like information that is usually stored in computers. And this number, 666, might be the Anti-Christ's personal code number that he enters into the different world systems because he establishes a world system of communications and a computer network.

D: *In Revelation it mentions it as the number of the beast. Is the Anti-Christ the beast that is referred to? Nostradamus said before that they could foresee him even as far back as Biblical times.*

J: He will be a beast in sheep's clothing. He will seem to be a sheep on the surface, but will actually be a horrendous beast within.

D: *Is this the meaning of some of the predictions in Revelation in the Bible?*

J: I'm communicating that to Nostradamus and he says, "I study the Vulgate Bible which was written in Latin. Because the translations of many Bibles are different, to read about the Revelations of Saint John is like reading an allegory."

D: *Then it is probably different from the Bible we have today. He said before that the Anti-Christ would make a lot of advances through the use of his golden tongue. He said that would be one way he will take over.*

J: Well, doesn't it make sense? He would help so many nations that have suffered economic loss and famine. By giving them grain and food and helping them to rebuild, he will be looked up to as a world server and a world savior.

D: *When he changes to become this evil being, is that when he starts taking over countries?*

J: He will have already set up a computer network that will leave countries vulnerable. He will be able to destroy their economic base by having access to information. Nostradamus is showing me a picture of a globe with a lot of threads surrounding it. He says, "He will have the master key to it all and will bring nations down to the ground by cutting off their communication with the rest of the world."

A member of the group asked if the Anti-Christ wanted to be like Napoleon and control everything.

J: He does not want to be Napoleon. Napoleon only wanted the vision of Europe united under him. The Anti-Christ wants the whole globe.

D: *Well, Hitler also wanted to take over the world.*

J: Yes, Hitler wanted to take over the world, but he did not succeed. None of these men will truly succeed, but haven't they all caused havoc?

Dn: *Will he be using psychic warfare and not just computers and technology? Will the resistance or vocal minority have problems because he will be able to psychically tune in to what they're doing against him?*

J: This is one area where he will have great powers. He will have the power to use his energies on a high level, to the point where he will even invent a computer that will function from a psychic brain level. A person will be able to turn it on by mentally commanding it, rather than even speaking to it. So he will be looked upon as a genius, for he will be very creative, inventive, and helpful.

D: *I imagine our country will have computers also. Will he be able to control all of them?*

J: He says all computers are networked at this *present* time throughout the world. Our communication systems, our satellite systems, and things of this type are all networked right now. Gaining the key to that system will give him a sense of power that he will use to unite the world systems in an attempt to help alleviate the economic chaos that is taking place. Networked communication systems will help him do it quickly and easily. Economic chaos will have taken place in the world and famine will have grown. So not only countries in the Third World will be suffering, but countries of the *developed* world will also be very hungry. By instituting plans and changes he will gain power through the power of communications.

D: *We already translated several of his quatrains that dealt with atomic explosions and wars, and I thought he meant this happened as the Anti-Christ took over these countries.*

J: No, not initially. He says it is through the communication network that he has gained power. He is like a child playing cat's cradle by pulling all the right strings.

D: *We also translated quatrains that said he would assassinate the leaders of the world.*

J: In a way he is assassinating them just by having them under his control.

D: *Well, won't the countries try to rebel later?*

J: They'll experience a lot of prosperity, you see, by using his system. Financial considerations will be given to them if they become part of his system and if they do not "play ball," they will be cut out and suffer as a result. Remember, he *is* a world server and a humanitarian. He will seem to be of light, but he will not be.

Dn: *What will he finally do to make people suffer?*

J: The resistance movement will gain in popularity, and when the mantle of complete evil takes over he will start exterminating the people he feels are useless to his system. This is when the chaos and the rebellion begin.

D: *Exterminating people?*

J: This is where he will cause difficulties. He will portray the future as being prosperous and bright. And then as the evil descends and he changes, he will try to wipe out people who have no economic benefit for his world scheme.

D: *Do you mean countries or what?*

J: He will wipe out groups of people. Just as Hitler exterminated the Jews, he'll exterminate people that he feels are not worthy to live on this planet: the sick, the poor, the enfeebled, and people who have no value in his eyes. Using his network, he will instigate mass euthanasia. There will be no escape because everything will be on file. For example, if one's son was retarded, or if one's mother was too old and unproductive, or if one's sister was mentally or emotionally unbalanced, they would all be slated for extermination.

This sounds a great deal like the plan Hitler had to control the world and produce the master race. Nostradamus said the Anti-Christ will study Hitler in great detail so he will be able to use him as a model, learning from his mistakes in order to succeed where Hitler had failed.

D: *By the time this happens he has the world under his spell.*

J: Yes. He says it's because the communication network will be so strong.

Dn: *Once he receives the mantle, how long will it be before he is overthrown? How long do we have to live with all this extermination and control?*

J: For a while. Nostradamus shakes his head and says, "I cannot say."

D: *Does he mean that by that time people can't fight back?*

J: Everything is crippled because he controls the communications network. As a result, he knows what is going on everywhere. We've become a computerized society at that point and everyone will have a certain number that will be stored in this main computer. This number will be indelibly tattooed on your hand, forearm or forehead, depending on what level of his system you belong to. The people in the upper echelon of his system will have this engraved on their forehead so they can walk in any place. The number will be automatically read, to bid them to enter. For most of us it will be indelibly engraved on our forearm or our hand. This will be done with a laser and will be painless. It will not look like a birthmark or a defect but will be invisible unless scanned by optical equipment. This way we will be able to go shopping, buy food, and enter certain places that are necessary to our work or career.

A member of the group wanted to know if the resistance movement would have any outside influences helping them combat this man, such as guardians from other planets or the higher planes.

J: There will be guardians from other sources. Keepers from all over the universe will be watching this drama. There is a great spiritual lesson to be learned as a spirit goes through complete annihilation. A cosmic law will be broken here, and it represents the extension of that energy. This is a very important lesson. So, many other beings from all over the universe will be gathered here to watch this spectacle.

I thought this sounded familiar. Then I remembered that in my book, *Keepers of the Garden,* my subject, Phil, said the same thing. That beings from throughout the universe were gathered to watch the events that were unfolding on Earth at this time. That these happenings had far more importance than anyone could imagine, and their effects would be cosmic in nature. At the time I was working with Phil on that book, I could not have imagined the gigantic scale these events would take.

D: *What is the cosmic law that will be broken? Can he clarify that?*
J: It's the cosmic law that represents being in harmony with the universe. The Anti-Christ will try to use the universe to make his *own* harmony; to become omnipotent in his own harmony. This is the cosmic law he will break. It's not very often that a soul is destroyed.
D: *Oh? I didn't think it was possible to destroy a soul. Does he mean that literally?*
J: It is not possible unless ... (*Pause*) This is more information than he wants to share.
D: *All right. I thought he might have meant it figuratively and not literally.*
J: No. He says this information is from higher levels that he has contacted, and that he can't reveal it at this time. This is not in our hands. It's up to a higher council or high spiritual beings who are observing this. Even though this power is being played out in the physical world, it is a very important spiritual lesson to be learned by more advanced souls or spirits, rather than the people of Earth.

A phrase kept running through my mind and it never seemed more appropriate than now. "What shall it profit a man if he gains the whole world and loses his immortal soul."

D: *Is there anything we can do as a resistance movement? Or should this drama actually play itself out?*

J: The drama will play itself out. The resistance movement will be aware of what is taking place, but people aren't going to listen to the underground. They will be renegades who are unable to fit into the society that is made by the courts or communication networks. They have to live as outlaws. They will be made up of people of many different financial and spiritual belief systems, but they will all be united to overthrow. *But* they will *not* be able to overthrow the Anti-Christ's network of communications, because if they do, their country will suffer immensely. As a result, these people will have to live like outcasts.

D: *Is this where the figure we know as Ogmios comes in?*

J: Ogmios will have a sense of destiny and will gather people around him from all over the world. They will collectively use their intuitive powers to make battle. I see them retaliating in psychic warfare. It will be more like giving the giant a headache.

D: *Instead of actual warfare?*

J: No, it will be played out. This is a drama that is being enacted not only for Earth people, but to teach more evolved beings. It is a part of their knowledge and soul growth. So we can't understand the many different layers that this story will have. (*Abruptly*) Nostradamus says he's tired now. He's still grieving. He says showing pictures in his magic mirror has been a better way of explaining his centuries. Don't fret, he says he will help you, Dolores, with the quatrains in the near future, but he wanted to give *this* vehicle an idea of how the Anti-Christ manipulates to become powerful. He says it has not really been explained in detail how the Anti-Christ conveys the sense of power he has in this life, but he was showing this vehicle how he would achieve this power.

D: *Yes, it seems so impossible that one man could attain that kind of power.*

J: He will have subordinates that also will be very powerful, but he will be the ring leader. He says it is similar to the concerts we have to help farmers and the famine stricken. People are networked together in different parts of the globe for a common goal. This is where he got the idea of how to connect them and unite the world.

D: *Is he using all of this in the plan he's developing?*

J: Yes. Nostradamus says he would like to be at peace now. He would like me to leave. He says, "It's wonderful to be of service to you and I will help you with more quatrains in the future, but for now I am in a bit of grief."

D: *It shows his dedication to the project to be able to put his grief aside for a little while. I appreciate it.*

J: He would like me to leave. I am in the mirror but I am moving to the tapestry. I'm in the Tapestry Room now, and it's just beautiful.

John was raised as a Catholic, but he is not as familiar with the Scriptures as I am. Thus, he did not know the implications in this session of the fulfillment of the Biblical prophecies in the book of Revelation. This part of the Bible is very heavily shrouded in symbolism, and people have had difficulty understanding it since the time it was written. It is supposedly a vision, which would explain the symbols. In Volume One Nostradamus said Saint John was seeing the same vision he had seen, and had described it the best he could. The Anti-Christ is not called by that name in Revelation, but the Beast seems to refer to the same man.

These are excerpts that seem to apply (Rev. 13:11–18):

"And I beheld another beast coming up out of the earth; and he had two horns like a lamb, and he spake as a dragon. And he doeth great wonders, so that he maketh fire come down from heaven on the Earth in the sight of men. And deceiveth them that dwell on the Earth by the means of those miracles which he had power to do ... saying to them that dwell on the Earth, that they should make an image to the beast. And he had power to give life unto the image of the beast, that the image of the beast should both speak, and cause that as many as would not worship the image of the beast should be killed. And he causeth all, both small and great, rich and poor, free and bond, to receive a mark in their right hand, or in their foreheads; and that no man might buy or sell, save he that had the mark, or the name of the beast, or the number of his name. Here is wisdom. Let him that hath understanding count the number of the beast: for it is the number of a man, and his number is Six hundred three-score and six (666)."

It is interesting that the George Lamsa translation of the Bible from the Aramaic reads almost like Nostradamus' predictions. Rev. 13:17–18:

"So that no man might buy or sell unless he who had the mark of the name of the beast or the code number of his name. Here is wisdom: Let him who has understanding decipher the code number of the beast; for it is the code number of the name of a man; and his number is six hundred and sixty-six (666)."

Chapters 14 and 15 of Revelation speak of a man who comes to help against the beast, and some of the verses could symbolically refer to the underground movement. During this time there are seven plagues delivered upon the Earth, each more terrible than the last, which create more and more turmoil upon the citizens of Earth. There seems to be no hope for mankind until the last plague is delivered at a place called Armageddon when a great voice from heaven cries out, "It is done."

The chapters after this refer to the doing away of the old world and the establishment of the 1000 years of peace which could refer to Nostradamus' description of the reign of the Great Genius who he sees coming after the time of troubles and restoring harmony to the world. (This is described in detail in Volume One.)

In my desperation to deny that what Nostradamus sees will come to pass, I find myself grasping at the fact that Nostradamus was familiar with the Bible of his day. He has said repeatedly that the saints and prophets have seen the same events that he has seen. I keep hoping that this partly influenced Nostradamus and that what he sees is an extension of these Biblical prophecies and will surely not happen. But there are too many correlations here to be coincidence. John's interpretation of the Anti-Christ's creation of a computer network is a better explanation of the number 666 than anyone else has been able to come up with by using logic.

Chapter 15

𝕹ostradamus' 𝕱ouse

BEFORE THIS SESSION BEGAN I asked John some questions about Nostradamus' house.

D: *What did he have in his study? Could you see anything?*

J: Yes, I saw a lot. He has shelves that have all different types of parchment scrolls on them with only a few books that are like our bound books.

D: *What about instruments that he uses?*

J: There were compass-like things, and he has quills that he uses to write. He has a whole glass … not a glass but a container filled with different quills of different shapes. He has a tripod-type of thing with a bowl that I noticed in a corner. I thought it was for heat because you could put a fire *in* the bowl. He also has a long table with two chairs that he works at, and there's a bench because sometimes this is where he talks to his students. He has a carved chest that he keeps locked.

D: *Hmm, I wonder what's in there.*

J: I haven't gotten to that yet.

D: *I was wondering if there was anything else he might use for his predictions, like the mirror and such.*

J: He uses the mirror and maybe the tripod with the bowl in it. The ironwork is fancy looking; it's detailed and looks very old. It looks like a brazier or something from the Roman period.

D: *I was wondering if there were any other kind of instruments he used to work with.*

J: I didn't see any laboratory instruments; no, nothing like that.

D: *Nothing that he would use for alchemy or anything like that?*

J: No, he has boxes of herbs, but that's in the next room.

D: *The room where he treats his patients?*

J: Right, the front room. See, this is the back study. He has a front study where he treats his patients; which has herbs and a type of bed in it. I'm not allowed in there. You know, it's not my … part.

D: *He doesn't want you to go into that part of the house.*

J: No. It's not where he wants me to go. While he was talking to me, I was checking out his study. It's not a very big room at all, kind of small by our standards.

After John was in trance, we began the session. First, I wanted to get a full description of the room.

J: Oh, he's at his desk today—it's not really a desk, it's a table—and he seems very absorbed in his writings.

D: *Did you want to look around the room before we contact him?*

J: Yes. To my left is the chest. It's really a square, carved box that has a key lock, but it's not really a key. It looks more like an icepick that locks it. It's very simple, and we could probably force it open if we wanted to. But I don't think Nostradamus would appreciate it. The chest is highly carved, and sometimes he puts things on it. Right next to it is a rack with small compartments in it where he puts scrolls of parchment. It's not paper like we have; it's parchment. And to the side of that there's a little window that looks like glass, but I don't think it is. It looks like a type of animal skin that's been tanned. It's opaque but it lets in light.

D: *Is it one solid piece?*

J: No, it's made up of little pieces with a type of filament in between.

D: *Is it like small squares?*

I was thinking of stained glass pieces that are leaded to hold them together. Apparently, this was something totally different.

J: No, they're not square—they're round. I get the word "marrow," but I don't think that's what it's made of.

D: *But you can't see through it.*

J: No. I can see light coming *through* it, but you can't see outside. To the right of that window is the little room he uses as his privy. In there is a big bucket of water and a big container of ash that he puts into the toilet. You know, after he finishes, he throws ash on top of it. It seems to have a slide that goes down into the earth. It doesn't smell because Nostradamus throws herbs down there once in a while, so there are no noxious fumes.

D: *Maybe he got the idea for his toilet from looking into the future.* (Laugh)

J: (*Laugh*) Yes, that might be right. And then there's the table with a big chair where he sits. He has a red, black and brown rug underneath the chair. Then there are clean rushes, like straw, on the floor. Underneath that is cold flagstone, and that's why the rushes are on the floor, to keep in the heat. Where I'm coming in from, there's a fireplace that completely warms the place. Usually I can't see it because this is the part of the room that I come through. In one corner behind the table is the tripod with the brazier bowl on it, and he has invoked spirits and people with this. He uses this in rituals, but he also uses it for heat. He moves it to the center of the room when it gets very cold.

This is very similar to the description of some of Nostradamus' methods of divination that was presented in his first two quatrains (CENTURY I-1 and 2): "Sitting along at night in secret study; it is placed on the brass tripod. A slight flame comes out of the emptiness and makes successful that which should not be believed in vain." "The wand in the hand is placed in the middle of the tripod's legs. With water he sprinkles both the hem of his garment and his foot. A voice, fear; he trembles in his robes. Divine splendor; the god sits nearby." These two quatrains were interpreted in Volume One, but they are self-evident and probably the easiest of all Nostradamus' quatrains to understand.

J: When it's very cold and he needs to be in this room, he lights a fire in the bowl. He builds a big fire in the fireplace and also lights this so he has good heat near him as he's writing. He will also wear mittens that have no fingers in them. The walls are made of something that looks like stucco. If you brush against it too much, it will fall off.

D: *Do you see instruments lying around?*

J: He keeps his instruments locked up because he has a nosy maid. He doesn't like her going through his things. He says, "Thank God she doesn't read, because she'd probably be in all my books." (*Laugh*) And what he calls books are actually his scrolls. He only has two or three books and they are hand copied.

D: *Are there any pictures or anything on the walls?*

J: The walls are bare, but above the chest are pegs that he hangs garments on.

D: *Where's the door that goes into the other room?*

J: It's on the left hand side right next to where ... the chest is on one side and ... oh, there's something else there. I don't remember seeing that yet. It looks like a ... I don't know *what* it is. I'm looking at it closely. (*Pause*)

D: *Next to the door or where?*

J: Well, on the other side of the door. On one side is the chest, and there's something else there. (*Mumbling to himself as he examined it.*) It's like a tripod, but it's not a tripod. It looks sort of like a candelabra except it's a lot bigger. It's about four or five feet tall and it has places for five candles ... or more ... five, six, seven, eight, nine, ten candles. I mean, you can really light it up. I think it's only used when it gets very dark and he has to work late at night.

D: *I was thinking that he had to have some kind of light.*

J: Uh-huh. He puts it in the center of the room to light up the whole room. He moves stuff around a lot. There are also a couple of benches near the table where his students sit when they come in to study with him.

D: *Is that the door that goes into the other part of the house?*

J: It goes into the front study where he keeps his medical supplies and he does his consultations.

D: *And we're not allowed to go into any other room but this study.*

J: No, he really doesn't want us to travel to any other room. There's some kind of a block or a barrier. It looks like either oil or salt on the door sill that prevents us from going into that area.

D: *Does it have any real power or is it just symbolic?*

J: I think it is both symbolic and powerful. He's put up an energy field. He does not want spirits of the future to go beyond that point. I've been able to *look* into that room, but I have not been able to go into that room.

D: *We want to respect his wishes.*

J: He's still writing at the desk. He's not aware that I'm here yet. Shall I let him know?

D: *Yes, if you will; then we can go ahead with our work.*

J: Okay. I appear in the mirror, he looks up from his writings and says, "Oh, hello. Yes, it's John from the future."

D: *Just out of curiosity, would you ask him what he keeps in the locked chest? Tell him we're curious.*

J: He's saying, "John ... (*the name was pronounced 'Jean' which is the French equivalent of John*)."

D: *He's pronouncing your name Jean?*

J: Yeah. He says that I am Jean. He smiles and says, "Jean, it's none of your business, but I'll tell you. I keep things in there I need to lock up because I have a nosy servant girl who gets into things. She tries to get into that chest because she thinks there must be a great amount of money in there. Well, I do store a bit of money in there because I have coins that go back to antiquity, but mostly, Jean, I have things that are very old in there." He keeps them locked up because with so many people ... He says, "I have three servants and four or five students, and things could come up missing very easily here." They're antiquities from the past, mostly from Roman and Greek times. He has an ancient Roman sword in there.

D: *Does he understand that we're just curious about the things in the room? He has nothing to fear from us.*

J: He understands who we are. He says, "It really has nothing to do with what we're working on. They're just antiquities that I've collected." He says sometimes he would go into the fields and find things, in ruins and by digging in the ground. He says the part of France where he lives was once a great Roman province. There are a lot of things that have been dug up by farmers planting, and he buys and collects them. He's like a collector of antiquities because he finds them interesting. The workmanship on these products is very refined compared to the workmanship of his own time, he says.

D: *Yes, I can understand that. I like things that are old also. What part of France is he living in? Can he tell you?*

J: He's showing me a map of France, and it looks like some place in the southern ... it's not near Paris. It's far from Paris and closer to Italy. I can't see the town exactly, but he says it's immaterial and not to bother with it.

D: *I thought I'd ask anyway. He knows he's dealing with very curious spirits here. (Laugh) There are people in our time that want to know about him and his life, and that's why we ask so many questions.*

When I did my research I found that Nostradamus spent most of his life in Salon which is located in the southeast corner of France near Italy and the Mediterranean Sea. As John said, it was a long way from Paris. It is located in the province of Provence and the area was conquered by the Romans in the second century B.C.E. At that time it was called Provincia Romana, from which the name of the province was derived. So it was entirely possible that Nostradamus was able to find Roman relics.

Section Two

The Translation

Chapter 16

The Translation Begins through John

WE HAD SUCCEEDED IN MAKING CONTACT once again, and we were now ready to continue translating his quatrains. We had been so successful operating through Brenda, and I had no idea if we could get the same results through John. There was the possibility we might get conflicting information that could jeopardize the entire project. Logically, it would seem to be impossible for two people to separately interpret these complicated puzzles and find the same answers, unless we were truly in contact with the mind that originated them. We were taking a chance and we knew it, but we were both willing to attempt the experiment.

I came across several quatrains which Nostradamus felt he could not clearly interpret through Brenda because of their astrological elements. He suggested these be put aside until we could work with John. These were the first quatrains I wanted to explore. Because some of them contained difficult phrases, it would be a real test for John, one he could not pass with his conscious calculating mind. The answers would have to come with the help of Nostradamus. Although it had worked twice before, the odds were definitely against our receiving the translations through a third person. But we were in contact with Nostradamus and our curiosity would not allow us to falter at this stage of the game.

I asked if he wanted me to read them the same way I had done with Brenda.

J: He says to repeat them first and if there is astrological data, he'll draw it out for us.

CENTURY I-42

Le dix Kalende d'Avril de faict Gothique,	The tenth day of the April Calends, calculated in Gothic fashion is
Resuscité encor par gens malins:	revived again by the wicked people.
Le feu estainct assemblé diabolique,	The fire is put out and the diabolic gathering seek the bones of the
Cherchant les os du d'Amant & Pselin.	demon of Psellus.

John asked me to repeat it. From the puzzled look on his face it was obvious that he, personally, had absolutely no idea what it meant. The translation of the quatrain then began to come through, obviously not from the mind of John but from a third party.

J: He says this quatrain has to do with the destruction of the church. During the time of troubles, in May of the mid- to late-1990s, the church will be going through difficult times. He says the pope at that time will be assassinated from within the church so the last pope can come into power, and this quatrain refers to that. He says that is all he can say right now concerning that quatrain.

D: *That word "Calends" was confusing. The translators say it's the first day of the Roman month.*

J: It's not April. It's in the first of May. He says he likes to play with words sometimes, and that was an anagram that he was kind of deceptive with. But it means the first of May. How do they interpret that quatrain?

D: *They have interpreted it as April. The translators think it refers to the institution of the Gregorian calendar system.*

J: He says, "Those people don't know what they're doing." It refers to the church and its interesting battles within itself. There will rise a pope that will be assassinated by his own kind, and this will be hidden. This will give the power to the last pope. He says to return to the part about the poison.

I was puzzled. There was no obvious reference to poison in the quatrain. I read the last part again. "Revised again by wicked people. The fire is put out and the diabolic gathering seek the bones of the demon of Psellus."

J: He says the pope will be killed by poison that will be absorbed into his bones. It will be a special type of poison that attacks the central nervous system and the skeletal system which will make it look like he went into shock or had a stroke. That is how they will present his death to the world. In this way the last pope of the Roman Catholic church will come into power.

D: *The translators are really off. Their interpretation refers to when Nostradamus began to write his prophecies.*

J: "Yes," he says, "you know we have argued about their inaccuracies before."
D: *(Laugh) Yes, I know. Sometimes he gets quite upset.*
J: He says, "No, I'm not upset. It's just that these people ... I don't know where their intelligence is."
D: *Well, they are using their common sense, that's all they can do.*
J: Yes, he says, but they are not using their intuitive memory. That would probably work better. He knows that in our time period many books will be written about him, but they will hardly contain any fathom of the truth of his words.
D: *Yes, that's it. Everyone is trying to find their own interpretations.*

CENTURY I-52

Les deux malins de Scorpion conjoinct,	Two evil influences in conjunction in Scorpio. The great lord is
Le grand seigneur meutri dedans sa salle:	murdered in his room. A newly appointed king persecutes the
Peste à l'Eglise par le nouveau roy joinct	Church, the lower (parts of) Europe and in the North.
L'Europe basse & Septentrionale.	

J: He says the two malefics are Mars and Saturn in the sign of Scorpio. This refers to the loss of the British monarch.
D: *Is this the great lord?*
J: The great lord is the British monarch that will be murdered by subservients, people who don't like his style or his government. He's a symbol, so they're not so much slaying the man as they are assassinating a symbol. He will be assassinated by the people of the IRA.
D: *(I didn't understand.) The people of who?*
J: If the IRA is no longer in conflict at the time this occurs, it will be a similar group of malcontents with similar motives. He says they will assassinate him after he becomes king.
D: *Could he tell us any more about the year? Or will you be able to find something out from that conjunction?*
J: He says this will take place after the year 2000 or about that time.
D: *Does this refer to whoever is king at that time?*
J: Yes, Prince Charles will be King Charles at that time, and this refers to him. Could you read the rest of the quatrain?
D: *"The newly appointed king persecutes the church. The lower parts of Europe and in the North."*
J: The death of this king will cause a lot of division in Ireland and England. The English people will put down the Catholic churches because they are usually a center for Irish people within the British Empire. This is where that quatrain will be fulfilled; it's their gathering places. People will know this group of malcontents assassinated the king because they will *glory* in it.

D: Is he showing you these events or telling you about them?
J: He's showing me pictures.
D: I was curious because he also showed the other vehicle pictures.

When we were able to obtain a 2000 ephemeris, we found that Mars and Saturn will be in exact conjunction in Scorpio on August 26, 2014. They enter this sign on July 27, 2014, and this configuration will last for a few months. During this time the King of England could be in grave danger.

CENTURY I-83

Le gent estrange divisera butins,	The alien nation will divide the
Saturne en Mars son regard	spoils. Saturn in dreadful aspect
furieux:	in Mars. Dreadful and foreign to
Horrible estrange aux	the Tuscans and Latins. Greeks
Tosquans & Latins,	who will wish to strike.
Grecs qui seront à frapper	
curieux.	

J: This quatrain describes the country we know as Turkey. It is the alien nation. He says Turkey is going to have a war with Greece shortly. He says Greece will ask for aid from Italy and the surrounding countries because Turkey will seem to be very dominating. They might even use nuclear weapons, not so much bombs, but those types of weapons. They will also use sophisticated technology from the Russians. The Russians will support Turkey during this uprising which will take place in the early 1990s. The "dreadful aspect" is either a Saturn square Mars or Mars square Saturn aspect. He says Mars square Saturn. I'm asking him where Saturn will be at that time. He says Saturn will be in its ruling position of Capricorn, and Mars will be in Aries. He says this will help me find out when this will happen.
D: "The alien nation will divide the spoils." Does that mean Russia is involved, or is he referring to one of the parties at war?
J: It represents Turkey because Turkey will contain so many internal factions. It will start a war so people will concentrate on the war rather than the internal problems that are taking place within their country.
D: Yes, that always gets their mind off it.
J: Right. He says it will cause a war with Greece who will want to annihilate Turkey. But while Turkey will have the support of the Russians, Greece will not have the support of other countries. It will ask for help from Italy, the United States and other countries, but we will all stay neutral. It will only last for a couple of months. It will be a short war in which there'll be fire in the great city of Athens. I asked if they are going to burn the Parthenon and he said, "No, I don't see the Parthenon being burnt *this* time."

This seems to go along with the predictions in Volume One that refer to the classical centers being destroyed during the time of troubles.

J: He repeats that Mars will be in the sign of Aries and Saturn will be in the sign of Capricorn.

It was later discovered that these signs would occur from May 31 through July 12, 1990 with an exact square between Saturn and Mars on July 1, 1990.

UPDATE: This quatrain and CENTURY III-90 *in Chapter 21 ("The Heart Attack") are connected and Nostradamus said they refer to the same event. The Dates given strongly suggest this is connected with the short Persian Gulf War which began building in the summer of 1990 and culminated in war by February 1991. The dates, countries involved (Turkey, Israel, Syria, Iran, United States, Russia, and the eastern Mediterranean area), and other details mentioned in the quatrains all seem to indicate this. The only part that doesn't fit is the mention of Greece in both quatrains. I discovered that Turkey and Greece have had ill feelings towards each other for centuries, going back to the Ottoman Empire, because of Greece being a Christian nation. It would not be inconceivable for trouble to develop there because the whole area seems ready to explode, and it wouldn't take much to set it off and draw Greece into the turmoil. I think this quatrain means that the seeds were sown in the middle of 1990, and they will sprout when the situation worsens in the middle 1990s (according to other quatrains). In this case 85 percent of the quatrain has been fulfilled and the remaining 15 percent is waiting on future events.*

CENTURY III-I

Apres combat & bataille navale,
Le grand Neptune à son plus
*   haut befroi:*
Rouge adversaire de peur
*   deviendra pasle*
Mettant le grand Ocean en effroi.

After the combat and naval battle, great Neptune in his highest belfry; the red adversary will become pale with fear, putting the great ocean into a state of terror.

J: He says this quatrain refers back to World War II and the Japanese advance on the Pacific.

D: *Does it refer to the naval battles there?*

J: Yes. He says Neptune was in the sign of Virgo in Libra at that time.

D: *Is that what is meant by the highest belfry?*

J: Yes. He says it corresponds to the entire time period of World War II.

D: *I thought the red adversary might refer to Mars. Is that correct?*

J: He says Mars was in bad aspect to Neptune at that time. It also represents the advance of the Soviets into China and China becoming a Communist country. He says it represents the 1940s.

D: *Then Neptune did refer to an astrological sign?*

J: He says he meant both the astrological sign as well as the archetype of the ruler of the ocean. When Neptune was in the sign of Libra and Virgo, and Mars was in square to that was when he saw the major naval battles take place. On these dates a lot of lives were lost, and Neptune rose up to carry the dead to the bottom of the ocean. He says this also represents the Soviet Union's advance to make China Communist.

Later, when John examined these signs in his ephemeris, he found the date referred to was the month of April 1944. My research disclosed that in 1944 some of the bloodiest naval battles in history were fought over captured islands in the Pacific.

It was also accurate that Russia was converting China into a Communist country during the 1940s. They used the people's preoccupation with the war with Japan to make their political inroads. Thus by 1949 the whole war-weary continent of China fell to the Communists and the Nationalist government fled to Taiwan.

I am including Brenda's interpretation of these next quatrains because it is interesting to compare how close her interpretation is to John's. It's obvious they were being shown nearly the same pictures, and each probably interpreted what they saw a bit differently. Since Nostradamus said there could be references to several different events within the same quatrain, they also could have seen various aspects of similar events he was trying to present. They are too similar to be coincidental, especially since the translators didn't even come close to what Brenda and John interpreted. I think this might explain any slight inconsistencies. Nostradamus has also explained that everyone will see the images a little differently and interpret them within the context of their own knowledge and experience.

CENTURY II-51

Le sang de juste à Londres fera faulte,	The blood of the just will be demanded of London burnt by fire
Bruslés par fouldres de vingt trois les six:	in three times twenty plus six.
La dame antique cherra de place haute,	The ancient lady will fall from her high position, and many of the
Des mesme secte plusieurs seront occis.	same denomination will be killed.

[*Brenda's interpretation.*]

B: He says this quatrain has a multiple meaning. "The blood of the just being killed by fire" refers to the terrorist attacks in London by the IRA. Because of fire bombs and other weapons, many innocent people will be wounded. He says the "ancient lady fallen from her high estate" refers to the Tower of London being destroyed. He says this is somewhat of a mixed-up quatrain because it refers to a lot of different *little* events that are all part of larger events taking place.

D: *When will the Tower of London be destroyed?*

B: He says it will be during the time of troubles. To find out more exactly when it will be, count from the time of the blitzkrieg during World

War II. (*Pause*) It's coming through confused. He says he's having difficulty getting time concepts across to us. The three times twenty plus six ... the way he worded it can refer to two different numbers. He says it can refer to either sixty-six or to seventy-eight, depending on how you read the number. He wrote it like that because three times twenty is sixty, plus six is sixty-six, or three times twenty plus six is seventy-eight.

This was something I would never have thought of, and neither had anyone else. The translators have interpreted the date to be 1666.

B: He says he used these numbers as ratios to represent particular planets in the horoscope. I believe he's referring to the ratios (seventy-eight and sixty-six) of their orbits around the sun. He says when they are in conjunction or in a particular relationship, it will indicate when this destruction will take place during the time of troubles. He says the line "the high lady will be taken from her high estate and others of the same denominations killed" refers to an event that has already happened. It's in the past from our viewpoint, but it's still in the future from his viewpoint. This event refers to the Catholic Church falling from power in England and England's identification with another church. The high lady and the high estate both refer to the Catholic Church. He says the priests of the Catholic Church were also killed during the warfare that resulted from England becoming a Protestant country.

D: *Do you think John will be able to understand those numbers from the information Nostradamus has given us?*

B: He says he should. If he needs more information feel free to contact him.

D: *The translators think this refers to the Great Fire of London in 1666.*

B: He says that it does, but that's not the only thing it refers to. Since that event is in the past from your point of view, he was telling you about other things unrelated to that event.

D: Then they are correct as far as they go. They thought it was interesting that he used those numbers. I'll show this to John to see if he can come up with the date. And if he has any more questions, we'll get back to you.

B: He says the numbers will correspond to a couple of the outer planets with much larger revolution times.

[*John's interpretation.*]

J: He says this quatrain refers to the war effort when the Anti-Christ's forces try to bomb London. The ancient lady represents Saint Paul's Cathedral because there was a temple dedicated to the *old* religion on that site, and within the bowels of the church is the ancient lady. They will discover her when the bombing takes place. That's *part* of what it means. The quatrain also predicts that Britain is going to have a lot of difficulties during the times of troubles because Christians will be persecuting Christians. There will be a lot of persecution among the wealthy, too. People will rise up against the rich, for they have hardly anything while the wealthy have it all. This will take place in the 1990s towards the turn of the century. That's the time period of these events.

D: *Can he explain the meaning of those numbers? Three times twenty plus six.*

J: (*Long pause.*) He says they are similar to an anagram, but they are numbers. He says they represent 1996.

D: *The only interpretation the translators could find was the Great Fire of London in 1666.*

J: Yes, he says this has been interpreted correctly to mean the fire in London, but it also represents things in the future, such as trouble in 1996 for the British people.

CENTURY III-4

Quand seront proches de defaut des lunaires,	When the downfall of the lunar ones is close they will not be very distant
De l'un à l'autre ne distant grandement,	from each other. Cold, drought, danger around the frontiers even
Froid, siccité, danger vers les frontieres,	where the oracle had its source.
Mesme ou l'oracle a prins commencement.	

[*Brenda's interpretation.*]

B: He says this quatrain refers to the establishment of space stations at the L-5 points in relation to the moon and the Earth. Space travelers must watch out for deep vacuum conditions in space. Regardless of their best preparations, even with the information from the computers, referred to here as the "oracle," they will still be unprepared for unexpected aspects of this environment. He referred to computers in general as an oracle because they will be using them to extrapolate unknown information based on presently known information.

D: *Before, I think you mentioned the establishment of L-5 space stations on the moon.*

B: They won't be *on* the moon but at the L-5 point! (*Exasperated*) He says if you only knew basic astronomy. This is the point between the moon and the Earth where the gravitational pull is equal from both directions. Less fuel is needed to keep the stations in position there since gravity will be doing the majority of the work.

D: *Okay. When he mentioned it before, he simply said L dash five space stations, so I assumed he meant on the moon.*

B: He says he is glad you have not printed that because it would make you a laughing stock. He says L-5 points are a very basic astronomical concept.

D: *"When the downfall of the lunar ones is close, they will not be very*

distant from each other." This predicts trouble with the space stations.
"Cold, drought" and so on, relates to the deep vacuums.

B: Yes. He says when these L-5 stations are established there will also be astronomical observatories being constructed on the lunar surface itself. It will be a joint project between the United States, Russia and England. The United States and England will be involved because they have the scientific information needed and Russia because they have the best scientists. Russia and the United States also have space technology. He says there will be accidents as there always are when new technology is being explored.

D: *Is this in the far future?*

B: Not as far as you would think.

D: *Does it happen in the time of the Great Genius?*

B: Yes, or before. He says the technology presently exists to do all of this but because of political and economic pressures created by the cabal, it cannot be done right now. So it's just a matter of getting the Anti-Christ and the cabal out of the way; then mankind can start doing these things. And later, the Genius will come.

CENTURY III-5

Pres loing defaut de deux grands
luminaires,
Qui surviendra entre l'Avril
& Mars:
O quel cherté nais deux grans
debonnaires,
Par terre & mer secourrant
toutes pars.

Then, after the eclipse of the two great stars which will occur between April & March. Oh, what a loss! But two great good influences will help on all sides by land and sea.

B: He says he could begin explaining this quatrain now, but it would be better to translate it with John, the astrologer, on hand. He also notes that it is somewhat related to the previous quatrain and he may want to treat them as a pair during the translation.

D: *Do you mean the quatrain about the space stations?*

B: Yes, he wants to cover them with John.

[*John's interpretation.*]

D: *Nostradamus told me that the next two quatrains are related. Should I read them together or separately?*

J: Read them together. (*I did so.*) He says they refer to the future, in the time period of 2000 or 2100. They are involved with space exploration and related topics. He says after the formation of the world government we will unite with other countries to have joint space explorations, around the moon and around another planet that might be on the other *side* of the moon. (*John seemed confused and he spoke to*

Nostradamus.) "Is that what you mean?" Okay. I understand what he means now. He says it's on the other side of the moon, meaning we have to go out beyond the moon. It also represents a time when we might have intelligent contact with extraterrestrials, working with them to build space stations and colonize space. This will be taking place in either the 21st or the 22nd century.

D: *Will this be after the time of the Anti-Christ?*

J: Oh, yes. He says this has nothing to do with the Anti-Christ. Space exploration, the colonization of space, and the joint effort of the Earth and another planetary system will take place in the mid-22nd century.

D: *The second quatrain says, "After the eclipse of the two great stars which will occur between April and March—oh! What a loss."*

J: He says this also takes place in the mid-22nd century. I'm getting the year 2158 or something like that.

D: *What does this have to do with the other quatrain?*

J: He says there might be some difficulties, and they might lose one of the base stations. But there will be help from another galaxy.

D: *Is that what he means by "Two great good influences will help on all sides on land and sea"?*

J: Yes. He means another planetary consciousness will contact the Earth. (*Abruptly*) He says that he is happy to be of service, but he would like to write in his book now.

D: *Is he done with us?*

J: Yes. He would like to write now. He says it's time to do his book meditation, as he called it, and he would like us to leave.

D: *Can I continue with the translation of the quatrains when we come again?*

J: Yes, he will be happy to be of service, but he would like to get back to his work now. He's got his quill out, and he wants to do some writing. He's saying something like, "Have a nice day," but it isn't "day" that he says. It's *event.*

D: *Have a nice event?* (Laugh)

J: I don't understand, but he's waving me off now. Okay, we'll see you later. Bye.

Since he was obviously dismissing us we had no choice but to leave. John immediately found himself back in the Tapestry Room.

D: *I keep wondering if when we read the quatrains does it trigger the picture he shows you or ...?*

J: Yes. We're sitting down at a table with the black mirror between us. I usually repeat the quatrain twice in my head, except I picture the words, and then he writes them. As he's writing, a picture appears in the mirror that he points to with his eyes.

D: *Do you think he was writing down the things we were talking about?*

J: I think there might be something to that theory. Maybe he wanted to write down what we were discussing before he forgot it.

D: *I'm curious whether or not we're helping him to write these quatrains.*

J: I think we are.

D: *I know he originally wrote them in French.*

J: Yes, but he says he's reading my mind in French.

D: *I'm not even sure if it has been translated correctly into English. But it's the reading of the quatrain that triggers the image. Then does he explain what it means?*

J: Yes, by showing it through the mirror.

D: *I've always wondered if it was the other way around; if he saw the picture and then wrote the quatrain.* (John shook his head.) *Then we really are helping him do this. But isn't this a big responsibility for us in our time period to be influencing what he's doing in the past? Is this allowed? Is it right or ethical?*

J: It's okay for us to do this. He is not only communicating with us, but with people from other parts of the future as well.

D: *Are they telling him what is happening?*

J: No. I see his tapestry thread connecting with other threads from all ages. So he has the ability to be in contact with people from other times as well as ours.

D: *Is that how he knows the events are happening?*

J: Yes, that's how he knows the future. He's his own time traveler. He's a great soul.

D: *I was wondering if we were influencing him in any way, and if it is wrong to do this?*

J: To a degree we are influencing him because all life influences life. The guardian of the tapestry is here now and he says, "Do not worry about that."

D: *I wouldn't want to influence him in the* wrong *way.*

J: No. He says you're not influencing anything in the wrong way.

D: *But is it ethical for us to, in a sense, write the quatrains for him? That's where I'm confused.*

J: He says not to worry about this. "As your consciousness evolves, you'll be able to understand parallel lives and the sense of time." A voice is saying, "Please, this stuff is beyond you. You people are working in your grammar school books and you're asking college graduate level questions."

D: *(Laugh) Okay. As long as they don't consider this interfering, because I don't want to have any* undue *influence.*

J: He says, "Do not worry. You are doing the best for all concerned."

Nostradamus had kept his promise that he would come through another vehicle. I didn't have to worry about losing contact with him. After all, he had picked *me*, not the other way around. The amazing thing about John's first interpretations was that they didn't deviate from the basic story Nostradamus was trying to convey to us. They didn't contradict Brenda's interpretations but merely added more pieces to the puzzle. This gave even more validity to the possibility that we were truly in contact with him. There can be no other explanation.

Chapter 17

The Fate of the Anti-Christ and the World

ALL THE TIME WE HAD BEEN WORKING with Brenda, one important question had remained unanswered. What was the fate of the Anti-Christ? We had seen the horror he would pour upon the world. And we saw that it apparently would progress to the point where there was no stopping him. But Nostradamus saw that the time of the Great Genius would follow, so we knew something had to happen to stop the madness. The answer was found unexpectedly in a quatrain that Brenda had had difficulty interpreting because it contained astrological data. Nostradamus suggested that John handle it, so I included it among the first quatrains to present to him.

CENTURY VIII-49

Saturn: au beuf joue en l'eau, Mars en fleiche,	Saturn in Taurus, Jupiter in Aquarius, Mars in Sagittarius, the
Six de Fevrier mortalité donra,	sixth of February brings death.
Ceux de Tardaigne à Briges si grand breche,	Those of Tardaigne so great a breach at Bruges, that the
Qu' à Ponteroso chef Barbarin mourra.	barbarian chief will die at Ponteroso.

J: (*He corrected my pronunciation of the names.*) He asks, "Didn't we review this one once before."

D: *Yes, we did, through Brenda. But there were some things that weren't clear, so he wanted an astrologer to go over the signs to help pinpoint a date.* (*He asked me to repeat the astrological signs.*) *Saturn in Taurus, Jupiter in Aquarius, Mars in Sagittarius, the 6th of February.*

J: He says this quatrain has to do with the Earth shift. It will take place in the early part of the 21st century, and many people will leave the planet at that time. This gives you an idea of when this event will take place.

D: Is this the major Earth shift? Will it come after the time of the Anti-Christ in the 21st century?

J: The Anti-Christ will still be in power. This is one of the ways a lot of his followers will leave the planet.

D: It says, "the barbarian chief will die at Ponteroso."

J: That represents the Anti-Christ's death.

D: Oh? We were curious about what happens to him.

J: He dies due to the Earth shift.

D: Nostradamus kept saying it was going to be a mysterious event, and he wouldn't tell us more.

J: This quatrain predicts the Earth shift when a lot of people will leave the planet, especially this evil being. He says in your time period you will see the world shift. He's giving me an image of the Earth. It seems as if our poles are moving faster, away from their present positions. As a result, there's a displacement of water.

D: Can he see what is happening to the Anti-Christ when this occurs?

J: He says the Anti-Christ will be swept away in a tidal wave. He and his army will be ready to strike and it will be humanity's last defense against him. Finally, he comes to naught by having an Earth shift take place. Because he believes that his power is omnipotent and that he can control the forces of the Earth—not just the Earth's *people*, but the dynamics of the Earth itself—he isn't counting on the tidal wave. No one can control the spirit of this planet. The planet rebels and shakes, and we see earthquakes and tidal waves that affect his army and bring him to his knees when he is swept away in a flood of water.

D: It's interesting that it will take something of that magnitude to stop him.

J: Well, the Anti-Christ believes that he has not just the people of the world in his grips, but also the spirit of the world. He's showing me a picture. I see an entire encampment of different types of airplanes, ships, and vehicles that I have never seen before. And it's all swept away by earthquakes and big water. It will happen very fast.

D: In the quatrain it says this will happen at Ponteroso. This is a word the translators don't understand. Can he explain the meaning of that word?

J: He says it refers to the Alpine area of northern Italy and Switzerland.

D: Is it the name of a place?

J: Yes. He says it is near the place where he will be swept away.

D: Do the astrological signs say when it will happen?

J: He says it will be in the early part of the 21st century. You should be able to find it.

D: Some of our ephemerides don't go that far.

J: You'll have access to whatever your needs are.

It would seem simple to find the date of the shift from the astrological data given, but it turned out to be more difficult than we anticipated. Part of the problem was caused by a mistake in Ms. Cheetham's translation, and trying to pinpoint this date became as complicated as a detective following clues to solve a mystery. This search is described in Chapter 29, "Finding the Date of the Shift." The date we arrived at is given there.

D: *Then that will be the end of the Anti-Christ's war.*

J: He says his followers will try to continue, but the suffering and pain of the Earth shift itself will cause people to put away their weapons and try to rebuild civilization.

D: *Will the Anti-Christ have a lot of world control by that time?*

J: Yes, it will be a time of climactic tensions among the people of the world, and a time for the Earth to renew itself.

D: *Will our country, the United States, ever be taken over by the Anti-Christ?*

J: No. He says the United States is out of the picture. The Anti-Christ mostly reigns in Europe. (*Pause*) But he's showing me a picture of the United States ... afterward. It's mostly islands.

D: *After the Earth shift?*

J: Yes. It looks like islands.

What John did next was extremely difficult. He attempted to describe the map as it was shown to him by Nostradamus. Looking at a topographic view of the United States without state boundaries is hard enough, but it is even more difficult to look at a land mass that had changed and try to determine what parts of the states were left. There were few landmarks to go by, and anyone would have difficulty. Therefore I do not expect this description to be totally accurate. I think John did an admirable job under the circumstances.

As I had no map to refer to, I relied on my knowledge of geography to ask questions.

J: There's a big island that begins with northern Quebec and New Brunswick, and it contains parts of northern Maine, northern New Hampshire, Vermont, northern New York state, and Pennsylvania. Below that is another island mass that goes south. I see it encompasses the southern Appalachians into West Virginia. There is land around Tennessee, North and South Carolina, northern Georgia, northern Alabama and Kentucky. This whole area is another land mass separated by a strait. Then this is separated by *wider* ocean from a huge island in the southwest that's almost circular. Iowa, Missouri, and Arkansas are all part of this major island. It also contains land from eastern Oklahoma, Kansas and Nebraska. Omaha is a seaport. It's also a big city.

D: *Saint Louis?*

J: No, I don't see Saint Louis. I see part of Missouri and Arkansas are cut in half, according to their present location in the 20th century. What is left is the northern reaches of what would be northwestern Arkansas, southwestern Missouri, and almost all of western Missouri. Iowa, parts of Minnesota, parts of the Dakotas, parts of Nebraska,

Kansas and Oklahoma make a big island that's almost continent size. This is where most of the commerce of the country will take place because it will be the largest land segment with water all around it. Above it I see the Pacific northwest and Alaska combined together as one whole land mass stretching down into northern Colorado and following the mountain chains through Colorado. That's another area that appears to be a continent. Most of Texas is under water, but a part of east Texas and eastern Oklahoma are attached to the large land mass that makes up the Midwest.

D: *Is the rest of Texas gone?*

J: The sea coast of Texas is gone, and only east Texas seems to be there. Northern Mexico seems to be just water, but the mountains of Arizona, New Mexico and California make up another land mass.

D: *Is California there?*

J: Parts of California are, but the southern part is not. The mountainous areas are there, but this is separated from New Mexico, Colorado and Utah by another strait. There are some islands that are off this area that were part of southern California where the mountains are high, but they're like channel islands. They're more like bird sanctuaries with just a few people.

D: *What about Florida?*

J: There's no Florida.

D: *Then what you are seeing looks like a series of islands with water in between. Is the Mississippi River part of the ocean?*

J: Yes, that's part of the ocean. The main land mass is where Missouri, Arkansas, parts of Kansas, parts of Nebraska, and Iowa are.

D: *I can imagine there would be a lot of cities destroyed. What about New York?*

J: New York is gone. Omaha seems to be a very big city. Knoxville, Tennessee, and Harrison, Arkansas are big cities. Jefferson City in Missouri is a big city. Des Moines is the big industrial and communications center. A lot of networkers come out of Des Moines and parts of northern Iowa. There will be a new city in northern Iowa that doesn't have a name yet, but it will be a seaport.

D: *It makes sense that land near the Great Lakes and the large rivers and gulfs would be the first to flood when this shift occurs.*

J: There will be a lot of water displacement when the continents raise again. The Hawaiian Islands are gone, as is most of Alaska, and the shift has made it a more tropical area.

D: *What about the northern parts of Canada?*

J: Those areas are other islands. They are more tropical because the polar cap has shifted creating a different climate.

I thought if we were so interested in the changes in our continent, there might be others in the world who would be interested in the re-shaping of their continents.

D: *What about South America?*

J: South America is completely changed. There is a long island that stretches from the very tip of its southern end all the way north through the whole of Central America. Around that it almost looks like a leaf shape, but it's a very narrow leaf. There's not much land. But there is new land that has risen up in the Caribbean that connects with this. There is a lot of water there which separates it from the islands of North America. It looks like the equator has shifted as well, because a lot of this area will be very moderate in climate but not tropical.

D: *Parts of new land in the Caribbean have joined with South America. Are there any other new land masses?*

J: Yes. There are new land masses in the middle of what was the Pacific and Atlantic Oceans that are continent size. These have moved up from the ocean bottom. The new land mass in the middle of the Atlantic Ocean is connected to Greenland, creating a new continent. There's water separating it from the islands that make up what was North America.

D: *Can he show us what the European and Asian continents will look like after this shift has taken place?*

J: Yes, he's showing me the globe. Most of India and the Arab peninsula seem to have gone but there are large islands that make up parts of Asia. Japan, the Philippines and that whole area of southeast Asia is gone, but the interior of what was Russia and China appears to be one huge land mass. Europe has scattered. It has islands running from the interior of what was Spain all the way to Norway. These areas are like a sprinkling of many islands, almost the way the islands are now off the coast of Greece. The two new large land masses are those out in the Pacific and the Atlantic Ocean.

D: *Is Europe separated by water from what we know of as Asia.*

J: Yes. There seems to be a lot of waters on its eastern boundary.

D: *What about England?*

J: Most of England is gone except for a segment of it. It has always been an island, but it's not as big as it once was.

D: *And the Mediterranean?*

J: The Mediterranean is gone. It is all ocean southward. Italy is not there any more. There are some parts of northern Italy, but most of it is not there. Most of Greece is still intact, surprisingly, but it's an island now. Most of eastern Europe is there, except for Poland. Poland is all water.

D: *What about Switzerland, Sweden ...*

J: There are parts of Switzerland, Sweden, and Norway, but they are all scattered like islands surrounded by water. The water isn't very deep though. It's only about 50 to 100 feet deep, so they're like islands in a lake. Most of Africa is gone except for some medium-size islands, mostly to the west.

D: *What about Antarctica?*

J: Antarctica is a land mass that seems to be connected to Australia in some way.

D: *It sounds to me as though the areas of the world that are now mountainous are the ones that will remain.*

J: Yes, it seems that way. Because when the Earth shift takes place, new land masses in the Atlantic and the Pacific Oceans will displace a lot of water.

D: *Would he be able to show you where the equator and the new poles are after the shift?*

J: It would be hard to describe because it really looks out of balance compared to our world.

D: *Okay. I think you've told me quite a bit anyway. Did you say that the climates of all these countries will change?*

J: Yes. The northern reaches will be tropical. Places like Alaska and Patagonia will be warm. Other places will be moderate. I don't see much cold weather. I don't see ice caps.

D: *Then it sounds like the United States will be mostly moderate. Is that true?*

J: Yes, it will be mostly a moderate climate.

D: *I'm glad we got an idea of what the world will look like at that time. But this raises a question for me. He sees that we are going to have drastic Earth changes, and yet he still sees space travel and exploration in our future. How are we going to continue with our technology after such disasters?*

J: He says there will be many people who will carry the new technology to these safe areas.

D: *I thought something like an Earth shift would be so drastic that it would just wipe out everything.*

J: He says there are many advances that will be made before all this takes place. The government already has places in the northwest where they can continue space exploration if there are major Earth changes. He says it will take almost 10 to 15 years for the technology to return to the level it was before the shift. But at the same time we will be making contact with extraterrestrials. He says other beings will be there to help during this time. They will help us advance in technology so we can help explore space. He says that they're a bit different from us, but they're still a part of us.

D: *I thought it sounded contradictory for us to be rebuilding after such terrible catastrophes and advancing at the same time. But he sees other beings helping us to rebuild the world after the Anti-Christ. I was afraid the shift would mean the end of everything. I thought he meant there would be no civilization left after this occurred because it would be so traumatic.*

J: There'll be a rebuilding and an economical use of the land. We will not exploit the land as we have in the past. I have a feeling

Nostradamus is telling us not to worry about this because other people and other guides from throughout the universe will help the people going through these transitions. I feel he says, "Do not worry. It is not your concern. Guardians are watching the planet." He shows me what looks like an angel.

D: *The important thing is that we will be able to rebuild our civilization.*

J: Yes. The cities will be much nicer. They will be cleaner. I don't see many cars or things of that type.

D: *Well, I wanted to find out the fate of the Anti-Christ because the whole time we've been working on these quatrains, we've been wondering what was going to happen to him. I guess it would take something of that magnitude to stop him.*

J: He tries to control the Earth's own spirit and she rebels. So he is brought down in her destruction.

I can appreciate how hard it was for John to obtain this type of information from looking at an unrecognizable map. Later, we decided to have an artist attempt to draw a map of this version of the world. This is explained in Chapter 28, "The Drawing of the Map."

𝕴T MIGHT BE IMPORTANT to again refer to the book of Revelation in the Bible and notice how it appears to apply to this prediction. The reader should remember that this Biblical book is full of symbolic references and must be interpreted in the same manner as the quatrains. Chapter 16 of Revelation begins with the pouring out upon the Earth of the last seven plagues by the seven angels.

Rev. 16:2–20: And the first (angel) went, and poured out his vial upon the Earth; and there fell a noisome and grievous sore upon the men which had the mark of the beast, and upon them which worshipped his image. And the second angel poured out his vial upon the sea; and it became as the blood of a dead man: and every living soul died in the sea. And the third angel poured out his vial upon the rivers and the fountains of waters; and they became blood. ... And the fourth angel poured out his vial upon the sun; and power was given unto him to scorch men with fire. And men were scorched with great heat, and blasphemed the name of God. And the fifth angel poured out his vial upon the seat of the beast; and his kingdom was full of darkness; and they gnawed their tongues for pain. And blasphemed the God of heaven because of their pains and their sores, and repented not of their deeds. And the sixth angel poured out his vial upon the great river Euphrates; and the water thereof was dried up, that the way of the kings of the east might be prepared. And I saw three unclean spirits like frogs come out of the mouth of the dragon, and out of the mouth of the beast, and out of the mouth of the false prophet. For they are the spirits of devils, working miracles, which go forth unto the kings of the Earth and of the whole world, to gather them to the battle of that great day of God Almighty. Behold, I come as a thief. Blessed is he that watchest, and keepeth his garments, lest he walk naked, and they see his shame. And he gathered them together into a place called in the Hebrew tongue Armageddon. And the seventh angel poured out his vial into the air; and there came a great voice out of the temple of heaven, from the throne, saying, It is done. And there were voices, and thunders, and lightnings; and there was a great earthquake, such as was not since men were upon the Earth, so mighty an earthquake, and so great. And the great city was divided into three parts, and the cities of the nations fell. And every island fled away, and the mountains were not found.

Chapter 18

The Injured Child

NOW THAT WE HAD TRANSLATED the quatrains containing astrological data, I wanted to continue. I asked if this would be possible. I explained, "We have the book of his quatrains that he published many years ago and we would like to work on their translation, if he is ready to continue with that work."

John remarked, "Indeed he is. He's sitting back in a chair now. He's told me to pull up a bench, too. He says, 'We can do a few. Don't worry.'"

I explained the procedure I had used with Brenda. I would read the quatrain and he would give me the interpretation. He had said he didn't want to bother with the quatrains dealing with the *far* past from our point of view. He wanted to concentrate on those involving our present and our future. These were more important. I wanted to know if he wished to continue with the same method.

J: He says, "Just read the quatrain and I'll tell you where to place it."

I decided to continue reading the quatrains in order from where I had left off with Brenda instead of picking some at random.

These will not be arranged chronologically in the following chapters because of the surrounding events that occurred within each session that persuaded me to leave the sessions intact. Only the quatrains pertaining to distant events that Nostradamus thought would not be pertinent to us have been deleted.

CENTURY III-40

Le grand theatre se viendra
se redresser,
Les des jettez & les rets ja tendus:
Trop le premier en glaz viendra
lasser,
Par ares prostrais de long
temps ja fendus.

The great theater will be raised up again, the dice thrown and the nets already cast. The great one who tolls the death knell will become too tired, destroyed by bows split a long time ago.

J: He says the theater raised up again was not referring to a theater with people on stage but a theater more like the Roman arenas with gladiators. He's writing. He just wrote all of that down, and now he's showing me this picture. It looks like our football stadiums or a coliseum except that people are *really* excited. They have motorcycles and all different types of vehicles, and they're *fighting* on them.

D: *Is this in our future?*

J: He says it's happening now. He says people get injured, but they don't go there to get injured. He's showing me pictures of speedways. The thrill of the crowd watching the disasters that sometimes take place at speedways, tractor-pulls and demolition derbies has been revived from the old theater. It's similar to the Roman crowds. He says to read the last part of the quatrain.

D: *"The dice thrown and the nets already cast."*

J: He says to look at how much money is spend and how much gambling takes place. He says it's like the resurrection of the ancient Roman gladiator games except it's not done with gladiators killing each other as much as it is with vehicles. He says a lot of money is bet and lost.

D: *The last line was "The great one who tolls the death knell will become too tired. Destroyed by bows split a long time ago."*

J: He says this relates to how people will perceive religion. Most religions in your time period will be going through the death knell as more light and understanding come into being. He says this quatrain is metaphorically connected. In his time they worshipped Jesus on the cross. He says this symbol will not be used in the future because it will be considered too horrifying. People will think it is barbaric and pagan to see suffering and death. This symbol will not be used in the religions of the future because it is negative. It represents death, destruction, pain, and despair when spiritually we're all eternal. So this quatrain represents the death of the image of the crucifixion. It's the end of people worshiping the crucifix, and especially Jesus *on* the crucifix.

D: *I agree with him there. But why are those two things together in one quatrain? Is there a connection between them?*

J: Yes, he says there's a big connection if you think about it. Religion has become a part of the masses and what the masses want is entertainment, just like they did in Rome. This quatrain represents giving people mass religion and mass entertainment. It's a picture of our world as it is right now. The people have not yet learned that the only way we grow spiritually is individually, and to find one's own sense of being one has to look within.

CENTURY III-41

Bossu sera esleu par le conseil,	The hunchback will be elected by
Plus hideux monstre en terre	the counsel, a more hideous
n'apperceu,	monster on Earth was never seen.
Le coup voulant crevera l'œil,	The deliberate shot will pierce his
Le traitre au Roi pour	eye, the traitor whom the king
fidelle reçu.	received as loyal.

J: He says this quatrain refers to the last pope. He's not really hunch-backed but has had difficulties with the curvature of his spine and with his legs.

D: *So this quatrain refers to his deformity?*

J: Right. He says he will align himself with the prevailing materialists and will seem to sell Europe short.

D: *What does that mean, "the deliberate shot will pierce his eye. The traitor whom the king received as loyal"?*

J: He's trying to show me a picture of something. It looks like the pope making a state visit. What happens is that a shot meant for the pope actually kills a king, a president, or someone in a position of power.

D: *They were shooting at this pope?*

J: Yes. They meant to kill the pope but they killed a dignitary high up in government, either a president or another ruler.

CENTURY III-42

L'enfant naistra à deux dents	The child will be born with two teeth
en la gorge,	in his mouth; stones will fall like rain
Pierres en Tuscie par pluie	in Tuscany. A few years later there
tomberont:	will be neither wheat nor barley,
Peu d'ans apres ne sera bled	to satisfy those who will weaken
ni orge,	from hunger.
Pour saouler ceux qui de	
faim failliront.	

J: He describes this as world-wide famine. Children will be born hungry, ready to eat, but will have no food. That is the symbolism of the "two teeth in his mouth." He says in his time Tuscany was a very great center of agriculture. I see a lot of farms, vineyards, and orchards but everything is bleached dry. The fields appear to be burnt by the sun. This represents world-wide famine.

D: *It says, "stones will fall like rain."*

J: He's giving me pictures of hailstorms destroying the food-producing areas of the United States, Russia, Europe, Central America, and Australia. He says there are world weather changes.

D: *Can you tell in what time period this will be taking place?*

J: I'm asking. He says, "Soon enough in your lifetime."

D: *Will it be before the Anti-Christ comes to power?*
J: Yes. He says this is one of the tools the Anti-Christ will use.

Tuscany is a region in north-central Italy. Even today this area is predominantly agricultural and highly productive, with almost no barren land. He is using it here as a symbol for productivity, and not singling out that area as the focus of the quatrain.

CENTURY III-44

Quand l'animal à l'homme domestique,	When the animal tamed by man begins to speak after great efforts
Apres grands peines & sauts viendra parler,	and difficulty, the lightning so harmful to the rod will be taken
De fouldre à vierge sera si malefique,	from the Earth and suspended in the air.
De terre prinse & suspendue en l'air.	

J: He's showing me a picture of a laboratory with monkeys, gorillas and other primates in it. I see scientists teaching them how to talk and ... (*surprised*) talk? Yes, talk! But they're not talking with their mouths. They're talking with their hands by using sign language. This represents the advancement of man's technology. He's showing me things that are taking place now in our time period. How scientists have been able to develop missiles, satellites, and rockets. He says this is what the quatrain applies to. Scientists teaching primates how to speak and communicate represents a spiritual advancement to a degree. The quatrain also represents what we would call technological advancement.
D: *What does the last part mean? "The lightning so harmful to the rod will be taken from the Earth and suspended in the air."*
J: They look like lasers. That's what we would call them. Obviously he doesn't have any idea what a laser is because lasers appear to him as lightning. He's seeing some type of military laser apparatus and also how lasers can be directed at the Earth to supply energy to different areas. So this also represents technological advancement.
D: *The translators say this quatrain refers to wireless communications and electricity.*
J: (*Laugh*) He says, "Oh, no, it's not that." He says the woman who wrote that book was using pure speculation. No, he shows me a laboratory scene where animals are communicating with their keepers in sign language. He says this is very important because it represents a spiritual advancement. You see, in his day animals were persecuted and killed because they were looked upon as dangerous. So he sees this as a wonderful advancement.
D: *You mean this type of animal was thought to be dangerous?*

J: They had *some* monkeys but not many. But animals in general were looked at with contempt. And now, this quatrain represents how man is now trying to understand the animal kingdom by trying to communicate with it.

D: *I know animals were used as beasts of burden in his day.*

J: Yes. He says people beat animals and hurt them. And in this vision he saw people now trying to understand them.

D: *It's easier to understand this quatrain when we see it from his perspective.*

This seemed to be a strange prediction, but when I began my research I found that it had already happened in our time. Some of the advances being made in conversing with primates are discussed in the October 1978 issue of *National Geographic*. In the 1960s Keith and Cathy Hayes worked with a chimpanzee for six years and succeeded in teaching it to orally speak several words. Then, R. Allen and Beatrice Gardner perceived that the chimp's difficulty in acquiring language was not stupidity, but rather an inability to control lips and tongue. They then decided to attempt to teach them the American Sign Language (AMESLAN) which is used by deaf Americans. With incredible patience they succeeded in teaching a chimpanzee to effectively communicate by using sign language. In 1972 Francine Patterson of Stanford University in California, began a similar project with a gorilla. The scientists were surprised to find that the gorilla was calmer and more deliberate in communicating than the chimpanzee. The apes are not only able to converse by use of sign language, but are now using computers with speech synthesizers. This was all totally unexpected and considered quite awesome because, by all accepted concepts of animal and human nature, the apes should not be able to do any of this. Traditionally, such behavior has been considered uniquely human. It would seem that Nostradamus was correct in defining this as a tremendous breakthrough in man's relation with the animal world.

CENTURY III-45

Les cinq estranges entrez dedans le temple	The five foreigners having entered the temple; their blood will desecrate the land. The example made of the Toulousians will be very hard, made by the man who comes to wipe out their laws.
Leur sang viendra la terre prophaner:	
Aux Tholousains sera bien dur example,	
D'un qui viendra les lois exterminer.	

J: This refers to a Jewish temple that is built in Israel. Moslem fanatics will try to desecrate it because it will be built on one of their sacred sites. He says this will be taking place in the 1990s after an earthquake hits the Holy Land. In the process of the quake, the Temple of the Dome of the Rock, which is the Moslem mosque or temple, will be destroyed. As a result a new Jewish temple will be built. And because it's being built on the site of their sacred mosque, Moslem fanatics disguised as Jews will desecrate the temple by committing ritual suicide within it. He says this will be a signal for the advancement of the Anti-Christ in the Arab world. This will be the war cry that will lead up to the battle of Armageddon.

D: *Is this one of the earthquakes that takes place during the time of upheavals?*

J: He says the earthquake will happen before this. Then the temple will be rebuilt. It will be a beautiful replica of the ancient temple of Solomon because the mosque was on the original site of Solomon's temple. It will be built very quickly and the Arabs won't have a chance to reclaim their sacred site. When it's completed it will be desecrated by the blood of infidels. The Jews will be considered infidels. This in turn is like a beacon for the Arab world, and for the leadership of the Anti-Christ which will be very active in the Arab world at that time.

D: *Is this "the man who comes to wipe out their laws"?*

J: That also refers to the Israeli army battling the Anti-Christ's forces.

D: *The translators say this refers to the battle of Toulouse in 1800.*

J: Well, Toulouse is another name for the French who will be involved in this.

D: *Is that what it means by, "the example made of the Toulousians"?*

J: Toulousians were also heretics in his time period, and this relates to that. He says in your time period you don't use the word "heretic," but he does. This is an area of France near where he lives and Toulouse was the center of the ... (*John had difficulty with the next word. It was strange to him.*) Albanians? Albain something. He says the church persecuted these people. The connection is that these other people will be fanatics, posing as French Jewish tourists who will come for the dedication of the temple. But they're not; they're Arabs and Moslems who commit ritual suicide on the steps of the temple to desecrate it.

D: *Then when he uses the word "Toulousians," he actually means "heretics." It's a meaning from his time period.*

J: Yes. He says in his time period Toulouse was a center of heretical ways against the church.

D: *They didn't even come close to that definition because this is something the interpreters didn't know about.*

Not surprisingly, my research revealed that Nostradamus was correct in his remarks about Toulouse. The city is located in southwestern France, and it could have been near him because he had once mentioned that he was living in southern France, a long way from Paris.

By the beginning of the 12th century, the Counts of Toulouse had such power that they controlled the greater part of southern France. During that time the *Albigensian* rebellion against the Church of Rome occurred. (*Albigensian apparently was the word John had trouble with.*) The revolt was supported by the Count of Toulouse, and as a result led to a siege of the city in 1211. Later it became the capital of the royal province of Languedoc, and the seat of the parliament (court) of Toulouse was founded in 1302. This court became known for its stern measures against religious heretics.

It was obvious that this information did not come from any of the minds of the participants in this experiment. It had great importance to Nostradamus because it was part of the history of the area in which he lived, and thus he used it as symbolism. This was also the reason why this translation had never occurred to any of the other interpreters—it was too obscure. Again it shows that the only way to understand the complexity of his predictions is to know the way his mind functioned during his lifetime, and to realize that he used things that were familiar to him. History and philosophy were very important to him.

While this book was being prepared for publication, articles appeared in the newspaper in May 1989 which seemed to apply to this quatrain. It stated that a group of Israeli rabbis were hoping to rebuild the ancient Jewish Temple in Jerusalem where Islamic shrines now stand. Quote: "The plan would place the Temple altar on what some ultra-religious Jews believe is its historical site. The spot is where the gold-topped Dome of the Rock now stands, a Jerusalem landmark and one of the holiest sites of Islam.

"The seemingly irreconcilable claim by Arabs and Jews to the area, known to Jews as the Temple Mount and to Arabs as Haram Al Sharif or 'Noble Enclosure,' is one of the most emotional issues of the Arab-Israeli conflict.

"Any attempt by Israel to reclaim it would be certain to stir tensions throughout the Moslem world. The government does not support the rabbis' plan to rebuild the Temple.

"The Temple Institute's 50 rabbis and artisans have made Temple vessels and produced a computerized blueprint of the shrine in preparation for rebuilding it on the site where it stood until 70 A.D. when the Romans destroyed it.

"In the centuries since the Temple's destruction, the 35-acre rectangular platform has become a sacred Islamic site, marking the spot where the Prophet Mohammed is said to have ascended to heaven. It encompasses the Dome of the Rock and Al Aqsa mosques—considered Islam's holiest places of worship after Mecca and Medina."

The group involved are dedicated to regaining Israeli control of the site and have collected more than $200,000, mostly from American Jews, to finance the project. They also said they would help the Moslems to move the two mosques to Mecca and rebuild them there.

So once again Nostradamus seemed to have seen a possible outcome involving a highly-charged emotional issue between two major religions. It also appeared likely that a temple could be built upon this controversial site.

CENTURY III-46

Le ciel (de Plancus le cité)
nous presage,
Par clers insignes & par
estoilles fixes:
Que de son change subit
s'aproche l'aage,
Ne pour son bien ne pour
ses malefices.

The heavens foretell, concerning the city of Lyons by means of clear skies and fixed stars, that suddenly the time of change approaches, neither for its good nor evil fortune.

J: This quatrain represents the destruction of the city of Lyons at the time of the Earth shift. He says it will be foreordained. Astrologers will know the change is imminent, but many places will not be saved during this time. (*Sadly*) He's sad because he has a strong tie to Lyons in his lifetime, and his beloved Lyons, as he says, will also go.

It must have been heart-breaking for him to see a place he was emotionally attached to destroyed and not be able to do anything, even with the knowledge from his vision.

J: I guess Lyons is one of his favorite cities. I get the impression he was educated there. (*Suddenly*) There's a knock at the door here.

I didn't understand. I thought he meant someone was knocking at the door of the apartment. Normally, noises wouldn't disturb him because he was completely cut off from our world. I looked at the others in the room. They shrugged. There was no disturbance in our time frame, so I continued.

D: *In the original French, instead of saying Lyons, he calls it "Plancus." The interpreters said it means the same thing, "so-called after Lyons' foundation by Lucius Manatius Plancus in 43 B.C.E." Does that make any sense to him?*
J: He says Lyons was an ancient Roman city. At one time it was the capital Roman city of this province.

Again research proves this. That city was the capital of the Segusians, a Gallic tribe, before Cæsar. It was occupied by Munatius Plancus in 43 B.C.E., and became the center of the political rule of Gaul because of its geographical position. This was local history that would only have significance to Nostradamus, but at least the translators were able to make the connection that Plancus referred to Lyons.

J: He says this quatrain also refers to the leadership of the French pope during the times of the Anti-Christ because he will also have a connection to Lyons.
D: *How does it refer to him?*
J: He says that he will be *from* Lyons, and the city will be very important to this French pope. (*Abruptly*) There's a knocking sound again. A

servant girl is coming in right now, and he's telling me to go back into the mirror because he has clients coming in.

D: *Then he won't be able to continue speaking with us?*

J: No. He says, "Please come back another time." He has a surgery to perform. The servant girl is asking him what needs to be done. What type of water needs to be boiled and what knives does he have? He says he doesn't like to perform surgeries. But this child's foot is all torn up, and it looks like it needs to be amputated. It looks very messy. He went out of the room and into the other study. I can't go in there, but I can watch through the open door. He has come back into the room now, and he says I have to leave.

D: *Did the servant girl knock or did she just come in?*

J: She knocked and then came in. He was somewhat upset about that, but the child needs attention right away. It's an emergency. He's run into the other room again, and he's holding the child's foot up in the air. He's screaming at everyone to get this and that. Now it's time for me to leave. I'm in the mirror.

D: *When he asks us to leave, we must obey his requests. That's very important. I don't want to offend him in any way.*

J: I'm out of it. He was nice about it. It just happened so fast.

D: *Well, he didn't know it was going to happen.*

J: No. He was enjoying our visit. He didn't realize what was happening when a whole group of people came rushing in carrying this child. There were four or five people, his wife and his servant girl, and two other men. They all crowded into the room. The child's foot looked like it was already completely torn off. And he said, "You have to leave."

D: *You said he doesn't like to perform surgery.*

J: He doesn't like to do it, but he had to take care of this. He held the child's foot in the air, to quench the flow of blood, I guess. Then he told the servant girl to boil water and his wife to boil his knives. He was commanding everyone to do all these different things and the child was bleeding and screaming at the same time. He was *really* screaming. It was a real emergency. So he said, "Please, let's stop for now." Now I'm out of the mirror and back at the Tapestry Room.

D: *I think we did very well. We were able to begin the translations from your point of view.*

J: (*He shuddered.*) The situation was so panicky.

D: *Well, we have no choice when something like that happens. With all of the excitement I don't think they would have noticed you anyway.*

J: No, no one noticed me, but he was copying down what I was saying and reading my mind. I communicated with him telepathically, and he wrote things down as I was talking. Now I'm back in the Tapestry Room with the guardian, and he says, "Oh! I see why you left now." He can see the event.

D: *Well, the guardian sees why we didn't stay as long as we wanted to.*

J: Nostradamus is out of my field of vision now.

D: *We want to respect his wishes because we are moving into his life unexpectedly at different times. So we want to be careful that we don't interfere.*

Chapter 19

Some Bad Wine

$\mathbb{J}$N THIS SESSION we arrived before Nostradamus.

J: He's coming into the study now and he's sitting down. He knows I'm in the room and he says, "Go to the mirror." When I appear in the mirror, he recognizes me and says he's happy to see me.

D: *Then in the beginning he senses you in the room but he doesn't know who it is.*

J: Yes, he feels a presence. He says, "Most people would think I am a necromancer, and that I call up the spirits of the dead, but I'm not. I know you spirits are eternal."

D: *So he doesn't really know which spirit it is until you look in the mirror?*

J: Yes, this is true, because other people's faces also appear in this mirror.

D: *Is he aware that we are alive in our time period and that we're speaking to him from the future?*

J: He has had a glimpse of what our life is like, but it's so different from his that it seems almost marvelous.

D: *But he knows he's not speaking with the dead.*

J: No. He understands the concept of spirituality. He's saying that he knows it is true there's no such thing as death.

D: *Does he know that we're alive in our time period conducting experiments to contact him?*

J: He says he understands that.

D: *Thus, we have the same limitations that he has.*

I opened the book to continue with the quatrains. I decided not to arrange John's interpretations in chronological order as I had with Brenda's, but to leave them the way they came through. When we contacted Nostradamus through Brenda we would meet in a shadowy special meeting place which was apparently located in another dimension. Thus, we were not personally involved with him. When he was called away or stopped communication we never knew the reason. But while working through John we became involved in a small portion of Nostradamus' life each time we visited him. I thought if I took the translations out of context it might take away from the impacts these visits had on us.

CENTURY III-47

Le vieux monarque dechassé
de son regne
Aux Orients son secours
ira querre:
Pour peur des croix ployera
son enseigne,
En Mitylene ira par port
& par terre.

The old king chased out of his realm will go to seek help from the people of the East: For fear of the crosses he will fold his banner; he will travel to Mitylene by land and sea.

J: He says this quatrain describes the Shah of Iran and the overthrow of his government. He says it's important to realize that any type of fundamentalist fascism will have effects upon people.

Nostradamus had told us through Brenda that if the quatrain predicted events that had occurred in our past he wished to skim over their meaning in order to spend time on the ones relevant to our immediate future. He re-emphasized this by repeating the same instructions through John. He would decide which ones he considered important for us to know more about.

The interpretation of this next quatrain seemed to be so controversial to me that I wrestled within myself about whether or not it should be included. I promised Nostradamus that I would be as true to his interpretations as possible, and that I wouldn't personally censor them. So I decided to leave it in, even though it doesn't represent my beliefs, and I hope it will prove to be untrue.

CENTURY III-48

Sept cens captifs estachez
rudement,
Pour la moitié meurtrir,
donné le sort:
Le proche espoir viendra
si promptement,
Mais non si tost qu'une
quinziesme mort.

Seven hundred captives roughly bound, the lots are drawn for half to be murdered; sudden hope will come so quickly, but not fast enough for about fifteen dead.

J: Could you please repeat that, he said. He's writing these down.
D: (Laugh) *I've often suspected that.* (I repeated it.)
J: He says this quatrain refers to the AIDS crisis. He's showing me a lot of different pictures in the mirror that depict how the disease began. He's showing me pictures of monkeys in the trees in Africa. A monkey

bite has spread an infection which is a mutation of some type of disease among monkeys. I see a woman being bit. She wasn't concerned about the monkey bite because they live in the wild. The disease mutated, changing inside of her, and she died very quickly. It is similar to rabies. She transmitted it to her husband because they had sex. He also died, but not before he had spread it through sex with other people. It's a big chain reaction. Then I see people lined up and being given money for their blood and plasma. They're going to a blood mobile in Africa. I see laboratories. This blood is being used in biological products, like medicines, and the disease has contaminated these products. It hasn't come from the blood so much as it has from the plasma and unsterile instruments. This is how it has spread. He's showing me how it affects the endocrine system. It will become a worldwide disease that will continue to spread. Then I see a lot of centers in the United States where it has been implanted among the people.

D: *What do you mean?*

J: I see people who are being tested. ... Ooh, I don't like what I see.

D: *Will it bother you to talk about it?*

J: Well, I see people who are at experiment stations, and drugs are being given to them to see their reactions. I see one man who is very effeminate-looking being given the drug. He in turn has gotten money from this experiment and is out partying with it. He's enjoying himself and spreading this disease. They *gave* him the disease! Seven hundred people were inoculated with a chemical ... or had a chemical reaction. And this base core group of 700 have since come in contact with others, spreading the disease until it becomes an epidemic.

D: *So that's why he wrote, "Seven hundred captives roughly bound, the lots are drawn for half to be murdered." Does he want to elaborate on "inoculated"? Who inoculated them?*

J: (*Softly and hesitantly.*) Your own government, he said.

I was shocked by this unexpected answer.

D: *Can he say why they would have done this?*

J: He says to look at religious intolerance.

D: *That seems to be a drastic thing to do.*

J: He says that's true.

D: *Didn't they know that it might spread?*

J: He said they were all paid volunteers who were tested with a new chemical they thought would treat hepatitis, and as a result this experiment went off the edge. The government believed they could contain it.

D: *Will doctors or scientists ever come up with a cure for AIDS?*

J: He said it will be very difficult since science created and hybridized this disease. Now I see the images go back to the monkey bite and the blood being used in scientific research. They mutated the disease and injected other people with it. "Fifteen dead" was his anagram for 15 years. He says 15 years will elapse between the first case until a cure is found. By that time it will be comparable to the plague of his time. It will wipe out a lot of people. This is *terrible!* It's genocide! It's gotten out of control, and that's why it's affecting more people. It wasn't supposed to spread; it was only supposed to affect certain groups of people.

D: *I'm trying to understand this. Was it done under the pretense of inoculating people for hepatitis or did they actually inoculate them with another virus?*

J: He says they were inoculated with chemicals as paid volunteers and chemical reactions left them very open to the disease.

D: *Did the government realize it was going to have this effect?*

J: (*Quietly*) Yes, the government realized. It was planned from the start.

D: *I thought you meant that it was an accident.*

J: I don't think I need to talk about this any more.

I didn't like the sound of it, so I wasn't anxious to pursue it further.

D: *All right. It's a touchy subject in our time. I wonder if I should even mention it. What does he think?*

J: He says that by the time your book comes out, this information will be common knowledge.

This information bothered me a great deal and I was anxious to move on to the next quatrain. In this work with the great seer I was constantly hearing things I would rather remain ignorant of.

This interpretation with its wild accusations against our own government seemed too horrible to consider until I happened to mention it to a group of people. One young man said it might not be such an absurd idea after all. He showed me a 1989 article in *Wildfire* magazine that seemed to confirm everything Nostradamus had revealed to John.

The article was condensed from a book published in 1988, *AIDS and the Doctors of Death: An Inquiry into the Origin of the AIDS Epidemic,* by Alan Cantwell, Jr., M.D. He is considered an expert in the field of cancer and AIDS microbiology. In his previous book, *AIDS: The Mystery and the Solution,* he was convinced that AIDS was merely a highly aggressive form of cancer. He changed his mind when he discovered the research of Dr. Robert Strecker. He is now convinced that the AIDS virus and epidemic were not accidents of nature, but were the result of a genetically engineered virus being deliberately unleashed. He believes the disease was created by splicing or mixing two different viruses together; which, when introduced into human beings, were capable of producing a "new" disease. He cited the experimental hepatitis B vaccine trials which began in New York City in the late 1970s and used gay men as volunteers. He said the *commercial* vaccine was safe, but that this was an *experimental* vaccine, and was not intended for the general public. Strecker said it was not a coincidence that the first cases of AIDS in the U.S. were discovered in Manhattan immediately following their experiments. As the trials were conducted in other cities into the 1980s the discovery of cases also followed there. As the number of cases mounted, the physicians were convinced they were seeing a new fatal disease. In his book Dr. Cantwell presents proof that the new AIDS virus did not exist in America before 1978 when the experiments began.

Dr. Cantwell says that Robert Gallo came up with the theory that the virus originated in central Africa in African green monkeys. The story said the monkey AIDS virus "jumped species," entered the black African population and then spread to Haiti. It was supposed to have spread from there to New York by gays who had had contact with infected men in Haiti.

Dr. Cantwell said he had been bothered by the idea that a virus could attack only gay men. It was impossible for such a thing to biologically happen, and yet it did happen. This made him suspicious that he might have stumbled onto the awful truth that the powerful culprit behind this was our own government, since these experiments were financed by grants from the Center for Disease Control (CDC), the National Institutes of Health (NIH), and the National Institute of Allergy and Infectious Diseases.

The entire project was under the control of Dr. Wolf Szmuness, a scientist who had defected from the Soviet Union. He had also conducted a hepatitis research project in Africa in 1973 where he used the Senegalese Army to secure blood specimens. This was prior to the experiment in New York City. Strecker believes there was foul play in Africa and Haiti, as well as in our own country and that the disease was "helped" along in those countries. He says, "Only a fool would fail to recognize the African 'connection' to AIDS." He thinks this connection involves a lot more than just green monkeys.

After finding this amazing correlation, I decided to include it in my book. It's comforting to find supportive evidence for these strange visions. I will leave it at this, allowing others to find their own conclusions. I have done my job as reporter.

CENTURY III-50

La republique de la grande cité	The people's government of the
A grand rigeur ne voudra	great city will not consent to severe
consentir:	repression. The king, summoned
Roi sortir hors par trompette cité.	by trumpets to leave the city,
L'eschelle ay mur, la cité repentir.	the ladder at the wall, the city
	will repent.

J: He says this quatrain refers to America and New York specifically. It concerns difficulties in the economy of the island. He's showing me a picture of New York and people are really crazy in the streets. It looks like the demonstrations that took place during the Vietnam war years.

He says it's a financial situation and that many of the businesses will go through a *big* change. He says some physical changes to the land mass could also be necessary. He's now telling me that it's not my problem; that it will work itself out.

D: *Is this in our future?*

J: He says it's in the very near future. It will happen in the next two years.

Could he have been seeing the stock market crash that occurred at the end of October 1987?

CENTURY III-52

En la campaigne sera si longue pluie, *Et en la Pouille si grand siccité:* *Coq verra l'Aigle, l'œsle mal accompli* *Par Lyon mise sera en extremité.*	In Campania there will be rain for so long and such a great drought in Apulia; the cock will see the Eagle, its wing badly finished put into difficulties by the Lion.

J: He says there are a lot of astrological symbols in this quatrain. Leo is prominent, and the sign of the cock. He says this predicts the beginning of a world drought. The drought will start in Campania, which is a segment of Italy, and it will spread around the world. The Campania area is the breadbasket of Europe, he says. A lot of food grows in its orchards, but there's not enough fresh water to take care of these plants.

Campania and Apulia are both located in Italy. They are both major agricultural areas which produce large quantities of food for export. It's interesting that he mentioned Apulia because the only crops that are grown there are those that can resist long dry spells or have short, early growing seasons. I think he is indicating a drought that will be severe enough to affect even an area like Apulia which is used to growing crops without much water. This is interesting symbolism.

J: There might be a nuclear power plant accident in northern Italy that will poison the land because he's showing me a picture of a nuclear power plant.

D: *What is the symbolism of the eagle?*

J: The eagle represents Scorpio. I'm getting a picture of a horoscope in my mind. He says that planets in square are negative or have discordant energy. *Now* I understand. He says part of this quatrain has already happened, but it happened very recently. He says because the water of the Rhine River was polluted, it will eventually affect the agriculture in part of Europe: Switzerland, Italy, and Yugoslavia. He says the water was poisoned and contaminated. This took place when Scorpio and Leo were not in good aspect to each other.

D: *Is the cock an astrological sign?*

J: No, not traditionally. He says, "I used the cock because there will be warnings before this takes place. Just as the cock, the bird of the morning, tells us that morning is here, there will be warnings. But people won't listen to them." The astrological symbols are the scorpion-eagle and the Leo-lion.

D: *"Its wing badly finished put into difficulties." Can you get any dates from the horoscope he's showing you there?*

J: Hmm. The dates I get indicate it might have happened sometime last year or the year before (1986). He says this will affect the soil and the ground water, and will poison the whole Campania area which will lead to drought later in the 1990s.

D: *The translators have interpreted those symbols to mean different countries.*

J: (*Smiling*) He says that's not true.

CENTURY III-54

L'un des plus grands fuira aux Espaignes	One of the great men will flee to Spain which will bleed with a great wound thereafter. Troops will pass over the high mountains devastating everything, then he will reign in peace.
Qu'en longue playe apres viendra saigner:	
Passant copies par les hautes montaignes,	
Devastant tout & puis en paix regner.	

J: He says this quatrain refers to the coming changes. I'm trying to get his idea across to you. He's showing me a picture of ... what is it? (*He seemed to be examining something.*) Some type of machine or gadget.

D: *What does it look like?*

J: It's very small and boxy. (*Pause*) I can't make sense out of what he's trying to explain. He says there will be saboteurs who will use this instrument to communicate with each other even though the information system knows everything about them. They'll be part of a hidden operation.

D: *The translators thought it dealt with General Franco and the Spanish Civil War in the 1930s.*

J: He says it could apply to that as well, but it also applies to the future. He says there are partisans who will do battle against the Anti-Christ and they will use this machine to interfere with information lines.

This apparently was referring to the Anti-Christ's control of the computer systems and the fact that people couldn't do anything without being monitored. So the underground will invent a jamming device which will allow them to bypass this system and have contact with each other.

CENTURY III-55

En l'an qu'un œil en France regnera,
La court sera à un bien facheux trouble:
Le grand de Blois son ami tuera,
Le regne mis en mal & doubte double.

In the year that France has a one-eyed king the court will be in very great trouble. The great man from Blois will kill his friend, the kingdom put into difficulty and double doubt.

J: He says there will arise a French President with a lazy or weak eye. During his stay in power it will be very difficult for people to grow spiritually. Many people will be persecuted during this time.

D: *The translators thought the quatrain referred to Henry II. He was a king who was wounded in the eye.*

J: No, this is a president who will come to power and damage France's economy by getting her into things she doesn't want to be involved with. This will happen within the next 10 years. (In Volume III there are two more quatrains [Nos. VI-3 and VII-34] that seem to refer to this same President.)

CENTURY III-56

Montauban, Nismes, Avignon & Besier,
Peste tonnere & gresle à fin de Mars:
De Paris pont, Lyon mur, Montpellier,
Depuis six cens & sept vingts trois pars.

Montauban, Nîmes, Avignon and Béziers, plague, lightning and hail at the end of March. Of the bridge at Paris, the wall at Lyons and Montpellier, since six hundred and seven score three pairs.

J: (*He correctly pronounced each name after me.*) This quatrain refers to a time in March when France will be at war. It will be a very cruel time for his beloved France to go through. He says it refers to World War II, and how easy it was for the Germans to take over the country. He uses the word "Allemande" (phonetic: *Al-le-man-day*).

D: *What does it mean?*

J: I guess it has something to do with the Germans. He says the word like he's going to spit it.

I looked it up later and the French word for Germany is Allemagne. It's similar to the word he used although it doesn't have the same pronunciation. In CENTURY III-78 (interpreted in Chapter 19, "The Heart Attack"), Nostradamus used "d'Alemaigne" to refer to Germans. Is this the same word that John was unfamiliar with?

I also found that in ancient Rome, Germany was composed of many tribes that made war against the neighboring countries. One of these groups was called the Alemanni, a confederation located on the upper Rhine and Danube rivers. In 357 C.E. (A.D.) the Roman emperor Julian [the Apostate] had to combat them when they broke through to Lyons. He later fought them in their own country. Since Lyons was one of Nostradamus' favorite cities, was he making a comparison between two similar events in history? Was the word he used "Alemanni" or "Allemagne," or an anagram symbolizing both?

J: He says in his time the Germans were not united. They were many different independent states and they will unite into one powerful state.

D: *What do the numbers mean, "Six hundred and seven score three pairs"?*

J: This refers to bombs. The Germans will threaten to bomb most of France's cities and annihilate them. They were going to blow up the main Paris bridge. This is why the French capitulated to the Germans, so their cities wouldn't be destroyed.

D: *The translators tried to convert those numbers into dates and had no luck with it. They said it was impossible because there were too many possible combinations.*

J: He says it refers to the number of bombs that were to be dropped on each city. They are symbolic numbers indicating a large amount of anything.

CENTURY III-57

Sept fois changer verrez gent
  Britannique
Taintz en sang en deux cents
  nonante an:
Franche non point par
  appuy Germanique,
Aries doubte son pole
  Bastarnien.

Seven times you will see the British nation change, dyed in blood for two hundred ninety years. Not at all free through German support, Aries fears for the protectorate of Poland.

J: Again, this quatrain refers to World War II, and he's showing me a picture of Great Britain teamed with France to protect Poland during the war.

D: *With the mention of Poland, I thought it probably had something to do with World War II.*

J: It was the downfall of the British Empire, he said. Now he's pointing to a map in his study, and he says, "Now no more ... no more power."

D: *After the war?*

J: Yes, he says so.

D: *Is that what two hundred ninety years means?*

J: He says they've had power for a long time.

England didn't begin to acquire the land that would become the British Colonial Empire until the early 17th century (the 1600s) when they began extended sea voyages. Land acquisition often involved wars and indeed was "dyed in blood." Their empire expanded until it circled the globe, then dwindled after World War II when they granted independence to various holdings. This would be roughly the 290 years that Nostradamus saw. Ms. Cheetham correctly interpreted this quatrain in her book.

CENTURY III-58

*Aupres du Rhin des
  Montaignes Noriques,
Naistra un grand de gens
  trop tard venu.
Qui defendra Saurome
  & Pannoniques,
Qu'on ne sçaura qu'il
  sera devenu.*

Near the Rhine from the Norican mountains will be born a great man of the people, come too late. He will defend Poland and Hungary and they will never know what became of him.

J: He says this quatrain refers to Ogmios, the Celtic Hercules, and where he will come from. People won't know of him because he will be a resistance leader during the troubled days of the Anti-Christ.

D: *The quatrain says, "they will never know what became of him."*

J: He says that refers to when he goes underground. After he's done what he's supposed to do, he doesn't want to draw attention to himself. He'll live the rest of his days in peace and serenity.

This quatrain described the fate of another one of our main characters.

CENTURY III-59

*Barbare empire par le tiers
  usurpé,
Le plus grand part de son
  sang mettre à mort:
Par mort senile par lui le
  quart frappé,
Pour peur que le sang par le
  sang ne soit mort.*

The barbarian empire is usurped by a third, the greater part of its people being put to death. The fourth man, senile, struck dead by his country, fears lest the line of his blood be dead.

J: This quatrain refers to the great Oriental nation of China and the different forms of government it has had in its history: emperors, mandarins, and now ... he says communalism, but he means communism.

It's interesting that he used that word. The definitions of communism and communalism are so close that apparently to his mind they were interchangeable.

From Webster's *New World Dictionary:*

COMMUNISM: 1A. A theory or system of the ownership of all property by the community as a whole. 1B. A theory or system of the ownership of the means of production (and distribution) by the community, with all members sharing in the work and the products. 2A. A political movement for establishing such a system. 2B. The doctrines, methods, *etc.* of the Communist parties. 3. Loosely, *communalism.*

COMMUNALISM: A theory or system of government in which communes have virtual autonomy (or self-government) within a federated state.

Our modern-day minds would not have used this term because we normally don't hear communism referred to by any other name.

J: Through all the variations of its leadership, the people of China have experienced a lot of devastation.

D: *Is he referring to communism when he says, "The fourth man, senile"?*

J: The fourth man represents both communism and the man who will be premier of China around this time. There will be more difficulties for China and she again will lose people. The word senile refers to both the state of the government and the premier who will probably be elderly by that time.

Note: When this was translated in 1987 there was no indication that the people desired a new form of government or that violence would erupt in China in May and June of 1989. I think this quatrain might refer to these events, and the nation's loss of people as it goes through a transition. In this reference, the line, "the fourth man, senile, struck dead by his country, fears lest the line of his blood be dead," would be most appropriate. It could signify a leader being killed symbolically and fearing that the form of government he represents will not continue. This quatrain is similar to CENTURY II-47 which was interpreted in Chapter 5, in which the leader of China appears to be symbolically murdered.

CENTURY III-61

La grand band & secte crucigere,	The great following of the sect of
Se dressera en Mesopotamie:	the cross will arise in Mesopotamia.
Du proche fleuve compagnie	Light company of the nearby river
legiere,	who will regard such a law as
Que telle loi tiendra pour	inimical.
ennemie.	

J: He predicts that there will be a band of Christians who will unite in the near east during the time of the Anti-Christ. These people will be involved in what we would call the "resistance movement."

CENTURY III-62

Proche del duero par mer
  Cyrrene close,
Viendra percer les grands
  monts Pyrenées:
La main plus courte & sa
  percee gloze,
A Carcassonne conduira
  ses menées.

Near the Douro closed by the
Cyrenian sea he will come to cross
the great mountains of the
Pyrenees. The shortest hand and
his opening noted he will take his
followers to Carcassonne.

J: He's writing this down. Could you please repeat it again?
D: *The translators have written in their book that they consider some of these lines to be untranslatable.*

I began repeating it, and he asked for the spelling of Cyrenian Sea.

D: *It's spelled differently in the French, C-y-r-r-e-n-e. Is that how he would pronounce it?*
J: He pronounces it like the word Syrian.
D: *It's not spelled like we would spell Syrian today.*
J: No. It represents Turkey. The word Cyrenian refers to the Anti-Christ's invasion of Europe through Spain and Greece. The Anti-Christ will take the possession of Cyprus away from the Turks when he first rises to power. He will also take over the ancient town of Carcassonne which is in southern France.

Could Cyrrene also be an anagram for Cyprus because the spelling is similar?

Carcassonne was known as the Old Cité in Nostradamus' day, so John was correct when he heard Nostradamus call it the "ancient town." This town also controls a major route in southern France; the easiest way from the Bay of Biscay to the Mediterranean. Is this the meaning of the line: "The shortest hand and his opening noted. He will take his followers to Carcassone." This could be why the Anti-Christ considers it a strategic point.

CENTURY III-64

Le chef de Perse remplira
  grande Olchade,
Classe Frireme contre gent
  Mahometique:
De Parthe, & Mede, & piller
  les Cyclades,
Repos long temps aux grand
  port Ionique.

The Persian leader will fill up great
Spain. A fleet of triremes against
the Mohammedans from Parthia
and Media, he will pillage the
Cyclades: then a long wait in the
great Ionian harbor.

J: This quatrain describes how the Anti-Christ will battle both the Mohammedans and the Islamic people in Iran and Iraq. It also tells of the war front in Europe which is near Greece. He said that's what the names represent.

Parthia and Media are ancient names for portions of the Persian Empire, the Cyclades are Greek islands, and the Ionian harbor also refers to Greece. This appears to be another piece of the puzzle, rounding out what we already know about the Anti-Christ's early campaign.

It was difficult for the translators to understand these quatrains because they were not aware of the larger picture that Nostradamus had shown us. They were looking at these quatrains as individual pieces.

J: (*Abruptly*) He's saying, "I have had enough." He appears to be melancholy today. (*Smiling*) Oh, I understand now. He's not feeling well. He says he drank some spoiled wine the evening before, and he's had a dull headache all day. He's taking things for it but he's just not feeling up to par. He says, "I think I am going to have to rest. I will leave now."

D: *These meetings take a lot out of him, too, I believe.*

J: He says, "I thought this draft that I took earlier would help me, but it's doing me no good. These questions you have are very important for *myself* as well as you. But I've got a headache. It hurts! *Se mal de ter* (phonetic)." And he points to his head and groans. (The French dictionary defines headache as: *Mal de tête.* Does this sound like "ter" when pronounced by a Frenchman?)

D: *Maybe you could help him feel better. Are you allowed to do that?*

J: No. He's very reluctant to have people from our dimension touch him. He doesn't like it.

D: *Okay. I thought maybe you could give him some energy.*

J: No. He says he's got some herbs in the other room that he's going to brew and take with some wine. (*John said afterward that Nostradamus used opium in this draft.*) Then he's going to take a nap. He thought the wine he drank last evening was aged, but actually it was spoiled. He says, "Please come back again. Hopefully I won't have this same *mal de ter.*" He's gone into the other room and shut the door and I'm back in the mirror.

Once again we had been abruptly dismissed with no choice but to come back to our present world.

Chapter 20

We Come at Night

J: I'm in the mirror. Nostradamus looks like he's drawing up horoscope charts. He's got ... it looks like a compass. It's not like ours in the 20th century. It looks like a very crude compass made of wood. Wait a minute! ... I don't think it's a horoscope; I think he's drawing a design. It's got circles, squares, and triangles ... but now he sees my face in the mirror, and he says, "Oh! You're here." He gave a surprised laugh. He's in a very good mood today. I can tell he's been very deep in thought. I'm asking him what he's doing with the designs and he says it has something to do with the arcs of different planetary energies. He's been working on the arc of energy emanating from Mars, and contemplating how it is affecting Europe at this time.

D: *In his time?*

J: Right. He says this arc of energy has caused some friction. Many of the nations, city states, and countries are embroiled in numerous wars. Since Mars rules war he wanted to know if Mars is emanating a lot of energy in this area of the world at this time.

D: *How does he know about these arcs of energy?*

J: He says he has studied many of the masters of old, like Ptolemy and Kricinimos. (*This was a difficult name to transcribe phonetically. It sounded like Krick-in-imos, Trick-in-imos, or possibly Kritimos.*) And many, many books have been made available to him. So he knows quite a bit about the astrology of the ancient Greek and Roman period.

When I did my research, I found that Claudius Ptolemy was the last great Greek astronomer who flourished in Alexandria during the 2d century C.E (A.D.). He contributed greatly to the survival of astrology. His most famous books, the *Almagest* and *Tetrabiblos,* were standard textbooks of astrology and astronomy for 1200 years after his time. This name was familiar to John, but not the other one. It's difficult working with transcriptions of tape recordings, and I must do the best I can with phonetic spellings of strange words. I searched through the encyclopedias but I could find no one whose name was even close to the phonetic pronunciation of Kricinimos or Tricinimos. I had given up until quite by chance I came across a name in *Origins of Astrology* by John Lindsay. I was trying to verify the old horoscope designs that John had seen Nostradamus using when the name "Kritodemos" jumped out at me. He was supposedly one of the pioneers and founders of astrology. Lindsay wrote that he was one of the very first Greeks to directly use Babylonian astrology or draw upon Babylonian sources. He was cited by other Greek astrologers and considered to be one of the most important authorities, but after his time period he was mostly ignored by later authors. This may explain his obscurity and the reason I couldn't find him in other reference books. It would also explain why a modern astrologer like John wouldn't recognize his name. He was quite familiar to Nostradamus, because he had studied the originators of astrology and had especially delved into the Babylonian style. This proved to be another example of a little-known fact that could not have come from our modern minds.

The Greeks applied astrology to all levels of the material world and assigned each sign of the zodiac to rule a part of the body. Medical astrology was so widely accepted that even in medieval times it was not considered possible for a physician to practice without the knowledge and use of astrology. After the fall of the Roman Empire, the Arabs developed divinatory astrology into a science. Astrology was taught in the universities of Europe from the 12th through 16th centuries. Medical astrology became mixed with divinatory astrology, and after a period of time became allied more closely with magic. It was not discredited until the 17th–18th centuries, after the time of Nostradamus. This explains why the practice was not condemned by the church during his time. It was an accepted part of a physician's training.

The invention of movable type resulted in the printing of books in the 1400s and permitted the publication of ephemerides and trigonometrical tables so the astrologer no longer had to know astronomy and higher mathematics to practice his art. Thus, the door was opened to anyone who could read, add, and subtract. The people who opposed astrology during Nostradamus' time were against unscrupulous astrologers more than the practice itself. Nostradamus apparently practiced it in the accepted way, but he also explored its other uses which was frowned upon by the church as dappling in magic. This was probably the part that he tried to keep hidden.

I found that in Sumeria and Babylonia records extend back to about 3000 B.C.E. At first astrology consisted solely of the observation and tabulation of solilunar data, and using that to predict the time and circumstances of their recurrence. These efforts were truly scientific in the modern sense of the word, and were followed by attempts to correlate the data with weather conditions. It was then a short step to connect the correlation with occurrences such as famine, natural disasters, war and peace, and victory and defeat. The next step carried it into the lives and fortunes of the rulers. *Collier's Encyclopedia* says, "The Babylonians' contribution to astronomical data is unquestioned. By the second century B.C.E. they were able to construct, in advance, ephemerides (tables of planetary positions in the signs, heliacal risings and settings, and times and places of conjunctions and oppositions of the planets.) Perhaps the major contribution of the Babylonians to later thought rests upon their conclusion, drawn from the invariable cycles of the celestial bodies, that the world is eternal." It seems entirely possible that Nostradamus had access to this type of ancient data, and that he had integrated it into the personal book he said he used to make his predictions. He said some of the information came from the Babylonians and dated back to about 3000 B.C.E.

D: *I thought it would be difficult to measure an arc of energy if you can't see it.*

J: He says there are formulas written by the ancient astrologers, but a lot of these works will be destroyed. Many were already destroyed when the Alexandrian library was burned. But some of this information was carried on by the people of the Arab world. He has talked with these people. "Even though I am a Christian and they are considered infidels, I am considered an infidel by them. We are men of science and we exchange ideas." In fact, he made a special trip to Malta to meet with some of these men.

D: *Was this when he was younger?*

J: He said this took place early in his life, but he was an adult at the time. He doesn't want to talk any more about that, but this is where he's gotten some of his information.

D: *I was curious about how he knew of these things.*

J: He says insatiable curiosity is important, but some things are best left unlearned or unknown. He says, "Enough!" He doesn't want to discuss it anymore.

Malta was under Muslim rule after the Arabs conquered it in 870 until 1090. In 1530 (the time of Nostradamus) the Holy Roman Emperor granted Malta to the Knights of St. John of Jerusalem. At first broadly international in its membership, the order soon became predominantly French. I think it would have been entirely possible for Nostradamus to meet with Arab astrologers on that island since there were probably many Arabs still living there. John thought it would have been unusual for Nostradamus to do this, and something he definitely would have kept secret. It probably would have caused trouble with the church if the Inquisition knew about it, and this might explain his hesitancy to discuss it.

J: He says he would like to hear more quatrains, but just a few today. He says it's important that we really think. He's been in a very deep contemplative state and his mind is full of facts and figures.

D: *Okay, then we'll take him away from his work for a little while. Let me know when he wants to stop.*

CENTURY III-66

Le grand Baillif d'Orleans
   mis à mort,
Sera par un de sang vindicatif.
De mort merite ne mourra,
   ne par sort,
Des pieds & mains mal le
   faisoit captif.
	The great Bailiff of Orleans is
	condemned to death by one
	vindictive for blood. He will not
	die a deserved death, nor one by
	jurors; they will keep him captive
	inefficiently (bound) by his hands
	and feet.

J: He says this quatrain deals with ancient history. It's not *ancient* history, but the events occur a hundred years before your present time. He says in French history, a military man was incarcerated wrongly because he was Jewish, and this was called the Dreyfus affair. He says he put "bailiff" in this quatrain indicating a man of power because this man was in the military. He's showing me a picture in the black mirror of military men in dress uniforms. He says this prophecy has already been fulfilled.

D: All right. We don't want to devote much time to past events.

I found that the Dreyfus Affair did occur about a hundred years in our past, in 1894. The military man, Captain Alfred Dreyfus, faced the prejudice of anti-Semitism at his trial and court martial because he was a Jew. This complicated case had a powerful influence upon the history of French socialism, and it weakened France in its role as a European and world state.

CENTURY III-67

Une nouvelle secte de
   Philosophes,
Mesprisant mort, or,
   honneurs & richesses:
Des monts Germains ne
   seront limitrophes,
A les ensuivre auront
   appuy & presses.
	A new set of philosophers despising
	death, gold, honors and riches will
	not be limited by the mountains of
	Germany, in their following will be
	crowds and support.

J: He says this quatrain refers to what we would call New Age philosophy. A very famous man in the metaphysical or New Age movement was born in Germany. This man was a spearhead of a whole new movement which will take us into the golden age that we refer to as the Age of Aquarius. The movement came out of Germany, but this man's philosophy will connect with the whole world. His ideas are very spiritually motivated and his followers will use them to develop other philosophies that will blend together as a New Age thought system. He's showing me a very beautiful cathedral. He's saying that as this man's spiritual energy grew, the darkness of Nazism also grew, in balance. The man was Rudolf Steiner. He says this quatrain refers to events that have already occurred, but these events influence your time period, the 20th century.

D: *The translators think this quatrain refers to the development of the Protestant sects.*

J: He laughed and said, "*All* churches are into money and honors. No, this has nothing to do with the Protestant sects." Again, he says, your translators are warping his quatrains with their own personal interests. He says, "Begone! Begone with them!" (*Laugh*) He says this quatrain refers to this spiritual leader. He has pointed this man out and he says, "As the Lords of Darkness were beginning to manifest through Nazism, they had to be kept in check with the Lords of Light manifesting through Rudolf Steiner's ability. He came from the mountains of Germany, and his philosophy has grown all over the world."

Rudolf Steiner did exist although I had never heard of him. I thought I was familiar with New Age thought, but this name was new to me. He died in 1925 and is described as an Austrian social philosopher. He lectured and wrote extensively. According to the encyclopedia, "He was the founder of anthroposophy, a doctrine explaining life in terms of man's inner nature and positing a faculty for spiritual perception and pure thinking independent of the senses."

CENTURY III-69

Grand excercite conduict par jouvenceau,	The great army led by a young man, will come to give itself up into the
Se viendra rendre aux mains des ennemis:	enemy's hands. But the old man born to the half pig will make
Mais la vieillard nay au demi-porceau,	Châlon and Mâcon into friends.
Fera Chalon & Mascon estre amis.	

J: (*He corrected my pronunciation.*) He says this quatrain again predicts the past. It refers to France surrendering to the Germans during World War II. I see that the half-pig represents Nazism to him. He says they were swine, swinish. The young man refers to all the noble young men of the French army who had to leave France during this time. He says it was a very bad time in French history. The older men who gave up also allowed the younger men to give up, creating a feeling of dishonor. He has a tear in his eye.

D: *That's because it will be a dark time for France in his future.*

J: Yes. He's very saddened about this.

CENTURY III-70

La grande Bretagne comprinse l'Angelterre, *Viendra par eaux si haut à inonder* *La ligue neufue d'Ausonne fera guerre,* *Que contre eux ils se viendront bander.*	Great Britain, including England, will be covered by very deep floods. The new league in Ausonne will make war so that they will ally against them.

J: He says this quatrain refers to a time in your future. Because of the Earth shift changes, Great Britain and most of the British Isles will be inundated by water. The British people will be flocking to high places in the Pennine mountains, as well as the mountains in middle Ireland, which will all be very small islands. They will be looking for more land, and they will move to territory around the Alps of France. They'll have connections with those people and while there may be a bit of a difference in life-styles and opinions, a lot of them will relocate to this area because their land will not be able to support them after the Earth change.

CENTURY III-71

Ceux dans les isles de longtemps asseigez, *Prendront vigeur force contre ennemis:* *Ceux par dehors mors de faim profligez,* *En plus grand faim que jamais seront mis.*	Those besieged in the islands for a long time will take strong measures against their enemies. Those outside, overcome, will die of hunger, by such starvation as has never occurred before.

J: He says this quatrain refers to many things. It refers to events that have already taken place in your time span. For instance when the Japanese took over different islands in the Pacific basin they starved people to support their war machine. But it also refers to a time in the future, when due to the Earth shift, a lot of land masses will become islands. At that time, people will have to learn how to use whatever resources are available to them to find food. As a result, a lot of people will starve; there also will be a lot of disease.

D: *The translators say it refers to the blockade of Britain during World War II and the concentration camps.*

J: No. He says they had the right idea, but the wrong place.

D: *They're half a world away.*

J: Right. He's showing me a picture of the globe. He says not many people in his time understand that there are other countries outside of Europe. They know of places like Cathay and India, but they don't realize other places exist, for instance, the Philippines and the Pacific Basin. New wonders are coming into being. Some have written about these new lands, but they're still fresh in the European mind. He says to read one more and then he has to retire. He says it's late at night now ... for him. He's writing these things as we are talking, and he says he needs his sleep. I'm looking out of the little window and there's a moon. He says, "I've been in my chamber now for many hours of the night." He's showing me a candlestick with different notches in it that represent hours. He says, "This is now moving into the eleventh hour of the day. It's time for my rest."

D: *We never know what time it is when we come because for us, it's the middle of the day. All right. We'll do just one more then.*

CENTURY III-72

Le bon vieillard tout vif enseveli,	The good old man is buried while
Pres du grand fleuve par	still alive, near a great river through
fausse souspeçon:	false suspicion. The newcomer is
Le nouveau vieux de	old, ennobled by wealth, having
richesse ennobli,	taken all the ransom gold on
Prins a chemin tout l'or	the way.
de la rançon.	

J: He says this quatrain refers to the killing of the great one who is the pope. The pope in the end times will be succeeded by a pope who rules the treasury and the finances of the Vatican. But the pope who would have been a great leader and a spiritual teacher will be stricken down early.

D: *Is this the pope we have at the present time?*

J: No. He says, "It's within your time span but ... I can't give you an exact date. But it will take place soon enough within the next two decades." This pope will be killed by his own kind.

D: *Is that all he wants to do with the quatrains?*

J: He says, "Thank you. It's time for me to go." He's getting up now and blowing out the candles in the room. He blew out the hour candle. He bows his head and says, "Please, we will meet again. In peace." He's leaving. He's gone out of the door.

D: *We have no way of knowing what time it is in his world when we appear like this. He's probably very tired if he's been in there for that long.*

J: Yes, he's been in his study for many hours. He was in contemplation a lot today. I'm out of his study now and back in the Tapestry Room.

This same thing used to happen while working with Brenda. Often Nostradamus would suddenly cut short our session. Then, we never knew the reason because we weren't directly connected with his life. These interruptions did not occur because Brenda or John were physically tired and wanted to stop the session, because after Nostradamus would leave we would continue to work on something else for the remainder of the time we had left.

Chapter 21

The Heart Attack

THIS SESSION WAS UNUSUAL because it marked the beginning of a strange sequence of events. We began coming into Nostradamus' life at different times. He was different ages, sometimes young, sometimes old. Sometimes he knew us, sometimes he did not. It was often confusing and we had no choice but to go along with it and allow the golden thread to deposit us where it wanted. I wondered if it was being controlled by the guardian because it certainly wasn't being controlled by us.

I considered arranging the quatrains in this book into some kind of chronological order, as I did in Volume One. But I thought if I did that it would take away from the sense of adventure, the sense of the unexpected we felt every time we had a session. We never knew what we would find as we came through the mirror.

J: He's writing in his book.
D: *Does he know you're there yet?*
J: No. I'm going to the mirror. "I didn't call for you today."
D: *Is that what he said?*
J: Yes. He said he's working on a codex of symbols, and that he didn't send for us. But he said, "Since you're here we will work."
D: *What are the symbols for?*
J: This is the ancient Hebrew system of cosmology called the "Kabbalah."

The Kabbalah is defined as: "The esoteric mystic lore of Judaism, based on an occult interpretation of the Bible and handed down as a secret doctrine to the initiated." Once again Nostradamus was delving into something the church would not have approved of, and something he would have kept hidden from the Inquisition.

D: *It sounds complicated.*
J: Yes. He's putting sand on the page that he has just finished writing. He says this will help the ink to dry. He's moved the book aside and said he will leave that so we can talk.

D: *All right. We would like to continue interpreting his quatrains if it's all right with him.*

J: He says he will try to be of service.

CENTURY III-73

Quand dans la regne parviendra la boiteux,
Competiteur aura proche bastard:
Lui & le regne viendront si fort roigneux,
Qu'ains qu'il guerisse son faict sera bien tard.

When the lame man comes into the kingdom, a bastard, close to him will compete with him. Both he and the kingdom will be greatly trimmed before he recovers, so that his action will be too late.

J: He says many of his quatrains pertain to the future as well as the past. This one refers to French history and also to the French pope.

D: *I thought so because he mentioned the lame man.*

J: He will have competition from within the papacy. He has stepped on many people's toes in his quest for the tiara of the pope.

D: *Who is the bastard?*

J: He's the illegitimate son of a cardinal who has moved from the priesthood into a cardinalship. He will be like a dog to this French pope, always at his heels. They won't get along. He will also remind him that through him he holds the papal tiara.

CENTURY III-74

Naples, Florence, Favence & Imole,
Seront en termes de telle fascherie:
Que pour complaire aux malheureux de Nolle
Plainct d'avoir faict à son chef moquerie.

Naples, Florence, Faenza and Imola will be on terms of such disagreement that to comply with the wretches of Nola they complain that they had mocked its chief.

J: He says this quatrain refers back to the time when the Italian states were coming together into the Italian nation. They were all city states at one time, and now they have united into the kingdom of Italy. This took place in the 1800s.

This was one of many small incidents concerning history that occurred during this experiment. It helped convince me that we were truly in touch with Nostradamus because if it is difficult for us to come up with dates in our own American history. It would be even more difficult to furnish dates dealing with European history. I had no idea when and if the Italian city states united into the kingdom of Italy. In our lifetime it has been known as one country, thus only someone familiar with European geography and history would be able to come up with the answers instantly. During research, I found that the proclamation of the Italian kingdom was begun in 1861. The final states of Rome and Venice were freed and one country was completed in 1870.

CENTURY III-76

En Germanie naistront diverses sectes,
S'approchant fort de l'heureux paganisme,
Le cœur captif & petites receptes,
Feront retour à payer le vrai disme.

Various sects will arise in Germany which will come near to a happy paganism. The heart captive, the returns small, they will return to pay the true tithe.

J: He says this quatrain refers to the near future. There will be a group of people who will arise out of Germany because of its wealth. He's showing me an image now in the mirror of something like a demonstration. He says they want to return to the simple ways of the past. They *are* a great group of people. It looks as if these demonstrators are at a nuclear power plant, and they're against war. They're protestors, that's what they are. Now I understand. This refers to the different protest movements that will be rising out of Germany and become world-wide. These people will influence other countries and other nations in Europe, and their influence will spread throughout the world. They are for peace and cleaning up pollution, and against nuclear weapons. They're much more organized than any of the similar organizations here in the United States. They will have the backing.

D: *The translators say this deals with the rising of the Protestant sects during the 16th century.*

J: Well, they're wrong. He says in his time Protestantism was actually controlled by only two sects. One was the Swiss Confederation and the other was the tenets of Martin Luther. He says, "How many sects can you get out of Martin Luther and his intolerance to the Roman church?" This didn't have anything to do with them. He can understand where they might get that idea because the group of protestors will *appear* similar to a sect. They have a sense of religious purpose, but they're devoted to their ideals. He says these people will demonstrate against the established order.

Comment: John Calvin is the person referred to as the Swiss Confederation. Both Calvin and Martin Luther were alive at the same time as Nostradamus.

D: *The translators were surprised when he gave an exact date in this next quatrain because not many quatrains include an actual date and month. They were curious and thought he might have made a mistake by leaving it in. Maybe he can explain it.*

CENTURY III-77

Le tiers climat sous Aries comprins,
L'an mil sept cens vingt & sept en Octobre:
Le Roy de Perse par ceux d'Egypte prins:
Conflit, mort, perte: à la croix grand approbre.

The third climate included under Aries, in the year 1727 in October the king of Persia, captured by those of Egypt: battle, death, loss: great shame to the cross.

J: Can you please repeat that slowly? I'm forming the words in my mind so he can hear them. He can read my mind telepathically. (*I repeated it slower.*) He says this quatrain refers to what will happen in the Arab world. He sees the Shazik (phonetic: Sha-zeek) Turks will conquer territory that was originally conquered by the Persians. They will take over the whole near east and spread into India. This quatrain deals with the Arab states' rise to power throughout that area of the world. He says the cross will suffer because the Arabs will not like Christians. This is part of the rise of the Turkish, Ottoman Turk, empire. And this did take place.

Research revealed that during the years 1726 to 1729, the Ottomans attacked Persia. This again validated a date given by Nostradamus, and one we would have been unfamiliar with.

D: *The translators wondered why he used an exact date. Usually, he tries to hide them.*

J: I asked him. He says it was a very clear interpretation that most people could figure out, and that's why he left the date in. In his time he can't mention many things concerning Europe, but this quatrain deals with another part of the world that Christians have no interest in. It was safe from the Inquisition because anything that mentions the death of Persians, Arabs or any group in the Moslem world, would cause the church to clap. They would accept things of this type. Anything that refers to the European states has to be obscure because of the political intrigue in his time. In fact, he's been asked to use his knowledge as an astrologer in this regard. He doesn't like to because he doesn't want to play sides. It gets to be a real pain, he says. He doesn't like court intrigue and political maneuverings. He's very much against that.

D: *I can understand. Let's move on to the next one.*

J: Hold it. *I'm* asking him a question.

D: *Okay. Go ahead.* (Pause) *What are you asking him?*

J: I'm asking if this is the mirror in which he showed Catherine de' Medici the portraits of the kings of France? He says, yes, this is correct; he carried that mirror with him to her court in Paris and showed her the succession of the kings.

D: *I didn't think he allowed any one else to see things in the mirror.*

J: It was not something he usually allows, but he says his servant girl saw it in her daily chores of cleaning this room, and she talked too much. She mentioned his mirror that was kept in a felt bag and that this was where Nostradamus got his predictions of the future. He was brought before a church official who respected and liked him, but this knowledge spread to Paris and to the ears of Catherine de' Medici. Because of this, she requested that he present to her a vision of the future. He had no choice. Since his servant girl caused him trouble, she's not working for him any longer. He had to cast her out and he's pretty indignant about the whole situation. "She caused me a lot of pain and sorrow, and almost divided my house. I paid her well," he says, "and her disloyalty is disgusting."

D: *I was surprised that he would allow someone else to see his mirror. He's usually trying to keep everything secret.*

J: Usually he keeps his things locked up in the box.

D: *In this case, he did take it to Paris with him.*

J: Yes, he took the mirror because it was requested. He says he's going to buy his next servant girl and make sure she has no tongue. There are servants like that. Just as people are blind and deaf, there are people who are mute, and he says his next servant girl will be mute. This happened recently so he's still upset.

I don't think this is the same servant girl he mentioned earlier because enough time has past that I wouldn't think she would still be a girl. Unless all servants were addressed that way regardless of their age. But it does appear that Nostradamus was constantly plagued with servant problems.

D: *I wonder what Catherine de' Medici thought. Did it surprise her to be able to see things in the mirror?*

J: Because she's used to court magicians, she wasn't really very surprised. To her, it was like magic and a bit of a novelty. When he told her that she would be the mother of *many* kings, she didn't like that. She felt uncomfortable because she saw that all of her sons wouldn't survive. They would become kings, but they would die in turn. She didn't appreciate knowing that, but she was generous and nice. He is saying she gave him some money and helped his reputation, but she's—*(broad smile)* well, he used the word "conniving"—very conniving for her power.

D: *She asked to see it, so it's her own fault if she didn't like it.*

CENTURY III-78

Le chef d'Escosse avec six
 d'Alemaigne,
Par gens de mer Orienteaux
 captif:
Traverseront le Calpre
 & Espaigne,
Present en Perse au nouveau
 Roy craintif.

The leader from Scotland with six
Germans will be captured by
Eastern seamen. They will pass
Gibraltar and Spain presented in
Persia to the new dreadful king.

J: He says this quatrain refers to the man who will be called the Anti-Christ. When he's coming to power, he will request communication experts from Scotland, but they will really be based out of London and Germany. They will be shipped to him and used as his brain support or his "brain trust."

D: *Won't these people have anything to say about it?*

J: They'll have something to say about it, but they grasp for gold. Nostradamus is showing me gold coins.

D: *I thought maybe they were going against their wishes.*

J: No. They're not being forced into anything. They go willingly because they're paid well. In fact, this is going to happen within the next 10 years. In 1991, he says, in April of that year.

D: *Then this happens when he's beginning to form his network.*

UPDATE: *I think this could refer to the countries in the Middle East trying to upgrade their weaponry and computer capabilities. During 1991 and 1992 there were many computer experts, as well as nuclear scientists, whose talents were being offered to the highest bidder due to the breakup of the Communist countries and worldwide economic problems.*

CENTURY III-79

L'ordre fatal sempiternal
 par chaisne,
Viendra tourner par
 ordre consequent:
Du port Phocen sera rompu
 la chaisne,
La cite prinse, l'ennemi quant
 & quant.

The fatal and eternal order of the
cycle will turn in due order. The
chains of Marseilles will be broken,
the city taken and the enemy at the
same time.

J: When the Earth shift and the downfall of the Anti-Christ occurs, there will be battling in the southern European war theater. When it takes place, Marseilles will go as well as the forces of the Anti-Christ.

D: *Is that what he means by the cycle?*

J: Yes. The end of the world. The end of the cycle is the end of the world as we know it. (*Strange how calmly he said that.*)

D: The end of our world, is that it?
J: As we know it.

No matter how many times I have heard this pronouncement, it still bothers me.

CENTURY III-80

Du regne Anglois l'indigne dechassé, *Le conseiller par ire mis à feu:* *Ses adhera iront si bas tracer,* *Que le batard sera demi receux.*	The unworthy man is chased out of the English kingdom. The counsellor through anger will be burnt. His followers will stoop to such depths that the pretender will almost be received.

J: In the near future there will be disgrace in the royal house of Windsor, and this quatrain pertains to that. It refers to the English monarchy in the future and the rise of the prime minister. The prime minister will not be killed or burnt, but—wait a minute, he's showing me a plane crash—he will be killed in a plane crash. But a bomb on the plane will cause it to crash. His death will cause a scandal in the royal family.
D: Will this happen soon?
J: It will happen in the 1990s.

CENTURY III-83

Les longs cheveux de la Gaule Celtique, *Accompaignez d'estranges nations:* *Mettront captif la gent Aquitanique,* *Pour succomber à Internitions.*	The long-haired people of Celtic Gaul, joined by foreign nations will capture the people of Aquitaine in order that they should succumb to their plans.

J: He's showing me an image of England but it's just a very small island now. I know it was a small island to begin with, but now it's vastly reduced. England will want to have land in parts of France after the Earth shift. They're trying to get more land and it's like a feud between these two countries. He says this has also happened in past history.

This sounds very similar to CENTURY III-70 in Chapter 17. The two quatrains may be related. Aquitaine was a former district of southwest France.

CENTURY III-84

La grand cité sera bien desolee,
Des habitans un seul n'y
  demoura:
Mur, sexe, temple &
  vierge violee,
Par fer, feu, peste, canon
  peuple mourra.

The great city will soon be quite deserted, not a single one of the inhabitants will remain. Wall, sex, temple and virgin violated, people will die from the sword, fire, plague and cannon shot.

J: He said this quatrain refers to the end of New York City. He says there will be destruction, but I don't see a fire. I see a nuclear-type of weapon being used, but it's not a *nuclear* weapon. It's a bomb that kills all of the people but doesn't hurt the buildings. It's a type of chemical warfare. It poisons the city, and it destroys life. That's what he's showing me. The bomb will be placed in New York harbor and will blow up the Statue of Liberty. This is what he means by the virgin defiled.

D: *The quatrain says, "people will die from sword, fire, plague and cannon shot."*

J: Obviously this is all of it combined in one. He probably couldn't describe chemical warfare, so he used that metaphor.

In the following quatrain he has one word capitalized and the translators don't know what it means. It could be an anagram.

CENTURY III-85

La cité prinse par tromperie
  & fraude,
Par le moyen d'un beau
  jeune attrappé:
Assaut donne Raubine pres
  de LAUDE,
Lui & tous morts pour avoir
  bien trompé.

The city is taken by trickery and deceit, captured by means of a handsome young man. An assault is made by Raubine near LAUDE, he and all of them dead, for having deceived so well.

J: He says this quatrain refers to the time of troubles when the Anti-Christ will take over southern Europe and the battles that are connected with that event.

D: *I thought he was the handsome young man. Why has he capitalized the word "Laude"?*

J: He says it's true, it's an anagram, but he's not going to tell me. (*Smiling*) He says, "I've been so much of a help to you with these. There are some things you'll have to figure out for yourselves." He says he would like us to think.

D: *Well, that gives us something to wonder about. There are still some puzzles left for us to figure out.*

CENTURY III-86

*Un chef d'Ausonne aux
  Espaignes ira,
Par mer fera arrest dedans
  Marseille:
Avant sa mort un long temps
  languira
Apres sa mort on verra grand
  merveille.*

A leader from Italy will go to Spain
by sea and he will make a stop at
Marseilles. He will linger a long
time before dying, after his death
great wonders will be seen.

J: He says this quatrain was a very easy one, but he couldn't write it out
at the time. It refers to the last pope and some of his travels. At the
end of his reign there begins a new world and a new way of looking
at religion and spirituality.

D: *There won't be any popes after him. Will he die at Marseilles?*

J: He says that's just a metaphor signifying his travels, he'll die in Rome.

CENTURY III-87

*Classe Gauloise n'approches
  de Corsegne,
Moins de Sardaigne tu
  t'en repentiras:
Trestout mourrez frustrez
  de l'aide grogne,
Sang nagera, captif ne me croiras.*

French fleet, do not approach
Corsica; even less Sardinia, you will
regret it. You will all die, the help
from the cape in vain, captive,
swimming in blood you will not
believe me.

J: This quatrain also refers to the time of troubles and the Anti-Christ.
He'll use the islands of Corsica and Sardinia as a base of operation to
attack France. Others who are aware of what is going on will try to
warn the French.

CENTURY III-90

*Le grand Satyre & Tigre
  d'Hyrcanie,
Don presenté à ceux de l'Occean:
Un chef de classe istra de
  Carmanie,
Qui prendra terre au Tyrren
  Phocean.*

The great Satyr and Tiger of
Hyrcania; gift presented to the
people of the Ocean: the leader of a
fleet will come forth from Carmania
and land at the Phocea of Tyre.

J: He says this quatrain refers to the Turkish-Greek war that will occur
soon enough. The Turks will try to sue for peace, and the Greek king
will be duped. The king and queen will be outraged by Turkey's
military might and its desire to control a lot of the Greek islands in the
Ægean Sea.

D: *He said before, the war wouldn't last very long.*

J: No. But this quatrain deals with this war in the eastern Mediterranean.
D: *What is the symbolism of the Satyr and the Tiger?*
J: He says the tiger represents Israel, and the Satyr represents the glory of ancient Greece. They will make an alliance and this will bottle up the Turks and Arabs who are trying to destroy Israel.

When I began my research I thought this might be a mistake. Hyrcania was a province of the ancient Persian Empire on the shores of the Caspian Sea. How could that relate to Israel? But I found two famous men named Hyrcanus who were very important to the early history of Israel. One was the founder of the monarchy of Judea which continued in his family until the accession of Herod. The other man was high-priest and king of the Jews. He was put to death by his successor, Herod, in 30 B.C.E. I am guessing that Nostradamus used the name Hyrcanie as an anagram for Hyrcanus. In this way it could refer to Isael, according to his convoluted way of thinking.

Carmania was a province of ancient Persia. Does that mean they will have more than a passing interest in this short war?

Tyre was an important seaport in ancient Phœnicia. Phœnicia was an ancient kingdom on the Mediterranean in modern Syria and Palestine. Phocean could be an anagram for Phœnicia. Again, this seems to be a hidden reference to Israel and the Arab world.

D: *It says "gift presented to the people of the Ocean," and ocean is capitalized.*
J: He says an alliance will be created between Greece and Israel against Turkey, and their ceremonies will be conducted on the water.

Nostradamus had indicated in another quatrain (CENTURY I-83, Chapter 16) that this war would occur soon, in the middle of the 1990s.

CENTURY III-91

L'arbre qu'estoit par long temps mort seché,	The tree which had been dead and withered for a long time will flourish again in one night. The Cronian king will be sickly. The prince with a damaged foot, fear of his enemies will make him hoist sail.
Dans une nuict viendra à reverdir:	
Cron Roy malade, Prince pied estaché,	
Criant d'ennemis fera voile bondir.	

D: *The translators have an interesting note in the book about the words "Cron Roi."*
J: Crown king. (*A long pause. John seemed puzzled.*) He's breaking his concentration with me. He's not there any more …
D: (*I didn't understand what he meant.*) *Doesn't he want to give you an interpretation for that quatrain?*
J: (*Puzzled*) He's broken off.

D: *Where is he?*
J: He's still at the table. (*Long pause*)
D: *What's the matter?*
J: (*Confused*) I don't know.
D: *What's he doing?*
J: It's like he's ... he's having a seizure. He's turning red and then blue. And it looks like ... I feel like something's wrong with his heart.
D: *Can you do anything to help him?* (This was a very helpless feeling.) *Are you allowed to?*
J: No, I'm not allowed to. I have to stay by the mirror. He's not going to die, but he's ... he's ... (*John must have felt very helpless, too.*)
D: *Is he still sitting in the chair?*
J: He's slumped over. (*Pause*) It looks like he's had a heart seizure.
D: *Are you allowed to send him any kind of energy or do anything that might help him?*
J: (*Pause*) There's a bell! It's near his door! ... I can't lift it. I can put my hand on the clanker inside the bell. I'm moving the bell. I can't lift it, but I'm moving it.
D: *Is it a very large bell?*
J: It's very heavy. Very heavy to *me*. It's not heavy to people. (*Pause*) I'm ringing it. ... I'm ringing the bell!

Later, he said he was able to make the clapper move inside the bell and this made it ring. It took a great deal of effort.

D: *Do you think anyone can hear it?*
J: Yes, people are now coming into the room ... his wife and a boy of about 17. They're running to him. Now there's a man about 30 who is also coming. He's listening to his heart and he's pumping him ... he's pumping him. (*Pause*) He's breathing. (*With a sense of relief.*) Nostradamus is breathing.

This was an emotional experience for John. It's bad enough to see someone in our physical state collapse from a heart attack or stroke and be helpless to do anything about it. It must have been even more frustrating to watch from the spiritual state. At least it didn't keep John from trying to help the man who had become our dear friend.

D: *Of course they're too busy to notice you're there.*
J: They don't see me at all. They are in panic. They thought he was dead.
D: *But he's breathing again now.*
J: He's breathing. His face is all flushed. It's red, and a blue color is there, too.
D: *Are they doing anything else to him?*
J: They've taken off his hat and opened up his tunic. And they're massaging him and pounding his chest. Now his eyes ... (*Abruptly*) I have to leave. The guardian of the tapestry is telling me I have to go. He's calling from the mirror, and I'm going back into the mirror. But he

said not to worry, Nostradamus will be okay. He has had heart trouble before. I'm in the mirror looking out. Now they're giving him some type of heart medicine in a glass of wine. (*Confidently*) He'll be okay. He's just old. He's older than the last time we were with him, and this must be a part of his aging process. I'm in the Tapestry Room now.

D: *Ask the guardian if we had anything to do with him having this stroke or heart attack.*

J: No, it's not your fault. The guardian says Nostradamus is an elderly man at this time. "He hasn't taken care of himself. He's a physician and he doesn't take his own advice. He should be taking a remedy for his heart and he hasn't done it. This terrible incident you have just witnessed will be a reminder to him that he has to take care of his vehicle."

D: *I just wanted to be sure that our visiting him didn't ...*

J: No, we didn't have anything to do with it. It's Nostradamus' life and part of the pattern that his soul has chosen, the guardian of the tapestry has just said. This was why Nostradamus was very unclear, at that point it was building up in him.

D: *Then if we go back again ... when we go back again, we should probably go to him when he's at a younger age, to avoid the problems he has as he gets older.*

J: Yes, the guardian says we will go to a point in his life where you can work with him, but he cannot predict the time when you will come into his life. He says you're being very presumptuous, and he doesn't like that. The guardian says you cannot be presumptuous on *any* life-form. He says by forcing our way into their lives we are doing negative good. (*Puzzled*) I don't understand what that means ... *negative* good?

D: *But I don't consider it forcing if he has asked us to come.*

J: No, he doesn't mean that. He says ... (*Laugh*) "Just don't make a pest of yourselves. Be nice." He says, "This was a very traumatic event that you witnessed and I don't think you will witness that again." But he says Nostradamus can only stay at a level that is receptive to our impulses for short periods of time. His sense of time that he sees us in the spirit form is *hours* compared to your sense of time which is *minutes*. It's as if this takes place in three or four hours in his sense of time, whereas in our sense of time it's maybe a bit longer than an hour. The guardian of the tapestry is explaining that it's a different sense of time because Nostradamus is reading my mind. It isn't instant communication all the time.

D: *But any time he wants to stop the communication, he does. So in that way I don't feel we're making him do something he doesn't want to do.*

J: He enjoys the presence of the spirits of the future so he tries to work with them. But the spirits of the future have to realize that their sense of time is not the same as his.

D: *We're doing this because he requested it.*

J: Oh, the spirit of the tapestry is well aware of that. He's just explaining time dimension distortion. (*Sigh*) He says we have to clear up this matter of time. That's the thing. He wants us to realize that each ·session we spend with him might seem to be 90 minutes, but is actually three or four hours to Nostradamus, which is a long time to take him away from his daily life. I don't understand how that can be.

D: *No, I don't either. But then there's a lot about this we don't understand.*

J: I'm trying to get a clearer viewpoint from the tapestry guardian. He says if it's hard for us to understand at this point, don't worry about it. But realize that there is an allotment of time. Nostradamus has a certain amount of hours that he can communicate with the spirits of the future. What you seem to say in ten minutes could actually be an hour to him.

D: *Well, he's also seeing a whole vision which could take longer.*

J: Yes, he's seeing these visions in his meditation, although sometimes they've been drug-induced by taking a bit of wine and opium.

D: *Oh? I suppose that makes him more open to it.*

J: Yes. The guardian says, "We will try to arrange for you to go into a better situation the next time you come."

D: *That's why I didn't think it would be presumptuous if we were to ask to come when he was younger, in a healthier state.*

J: No, he says that would be better. The guardian is a very loving spirit. It's just that he has a lot of work to do to keep this tapestry in shape. He has a lot of responsibility. He says sometimes these mishaps occur, but he didn't realize when I left on the thread that I was coming in at the point where Nostradamus suffers from a heart attack. He says, "Next time you come, we'll make sure that Nostradamus is in the right state of mind, and that he's not going to be ill." He says it's time for us to leave now.

This was quite an experience. And it brings up many questions. Did John actually save Nostradamus' life by ringing the bell? Was that the reason behind us being there at that precise time, so we could help? Apparently no one in the room questioned the ringing of the bell because of the confusion. Would he have died if John had not summoned them? These people were used to him spending hours undisturbed in his study, so no one would have checked on him. John said he had not seen the bell hanging on the wall by the door during the sessions when Nostradamus was younger. Maybe he had it put up as he grew older so he could summon help if he needed it.

Nostradamus did say, "I did not call for you today." Maybe at this stage in his life he had finished the quatrains and didn't see the spirits from the future as often as he had when he was younger. Whatever the reasons, this was one experience we did not wish to repeat.

Chapter 22

The Hidden Room

AFTER THE TRAUMATIC EXPERIENCE during the last session, we wanted to try to contact Nostradamus at a time in his life when he was in better health.

J: The guardian says, "You want to go to visit Nostradamus now, don't you?"

D: *Yes, and we don't want to repeat the experience we had last time. We would prefer a day when he has time to talk to us, and a day when he's in good physical health.*

J: Okay, I'm on the beam. ... I am there now. (*Smiling*) Nostradamus is putting all kinds of stuff away.

D: *What do you mean?*

J: Oh, he's got the door to the study open and he's in the other room. He's putting stuff away like we would put away groceries. He's got herbs and incense and all kinds of stuff. Now he's coming back into the room. Oh, he looks good today. He's very chipper. We came at a good time in his life. He's a lot younger looking. His hair has gray in it, but he's probably in his forties.

D: *That's better. We don't want anything to happen like last time.*

J: (*Seriously*) I can't talk about that.

D: *About what?*

J: About what happened last time.

Apparently Nostradamus was not allowed to know about the incident in his future when he would suffer a near-fatal heart attack. In this case we possessed knowledge about him that we were forbidden to transmit.

D: *Can you let him know that we're here?*

J: He sees me in the mirror, but he's busy. He's working and says, "I'll be right there. (*Laugh*) Let me get my paper, my books, and my scroll here, and then my sand and my ink." He's setting that all up. Now he's going into his kitchen area.

D: *Is that another room?*

J: Yes. He's telling his wife he doesn't want to be disturbed now. And he's come back through the studies and he's locking the door.

D: *That's good, maybe we'll be able to work today.*
J: Yes, he's feeling very good.
D: *Then would he like to continue with the translation of the quatrains?*
J: Yes, he says, "Go ahead."

CENTURY III-91

L'arbre qu'estoit par long
   temps mort seché,
Dans une nuict viendra
   à reverdir:
Cron Roy malade, Prince
   pied estaché,
Criant d'ennemis fera
   voile bondir.

The tree which has been dead and
withered for a long time will flourish
again in one night. The Cronian king
will be sickly. The prince with a
damaged foot, fear of his enemies
will make him hoist sail.

This was the quatrain I was reading when Nostradamus had the heart attack during the last session. We were unable to interpret it then, so I began with it.

J: The Cronian king. How do you spell Cronian?
D: *This is something the translators don't understand. In the French he has "Cron Roy," and they've translated it as "Cronian." In their translation they think the Latin Cronus may refer to Saturn.*
J: No, it doesn't, he says. It describes the royal family of England at the present time. It's about Prince Charles and the Cronian king, who is actually—Cron is more what he had in mind. He says it represents a *woman* king; an older woman king. He says the British royal family has lost some of its prestige and power in this century, but this will change shortly when the prince—who has had trouble with his foot or will have trouble with his foot—gains control. He will hoist sail to help the royal family gain prestige and power. It doesn't mean he's going to sail away. The tree which had withered will now blossom again.
D: *I can see the symbolism there. They've had a woman queen for a long time now.*

CENTURY III-93

Dans Avignon tout le Chef
   de l'empire
Fera arrest pour Paris desolé:
Tricast tiendra l'Annibalique ire,
Lyon par change sera mel
   consolé.

In Avignon, the leader of all the
Empire will make a stop because
Paris is deserted. Tricast will
contain the African anger, the
Lion will be poorly consoled by
the change.

John repeated each line aloud after me.

J: He says this quatrain refers to two things. It refers to the Nazis and the takeover of France, and how the lion, which represents London,

England, will have some real problems during this time. It also represents the problems that will be created by the Anti-Christ—the word he uses is world destroyer—when he marches through southern France near Avignon. He says Avignon was a very important city in his day because it was the seat of the papacy at one point; within a couple of hundred years of his time. It was an important city then, although it's not nearly as important in your time frame.

Again Nostradamus was correct with his knowledge of local French history. Because of troubled times that were devastating Italy, the Pope moved the seat of the papacy to Avignon. The popes remained there for 68 years, from 1309 to 1377, within 200 years of Nostradamus' time.

J: He says this quatrain indicates the route the Anti-Christ will use when he marches through southern France. Paris will be deserted because he will threaten to bomb it, as he has bombed Rome and Athens. He will set up camp outside of what is now Avignon and England won't be able to do a thing because she'll be threatened next.

D: *Then the lion represents England in both interpretations.*

J: And Paris was also deserted during World War II.

D: *Can he give you a time period of when the Anti-Christ will cause problems, or is he just showing you a picture?*

J: He says this will all take place during his reign of terror, as he calls it.

CENTURY III-96

Chef de Fosan aura gorge coupee,	The leader from Fossano will have his throat cut by the man who
Par le ducteur du limier & laurier:	exercised the bloodhounds and greyhounds. The deed will be
La faict patre par ceux de mont Tarpee,	committed by those of the Tarpean rock, when Saturn is in Leo on
Saturne en Leo 13 de Fevrier.	13th February.

He asked for spelling and then corrected my pronunciation.

J: This will happen after the year 2000. It relates to factions that will be fighting each other after the Anti-Christ. A bit of turmoil during this time period will cause one of the leaders to be assassinated by a faction that still holds the beliefs of the Anti-Christ, even though the Anti-Christ is no longer on Earth. These people will cause difficulties during this period, but out of this will come one world government, he says.

D: *I thought that after the Anti-Christ died people would have no more desire for war.*

J: Well, it's more political maneuverings, he's saying. Shifting loyalties will cause this man to be killed.

D: *What is the symbolism of the bloodhounds and the greyhounds?*

J: The bloodhounds are war dogs. That's how he sees them. They're dogs that pick up the scent of an animal that has been wounded in order to find it and kill it. They'll devour it if they're not stopped. The greyhound is another hunting dog, but it's more noble because it listens to what it's guided to. This symbolism refers to the different types of factions that will exist at the time.

D: *If you were to look up those astrological signs, would that give us the date?*

J: He says to look in an ephemeris after the year 2000.

Later, when John was able to find the 2000 ephemeris he calculated the date as February 13, 2036, when Saturn is in Leo and Jupiter is in Taurus.

There is interesting symbolism in Nostradamus' referral to the Tarpean Rock. This was a rock on the Capitoline Hill in Rome, from which the Republican Romans hurled state criminals. This appears to be another case of Nostradamus referring to Roman history as a cross reference. Would this mean that the murder was committed by those who were considered to be criminals or rebels against the established order?

CENTURY III-98

Deux royals freres si fort guerroierent, *Qu'entre eux sera la guerre si mortelle:* *Qu'un chacun places fortes occuperont,* *De regne & vie sera leur grand querelle.*	Two royal brothers will fight so fiercely and the feud between them will be so deadly that both will live in fortified places. Their great quarrel will concern their lives and the kingdom.

J: This quatrain applies to many rulers throughout history, but we will especially see these events occur in our time period between the sons of Prince Charles of England.

D: *Does he mean that there will be problems between these two?*

J: There is already sibling rivalry now, he says. This problem has already begun and they're only babies.

D: *Then this quatrain predicts future events, but some have already happened.*

J: Yes. This has happened many times in different countries, like Russia and England in the first part of our century. He's saying that this represents turmoil that occurs from his time up through our time until the new world order.

CENTURY III-99

Aux champs herbeux d'Alein et du Vaineigne,	In the green field of Alleins and Vernegues of the Luberon moun-
Du mont Lebrou proche de la Durance,	tains near Durance, the fighting on both sides will be so bitter for the
Camps de deux parts conflict sera si aigre	armies that Mesopotamia shall cease to be found in France.
Mesopotamie defaillira en la France	

He repeated portions after me and corrected my pronunciation of the names.

J: He says this quatrain refers to the fighting that will occur when the Anti-Christ's forces try to capture Switzerland. He won't be success-ful but he will destroy a part of France in trying. A bomb will be launched to destroy Geneva and Zurich, but instead it will land in France and cause contamination.

D: *Is this atomic contamination?*

J: It's not necessarily atomic; it kills people but doesn't kill the landscape.

This is similar to the quatrain describing the destruction of New York (CENTURY III-84 in Chapter 21).

D: *He uses a lot of names in the quatrain.*

J: In his time these were all names of places in France. There are anagrams in there as well, he said.

D: *Anagrams of other place names?*

J: Well, he's showing me a map of Switzerland and pointing out the French and Swiss border area.

CENTURY IV-1

Cela du reste de sang non espandu,	The remaining blood will not be spilt, Venice seeks for help to be
Venise quiert secours estre donné,	given; Having waited for a very long time the city is handed over at the
Apres avoir bien long temps attendu,	first trumpet blast.
Cité livrée au premier cornet sonné.	

J: He says Venice was a great maritime state in his time. In your time period, it's slowly sinking into the marsh of the lagoon. He says this quatrain represents the downfall of this beautiful jewel of a city. Because of the changes that are taking place and the rising of the oceans, most of Venice will soon be under water. This will be especially critical in the 1990s because he's showing me water rising up and up.

D: *They're trying to do something now to keep it from sinking. Do you think it will be successful?*

J: To a degree, he says, but with the Earth shift it will be covered completely. He shows me the Earth and that area is all under water.

I found that in Nostradamus' time Venice was the greatest maritime state in the Western world. It was powerful in European politics and the center of intense cultural activity. Indeed, he must have felt saddened to see it sink.

CENTURY IV-3

D'Arras & Bourges, de Brodes grans enseignes,
Un plus grand nombre de Gascons batre à pied,
Ceux long du Rosne saigneront les Espaignes:
Proche du mont ou Sagonte s'assied.

From Arras and Bourges great banners from the Dark Ones, a greater number of Gascons fight on foot. Those along the Rhône will make the Spanish bleed. Near the mountain seat of Sagunto.

He again corrected my pronunciation.

J: He says this quatrain refers to the time of troubles and how the Anti-Christ will take over most of France, but not Paris. He will conquer most of the southern section of France and try to spread into Italy as well as Spain. By this time he has already blown up Rome and he will concentrate on this part of France because it's a very rich agricultural area. This is where all our luxury foods come from. He's showing me a truffle, geese, and things like that. He says this will be a very important time.

D: *I assume the dark ones represent the members of the Anti-Christ's forces, but it says "a great number of gascons fight on foot." Who are the gascons?*

J: Gascony was a province of France in that time, so the gascons symbolize the *free* French because they're from the north.

CENTURY IV-4

L'impotent Prince faché, plaincts & querelles,
De rapts & pille, par coqz & par Libiques:
Grand est par terre par mer infinies voilles
Seule Italie sera chassont Celtiques.

The powerless Prince is angered, complaints & quarrels, rape and pillage, by the cock and by the Libyans. It is great on land, at sea innumerable sails; Italy alone will be driving out the Celts.

J: He says this quatrain refers to a time in your century when a prince from an old house will want power, but he won't get it.

D: *Does he know what country?*

J: He says it's in the Arab states. It's difficult to see. He says, "I don't understand all the names of your new countries." He's being very vague.

D: *Who is the cock in this case?*

J: (*Surprised*) Egypt. I don't know how ...

D: *It says, "Italy alone will be driving out the Celts." Who are the Celts in this quatrain?*

He hesitated as though Nostradamus wasn't answering him and then he continued.

J: The Celts were the ancient tribe that inhabited the Italian peninsula before the Romans and the Etruscans. He said you should know your Roman history. He says, "We know it very well—you should, too." He's pointing at me.

D: *He has told me that before. I know we should be more familiar with Roman history, but there's a lot of later history that has replaced it.*

J: He says, "I want to see the brilliancies of *your* mind." (*Laugh*) He says to look in your Roman history for the clue and then we'll discuss this quatrain again.

D: *Why wasn't he speaking a moment ago. Was something bothering him?*

J: He was deep in contemplation. He gets kind of "spacey." I guess that's what it's called.

D: *Well, we had a loud noise here* (a lawn-mower outside the window) *and I thought maybe that was bothering him.*

J: No, it wouldn't bother him. He doesn't hear anything in my dimension. (*Abruptly*) He doesn't want to interpret any more quatrains. He's just put down his pen. He says, "If you want more information we can look in the mirror. What would you like to hear about? That last quatrain made me think about a lot of things."

D: *Anything in particular?*

J: He says, "Study Roman history. We have to study it in our time so you should study it in yours. It was part of your civilization as well as mine."

D: *Yes. But so much more time has passed between then and now, that it has kind of fallen into the background. People don't use it as much as they should, I guess. If he doesn't want to talk about the quatrains, does he have anything in particular he would like to show us in the mirror?*

J: He doesn't ... he says we'll put them away for now. He's in a very cheerful mood. He's saying that he has another room upstairs and asks if I would like to see it.

This was a surprise. We had never been allowed in the rest of the house.

D: *Can we do that?*

J: Yes, he's taking me upstairs and into the other room. It's a very tiny ritual room. This is where he keeps all of his magical instruments and such, but he doesn't keep the mirror here. He has a lot of hangings on the walls, and it's really beautiful. The room's about the size of my bathroom; no, it's a bit bigger than that. It's about nine or ten feet on each side. You couldn't put a bed in it, but there's a magic circle on the floor. He has different types of scrolls, books, a big incense burner, and a chair that has cross-beam legs like this (*hand motions*) on the bottom part. It's off to the side. This is where he comes to meditate and pray. He's a very spiritual man. He says it's very important for people to pray.

D: *What do the wall hangings look like?*

J: Oh, they're beautiful, and they're made of something like velvet. Some are embroidered and some are woven like tapestry. They have all different types of occult symbols on them. I asked him who made them and he said, "That's *my* secret." (*Laugh*) He has to keep this room hidden. It has a heavy lock on the door and it's considered his storeroom for money and valuables. His wife can see it, but the servant girl can't because she would use it to denounce him as a witch. It's his religious retreat and he just wanted to let me know he was thinking about it. He's saying, "I like to sit in here and pray for my ancestors to bless my life and my family's lives." He would like me to leave now. He says he would like to pray.

D: *Was that the only thing he wanted to do, just show you that room?*

J: I don't know why, but he wanted to bring me here. He wants to pray, and he says that—oh, I understand now. You see, at times he gets feelings that we might not be good; that we're evil spirits.

D: *I can understand why he might feel that.*

J: He feels that if we pray with him, he would know. I'm praying with him now. I'm reciting the Lord's Prayer with him.

John recited it softly. I said it mentally with him.

D: *Does he say it the same way we do?*

J: No, it's a little different, but it's similar. It's a test he was doing. He says, "I know now you're not an evil spirit because you couldn't say that prayer if you were." He wants us to leave now.

His mention of evil spirits sparked my curiosity and I wanted to pursue that.

D: *Can you ask him if he's had ...*

J: He doesn't want to talk. He's got a scroll out and he's reciting words from it, praying.

D: *I was just curious if any spirits ...*

J: I'm back in the Tapestry Room. The guardian pulled me back. The guardian is talking to me now, "He doesn't want you there. It's very important that he pray. Prayer uplifts man." Nostradamus wanted to test us because he's had some incidents where he's "gotten involved with demons."

D: *That's what I was curious about.*

J: Some negative spirits have come through the mirror, the guardian has said. "Prayer is very important because prayer is when we *talk* to God. When we meditate we listen to what God has to say in return," he says.

D: *I thought it was unusual that we were allowed in another part of his house.*

J: He wanted to see if we were negative spirits, and if we *were* negative spirits, he had salt on the floor. *(Laugh)* I knew that. But that's why he wanted to see if we would pray, to praise the Creator, as he said.

D: *I would have thought by now that he would know we are positive spirits. I would hope so. We've been coming for quite a while.*

J: You see, it's not consistent. We don't come every day at a certain time. We come through at different times in his life. The guardian says he has had some difficulty with negative spirits.

D: *Well, I'm glad we passed the test.*

J: Yes. The guardian says you'll do wonderfully.

I also believe the guardian would not have allowed us to find Nostradamus through the tapestry if he had picked up on any negativity from us. He had said in the beginning that he knew our motives better than we knew them ourselves.

Chapter 23

ℵ̩ostradamus' First Contact

AT THE BEGINNING OF THIS SESSION as John came through the mirror he unexpectedly jerked back in surprise and exclaimed, "He's *tapping* on it!"

D: Tapping on it?

J: Yes. He has a wand. It looks like a magician's wand, but it's bigger than our magicians would use in the 20th century. It's about 18 inches long, but it's thick. It looks like an ash tree limb that has been filed down and painted. I thought it had cabalistic designs on it, but they are Hebrew letters. He has his name written on it in Hebrew.

D: And he tapped on the mirror with it?

J: Yes. He tapped on the mirror like that. (*He waved his hand like an orchestra leader tapping on the podium with a baton.*)

D: Why did he do that?

J: It looks like he's in the middle of some type of magical ceremony. On the ground beneath his feet is a circle with a pentagram on it and many different Hebrew characters. The circle is on the floor near the table, and there are two candles inside the circle. The mirror's on the table. He tapped the mirror like this (*hand motions*) and said, (*surprised*) "Oh! You are one of the spirits, aren't you?" And I said, "Yes, I'm one of the spirits."

D: Do you think he was trying to call a spirit from the mirror using this ceremony?

J: Yes.

D: I guess he didn't know he was going to get us.

J: No, he was looking for spirits to help him work on his book.

D: Then we happened along at the right time. I wonder if there are any other spirits who would have come through if we hadn't shown up?

J: Yes, there are.

D: There are? Where are they?

J: One is my spirit guide, and there is a whole chorus of spirits that have been called. They're watching. The ceremony is done in the name of God, so only good spirits can come through.

D: *Do they care if we're the ones who talk to him? Somebody else might have been here first.*

J: No, they don't mind. They're curious. Nostradamus is very young looking. He has a lot of dark hair with just a little gray in it. I would say he looks as if he's in his late thirties or early forties.

D: *Do you think this might be one of the first times he has called for spirits to come forth?*

J: Yes, I think so. He's a little shocked. He's ... (*smiling broadly*) a little nervous.

D: *(Laugh) Maybe this was his first experiment of this type.*

J: No, it's not his first experiment, but it's the first time he's seen a visualization coming out of the mirror. I think he's just gotten the mirror.

D: *If he's a bit nervous, maybe you should talk to him, to make him feel better.*

J: I'm talking with him telepathically. I'm telling him I've come with love and light for him and that we want to be of service to him. We'll also help him with his book.

D: *What does he say?*

J: Merci, thank you.

D: *Is he still afraid?*

J: He's not moving from that circle. (*We found this amusing.*) But he's got equipment. He's got a book ... no, it's not a book, it's a scroll that he has quills for.

D: *Well, I don't blame him for being cautious. I think this would be strange.*

J: (*Abruptly*) He has some type of skin problem.

D: *What do you mean?*

J: I don't know. It looks like he has a rash on his face. I think it's from a drug reaction. It's probably hives or a similar allergic reaction. He was scratching his face like this. (*John scratched in his beard and on his cheeks above his beard.*)

D: *Do you think he takes drugs?*

J: He only takes them for health. He doesn't abuse drugs like we do in the 20th century. He says he'll have a glass of wine or two, but he doesn't abuse it. He's saying something, but I don't understand it. "Drunkenness is the ..." It's a proverb or something like that. "Drunkenness is allowing demons to talk through you."

D: *I thought he may take some drugs and not realize the effects they can have.*

J: No, he says he knows quite a bit about what he calls "pharmacopœia."

The word was strange to me, but I suspected it referred to a pharmacy or drugs. Definition: An official book with a list of drugs and medicines and a description of their properties, preparation, *etc.*

D: *If this is the first time he's seen us, he might be curious. Does he want to ask us anything?*

J: He's asking us who will be the next ruler of France.

I almost laughed. What a typical first question that people always ask of spirits. It was also a question we asked of him when he wanted to know what we wished to see in the mirror. We asked about our next president. He had chided us at that time for asking such a trivial question because he said that rulers come and go. But here Nostradamus proved to us that in his early days of experimentation his curiosity followed the same human direction as ours. It was funny. Here he was asking us the same type of question he had later criticized us for. But I wondered how John would answer it. I certainly couldn't remember who the ruler was in his time, even if I ever knew. That was ancient history and the only way for me to answer would be to find an encyclopedia in a hurry and look it up. It would be difficult to put Nostradamus on hold while we did that. John said later that in his conscious state he didn't know the answer either, but his response came from somewhere.

D: *Do you know? Can you help him with that?*

J: I'm telling him that it's not going to be the present dauphin, but it will be one of his brothers.

D: *Hmm. I don't even remember who the king was at that time. Will you tell him we are from farther in the future and that information is very old history to us?*

J: Yes. He laughed when I said that.

D: *Why?*

J: Well, he just can't comprehend 500 years from his time period.

D: *You could tell him that his book is already published and that we're reading it. People have been puzzled by it for 400 years.*

J: Well, he's happy to know that it will last that long, but he's reluctant to talk about his own future. He doesn't want to know anything about that.

D: *Okay. Has he begun to write his book of quatrains yet?*

J: No. He's done research for a book on the Kabbalah. He's also been working on an astrological book of data for a *very* long time, he says, and he's pointing to that huge calfskin book that has loose-leaf papers in it. He's spent a lot of time on that. But he's also a doctor so he spends time healing as well. He's also thinking of writing a book on some type of philosophy. You see, at this time they're translating most of the great works of ancient Greece and Rome from Greek and Latin into either English or French. He's involved in that, too.

D: *Then he hasn't really started to write his quatrains.*

This could present a problem if he hadn't begun writing them or if he hadn't even thought about them yet. If I read them, they might be as much of a puzzle to him as they were to us. I expected that he would only be confused because he would have no idea what they were. Unless ... unless we really *were* helping him to write them.

D: *Well, I wanted to read some quatrains and have him explain them. Do you think it will do any good?*

J: "By all means," he says, "let's try it." I've just told him about the qua-
trains and the prophecies that will be attributed to him in the future.
He has a very perplexed look on his face, but he says, "I'll try, I'll try."
(*It was a confused tone of voice. I laughed.*)

D: *In 400 years no one has been able to fully understand them. So that's
what we're trying to do, translate them. That's why we went to the
source; if he can understand such a concept.*

J: He says, "I'll try." (*With a resigned shrug of his shoulders.*)

D: *Did he want to ask you any more questions other than who the next
ruler of France was going to be?*

J: That's all for now.

D: *All right. I will read one to see if he can interpret it for us. We can see
his reaction anyway.*

CENTURY IV-5

Croix paix, soubz un accompli
   divin verbe,
L'Espaigne & Gaule seront
   unis ensemble:
Grand clade proche, &
   combat tresacerbe,
Cœur si hardi ne sera
   qui ne tremble.
	Cross, peace under one the divine
	word achieved. Spain and Gaul will
	be united. A great disaster is
	close, the fighting very ferocious,
	no heart so brave as will not
	tremble.

J: He says in the future there will rise a spiritual party of people who
won't be interested in politics, but in humanitarian and compassion-
ate work. This party will be formed during the time of troubles.

D: *What does it mean, "Spain and Gaul will be united"?*

J: Gaul was the ancient word for France. This relates to a territory that
will appear at that time. There will be many islands and rocky lands
in Spain, not like it is now. Thus, people of spiritual consciousness will
immigrate to this territory and form a spiritual party to be of service
to the world and to the one world government.

It appeared that Nostradamus was able to translate the quatrains even
though he didn't understand what was happening.

D: *When I read him the quatrain, was he able to see a picture?*

J: Yes, he was able to see it. He said, "All of this is very familiar, but I
don't know why." I guess he's getting a taste of simultaneous time but
doesn't realize it.

D: *I wondered what his reaction would be. It's a bit confusing to him, I'll
bet. At least he seems to know what the quatrain means. All right.
Let's go on and see his reactions.*

CENTURY IV-6

D'habits nouveaux apres
faicte la treuve,
Malice tramme & machination:
Premier mourra qui en
fera la preuve,
Couleur venise insidation.

After the truce is made, new
clothes will be put on, malice,
conspiracy and plotting. He who
will prove it is the first to die, the
color of Venetian treachery.

D: The translators say this quatrain is very obscure. They don't under-
stand it.
J: He's showing me a picture of the Kaiser during World War I, and he
says this quatrain refers to the rise of that war and the militarism of
Germany during that time. The powder keg of World War I was set
off by the assassination of Archduke Ferdinand. The man who killed
him lived in Venice for a while at one point and got his training, supplies, and money in Venice. This is the Venetian connection.
D: That would be in our past.

I was unable to find whether or not the man who assassinated Archduke Ferdinand had any connections with Venice. To this day there are
still many unknown facts concerning the murders. The question of who
was behind them and who supplied them has never been satisfactorily
answered. Nostradamus may have seen more details about the incident
than were available to the investigators.

CENTURY IV-7

Le mineur filz du grand
& hai Prince,
De lepre aura à vingt ans
grande tache,
De deuil sa mere mourra
bien triste & mince,
Et il mourra là où tombe
cher lache.

The younger son of a great and
hated prince, will be greatly marked
by leprosy by the time he is 20.
His mother will die of grief, very
sad and thin, and he will die when
the cowardly flesh falls (from
his bones).

D: The translators take this very literally, but they don't understand it.
J: Hmm. This is a very interesting quatrain.
D: It has interesting symbolism anyway. What do you see?
J: This quatrain involves a president in our near future. His son will die
of AIDS. This will be during the AIDS crisis of the late 1980s and the
mid-1990s. AIDS will be similar to the Black Plague of his day, he says.
One of our president-elect's sons, who won't be even 20, will succumb
to this disease. He's showing me sores on the person's body that are
purple, like the plague, and he says: this is how his flesh will rot from
his body. He's scratching his head. He says, "The Black Death, or as

we call it, 'Mort de Mal, Sick Death' is worse than this because it is
very painful. But this is also a plague."

D: *Did he call it leprosy because that was the only thing he could identify
   it with?*

J: Yes, because it looks as if the sores on the body are disintegrating.

D: *That was the only way he could interpret it then. Hmm, that's very
   interesting. Will it be in our near future?*

J: Very soon, he says. He asks, "You people are from the mid-20th
   century, aren't you?" And I said, "Yes."

D: *It is now toward the end of the 20th century here.*

J: "I also have spirits come from the 23rd century," he said.

It appeared that interest in Nostradamus' quatrains will not diminish
if people are still seeking him out 300 years from our time.

D: *It says, "the younger son of a great and* hated *prince." It doesn't sound
   like he will be a very popular president. Does he have an explanation
   for why he uses that word?*

J: (*Smiling*) All mankind hates its rulers. That's what he just said. Even
   the noblest leader was persecuted and crucified.

D: That's true.

He was obviously referring to Jesus.

When I was putting together the first volume of this work, I saw something in a quatrain that Brenda had interpreted that I believe might correspond to this one. I will repeat part of it here.

CENTURY II-53

La grande peste de cité maritime,	The great plague in the maritime
Ne cessera que mort ne	city will not stop until death is
soit vengée	avenged by the blood of a just man
Du juste sang par pris	taken and condemned for no crime;
damné sans crime,	the great lady is outraged by the
De la grand dame par	pretense.
feincte n'outragée.	

Nostradamus explained in Volume One that this quatrain referred to
both the Black Plague that struck London and to the present plague called
AIDS. He said it would spread like wildfire over the whole country and
affect a large portion of the population. I asked him to clarify the part
which says, "The plague will not stop until death is avenged with the
blood of a just man taken and condemned for no crime."

He said that if he were to try to explain that part it really wouldn't
make any sense, but that it would become clear in time. I thought it
referred to a cure, but he said that a cure would not be found in time for
this plague. Death would just have to run its course.

These two quatrains are so similar in content that I wonder if they refer to the same thing. The plague wouldn't be stopped until the son of the President of the United States was affected. That event would surely spur the search for a cure like nothing else. This would also fit the time frame of 15 years before a cure would be found which Nostradamus indicated in CENTURY III-48, Chapter 19.

CENTURY IV-8

La grand cité d'assaut prompt & repentin,	The great city will be surprised at night by a sudden and quick assault.
Surprins de nuict, gardes interrompus:	The guards interrupted; the watch and guards of St. Quintin slaugh-
Les excubies & vielles sainct Quintin,	tered, the guards and the gates broken down.
Trucidés gardes & les pourtails rompus.	

J: Could you please repeat that? He's having difficulty writing it down. (*I repeated it.*) In his time the great city was Rome. This quatrain refers to the destruction of Rome during the crisis of the Anti-Christ.

D: *What is St. Quintin?*

J: He is the keeper of the door of the Vatican.

I found that St. Quintin was a Roman living in 286 C.E. He was tortured and decapitated because he refused to leave Christianity and return to worshipping Roman gods. There is an elaborate legend surrounding him, but I could find no mention of him being considered the "keeper of the door of the Vatican." Maybe this was what he was called in Nostradamus' time. Today we refer to St. Peter as keeping watch at the gates of Heaven, but St. Quintin is little known.

D: *The translators relate this quatrain to a city called St. Quentin even though it's spelled differently.*

J: (*Pause*) He doesn't understand.

D: *I said, the translators, the ones who have translated these quatrains in our time have associated this quatrain with a city called St. Quentin, but the name is spelled a bit differently.*

J: He said, "*Who* are these people?" (*I laughed.*) He's pretty angry. He doesn't like hearing about them.

D: *They are people in our time who will try to understand his writings because they are puzzles.*

J: Yes. He said the spirit from the 23rd century has told him this.

Apparently the idea of people misinterpreting his work angered him even though he hadn't written the quatrains yet.

D: *So that quatrain referred to the fall of Rome during the time of troubles.*

CENTURY IV-9

Le chef du camp au milieu
de la presse,
D'un coup de fleche sera
blessé aux cuisses,
Lors que Geneve eu larmes
& detresse,
Sera trahi par Lozan & Souisses.

The leader of the army in the middle of the crowd is wounded in the thighs with an arrow. When Geneva in trouble and distress is betrayed by Lausanne and the Swiss.

J: This event took place during the Swiss confederation. In other words, this quatrain applies to the different cantons and provinces before they became the union of Switzerland. It happened a few centuries ago.

D: *What is the meaning of this line about the leader? "In the middle of the crowd, wounded in the thighs with an arrow."*

J: That happened to one of the top generals consolidating the Swiss.

D: *Then this occurred in our past.*

J: Yes. He says it was almost in his time.

Again he was correct with his historical footnotes that we would have no knowledge of. In Nostradamus' time, Switzerland was composed of many different cantons and provinces. It was called the Swiss Confederation. During that time they were trying to consolidate and emerge as an independent country. By the middle of the 1600s they were recognized by all of the European states. So this did occur near his time although it was after his death. Two hundred years ago their constitution established a strong central government for the first time in Swiss history. So he was also correct when he said that this occurred a few centuries before our time.

CENTURY IV-10

Le jeune prince accusé
faulsement,
Mettra en trouble le camp
& en querelles:
Meutri le chef pour le
soustenement,
Sceptre appaiser: puis
guerir escrouelles.

The young Prince, falsely accused will put the camp into quarrels and trouble. The leader is murdered for his support to appease the crown: then he cures the king's evil.

J: This quatrain refers to England in the future. There will be difficulties in the line of succession of Prince Charles' children who are living at the present time.

D: *What does he mean, "the leader is murdered"?*

J: He says it's not good to predict other people's deaths.

D: *He doesn't like to talk about that?*

J: He says it's not good for you to talk about that right now. This quatrain has something to do with the line of succession to England's throne.

D: *Tell him that a lot of his prophecies deal with death, and it would be difficult for me to find some that didn't. That's the trouble—some of them are very morbid.*

J: Talking about death upsets him.

D: *Okay. If there are any he doesn't want to talk about, just let me know.*

It seems that Nostradamus also had to come to terms with his visions and develop an objective attitude as his abilities progressed.

CENTURY IV-11

Celui qu'aura gouvert de la grand cappe,	He who will have government of the great cloak will be led to execute in certain cases. The twelve red ones will come to spoil the cover, under murder, murder will be perpetrated.
Sera induict à quelques cas patrer	
Les douze rouges viendront fouiller la nappe.	
Soubz meutre, meutre se viendra perpetrer.	

J: This quatrain refers to the rise of the Tsar and the Russian aristocracy and its putdown by the Communist party at that time.

D: *Who are the twelve red ones?*

J: Red soldiers.

D: *"The government of the great cloak." Does that refer to communism?*

J: No. The aristocracy of Russia lived under a great cloak. A cloak is supposed to protect someone, but only a few people were protected by this cloak. The rest were left to fend for themselves.

D: *"The twelve red ones will come to spoil the cover."*

J: This line represents the march of liberation by the Marxist and Communist party.

D: *The translators associate it with the pope and his twelve cardinals.*

CENTURY IV-12

Le camp plus grand de route mis en fuite,	The greatest army on the march put to flight will scarcely be pursued further. The army reassembled and the legion reduced, they will then be driven out of France completely.
Guaires plus outre ne sera pourchassé:	
Ost recampé, & legion reduicte,	
Puis hors ses Gaules du tout sera chassé.	

John repeated this aloud line by line after me.

J: All of this refers to the United States and events in the recent past. France's NATO treaty will be broken with us as we go through economic difficulties. He's saying this quatrain refers to how we were the greatest war nation on Earth, but humble Vietnam showed us that the giant can be overtaken. This quatrain describes how America suffered through Vietnam.

D: *It says they will be driven out of France completely.*

J: In the near future, France, by a popular decree, won't allow our air bases or our nuclear weapons in their country.

*UPDATE: In 1992 it came to light that this quatrain may be on the verge of coming true. The new unified Germany has begun a program which observers interpret as a call for Europe to move away from its American influences. To underscore this point, Germany and France have established a 50,000-man joint army that apparently will operate independently of NATO. These same nations have shown contempt for international restrictions on the proliferation of weapons of mass destruction. Also, as Nostradamus predicted in one of his quatrains, a small but increasingly vocal neo-Nazi movement is arising among Germany's youth (*CENTURY I-61, *Volume One).*

CENTURY IV-13

De plus grand perte nouvelles raportées,	**News of the great loss is brought;** **the report will astonish the camp.**
Le raport fait le camp s'estonnera:	**Bands unite against those revolting,**
Bandes unies encontre revoltées,	**the double phalanx will forsake the**
Double phalange grand abandonnera.	**great one.**

Again John repeated the quatrain line for line after me. I had trouble with the word "phalanx" and started to spell it, but he interrupted me. He said he knew what it meant and then he pronounced it correctly.

J: This quatrain creates a picture of a civil war that will occur in America's future. It will involve fundamentalist Christians, New Age sects, and all kinds of religious persecution. He says there is religious persecution in his day, and you will witness it again in the late 20th century. (I didn't like the sound of that.)

D: *What is the meaning of the word "phalanx"?*

J: A phalanx is a column of soldiers. These Christians will see themselves as soldiers of Christ, when actually they are soldiers of their own exorbitant lust to rape, rule, and rob. (*Abruptly*) He doesn't want to talk any more. Something is happening to his magic circle. He needs to leave this place.

D: *Did it disturb him to see all of these things?*

J: Well, he's not used to it. He's not used to *us*. You see, this is one of the first times we've come through. He sees the vision in the mirror, and he has this wand that he points with. That's how I'm communicating with him, by being in the circle with him. But his spell is over, and he says, "It's over, you have to leave."

D: So that's all he wants to handle at this time?

J: He's been writing in this scroll and he's very intrigued, but he's ... ambivalent. He wants us to leave. He's calling ... "In the name of Jehovah, Elohim, I ask that you spirits go back to your place."

D: Okay, we respect that.

J: I'm in the Tapestry Room now.

D: It shows how powerful his spells are.

J: Yes. If I had stuck around there, I would have been zapped with something like electricity.

D: (Laugh) Did you have to stay within that circle on the floor?

J: Yes. It was very strange.

D: What do you mean?

J: Well, as a spirit of the future, it was basically my first meeting with him. *(Confused)* I don't know what this is or how it's done.

D: Well, it must have startled him. Maybe he really wasn't expecting what happened.

J: Yes, I think that was it. The guardian of the tapestry is here. Do you want to speak with him?

D: I'm curious. Does he think we disturbed Nostradamus because it was one of our first meetings?

J: No, it didn't disturb him, the guardian is saying. It's just that people who undertake to use the forces of nature while still in the human incarnation have to be prepared for some unusual results. He says that with a smile.

D: So when they're able to do these things, they simply have to be prepared to take the consequences. The circle and his invocation, when he asked you to leave, were powerful. That's very important. That means we can also use these things to protect ourselves.

J: This is true.

I don't think there is any clear explanation for what happened in this session. Our experiences continue to add credence to the theory of simultaneous time which is the idea that everything is happening at once instead of proceeding on a linear plane. If this is the explanation, it still doesn't make it any easier to understand.

This time Nostradamus didn't recognize us and he seemed to be afraid, even though he was willing to attempt a daring experiment to contact spirits from the beyond. This was a radical and dangerous thing for him to do in his time. Apparently his curiosity was as great as ours, and he took greater chances than we could even imagine.

Our part in this strange scenario seemed easy compared to what he subjected himself to. At this time in his life he seemed to be totally unaware of the quatrains and wasn't even planning to write a book about them. When I read a few to him he said he experienced a sense of *déjà vu*, the feeling of having heard it somewhere before. I imagine this was very confusing to him. For once, we were more informed than he was because we had already participated with him in his future. This entire episode was strange. It couldn't have been anticipated because we didn't know where the golden thread would deposit us in Nostradamus' life. We seemed to be on a wild swing back and forth through time, with our only goal being to contact Nostradamus, no matter what phase of his life we happened to enter. Something like this was too complicated for our Earth minds to comprehend. I was glad the guardian seemed to be in charge of things. He was the only one who wasn't confused about what was happening. He just kept telling us to, "Do it! Don't ask questions! It's too complicated for you to understand anyway. So just do your job and it will all work out for the best." So we, as pawns or puppets, have no choice but to continue to work on a plan that was apparently mapped out on a grand scale incomprehensible to mortals.

Chapter 24

Nostradamus' Philosophy

J: I've appeared through the mirror, and now I'm in his room. I'd say he's in his early fifties. He's got gray in his hair and in his beard. He's seriously pondering his writing at the present time, and he's writing about some type of philosophy. I don't know what it's about. He says it's his own private work and none of our business. (*Laugh*) That's what he said, "It's none of your business. It's my own private philosophy. I might not even publish it, but it's something I need to work on."

D: *Well, is it all right if he works with us for a while?*

J: Yes. He's prepared, he says. He's taking out another big book that he writes quatrains in.

Since he was prepared, we continued with the quatrains.

CENTURY IV-14

La mort subite du premier personnage.	The sudden death of the leading personnage will have changed and
Aura changé & mis un autre au regne:	put another to rule. Soon, but too late come to high position, of young
Tost, tard venu à si haut & bas aage,	age, by land and sea it will be necessary to fear him.
Que terre & mer faudre que on la craigne.	

J: He says this quatrain refers to the first Anti-Christ, Napoleon, and how he will come at a time when France will have trouble changing from the monarchy into a republic. He says it also could apply to the future as well. There will be a leader born after the time of troubles who will be young for his age, but an advanced being. He will be feared, but it won't be the same sense of fear you have at the present time. He is the embodiment of a great spirit. It will be like the return of Christ. Nostradamus says he's not like Jesus, the Christ, but the situation is very similar.

D: *Would this relate to the figure we've spoken of before, the Great Genius?*

J: Yes. This quatrain refers to both Napoleon and him. But the Great Genius won't be *feared,* he will be respected. He says that's how the quatrain would be translated for him.

D: *The translators thought it referred to John F. Kennedy, a president in our time. They have tried to relate a lot of the quatrains to the Kennedy family.*

J: The translators are obsessed with them, aren't they? There are quatrains that do apply to the Kennedys, but not as many as they think. He says, "I knew they would be important men in your time period, but their power has waned. They were incarnations of the Roman Gracchus brothers."

This sounded like: Gracius (phonetically). This was how I pronounced it since it was an unknown name to me and the others in the room. Research later revealed that it was Gracchus, remarkably similar in sound.

D: *Gracchus brothers? I'm not familiar with those people.*

J: (*Abruptly*) "Dolores! You *need* to study your mythology! And your history!" That's what he's saying.

I was being chastised again for my ignorance.

D: *(Laugh) I know, but it's not as important in our time.*

J: He says a lot of the things he refers to are from that time period because that was the mark of a classical education in his day. But he understands that we study different subjects, like algebra and geometry, which he is just learning about.

D: *We learn about science and computers and things he wouldn't even understand. So we've pushed mythology and ancient history to the background.*

J: But it would be good for you to review these subjects so you will understand his further works. That's what he's saying.

D: *Yes, I'll do research. But the Kennedys are the reincarnation of the Gracchus brothers?*

J: He says, "Yes, I do believe in reincarnation now. For a long time it was very hard for me to accept. But now that I see the transmigration of souls from the mirror, I can understand its process."

D: *Maybe now it's easier for him to understand where we are coming from? Can he see the connection I had with his student when we were first contacted?*

J: Yes. He's older in life, and he's learned a lot and grown in his own way.

Research revealed that he was again referring to ancient Roman history. Tiberius and Gaius Gracchus, called the *Gracchi,* were two brothers who attempted to institute political and social reforms in Rome during the second century B.C.E. There are several parallels between the lives of these brothers and the lives of the Kennedy brothers. Most notable was their attempt to pass legislation that would benefit the average person. They were faced with problems such as, a crisis in military manpower, and a poor and unemployed rabble in Rome. They had opposition to their way of thinking. Tiberius was killed during a riot when he attempted to run for a second year as tribune, an act that was considered unconstitutional. His brother, Gaius, tried to avenge his brother's murder by entering politics and proceeding with his brother's plans. Gaius was considered to be more of a rabble rouser where his brother had been more dignified. During his career Gaius became so popular that he was declared the uncrowned king of Rome. A few years into his popularity he made the fatal mistake of submitting a very unpopular piece of legislation. Again, a riot broke out, and Gaius committed suicide while being pursued through the streets of Rome by a senatorial posse. Perhaps he did it to escape the same fate as his brother. Two thousand of his followers were executed after his death. The time period of the Gracchi is called the Roman Revolution.

I have not included all of this information under the assumption that I believe the Kennedys were the reincarnation of the Gracchi, although their story is full of similarities. I have included it because it was an incident in ancient Roman history which no one in the room was familiar with, and the parallels which Nostradamus referred to cannot be coincidence. Again, if this did not come from the mind of Nostradamus, where did it come from? It emphasizes his constant referral to Roman history and mythology which he used to explain his quatrains and throw the Inquisition off the track. They merely assumed he was writing about ancient history, and could not see his sly inferences to prophecy. These small details were remarkable and never failed to astound me when I did my research.

CENTURY IV-15

D'où pensera faire venir famine,	From the place where he will think
De là viendra le rassasiement:	to bring famine, from there will
L'œil de la mer par avare canine	come the relief. The eye of the sea,
Pour de l'un l'autre dorna huile,	like a covetous dog; the one will give
froment.	oil and wheat to the other.

J: He says this quatrain refers to the karmic relationship that lies between the Soviet Union and the United States. The eye of the storm, he's showing me a place that ...

I corrected him although his wording also proved to be appropriate. "The eye of the *sea.*"

J: The eye of the sea. He's showing me a place in the Pacific Ocean off the coast of Lima, Peru. He says this environmental feature *has been* affected by mankind and that it wasn't present in his time period.

D: *What does he mean by environmental feature?*

J: It looks like the eye of a hurricane. He says it causes weather patterns to fluctuate in the United States, and it has been controlled by man. There are weather control studies that are being conducted by the United States, as well as the Soviet Union. The reason why America is a great nation is because of her food supply; this is her wealth. Russia has a hard time because of its harsh climate. So the Soviet Union will try to strip America of its wealth by manipulating the weather. Thus, they will feel that they're given parity with the United States. They have planned this storm center. It has been in the making for the last four years and they think it will cause destruction or famine for the United States. In actuality it won't, because the United States will offset it using its own scientists and engineering. As a result, there will be better trade and friendship between these two countries in the future.

D: *Can he give a time when this will happen?*

J: Yes. It's been happening since 1945.

D: *Have they been experimenting with controlling the weather that long? It seems strange to think they can do that.*

J: He's saying that in your lifetime you've seen them seed clouds to produce rain. This is a practice that was begun earlier in your century. He's not saying all this, but he's showing me in the mirror.

D: *Is it similar to cloud seeding?*

J: They use all different types of methods. Also there's space technology and satellites that affect the weather.

D: *These are things that we don't know about, as a rule.*

J: You should!

D: *I mean there are many things that are kept secret from the people. The government doesn't tell us everything. What did he mean by karmic relationships between our country and Russia?*

J: There are strong ties between the two nations. He says, "Just like England and France have a strong tie. We've fought and argued and had difficulties with England. We are part of its balance." You see, part of his philosophical treatise is on karmic ties and that's why he made that correlation.

D: *I'm not used to thinking of karmic ties between nations.*

J: Everything has a karmic balance, doesn't it? It's the law of cause and effect or the law of retribution. Nations, races, even the planet has a sense of karma. As do all living things from the smallest blade of grass, through the minerals, rocks, and oil to the animals. All animated and inanimate things have a sense of purpose, he says. He's showing me a big green field and all of the connections within it.

D: *The translators thought this quatrain dealt with submarines because of his mention of the eye of the sea.*

J: No, he says they've got that wrong. They take things too literally. He says it doesn't mean that. It represents the eye of the sea which is an area of the sea. The area he's showing me is what they call "El Niño."

D: *I thought that might be what he was referring to.*

J: And this is also eye of the sea. He said this isn't really an anagram, but there's a correlation between "eye of the sea" and the Spanish word "El Niño." This phenomenon has been geophysically (he had difficulty with that word) manufactured by the Soviets. He says they have used submarines as well as surface ships in that area to create this weather pattern that can bring havoc to America, especially in its grain basket.

D: *There have been questions about El Niño. Meteorologists think it occurs more often and at times of the year it's not supposed to.*

J: Realize that it's being manipulated by scientific men. He's not telling me this, he's showing me in the black mirror.

El Niño is a weather phenomenon characterized by a warm coastal current that flows south along the coasts of Ecuador and Peru about Christmas time. The warm surface waters and biological disturbances associated with El Niño extend southward to Chile and northward to British Columbia. Its name is derived from the Spanish *el niño Jesus* ("the Christ child"). It's the largest irregularity in the year-to-year fluctuations of the oceanic and atmospheric systems. It usually starts around Christmas and lasts for a few weeks, but major events may last longer. Various catastrophes are associated with major El Niños, including torrential rains and flooding along the normally dry coast, the absence of fish, and the starvation of fish-eating seabirds. In 1972 El Niño led to a collapse of the once-large Peruvian anchovy fishery. Other disturbances in the El Niño can affect much of the globe. Australia and parts of Indonesia suffer drought; winter weather over North America is abnormal; storms over the North Pacific increase; and patterns of hurricane occurrence change.

In 1987 El Niño dominated the weather news. Unusually warm waters in the equatorial Pacific Ocean altered atmospheric circulation and the results were felt throughout the world. This situation was detected early in the year and was carefully monitored. The lack of monsoon rain in India caused serious food shortages, and the government had to import rice to prevent starvation. In the past, a failure of the monsoon would have resulted in famine and the deaths of thousands. Now, however, El Niños can be predicted six to nine months before they occur, giving governments time to plan so they can alleviate the hardships this weather phenomenon can cause.

The inference by Nostradamus that a weather feature of such proportions can be manipulated by man is almost unfathomable. But then it's not any more preposterous than the many other things we have been shown. It was often difficult for me to not pass judgment, and to merely report without comment. I had to remember that these things must have seemed even more unbelievable to Nostradamus than they do to us.

CENTURY IV-16

La cité franche de liberté
fait serve,
Des profligés & resveurs
faict asile:
Le Roy changé à eux non
si proterve
De cent seront devenus
plus de mille.

The free city of liberty is enslaved, it becomes the refuge of profligates and dreamers. The king changes and is not so ferocious towards them. From one hundred they will become more than a thousand.

J: He says this quatrain refers to the blossoming of Paris as a cultural center.
D: *Did this happen in our past?*
J: Yes. You see, Paris was an administrative and a religious center in his time period, but in the late 1800s Paris changed to become the art capital of the world. It was a very important place for art and culture. He also says that kings resent artisans and creative people, unless their gifts are used for their service. He says this quatrain predicts change from one king to another king, from an old monarchy type of establishment into a more free democratic process.
D: *Then the numbers don't have any significance, except to represent the growth of the ...*
J: The birth of the French capital as a cultural center.
D: *The translators didn't relate it to that at all.*

CENTURY IV-17

Changer à Beaune, Nuy,
Chalons & Dijon,
Le duc voulant amander
la Barrée
Marchant pres fleuve, poisson,
bec de plongeon,
Vers la queue; porte sera serrée.

Changes at Beaune, Nuits, Chalon & Dijon, the Duke wishes to improve the Carmelites. Walking near the river, a fish, a diving (bird's) beak, towards the tail; the gate will be locked.

He repeated each name after me and correctly pronounced each one.

J: He's showing me a map of France, and he's directing me to the Bay of Biscayne area. He says many people don't realize it but the French at this time in your century have a great arsenal of water ... *(unsure how to describe it)* a water thing ... a water armada. He's showing me ships, but they look like the ships of old rather than new ships. He says this quatrain refers to the fortification of this entire area. It's been taking place, but it will go abruptly forward in the future. The towns that are named will be near major military installations for the French army because the French are going to cut themselves free of what we know as NATO. They will take on their own national defense by strengthening these areas.

D: *What does he mean by the Carmelites?*

J: He says you wouldn't realize this because you don't study history, but many of the Carmelites were repentant warriors. He says they gave up military life in their pursuit of a religious life. This has important symbolism because the retired military of the France of the 20th century will want to expand and separate itself from other nations.

The Carmelites were members of a Roman Catholic religious order. They were originally a group of hermits. As their numbers grew they were still under severe regulations and lived a solitary, isolated life. Perhaps, as Nostradamus indicates, the repentant warriors chose this type of life to repay for the violence they had caused. After Nostradamus' time the religious orders became more outgoing and changed their strict regulations. His interpretation of this quatrain correlates to what he knew of the order during his lifetime, thus the symbolism.

D: *The translators think this part is very obscure, "Walking near the river, a fish, a diving bird's beak towards the tail. The gate will be locked."*

J: This refers to ... it's not so much an armada. He's showing me military fortifications.

D: *Is that the fish and the diving bird's beak?*

J: It's like a submarine. You know, submarines and airplanes and such. The best way for him to describe this equipment was in metaphors of animals that he was familiar with.

D: *Yes, that makes sense. And "the gate will be locked." What does that mean?*

J: It means this is only going to be *France's* armada.

D: *And they won't need the other nations or NATO.*

J: Right. They will take on their own defense.

D: *The translators didn't understand that one at all. They said they couldn't make anything out of it.*

CENTURY IV-18

Des plus lettrés dessus les faits celestes	Some of the most learned men in the heavenly arts will be reprimanded by ignorant Princes; punished by an Edict, driven out as scoundrels and put to death wherever they are found.
Seront par princes ignorans reprouvés:	
Punis d'Edit, chassez comme scelestes,	
Et mis à mort là où seront trouvés.	

J: He says this quatrain should be very obvious. It refers to the debasement of astrology after his time.

D: *The heavenly arts refers to astrology.*

J: Yes. He says a fellow Frenchman—and he's giving me the name,

Voltaire—will help to discredit astrology, and popularize a whole new philosophical viewpoint. He says as a result astrologers will be persecuted.

Voltaire lived more than a century after the time of Nostradamus. He was a philosopher and a prolific author. He was one of the fathers of the Enlightenment, which is also called "The Age of Reason." As new philosophies were developed everything was under attack. He wrote on many subjects, including religious freedom and penal reform, and his works are still popular today. *Collier's Encyclopedia* says, "His whole life was devoted to protest against existing evils." So it's possible that he also wrote against the once respected field of astrology.

D: This is similar to what the translators said. "Shades of the Inquisition linger over this verse, for in fact astrologers were never as grossly persecuted after Nostradamus' death as they were during the century before."

I have already indicated from my research that astrologers were not persecuted in Nostradamus' time unless they overstepped their boundaries to dapple in magic. They were usually highly respected and tolerated. Astrology was an absolute necessity for a physician. Nostradamus indicated that the persecution and misunderstanding would happen *after* his time. This was something I would not have suspected.

J: He says it's tricky being an astrologer in his time period, because if you're good you can predict many events and your clients will look up to you. But the church frowns on it because the church wants power. It wants *the* power.

D: That makes sense. The translators were right, this quatrain does deal with astrology.

J: Yes, it does.

CENTURY IV-20

Paix uberté long temps lieu louera;	Peace and plenty for a long time the place will praise: the fleur de lis
Par tout son regne desert la fleur de lis:	deserted throughout the kingdom. Bodies dead by water, they will be
Corps morts d'eau, terre là lou apportera,	brought to land there, waiting in vain for the opportunity of being
Sperants vain heur d'estre là ensevelis.	buried.

J: He says this quatrain refers to the far future. After the Earth shift takes place—he's showing me the Earth shift—a part of France will disappear. France as a national entity will be gone because *all* people will come together. Many bodies will be washed ashore in a new land that will have peace, happiness, and prosperity. But the bodies of those that have died during the cataclysm will need to be buried.

CENTURY IV-22

*La grand copie qui sera
deschasée,
Dans un moment fera
besoing au Roi,
La foi promise de loing
sera faulsée
Nud se verra en piteux desarroi.*

The great army which will be driven out at one moment will be needed by the King. The faith promised from afar will be broken, he will see himself with nothing, in pitiful disorder.

J: Could you please repeat that because he's writing this one down.

I repeated it and John said each phrase after me.

J: This quatrain refers to Charles de Gaulle. He was not a king of France, but he became president even though he was not well liked. He was influential in driving the Nazis from his beloved France.

D: *Yes, he was.*

J: But he wasn't rewarded with the presidency until much later in his career. This is why he was sometimes a very bitter man.

D: *We are familiar with him in our time period.*

CENTURY IV-23

*La legion dans la marine classe,
Calcine, Magnes soulphre,
& paix bruslera:
Le long repos de l'asseuree place,
Port Selyn, Hercle feu les
consumera.*

The legion in the marine fleet will burn, lime, magnesia, sulphur and pitch. The long rest in a safe place; Port Selin, Monaco will be consumed by fire.

J: He says this quatrain refers to Asia. He's pointing to Asia on his map. It describes some type of naval accident that will affect the island of ...

John had difficulty with the pronunciation of the name. He went through several tries before he settled on Macao.

J: He's showing me an English ship. It will explode in their harbor causing a lot of damage to the city.

D: *Is this what he means by the list of chemicals?*

J: Yes. He says these chemicals will be found inside the ship and will cause it to explode. There will be some type of accident and the resulting fire will also burn the port city of Macao.

This would appear to be a mistake, since I had definitely read the word "Monaco" from the quatrain. Monaco is located on the coast of the Mediterranean, a long way from Macao, which is near Hong Kong. It seemed to be contradictory, and I thought we had finally come across something that could be challenged by skeptics. But upon closer look, Monaco is the translator's name for the city. In the original quatrain the word is "Hercle," which was translated as "Latin, Herculeis Monacei, another name for Monaco." This is Ms. Cheetham's own interpretation. In other books on the quatrains the word "Hercle" is missing. If John were being influenced by my reading of the quatrain, it would have most certainly made him connect it with Monaco instead of Macao. This emphasizes beyond a doubt that John was not using his reasoning mind but was reporting what Nostradamus was showing him in the magic mirror.

D: Will there be any loss of life?

J: Yes, many lives will be lost. This will happen soon enough ... in the early 1990s actually.

D: The translators thought it might refer to "Greek fire," if he knows what that is.

J: (*Nonchalantly*) Yes, he said he's made it before.

D: He has? That's what they thought he was referring to.

J: (*A disgusted tone of voice.*) No! He says that stuff has been around for centuries. The Greeks and Romans used it on their war galleys. The Venetians are *known* for using this all the time to conquer new lands for trade.

D: They thought he might have been giving the recipe for Greek fire.

J: (*Laugh*) He says, "Why? Anyone who has any type of knowledge *knows* the recipe for it."

Greek fire was a famous secret weapon used by the ancient Greeks and Byzantines in their naval battles. It was a combination of various flammable chemicals which were ejected from tubes onto enemy ships or would ignite upon contact with the water. But in our day the exact ingredients have only been guessed at. It appears that it was not a secret to the scholars of Nostradamus' day.

CENTURY IV-24

Oui soubs terre saincte
    dame voix fainte,
Humaine flamme pour
    divine voix luire:
Fera les seuls de leur sang
    terre tainte,
Et les saincts temples pour
    les impurs destruire.

The faint voice of a woman is heard under the holy ground. Human flame shines for the divine voice. It will cause the earth to be stained with the blood of celibates and destroy the holy temples for the wicked.

J: He says women will rise to power in your century. They will bring about the destruction of the established religious and financial institutions of their time. He says this quatrain also refers to the great mother, the Earth herself, and her rebellion against being harnessed.

D: What will the women do to bring this about?

J: It's through their beliefs.

D: *It sounds like he's a bit of a chauvinist.*

J: Yes, he is, very much so. You know that. But I don't want to talk about that; he doesn't appreciate it.

D: *Okay. But he does think women are going to bring about these events.*

J: Yes, he believes women will become more powerful. You see, in his time women were treated like donkeys. You know, load this up, cook this, do this, and do that. Even he has that attitude. Women weren't given an education back then unless they were very rich, or they were from a noble house that had tutors. And tutors were only for the nobility, like kings, queens, princesses, and dukes. So women as a whole were not educated.

D: *Well, I can appreciate his beliefs based on his time period. That doesn't bother me.*

J: He said don't worry about it, "It's okay."

D: *Will this happen within our lifetime?*

J: He says the quatrain represents the unleashing of the female energies of the universe. That's the best way to describe it. He shows me a Virgin Mary image, but it's not the Virgin Mary. It represents the eternal female aspect of God.

CENTURY IV-26

*Lou grand eyssame se levera
d'abelhos,
Que non sauran don te siegen
venguddos:
De nuech l'embousque, lou
gach dessous las treilhos
Cuitad trahido per cinq
lengos non nudos.*

The great swarm of bees will arise but no one will know whence they have come, the ambush at night, the sentinel under the vines, a city handed over by five tongues not naked.

He repeated each phrase aloud again after me, and asked for a spelling of the word "tongues."

J: He says this quatrain refers to an attack on a naval city. It looks like Pearl Harbor. This quatrain refers to that event, but he says it will also happen elsewhere. It will be a sneak attack, and it won't happen in America but in India. An Indian naval base will be attacked by night.

D: *Does he know who they will be attacked by?*

J: Persians. That's what he says, "Them Persians!"

D: *Are they the swarm of bees?*

J: Yes, the bees represent the Persians who will overtake this place and destroy it.

D: *I want to understand some of his symbolism. "The sentinel under the vines." What does that mean?*

J: It symbolizes a sentry under palm trees.

D: *And "a city handed over by five tongues, not naked"?*

J: The city will be handed over by the people in power.
D: *Does "five tongues" have any significance?*
J: This is why the quatrain refers to India. India has five major languages.
D: *"Not naked"?*
J: There's one national tongue in India with many dialects, and there are even more completely different languages. That's what he said.
D: *We don't know these things, so by working with him we become educated. Can he tell us when this might happen?*
J: He says before the end of your century.
D: *Will this be a part of the Anti-Christ's war?*
J: Yes, he says this relates to those events.

CENTURY IV-27

Salon, Mansol, Tarascon de *SEX. l'arc,* *Ou est debout encor la piramide:* *Viendront livrer le Prince* *Dannemarc,* *Rachat honni au temple* *d'Artemide.*	Salon, Mansol, Tarascon, the arch of SEX: where the pyramid is still standing. They will come to deliver the Prince of Denmark, a shameful ransom to the temple of Artemis.

J: Nostradamus lives in Salon.
D: *Oh, does he?*

He was referring to one of the cities named. This was just the type of comment a real person would make.

J: He says there is going to be an archæological investigation at the Great Pyramids that will uncover many secrets. The way it will be bankrolled will be through a person of the noble house of Denmark.
D: *Will he finance it?*
J: Yes, but won't get much in return for what he's put into it, so he'll be deceived. The French will take all the credit for it. He says, "There we are, a belligerent race of beings. (*Chuckle*) We take all the credit when we want to."
D: *Why does he name those cities?*
J: The cities are all located in southern France and they represent the different areas that the archæologists will come from.
D: *Well, the translators think "the arch of SEX" is an anagram, but they don't understand it. What does he mean by that?*
J: It's not an anagram. Think for a minute what an arch of sex is, and he'll say.

I was sure I couldn't come up with an answer, unless it was possibly a symbolic reference to a woman's sexual organs. He might have felt ill at ease discussing that with a woman, but I didn't want to be the one to bring up sexual innuendos.

D: *I'm sorry. I'm coming up with nothing. I'm trying to see how it's connected to the Pyramids. (Pause) Why? Does it bother him to tell me what it means?*

J: No, he's laughing now.

D: *(Laugh) Well, he's made his meanings very obscure, I'll tell you that.*

J: He says the arch of sex simply refers to womankind. There will be female members of this archæological team.

D: *Is that why it's capitalized? It's unusual?*

J: Right! Women didn't have these types of positions in his time.

D: *Because they didn't have the knowledge.*

J: Right. And that's why it's important. The clue was the arch of SEX and also the temple of Artemis. He says you should have gotten that quickly.

This would be funny if it wasn't so serious. Nostradamus certainly gives me credit for a lot more knowledge than I actually have, especially when dealing with mythology.

J: Remember, the moon goddess was worshipped in the temple of Artemis. And who worships the moon goddess?

D: *Women? Okay.* Now, *it's clear! But just by looking at it, it's not.*

J: He's laughing.

D: *That's why we need him to explain these things. I can see it now, but not even the translators understood it. They were associating the symbol with some historical monuments that had SEX as part of their inscription.*

J: He says, "In your time people are obsessed with sex. In *our* time we enjoy it, but it's not a big issue. I see how it is." He has a vision of our future. *(Laugh)* He's seeing porno shops and prostitutes, and he says, "We even have prostitutes in Salon as well as in Marseilles, but they are honest about what they do." He says it's not an obsession; it's just a part of life.

D: *This is why it's difficult for people to understand his quatrains. He has a different way of thinking and a different frame of mind.*

J: This is true.

D: *So the archæologists are going to find out more secrets about the pyramids. Does he have a time frame on that?*

J: He says it's very soon in your future. And there'll be French women involved with this archæological study.

D: *That would be a great discovery. It has been long awaited. We know there are many secrets about the pyramids.*

J: This is true.

CENTURY IV-32

Es lieux & temps chair un *poisson donra lieu,* *La loi commune sera faicte* *au contraire:* *Vieux tiendra fort plus osté* *du millieu,* *Le Pánta chiona philòn mis* *fort arriere.*	In those times and places that meat gives way to fish the common law will be made in opposition. The old (order) will hold strong, then removed from the scene, then All Things common among Friends put far behind.

J: He says this quatrain refers to the growth and development of Communism in the Soviet Union.

D: *"In places that meat gives way to fish"?*

J: This represents the wilds. He's showing me a picture of tundra, ice, and snow.

D: *What does he mean by "giving way to fish"?*

J: The land goes toward the Arctic Ocean and that type of water.

D: *He's referring to the area then. It's a way of saying "Russia."*

J: To him it is. It's one of his hidden meanings. But it represents the Soviet Union and the rise of Communism.

D: *The translators have Friends capitalized, and say that refers to Communism. They've come close to interpreting it, but they think it represents the* decline *of Communism.*

J: *Wishful* thinking!

D: *(Laugh) Then it's not about to decline that quickly?*

J: No, it will go through an improvement. He says the basic principles of what he understands about Communism are good, but any power that manipulates other people is not good. He says, "We have kings in our time. You will have dictators and presidents in yours. The world doesn't change that much, even after centuries."

UPDATE: In Volume Three of this work Nostradamus translated quatrains predicting the fall of the Berlin Wall. He also said the various satellite countries of the Soviet Union would start rebelling, and would gain their freedom, some peacefully and some through violence. He said the Soviet Union would be reduced to its original size of Russia and Siberia. He also said that when Russia began to display economic problems the rest of the world would follow. He indicated that if America tried to help Russia with their money woes, it would wreck our economy also.

J: *(Abruptly)* He's saying that it's time for me to leave. He's pulled out his pipe, and he said, "I need my solace now."

D: *We have done quite a few today and I really appreciate it.*

J: He says we can do more at another time. He also says that you'll have other guides to help you.

I wasn't so sure about that. I was well aware that time was growing short, as John would soon be moving to Florida.

D: *Is he aware that this vehicle is leaving, and that we might only have time for one more session.*

J: He says he understands. He sees me as a spirit and not as an individual. He says, "Other spirits come and go, but we will accomplish what we need to." He has lit up his pipe and is taking a big puff. I'm in the mirror. I'm going back. Bye!

D: *(Laugh) Bye-bye! I just hope he'll talk to whomever I bring.*

J: He said, "Don't worry, have them come through the mirror." That's the last thing he said. Guide them to his mirror and then come through it. He said this will be handy. Now he's gone, and I'm in the Tapestry Room.

D: *We've done quite a bit today. I'm surprised. He stayed with us longer than he normally does.*

J: He had a clay pipe.

John's hand motions indicated that it was a long pipe, with a curved stem maybe a foot long and a small bowl.

J: He put tobacco and herbs in it and he wanted to smoke. He was feeling *fine*, relaxing, and studying what we have talked about and helped him write.

D: *To me it still seems strange to think that we are helping him to write his quatrains. This is confusing to our human minds.*

J: *(Very authoritatively.)* "It's not a question for you to comprehend at this point in your existence." That's what the guardian of the tapestry is saying.

D: *(Laugh) Just do it and not ask questions?*

J: *(Laugh)* Yes. That's basically what he's saying. He says in time you'll understand, but right now you may not. He says just to continue your good work.

D: *(Resolved) Okay. The main thing is that we're not interfering. We have been told to do this.*

J: Yes, he understands. He's studied this case very closely in detail.

D: *I wish I knew it in detail. (Laugh) I feel like I'm just a pawn in the middle of all this. Is it really like that?*

J: He says he can't talk about that right now. He doesn't want to say anything to discourage you or to elate you. "Just *do* it!" He says, "Whatever I say could be used either for good or bad or against, and I don't have the time."

D: Okay. I'm in the middle of this, not knowing where it's going or what I'm supposed to be doing. I'm doing my part, I guess, and all the other people involved are just doing theirs. Is that right? *(No answer.)* We'll leave it that way then.

Apparently he wouldn't discuss it any more; "end of discussion, subject closed."

IT'S STRANGE how quickly things become commonplace. When I first suspected that we might be helping him to write the quatrains, it was very disturbing. It was mind-boggling. And only a month later, the whole thing was accepted and acknowledged as an important job. It now seemed normal to accept it instead of being frightened by it and trying to run from it. It apparently had been decided on some other level. For all we know we were part of that decision making.

Chapter 25

The New Baby

THIS WAS OUR LAST SESSION with John because he was moving to Florida in two days. I was hoping it would be productive before we bid Nostradamus a fond farewell once again. John said he might return for a visit and we could work then, but I knew from experience not to count on that. Strangely enough, when my subjects left they went *far* away, as though their part in this project, their karmic connection, was finished and they had to completely sever their ties to it. Only my part in this scenario remained constant. It *did* seem too perfectly orchestrated to be happening by chance.

So for the last time I used the keyword and instructed John to follow the golden thread to Nostradamus. As he came through the mirror he saw Nostradamus dressed very differently from his usual informal clothes. John spent some time trying to describe the strange hat Nostradamus was wearing. He had difficulty because he was not familiar with it. "It's a funny-looking hat. It's round ... and thick. The material is bunched down, and it looks like a big plate with a little cap underneath it and flaps over the ears. He's also wearing voluminous robes today because it looks like it's cold where he is."

This sounded somewhat similar to the hat Nostradamus is shown wearing in various portraits.

John noticed that Nostradamus was drawing up a horoscope.

J: (*Smiling*) He sees me coming through the mirror and he says, "This is a momentous day. My wife has just given birth to a child." I asked, "Is this your first wife?" He said, "No, it's my second wife, and I'm doing my son's horoscope. I don't have much time today so I can only work with you a bit. I have to attend the celebration of my son's birth. That's why I'm dressed this way. I've got important guests coming to my house from all over Salon. These are old friends who know the unhappiness I felt when I lost my other family. I'm very excited. I'm drawing up the horoscope." (*Smiling*) He's a proud father wearing his *best* clothes. His robe is a rich wine-colored velvet with white lace sleeves underneath it. He's even got ribbons above his knees. He says, "But I can't spend very much time with you today because my guests will be arriving shortly."

D: Well, we're excited and happy for him, too. Is this his first child by this wife?

J: Yes, this is their first child. Her parents are also traveling to this celebration.

D: Can he tell us what date is on the horoscope he's drawing up?

J: I'm not sure. Their writing is very different from ours, and it's difficult to read his numerals. It looks like 1557 or 1551, but it could be 1547 or 1541. It is ... November. I know the month is November, but I'm not sure of the year.

D: Is the horoscope drawn the way you've seen him do it before?

J: No, it's different from the other horoscope I saw. It's a diamond shape again, but it's inside of a square. He's telling me he uses three forms for horoscopes: a three-diamond pattern, a square within the diamond shape, and a round wheel. He says the ancients used the square and diamond patterns in their horoscopes. (*Proudly*) He says, "I've got a son that can carry on my name. I am so happy and excited. It's just wonderful." He's in seventh heaven. It looks like he's in his forties.

I gave John post-hypnotic instructions that he would be able to duplicate the pattern of the horoscope after he awakened.

D: Maybe we can do a few quatrains before he has to go.

J: He says we can do only a couple because it's important to him to get to the gathering.

This would have to happen in our last session. *We* had plenty of time to work but Nostradamus didn't. In a case like this you feel like an unwelcome guest that has dropped in at an inopportune time.

D: I wish we had more control over what days we come.

J: This is a very happy day in his life.

D: And we're very happy for him, but we never know when we're going to pop in on him. Let's see what we can do in the limited time that we have. There's one quatrain I want to ask him about first because it includes astrological signs.

CENTURY V-23

Les deux contens seront unis ensemble,	The two contented men are united together when most (planets) are
Quand la pluspart à Mars seront conjoinct.	conjunct with Mars. The African leader trembles in terror. The twin
Le grand d'Affrique en effrayeur & tremble:	alliance scattered by the fleet.
DUUMVIRAT par la classe desjoinct.	

J: He took out a cloth and rubbed it against the black mirror, and he says, "This is going to happen soon enough in your lives. You people function in 1987. (*Unbelievably*) Ahh! Almost *400* years in the future from me." He says this prophecy will be fulfilled in Africa. Mars, Saturn, other planets, the Sun, and the Moon will be in the sign of Sagittarius at this time. He says it will happen when there's a new moon in Sagittarius conjuncting Mars and Saturn. (*Sigh*) He says Mars might not be in Sagittarius, it might be in Scorpio, but close enough to this energy that it will be affected. He says during this time there will be an attempt to overthrow the Libyan government.

D: *Is this what he means by "the African leader trembles in terror"?*

J: Yes. (*Confused*) It sounds like this has already taken place. He's showing me bombs and the American fleet battling with Libya who is now trembling. She's not the great power she thought she was going to be.

Nostradamus then tried to clarify the astrological signs, but it only became more confusing. Was this confusion caused because he was working on the baby's horoscope and the quatrain was distracting him?

J: He says not to worry about the astrological portents. He says, "Look at what the mirror shows. It shows the Mediterranean. Here in the Mediterranean is Libya. Libya is trying to expand and take over the countries around her, those to the east, the west, and the south. She wants to carve an empire in the top half of the African continent." He's using a pointer to show me this sphere of influence and he says, "This is Libya here, and right here are the twins. The twins represent the United States which scatters his force and power. There are clandestine operations by your government of the United States of America."

D: *What does he mean?*

J: He says, "Your government is working in other countries to prevent this sphere of influence from growing and this causes the African prince—the African *king*—to tremble."

The astrological findings showed that the most likely date for this event would be December 20, 1987. This is based on the Sun, the new moon, Saturn, and Uranus all being located in Sagittarius, and Mars in Scorpio. There was confusion about these signs, but I believe Nostradamus indicated the event has already occurred. Actually, it's still in the process of happening. The United States involvement with Libya is still very much in current world news.

After looking through my Collier's Encyclopedia Yearbooks it became apparent that Nostradamus was correct when he said that our government might be involved in clandestine operations against Libya. He was also correct when he said that Libya was trying to expand into neighboring countries. The 1987 Yearbook reported that it had been revealed that the United States State Department had succeeded in heading off a White

House-sponsored plan for a joint U.S.-Egyptian military attack on Libya in 1985. The plan, devised by the National Security Council, called for Egypt to attack Libya, seize half of the country with U.S. air support, and depose Muammar al-Qaddafi. This plan was never carried out. But the United States did support Chad in its war with Libya in the belief that a Libyan defeat would precipitate Qaddafi's downfall.

In 1986, Libya and the U.S. engaged in armed conflict. In March, Libya attacked U.S. planes and vessels when Qaddafi claimed they had entered his territorial waters. The U.S. retaliated by attacking Libyan ships and a missile site.

Terrorism became a problem on a global scale in 1986, and it was known to be a declared state policy by Qaddafi. Thus, after several terrorist attacks in Europe had taken many lives, the U.S. claimed they had evidence of Libyan involvement. It was difficult to get the support from other countries because of their oil interests in Libya, but in April the U.S. bombed Qaddafi's headquarters killing several people. Most countries criticized this action. It was hoped that because of all of the problems, the government of Libya would be overthrown from within. At this time there was constant pressure from the U.S. and other countries to keep Libya from expanding her influence to other countries.

In 1987, the Chad war spilled over the border into Libya and a ceasefire was declared. It was suggested that Qaddafi recognized the impossibility of a Libyan victory because of the French and U.S. backing of Chad.

In 1988, the U.S. asserted that Libya was developing a huge plant to manufacture chemical weapons, while Qaddafi claimed it was to make drugs.

It's obvious that uneasy conditions still exist between the U.S. and Libya. The astrological signs given by Nostradamus might infer that the conditions described in the quatrain were prevalent during the late 1980s. It appears that he saw the politics behind what was going on while the world in general was ignorant of it. It was certainly a situation that I was unaware of until his remarks prompted me to do research.

UPDATE: The area of the Middle East was described by Nostradamus as a thunderstorm brewing just beneath the horizon, a time bomb waiting to explode. The following quote was made by Muammar al-Qaddafi in April 1990, and shows the unstable conditions in the area. "If we had a deterrent force of missiles able to reach New York we would have directed them at that very moment. (During the 1986 bombing raid on Libya by the U.S.) We therefore must have this force so that the Americans and others would not think to attack us once again."

D: Why does he refer to the United States as the twins?

J: He says it is remarkable. Because he knows the future, he knows that I will live in a populous country made up of individual states which have all united. He's aware that Gemini is very prominent in the horoscope of this continent of the United States. In other words, the twin effect. He says, "You have twin cities, great cities on each coast. There's positive and negative. You have great heat in the south, and great cold in the north. There's always a twin pattern or balance of opposites."

D: *Is that what it means in the first sentence? "The two contented men are united together."*

J: Yes. He says this again refers to Gemini.

D: *Then this all refers to the United States. The translators thought it represented two allies but it has nothing to do with that at all.*

J: No. He says it actually represents two men. Don't look at your president, he doesn't have the power. There are two men who control the whole world situation right now in your time. He says one is based in New York and one is based in—he points to London on his world map. And these two men, he says, are very, *very* powerful. They're very well hidden, but they control most of the economy of both the known world and the third world.

D: *This is not known to the average person.*

J: No. (*Sigh*) He says, "I'm giving you this information because it's important."

D: *Do the governments know about these two men?*

J: They *control* governments. He's showing me the man in New York who looks like your average business executive. He has glasses and is about 55. He has a lot of power but it's all hidden. He manipulates different agencies of the U.S. government and other countries, because he has the power to do so. The man in London is the same way. They are real men who are the hidden leaders. He says they're going to create problems, not because they want money, because they have all the money they could wish for—he's showing me *tons* of gold—but because they want power and control. He says these are the men who will set the stage for the Anti-Christ.

D: *Then Arab leaders aren't the only ones who will help the Anti-Christ in this way.*

J: No. He says these people will take him into their organization and rapidly advance his position. He says, "In your time this might be very dangerous information, *but,* I believe people should know."

This sounded like Brenda's referral in Volume One to the mysterious cabal: a group of secret people who are behind the governments of the world and who have been controlling things for many generations.

J: He says these two men are the leaders of the world, but you don't know of them. You don't even know their names. The media doesn't know of them. They're kept clandestine, but they have great influence, especially on the presidents and leaders of the different world governments. In fact, they're trying to manipulate the government of the Soviet Union to bring another leader into the net.

D: *It's hard to understand how they can control so much and not be known. How can they keep it out of the media?*

J: He says they *control* part of the media and can do anything they want. Their power is enormous. He's showing me a picture of the globe with lines on it that he has drawn, and everything is tied together. These men are the movers and shakers of the world. That's what he said. (*Smiling*) He shows me that they are shaking the world. He says, "We believe these souls are incarnations of people who have had power in other lifetimes, and now they're making their final bid for world dominion. They're really the power behind the throne."

D: *Did they have something to do with Libya?*

J: He says, "Those two are the connected men that I see. They have a plan to control the world, and it's all falling into place. *But,* the *true* controller of the world will be *this* man." And he showed me ...

D: *The one we know as the Anti-Christ?*

J: Right. But he says we won't deal with him at this time.

D: *No, we don't want to deal with him.*

I certainly didn't want to take the chance of a replay of what happened the last time we looked in on his life.

J: He says these two men will bring the Anti-Christ figure into their power network. And the Anti-Christ will topple *them.* (*Emphatically*) *He will topple* them.

D: *Their plan will backfire on them.*

J: The mirror's black now. He's saying, "Go on to another quatrain because I have gatherings coming."

This is essentially the same information given by Brenda. She also described in Volume One how the cabal will want the Anti-Christ within their group thinking they will control *him.* And he ends up destroying them in his bid for world superiority, not realizing that he really needed *them.* A case of "cutting off your nose to spite your face."

CENTURY IV-34

Le grand mené captif	The great man led captive from a
d'estrange terre,	foreign land, chained in gold,
D'or enchainé ay Roy	offered to King Chyren. He who
CHYREN offert:	in Ausonia, Milan, will lose the war
Qui dans Ausone, Milan	and all his army put to fire and
perdra la guerre,	sword.
Et tout son ost mis à feu & à fer.	

D: *He has the word CHYREN in capitals. The translators think it's an anagram.*

He asked for the spelling of Chyren and Ausonia.

J: He's trying to write ... you see, now he's back in his book and he's got his pen out. He says, "Let's get it from the top."

I repeated it and John said each phrase aloud after me.

J: (*A resolved tone of voice.*) "Here it comes again. He's showing me the mirror. He says the place is Cyrenia, and he's showing me where it is. This quatrain again deals with North Africa, represented by King Chyren. He says a very important diplomat from a very important government will be taken hostage, and this will happen in the 1990s. He says, "I believe he will be a European hostage from a wealthy nation." I see chains of gold. This quatrain also refers to the Anti-Christ who will gain control of North Africa. This is during one of the Anti-Christ's final battles before moving into Europe. He will take this man hostage and will promise to negotiate for his release but instead he will be barbaric to this captive. Because of his atrocities this captive will be destroyed. He says Ausonia and Milan are in northern Italy. Ausonia is almost in Switzerland, in the Alps. He says the man will come from this area. This important man who will be held captive might be Swiss. You see, the Anti-Christ wants the money that is in Swiss banks. He wants it *all.* He believes that by having all that bullion he can control the world, but they're going to fight him to the last man.

D: *He doesn't think small, does he?*

J: No, he doesn't think small. He wants it *all.*

D: *Is that why he's meeting with this man?*

J: Yes. He's going to meet with this man and try to use the hostage situation to get the money, but the resistance in Europe will be quite strong. It will be quite a battle. They will send a nuclear weapon against him, and this will destroy his army. But he'll retreat deeper into the Near East. When he appears again he will be more powerful than ever. He says this will happen in the mid-1990s.

D: *The translators think Chyren is an anagram for King Henri.*

J: (*Laugh*) He says, no. He says to look at your history and see where Cyrenia was.

D: (Laugh) *I don't know where it was.*

J: He's showing me that Cyrenia is between Egypt and Libya, along the North African coast. Again he says you must study your ancient history.

Should I have been surprised that he was correct again? I think he was referring to Cyrenaica because he used this name several times when translating through Brenda, to represent the Anti-Christ and North African countries. Cyrenaica today is a part of Libya. In ancient times it was much larger and a part of Egypt for a time. Thus, when he showed John the map it was the location of Cyrenaica in ancient times. He used it to symbolize that area of North Africa and also as an anagram for the

Anti-Christ. Interestingly, during ancient times Cyrene was the chief populated center of Cyrenaica. Both names clearly fit with his anagram "King Chyren." The translators, by suggesting it was an anagram for King Henri, are completely missing the point that Nostradamus used ancient history profusely in symbolic reference.

J: He says one more quatrain, and then he has to leave.

CENTURY IV-35

Le feu estaint, les vierges trahiront *La plus grand part de la bande nouvelle:* *Fouldre à fer, lance les seulz Roi garderont* *Etrusque & Corse, de nuict gorge allumelle.*	The fire put out, the virgins will betray the greater part of the new band; lightning in sword, lances alone will guard the king, Tuscany and Corsica, by night throats slit.

J: He says this quatrain indicates that the European beachheads will be in Corsica as well as in Tuscany, which is in northern Italy. He's showing me these areas on the map and he says they are going to be very important in the future. They will be the beachheads that the Anti-Christ's forces will use to come into Europe. He says the king he refers to is King Charles. Britain will be upset because the Anti-Christ will try to take Gibraltar, but the British people will stand at attention. In other words, they will protect their own very well. But the Europeans, especially the Italians, will have a very difficult time. Corsica and the French will also have trouble. Actually, the French will probably make an alliance with the Anti-Christ. He points to France and wipes a tear from his eye. He says it's one of her biggest mistakes because this will give the Anti-Christ a hold so he can conquer his real objective, Switzerland and southern Germany which will be the great industrial areas of the 1990s. He says this quatrain applies to all of this activity.

D: *What does this part mean, "the virgins will betray the greater part of the new band"?*

J: (*Smiling*) He says, "Knowing your days, there aren't many virgins. (*Laugh*) But the true virgins who do exist in your culture are religious figures." It means they will use religious people as a front. In other words, the enemies of Europe at this time will use nuns and other religious figures to infiltrate these countries. This is where the virgins are betrayed because they think they are working for a good cause when actually they're going to be "used" to help destroy Europe.

D: *What does that first part mean, "the fire put out"?*

J: The fire put out means they had bombed Rome.

D: *It also says, "lightning in sword, lances alone will guard the king." What is that?*

J: He says King Charles will be protected by superior weapons. You see, this will be a full-scale attack against southern Europe. They will attack Gibraltar. They won't attack France because they will want an alliance with France, but they'll attack Italy, Switzerland, southern Germany, Austria, and Yugoslavia. This whole area will become a battleground. He says they will also try to conquer London, but England will have superior weapons.

This relates to quatrains interpreted by Brenda in Volume One that refer to sea battles at Gibraltar. She also related the war plans of the Anti-Christ in the exact same way.

J: He says, "This will all take place in the mid-1990s. *You* will see this in your lifetime."

D: *I don't know if we want to see all of this. It's one thing to know about these things, and another thing to think they will happen. We hope they won't.*

J: (*A big smile*) Ahh!

D: *What?*

J: Well, I can't believe it, but … he's looking in the mirror at what his son's life is going to be like. He sees his son growing up to be a credit to him. And he's very happy. (*Abruptly*) Here comes his wife into the room with the maid servant who's carrying the baby. It's all dressed up in a gown with lots of … well, it looks like a little mummy actually. (*Laugh*)

D: (Laugh) *What do you mean?*

J: He's a cute little baby but he's all bundled up. Like this … (*He criss-crossed his hands across his chest.*) His hands are up against his chest like this, and he's all bundled up. He has on a long christening robe and a little white cap that has scalloped edges around it. Nostradamus' wife looks exhausted. And he's saying, "It's time for you to leave. My wife has come." He looks into the mirror at me, and he says, "But isn't my baby beautiful?" (*A big smile*) He's a very proud father. His wife looks like she just went through hell. She looks drained because she has pale skin. Her headdress and her clothes are very elaborate. They're a rich emerald green velveteen.

D: *I wonder why they're having the celebration so quickly. Why can't they let his wife rest first?*

J: I asked that question. I asked, "How come she's up?" And he says it was a very easy delivery. The baby was born early this morning. This is the afternoon, and she's rested now. She looks a bit wane, but he said it was an easy delivery. He says, "That's one of the reasons I married her, because she has good hips. (*Laugh*) Good hips and she can carry children very well." He says she was more concerned about cleaning the house than resting. (*Laugh*) He's very proud of her and he sent out the word that they're going to have a celebrating feast.

They will take the baby to be baptized tomorrow. He says this is a momentous occasion because it represents the birth of an heir for *him*. Also, its grandparents (his wife's parents) are wealthy and he's establishing a sense of dynasty. That's why it's a very important event for them. There's going to be a big party. He says, "I killed a couple of the sheep and an oxen. They're being prepared." He says this is the first time his servant girl has shown *any* interest in doing anything right. It takes a baby to be born. But the house is decorated with fall flower arrangements. He also has three girls working around the house, and men in the courtyard bringing in a cask of wine.

D: *We're very happy for him and we're glad he took some time to talk with us.*
J: He says, "You can contact me again. Please, it's very important that you do. I am here to be of service. You have to realize though that I do have a life. My life goes on, but I am happy to be of service to you all."
D: *Oh, yes, we realize that. We don't want to intrude. We have our own lives also.*
J: He's closing the door now. He left.
D: *Well, I think it was nice that he took some time to be with us anyway. It was an important day for him.*

THIS WAS OUR LAST VISIT with Nostradamus and I was glad that it ended on such a happy note. I had to admit I would miss him. Through John we had become quite familiar with Nostradamus' personality and his personal life as well. We had come to consider this gruff disciplinarian a dear friend and a wonderful person. I'm sure that John would not soon forget his remarkable association with this great man.

One of the most amazing aspects of the interpretations that came through John is that there were no contradictions between what he was shown and what Brenda saw. It was as if there had been no interruptions. The same main characters were carried forward. The Anti-Christ, Ogmios, the last Pope, the Great Genius, and even the shadowy figures of the secret cabal continued to carry out their roles in this scenario. The future plot line that Nostradamus saw also continued with no deviation. More details and pieces were added, and some aspects were expounded upon and clarified, but there was no alteration. Even the same symbolism and anagrams were used. The odds on such a thing happening by coincidence must be incalculable.

Chapter 26

A Karmic Debt Repaid

$\mathbb{W}$HEN NOSTRADAMUS TOLD ME I would need a "drawer of horoscopes" to help interpret the quatrains, I knew I would have to find a special person. There are many people who understand astrology, but not as many who are also interested in metaphysics. There are fewer still who would be willing to work on such a strange project with an open mind. The idea of working with a prophet who had been dead for 400 years is undoubtedly in the realm of the bizarre. So the astrologer had to be someone who would accept such a strange assignment as common place, and be willing to follow out-of-the-ordinary instructions in regards to symbolism and archaic astrological interpretations. I wanted a professional, but I knew it would be difficult to approach an expert with such a weird proposition.

I needn't have worried about it. I was unaware at the time that the solution was already in the works and completely out of my hands. When John Feeley accompanied his friends to our metaphysical meeting he said he had the strongest feeling that he was there for a reason, but he didn't know what that reason was. When he found out what I was working on, the answer was clear: he was to help me with this project. He said as an astrologer he had always been interested in Nostradamus and was fascinated by the mystery that surrounded him. This was a chance that was too good for him to pass up. I believe his curiosity was as strong as mine.

At that time we did not suspect that something more was at stake. An arrangement had been made on the other side for the repaying of a large karmic debt. John himself was not aware of it until all the bits and pieces of the puzzle began to fit together. When he found that he was also able to help with the interpretations of the quatrains, the logic behind it began to surface.

Like a heavy fog lifting, the purpose of our coming together became crystal clear to John, but would have remained oblivious to anyone who wasn't directly involved with this project. A memory that had been stirred by a past life regression held the key.

Four years before I met John he tried past life regression on his own by using hypnotic regression tapes. These can be used in the privacy of one's own home by following simple instructions. By using this method he unearthed a very strong past life memory from the hidden recesses of his mind. It came forth with an extraordinary amount of detail. It is now incorporated into his present existence and is as much a part of his own personal history as are his childhood memories.

This often happens when a subject is able to relive and identify with a past life. It defies all logical explanation and many so-called "experts" would say there is no evidence to support the memory, but the subject does not need any proof. He knows, from some reservoir deep inside of him, that it sounds "right," and that it explains events and situations in his present life that could not be explained by so-called "logical" methods. Thus, it becomes a part of his history and is very basic and vivid to him.

I worked with one subject who explained this very well. Under regressive hypnosis she had relived a lifetime in France. A few weeks later she was in a store and overheard some women talking about a recent visit to Paris. Without even thinking she almost blurted out that she used to live in Paris. The impulse was so strong that she had to bite her lip. The women would never have understood that she had indeed lived there, but it had been 200 years ago. What seemed so natural to her would have been bizarre to them. This illustrates how closely people identify with these memories once they are revived and accepted. I know because I can remember a lifetime where I was a monk sitting for hours in a cold monastery library copying and re-copying Scripture. Occasionally I was able to conceal some forbidden text from the shelves within my robe, to be read later by candlelight undetected in my cell. My curiosity and craving for knowledge was as strong then as it is now.

This was the case with John. He knew many details about his past life and they seemed very natural to him. After working with Nostradamus he could finally apply this memory to his present life and escape the karma that lifetime had represented to his subconscious.

This is the story of the memory in his words:

MY NAME WAS FRANZ WEBBER and I was born in the late 1880s into a wealthy family in Germany. My father escaped the First World War by moving the family, prior to the war, to Switzerland, where I was educated and grew up. I went to the University of Basel at Basel, Switzerland. While I was earning my degree at the university, I visited a woman astrologer. It's interesting that it was again a *woman* astrologer. (He was referring to his being taught by a woman astrologer, Isabelle Hickey, in his present life.) She did a horoscope for me. I became interested in this and she recommended books for me to read. Because I was educated in a university background, it was very easy for me to assimilate this information. I was also wealthy enough to buy the different books and materials needed to draw up horoscopes, and I began to do this on my own. I think the best astrologers are self-taught, and that's why it was important for me to take classes now in this lifetime because I was mostly self-taught in that one. I know I got most of my basic knowledge from that lifetime, and that's why it was so easy for me to assimilate it in this lifetime. (He snapped his fingers.) It was right there. But in that life I wasn't only interested in horoscopes. I also learned about the rune stones and things of that nature which were very Germanic. Even in this lifetime I am fascinated with all of those things.

I was strongly attracted to the German Romantic movement that took place during the 1890s and the turn of the century. I was at one time a follower of Rudolf Steiner and was abreast of the affairs that were taking place in Germany, Italy, France, and throughout the whole European continent. As the Nazis began their rise to power I was intrigued by them. Because of the glorification of Germanic life-style, I really got hung up on it. I was especially caught up in their propaganda, so it was not strange that I decided to return to Germany and work with them on the development of the new government. I became a Nazi and helped in the Bureau of Information in Berlin, which was actually the propaganda department. They wanted to utilize my knowledge of astrology. Hitler believed in astrology and had many people helping him with this. He used all types of esoteric information. About this time Hitler decided he wanted to use the Nostradamus quatrains to show how Germany was going to conquer the world. I was instrumental in dissimulating information about Nostradamus. I was one of the people who worked in the ministry of information which dealt with this material. They were twisting the interpretations around to fit their cause. You see, the Germans were very interested in it, and they still are interested in what they call "the occult sciences." The bureau would use these interpretations in radio broadcasts as propaganda. They would say, "Nostradamus predicted that Germany would rise to power and here's the quatrain." Then they would recite a quatrain, for example one that described Paris falling. "Look at how fast Paris is falling. We control the whole continent now. We are a thousand-year Reich. He predicted us."

It didn't bother me to be rewriting them, actually I felt the cause was worth it. You see, I really believed in the Nazi system. We published a book of Nostradamus' centuries that were in German, changing them around to fit the circumstances and making them flatter the German regime. We were creating a national religion. One of the purposes for using the science of astrology and such was to create a belief system for the Nazis, for the master race. This was our basic program.

I was a member of the Thule Society and involved with a lot of these people because I had one thing they didn't; I had great wealth. I was born into a very wealthy family and felt I could do anything. This is why I have to learn humility in this lifetime because in that lifetime I was very abusive. I was a very arrogant and stern person.

Then something happened to change my attitude about the glorious Nazi power. I found out how people were being destroyed and that brutality was taking place. What happened was that my wife brought home a lampshade made from human skin. She wanted to replace a lampshade so she brought this one home. I noticed the texture of it. I thought it was leather, but then I found out what it really was ... human skin. I demanded to know where she had gotten it. She said it had come from one of my commander's wives, and that these were being made in Dachau. I thought it was a grotesque thing and I became very angry. That put me on the track that something macabre was going on. After that I became very disillusioned with the Nazis, especially regarding how the Jewish issue was being settled. I then realized that these were very sick people. So I became involved in a plot to overthrow Hitler and bomb his office during a council meeting. Because of that, I was shot in the heart by a Gestapo agent as a traitor to the Third Reich. My wife was also killed.

(Is it a coincidence that when John had a chest x-ray there was a small hole in his sternum [breast bone]? The doctor had no explanation for it and considered it a birth defect. There is no mark on John's skin. Coincidence?)

He continued: It's interesting that a lot of people I have known in *this* lifetime had also taken part in that one. My present brothers were involved and were all killed during a bombing raid on Berlin in that life. Perhaps one of the most startling corroborations was when I found out that a friend of mine in Dallas was also involved with that German life. He didn't know anything about my experience, but through a past-life regression of his own he found out that he was the German radio announcer who read my copy. I would give him the script of the radio programs. He was involved with spreading the propaganda in that way. We found there were many similarities between his memories and mine. In this lifetime my friend speaks fluent German. It came very easily for him, and he now knows it was because he had to speak different German dialects on the radio broadcasts that were being transmitted throughout Germany.

After these memories came forth four years ago I didn't seek out Nostradamus. It wasn't that important to me. I found it interesting that I was also into astrology in this life, and it helped to explain why it had come so easily to me. I knew *of* his prophecies but I didn't study them. Obviously I must have read them in that lifetime, but I didn't in this one. I never would have thought I would be doing something like *this* (being involved with the interpretations), because I didn't make that kind of connection until now. So I feel that by working with you on this Nostradamus material, I am making up for the things I misused once before. Now that I have met him, I would like to study his life and read a biography about him. But I won't; simply because I don't want to influence any information that may come out. I have found this to be very interesting work. I believe I'm fulfilling a sense of karmic destiny by working to clarify the interpretation of these quatrains. I also think that's why I'm into astrology as much as I am and why I try to help people with it. Maybe some people in war-time Germany believed my prophecies, which were nothing but lies, and this is a way to clear that up. I did it then for the regime of the Nazis, and now I'm doing it from a spiritual source.

WHEN I BEGAN MY RESEARCH for this book at the end of 1988 I found a few books that mentioned that Nostradamus' quatrains had been used for propaganda purposes during World War II. So maybe the idea wasn't as far fetched as it sounded. In one of these I found a reference to an obscure book, *Nostradamus and the Nazis,* by Ellic Howe. I thought this might contain information that related to John's regression memories. The interlibrary loan department at the university where I do my research finally tracked the book down and found that only one copy was available in the United States. The copy that I received came from the Library of Congress. Remarks on the inside cover explained its rarity. It was privately published in England as an example of a particular type of printing process and binding technique, and was never sold to the general public.

The author did a lot of research on Karl Krafft who was reported to be Hitler's main astrologer during the early days of World War II. It should come as no surprise that Hitler was interested in occult matters, as he seemed to have been influenced by the strange and unusual all of his life. When the British heard that he was employing astrologers to advise him, they obtained the use of Louis de Wohl, so they might know what advice Hitler was being given. Karl Krafft has been mentioned as the most prominent, but Howe's book indicates that there were several other astrologers used by the Nazis, under the control of the Propaganda Ministry. Simultaneously, the Nazis were arresting astrologers and confiscating their books, but also hiring certain ones to work privately to help promote their cause. On the surface this seemed to be a contradiction, but it appeared that they wanted total control over anything they were involved in. And Hitler's regime was certainly anything but logical.

It's an interesting coincidence that Krafft was also educated at the University of Basel and had become interested in astrology while in Switzerland. It was possible that he and Franz Webber (John) may have known each other during that time or could have met. There was a surge of interest in the occult sciences during that period between the two wars.

When Dr. Goebbels became interested in the Nostradamus' quatrains (he had been made aware of the similarity between the prophecies and the development of the Third Reich), he suggested that they could be used for propaganda and psychological warfare purposes. This was when egotistical and neurotic Krafft was hired to work on them. When the meaning in the quatrain was not specific enough, he was told to alter it so it would favor the Nazis. They argued that since the quatrains were so difficult to interpret anyway that no one would ever know the difference. It was suggested in Howe's book that Krafft didn't really like the idea of corrupting them. Quote: "All that Dr. Goebbels wanted was propaganda material based upon Nostradamus' predictions. But Krafft and I both agreed that it would be an offense against the spirit, as it were, of Nostradamus if we tampered with his prophecies and if we did this he would bitterly reproach us from the grave. So we did our best only to provide material that appeared to be sensible and to the point."

Krafft was finding it increasingly more difficult to satisfy his task-masters. It was suggested in the book that his interpretations were being rewritten or adapted by a hack propaganda writer within the Ministry who probably did not share Krafft's reverence for the prophet's work. The Propaganda Ministry began the production of "black" psychological warfare material for dissemination in France by means of radio broadcasts and printed leaflets. Brochures containing appropriately threatening quatrains were dropped from aircraft. These were crude forgeries which predicted that Hitler would be victorious. There were a limited number of booklets published that contained the German translation of selected quatrains. The British retaliated by composing their own versions of the quatrains and had Allied pilots drop them over France and Belgium as anti-German propaganda.

Krafft became increasingly unwilling to participate in the project and was finally arrested and taken to a concentration camp with other astrologers who had suffered the same fate. It was intimated that the Nostradamus project stopped after that, but I'm inclined to think that it continued in secret and that perhaps John had been a member of the group that carried this on within the Ministry. The basis for my assumption is Howe's mention of the Thule Society's involvement with the Propaganda Ministry. A collection of spiritualist mediums, psychics, pendulum practitioners, astrologers, astronomers, and mathematicians were gathered to help the German war effort by using their unique psychic powers. John said he was a member of the Thule Society in that lifetime.

I could find nothing in the book that contradicted what John said about the Nazi involvement with Nostradamus. It was a short-lived propaganda method used during those hectic years.

MAYBE THE KARMIC DEBT of Franz Webber was being repaid by John working with me on this project. In his lifetime in Germany he used his knowledge to help the second Anti-Christ, Hitler, in conquering the world. Now perhaps it is his karma to use it to help defeat the third Anti-Christ in his ambitions of conquering the world. In both cases John used the quatrains, the first time in a negative way, and this time in a positive way. It also appeared that he owed a debt to Nostradamus to compensate for the damage he had done to him by corrupting his work. Now he had to repair that and to clear his good name by trying to interpret the quatrains as accurately as possible.

It seems that the wheel of destiny is constantly turning, bringing people into contact with each other and then turning them away again into other directions. But that brief passing can have more momentous importance to the souls involved than we can possibly realize. It's a good thing that someone on the other side is in charge of keeping track of all this. It's far too complex for a mere human to handle. At least the karmic debt now appears to be settled, and the results of John's efforts may be even more far-reaching than the damaging broadcasts in Germany.

Chapter 27

The World of the Future?

ᴀFTER WEEKS OF DELVING into the fate of the Earth and exploring the events destined for humanity during the next hundred years, the concept was depressing. The idea makes an interesting story, but I cannot in my own mind admit the possibility of humans sinking to such depths of depravity. I choose to believe that Nostradamus was correct when he said "forewarned is forearmed," and that by showing us the most horrible scenario possible maybe we will do something to prevent it from happening. But even with all of this information, is it possible for us to do anything to forestall future events? Can humans change the course of the world? I believe more in the eternal hope within one's soul than the eternal blackness of the dark side. The only way we can know for certain is to watch the future as it unfolds and to be aware of any clues that our world is headed toward what Nostradamus saw in his black mirror.

John also wondered if what he had seen could possibly come to pass. He telephoned me unexpectedly. He has been packing his belongings for storage when he got a sudden inspiration. He said, "Take me into the future to the life I will be living at that time, and let's see what the world is like."

I had never tried this before. It sounded strange, but if there is no such thing as time why couldn't we go forward as well as backward. I had regressed hundreds of people into past lives and they had relived them vividly. Why wouldn't it work just as well to *pro*gress someone into the future? When using this type of hypnosis any exciting challenge can be followed up on, and the impossible soon becomes commonplace. It was worth a try, and it was one of the last things John wanted to try before leaving for Florida.

This last session was held once again among the disarray of packing boxes, just as Elena's had been. It was beginning to be familiar and appropriate surroundings. We decided to move John ahead 100 years, to 2087, and see if he would be alive at that time.

When I finished counting, he found himself in the body of a woman who was looking out of the window or spaceport of a spaceship. He drew back to act as an observer and he described her. "She's about 30 years old and very pretty. She has blond hair, blue eyes, and is very statuesque. She's dressed in what looks like a space suit. Yes, it's a space suit but it's not bulky like our present space suits. It doesn't hug her body either; it's loose. She just told me that she's in what we would call an extra-terrestrial's vehicle, a craft from a different planet. She's going on a federation mission to that planet with other people from Earth. This is the first mission. The craft is traveling faster than the speed of light, so things look like a blur out the window. She's reflective and I can pick up her thoughts."

D: *Is this a large spacecraft?*

J: No, it's not very large. It's similar to a commuter bus. That's what she's saying. They're headed into the star system of Sirius. There are three planets there that are very important and are the reason for this mission. They are taking things, like crystals, that are of value to these other planets to use as trade items.

D: *You said there are other people with her?*

J: There are about seven or eight other people, and they're talking, exchanging ideas, and having a good time. They're very excited that they're the first party of earthlings who will be going to another galaxy.

D: *Does she know how this trip was arranged?*

J: Yes, she was born a natural healer, and at a very early age they knew of her healing talents. As a result, she studied under people versed in different forms of healing. She's what we would call a "doctor," except she's not like our typical medical doctors because she uses crystals, her mental powers, and visualization. She's a very astute woman. She's married to one of the men on the ship.

D: *Does he have any special talent?*

J: He's interested in studying the architecture of these different planets in the Sirius star range because this is his field. Some of the planets have the same gravity as Earth while others do not. He wants to see the different methods of construction to get ideas for new structures to be built not only on the Earth itself, but also in space.

D: *How was this trip arranged? Was it the Earth's idea to do this?*

J: No. They've had contact with these extraterrestrials. There are two of them on board who are piloting the ship. You can tell they are not from our planet, but they look humanoid and wear similar clothing. They're *bald*, have protruding eyes, and their ears are closer, almost inside their heads. There's a spiral structure in their ear, similar to a chambered nautilus shell. Their noses have two nostrils but are a bit flatter. Other than those differences, they look very much like humans.

D: *Are these aliens large people or small people?*

J: They're medium in height. Their skin isn't white but more of a golden brown color. Their heads aren't shiny because they're bald, but they have an unusual cranium development. They're different looking, but they're not ugly, and they project such a loving nature that we find them very irresistible.

D: *Can you see their hands? Is there any difference there?*

J: Yes, there's a bit of a difference. Their fingers are very thin and tapered with cone-shaped tips and they don't have fingernails. It doesn't look like they have hair or fingernails, or any extra things like that on their body.

D: *Are these people from the Sirius star system?*

J: Yes. They're quite handsome people. They communicate with each other and with the other people on the ship telepathically. They're talking about the different things they're going to explore and each person's mission. There's a great sense of love onboard this craft, and these people touch and hug a lot. Everyone's in a very happy mood. They have a circle meditation, and this is how they communicate with the people back on Earth. It's a wonderful gathering of people who are very excited because they're the first ones to go on this kind of journey.

D: *Was this mission worked out with the governments of Earth?*

J: Earth now has one government. It's called One World Government, and its headquarters are in what used to be ... (*surprised*) Omaha! That's where she lived, outside of the Omaha area. That's one of the biggest planetary centers. They're not called cities anymore; they're called planetary centers. The message went out from Omaha that people were invited to go on this mission. She was selected because of her healing talents. Zarea (*phonetic*)—that's her name—is going to do healing and medical work. Her husband, Huran (*phonetic*), is going to research architecture and engineering.

D: *Each one probably has a certain talent.*

J: Yes. There's a black man, a man from India, and an Oriental woman who's going to study their art and culture. The black man is going to study their flora and fauna, while the Indian man is going to discover their philosophical truths. They each have a different skill, but they're all interested in exploration and the creation of new colonies in space, because now there's not much land area on the Earth.

D: *Why isn't there?*

J: Well, there's just not. They believe that to support the population increase which will occur a hundred years in the future, that they will have to colonize space around this planet. They're also planning to live for a long time. They know they will see things that will exist for a long time to come, and this is very important to them. This is why they're visiting other worlds. She says they are also thinking of colonizing part of the moon and a part of Mars.

D: *Why isn't there much land area? Is it because of overcrowding?*

J: No, the ocean is just everywhere. That's what she said. Most of the Earth is mainly islands with a few major continents. The majority of the Earth is even more ocean than it was at the time of the shift, she said.

Apparently this was after the great Earth shift predicted by Nostradamus.

D: *Has the Earth been involved in space travel?*

J: During the shift, contact was made with these people who have helped them form the planetary centers.

D: *Have they been working with them for a while?*

J: Yes. They've been working with them for the last ... 80 years.

D: *Was the Earth involved in their own space program with space ships?*

J: Not really. After the earth shift, most of the areas studying space exploration were under water. But in the northwest is a large island, an area called "Seal Center." It's remnants of what was Seattle and Tacoma, Washington. East of there was an area where space exploration study remained after the earth shift. As a result, there's a space port they call "Surveilas" (*phonetic*).

D: *What does that mean?*

J: I don't know. The landing area, Surveilas, is the space port where they transport the crafts. This is where the UFOs—what we would call UFOs—land. This area in the northwest is part of what they call the "northwest island." This was once a part of the United States before most of it sank, but they don't call it by its old name. You see, a planetary consciousness is taking place. The United States is now part of the one world government system. She's looking at a map, and she sees what the Earth once looked like and what it looks like now. Most of the world that we know is under water.

D: *Have the polar caps reformed on the Earth?*

J: No, the polar caps aren't there.

D: *We thought that after the shift the ice caps would form again and this would take up some of the water.*

J: No. She says that's why land resources are very limited. Because of the pollution and the destructiveness that went on, the living being of the planet itself is now only 10 percent land mass and 90 percent ocean.

D: *Are some of the land masses still polluted?*

J: Most of them have been cleaned up by the interconnection and working with people from other galaxies. They have helped to regenerate what land is still available. She says as a result of a tragic nuclear accident, one *huge* area in what was Asia—she calls it the Asian island—has *no* land that can be used. She says, "We've been thinking of flooding this area, but we know it would poison the ocean." She says it's 300 square miles of "radioactive city." No one lives in this area except people who don't want to change or who want to go back to the old system. As a result there are some types of mutations that take place among their births. She's showing me the area ... it's somewhere in Asia.

D: *What caused this nuclear accident?*

J: It happened during the shift. It wasn't a nuclear war, but an accident. When the Earth shifted, it broke up an atomic reactor. It went almost completely down into the core before it calmed down. As a result, it poisoned the whole area.

D: *I thought it might have been something that happened before the shift.*

J: No. In her sense of history there was no nuclear war. She says the threat was always there, but it didn't happen.

D: *Does she know anything about the wars that happened before the shift? How far back does their history go?*

J: They don't talk much about what they call the "old world." It was full of brutality, injustice, and hate. They don't want to give credence to any of these negative emotions and feelings. So they really date everything from what they call "One World Government." That took place in 2039. Twenty thirty-nine was ten years after the shift. (This was certainly disturbing knowledge.)

D: *Do they have anything that dates back to the old world?*

J: Yes, there are some buildings and such that are kept up. In fact, they even have a recreation area of what an American village of the 1980s looked like. (*Laugh*) You know, a supermarket, a mall, and parking lots with cars. They also have a colonial village with things from that time. It's similar to a living museum. They use it to instruct their children on the different ages that humans have gone through. But now, humans are spiritual beings who are enlightened. They understand the knowledge from all of these periods they've already lived through. We are at the pinnacle of a new time, she says.

D: *Then they didn't just do away with all of the old world.*

J: No. In fact, people still live in houses that were built during that time that survived the earth shift. But they think the quality of life then was very primitive and barbaric so they look on it with a sense of distaste. It's the way we would feel about primitives that still hunt heads in New Guinea.

D: *(Laugh) Yes, I can see that. So they really don't study the old histories.*

J: Most of them are spiritually enlightened beings who know what they have been like in previous lifetimes, so they know their cycle. Everybody unites in spiritual intercourse with each other to heal the planet and make up for all the losses when the shift occurred. There aren't many people on Earth. She says there are ... about 120 million people on the Earth right now in 2087.

According to statistics, the world population in 1987 was five billion. The population of the United States was 245 million, and there were over one billion people in China. The experts predict that, in spite of attempts at birth control, another billion people will be added to the planet by 1998. This is a phenomenal growth rate. The population is expected to double to more than ten billion people within the next four decades. If the disasters which Nostradamus saw, and which John was reporting from his vantage point in the future, are correct, it would mean that a tremendous loss of life would have to occur in order for the world population to shrink to 120 million people.

D: *Did the majority perish when the Earth shifted?*

J: Many, many people were lost to the Earth shift and many more people died in the transition because of disease and things of this type.

D: *What does she mean by the transition?*

J: The Earth change.

D: *After the Earth shift?*

J: Yes. She said many people died because it was not an easy time. Diseases were running rampant, and if it weren't for the help of the extraterrestrials, the planet could have perished. But the extraterrestrials came to heal as well as to educate people and to show them new technology.

D: *But they predict that in the next hundred years their population will increase.*

J: Yes, that's why they're looking for new land elsewhere, because the Earth is only 10 percent land mass now. They have to look outside of the Earth itself and explore space.

D: *Have other extraterrestrial beings contacted them besides this group on the ship?*

J: Yes. People from Sirius, Aldebaran, Betelgeuse, or about 15 other star systems have contacted us. Now we're part of the galactic federation. We're one of its newest members. The requirement for membership into the galactic federation is to know the plan of the Creator, to follow that plan, and to be part of one galaxy consciousness. And only advanced beings are allowed to incarnate into this.

D: *Were all of these extraterrestrial helpers of the highest intentions? I was wondering if any of the people who came from other planets were negative?*

J: Well, there is another federation that could be considered negative. They're from a solar system that is about 300 light years from our central planet, the Sun. They were around at the time of the Earth shift, but they were prevented from taking part in the rescue by the force fields of all these other members of the United Federation.

D: *Did the people of that federation have any connection with Earth before this?*

J: That federation had been influencing the planet prior to the shift, yes. In the old world they were called "demons," but in actuality they are a force within the universe. As you know, the universe is eternal and unlimited, but there are negative entities.

D: *Then when the shift occurred, did they want to help or were they going to be disruptive?*

J: They were prevented from doing anything at that time, but they have
     control over worlds that are still evolving into spiritual and human
     consciousness.

D: *I was curious about that because I thought there might have been some*
     beings around during the time of these great upheavals that were not
     all positive. Has all of this space travel been done with the extraterres-
     trials' vehicles?

J: Basically. The extraterrestrials are helping us on Earth to build our
     own propulsion power drives and such, so we'll have our own
     vehicles. They're really helpful and wonderful. They helped us form
     the One World Government because they reinvented the communica-
     tion lines between the different islands.

D: *Do you know what type of power these ships use?*

J: It's electrical-magnetic.

D: *Is it the same basic principle as our cars and motors?*

J: It's a pure energy that is collected in ... (*carefully as though it was a*
     strange word) photovoltaic cells from the sun. This energy is trans-
     muted into vehicles like this space ship that I am in now.

D: *Is this the only power source that's used?*

J: No, there are other power sources that are used on Earth, but I can't
     identify the names of them. She's a healer—that's not her field. Her
     husband is into it, but I'm not in his consciousness. It seems to be
     photo-electric energy and such.

D: Is it still effective even after they leave our solar system? I thought that
     if the power was coming from our sun, that leaving the ...

John grimaced and groaned, obviously displaying signs of physical
discomfort.

J: I'm getting uncomfortable. I have to leave this space vehicle. It's
     going into what they call ... a different dimension and I can't go into
     that area.

Because of John's obvious physical and mental discomfort, I brought
him back to full consciousness.

Upon awakening he said the woman was aware that he was there in
the ship, and knew he was getting information from her. It didn't bother
her because in that time period they were psychic and knew about their
past lives. She just accepted him as one of her other selves.

THIS WAS THE FUTURE WORLD that John envisioned he would be living
in. It corresponded amazingly to the world Nostradamus saw in his
visions through the black mirror, his window to the future. I was pleased
to find out that human beings had survived the catastrophes and rebuilt
their world. We had also made contact with the people of space and had
our eyes on the stars. The indomitable human spirit had triumphed and

the world did not perish, even though it had undergone a great change. My main concern was whether or not humankind would perish, or if the remaining humans would have to return to primitive life in order to survive. In either case all our progress would be lost. It appeared that with the help of the aliens, we would not only keep our technology but advance into a world completely beyond our present-day imagination.

This was the future as seen by John. But was this *our* future, or only one *possible* future out of many that could occur along the network of time lines and nexus, as Nostradamus called them? He had explained that time could go in many different directions and there could be different results according to decisions made along the way. Which will it be? We won't know until we reach *our* future and maybe it's better that way.

THIS WAS THE LAST SESSION we were able to have with John. He moved to Florida in the summer of 1987 to continue his life in another direction. Apparently his part in this strange scenario was complete. He would be able to work with any astrological information I might receive or to clarify things, but it would have to be done by correspondence.

Brenda was only able to work sporadically after this and then only for short periods. When I work with people over a long period of time their normal life always takes precedence. They either experience psychic burn-out or they tire of the experiment. It's never their main interest anyway; just a curious sideline. It shows they have no interest in perpetrating a hoax either because this experiment is not a motivating force in their life. This is just as well because their main focus should be on living as normal a life as possible. It began to appear that I was the only continuing stabilizing energy moving through this. Maybe I was the true catalyst that Nostradamus was using to bring his interpretations to our time period.

Things slowed down after John left and for several months I was unable to gather any new information about the quatrains. I devoted my time to organizing the material and preparing this book. I was in limbo, but I had enough confidence in Nostradamus to know that he would find another channel to reach him so we could interpret the meanings of the remaining 500 quatrains that had not been covered. The impossible had been achieved so many times in the last year that I knew the project would continue. He had proven this by communicating through three different vehicles in less than a year. Since I could only wait and see what route it would take next, I prepared the material, confident that he would surface again in some other way. This was his promise, that I would be able to reach him through anyone that I worked with. I like to finish what I start, even a job of this magnitude, but I knew that if I tried to direct it, I would only meet with depression and frustration. Many of my subjects were capable of deep trance levels, but for one reason or another they did not seem to be the ones to work with on this project. I have now returned to work on the myriad of other projects that I am involved in.

This second book is finished. So if he *did* intend for us to translate the rest of the quatrains, then God willing, another channel will come forth and a third book will be written.

Section Three

Work in
the Aftermath

Chapter 28

The Drawing of the Map

In THE SPRING OF 1989 the first volume of this work was off the press. I then devoted my attention to the preparation of this second volume. People expressed an interest in the map that Nostradamus had shown to John, and they wondered what the United States and the rest of the world would look like after the Earth shift. There was speculation about exactly which portions would be left above water. John was the only one who had seen the map and he did the best he could to describe what he was being shown, as I reported in Chapter 17. I now wondered if it would be possible to have an artist draw a map following John's description so we could see the actual shape of the world of the future. The publisher agreed that to include such a map in this book would satisfy people's curiosity.

I discussed it with an artist friend, Beverly Wilkinson, who wanted to attempt the unusual project. She is a native of Louisiana who has studied art in both the United States and Italy. She felt that the only way to work with such a terrifying concept was to treat it as an interesting story, and not an absolute truth. We intended to concentrate first on the United States. If she were able to draw that map, then she would try to draw the other continents. It was an interesting prospect, but there were unforeseen problems.

At our first meeting she and I spent several hours going over the transcript of John's session, comparing it with a topographic map of the United States. Laboriously, we tried to distinguish which states would be left above water. John indicated that the higher mountainous areas would survive because of their elevations. Other areas did not seem to follow such simple rules. He had been most emphatic that a large land segment would be located in the interior of the United States, composed of parts of Arkansas, Missouri, Oklahoma, Nebraska, *etc.* But some of this area did not have a very high elevation. We couldn't understand why the rising waters of the Great Lakes, the Mississippi River, and water coming down from Canada wouldn't cover this area also. There were contradictions, and we realized it was impossible to draw the map based solely on the elevation of a certain area. The artist also felt that she would need more information before she could begin to draw the map.

She said she wished I had asked John more questions, but when that session was conducted in 1987 I didn't use a map as a reference. I simply asked questions based on my meager knowledge of geography. Hindsight is wonderful, but my work is spontaneous and the unexpected is commonplace. Since John was now living in Florida, it was impossible to get any more information from him, and we felt uncomfortable drawing the map based on the information we had. Beverly was involved in several other art projects, so she would have a few months to ponder the problem before she had to begin the actual drawing.

Then, a week later, an idea occurred to me. I wondered if it would be possible for a subject to go into trance and have Nostradamus show them the same map that John had seen. My thoughts immediately returned to Brenda as the most logical person to attempt this. She had been the most reliable link with the great master, and certainly knew his mind and idiosyncrasies better than anyone else. But that was before she experienced what I call "psychic burnout." The project had been a burden and she had decided not to continue. I hadn't worked with her for almost two years. It was always in the back of my mind that our work would resume when the proper time came, but I certainly didn't want to push her into anything that she didn't want to do.

When I called and explained the situation involved drawing the maps, she was interested and agreed to have a session. It certainly wouldn't be as tedious and demanding as the interpretation of the quatrains.

I was uncertain how to proceed, but I obtained copies of blank maps for her to draw on and I took an atlas so I would be prepared if I had to ask questions regarding geography. I didn't want to be caught off guard again.

We set up an appointment for the session, and when I arrived we discussed how to proceed. In other sessions I have had the subject open their eyes while still in trance and draw or write for me. I have obtained some interesting results while doing this and although I normally conduct my sessions with the subject lying down, we decided to have Brenda sit up as it is difficult to draw or write while lying down. We positioned the maps on a clipboard and arranged writing materials on a nearby table. In this way she might be able to sketch roughly what she was seeing, instead of my referring to the countries and states in the atlas. If it didn't work she could always return to naming the areas as John had done.

As Brenda settled into position, she jokingly remarked, "Remember, I'm a music student, not an artist. I won't promise anything."

Even though it had been almost two years since the familiar keyword had been used, it was as though no time at all had passed. When I said the word she slipped immediately into a comfortable deep state of trance, and we were ready to begin our work again.

She found Nostradamus waiting as though there had been no interruption in our meetings. Normally Brenda had conversed with him in the misty dimension which he referred to as "the special meeting place." This time it was different. She found him in the library on the spirit plane. I don't know why this should have surprised me. If I had been able to locate this special place through many of my subjects, surely a man of Nostradamus' abilities and intellect would also have no trouble. It must surely have been an excellent source of knowledge for his work. Even though we seemed to be in a different portion of the library, I assumed it was the same place John had visited. This portion resembled a Victorian library setting. The wooden floors and shelves gleamed with a highly polished sheen and the books were bound in beautiful leather. Brenda explained that these books contained all the information in the entire universe. She also explained a curious aspect to this library. If you wanted to be alone you could have the entire place to yourself, but if you wanted company, others would be there.

Nostradamus seemed to be more relaxed during this visit. He was leaning back in a large comfortable chair with his feet crossed at the ankles. He told us this was one of his favorite places, and while exploring it he had discovered what libraries of the future would be like. Instead of books on shelves he had seen computer terminals and printers.

Brenda said, "He thinks it's very marvelous. He says, at last you've cheated the dust, the mice and the dampness of the weather." Those were all enemies of his own library on the earthly plane.

He said he chose this setting because he anticipated our questions. He pointed to a large world globe which sat on a nearby table, and indicated he would be able to use that to relay the information to Brenda's mind. According to him, Brenda should have no trouble sketching the areas on our blank maps as he pointed them out to her on the globe. He instructed me to keep quiet, because he would be giving her a verbal commentary and they would both be concentrating. He said he would stop occasionally and give me a chance to ask questions.

B: He says it's difficult to distinguish the specific effects of an axis shift because so many changes will be taking place in the world. He didn't concentrate on details because he was busy warning about the larger things which he reported in his quatrains. There will be changes world-wide, and he's willing to show you changes in the parts of the globe that he knows are *terra incognita* (Latin: hidden or unknown land). Those are the areas that were unknown to explorers of his time, but are known to us. For instance, they're not very familiar with Asia, and they don't know anything at all about Australia or Antarctica. He suggests that we begin with the continent of Africa. He says I can open my eyes to sketch and if I need to close my eyes to see him more clearly, then that's okay too.

She then opened her eyes and gazed with a glassy stare at the map. When I have someone open their eyes while in trance, they seem to have the blank stare of someone who is half-asleep or drugged. During this type of procedure they are oblivious of anything else in the room except what they are concentrating on. She selected a pencil and a large eraser from the table, and began to sketch. He asked me not to speak, so I quietly watched her, doing nothing to interrupt their concentration. She alternated between sketching and occasionally closing her eyes. She appeared to be watching something and listening to his voice. The drawing proceeded rapidly as the pencil moved confidently across the paper, seemingly guided by an unseen hand. I breathed a sigh of relief. It appeared that we would accomplish this after all. When the drawing on the African map was finished he began to give commentary.

B: He says that when the axis shifts it will cause many earthquakes to occur and volcanoes to erupt. Thus, not only will the water rise and some land sink, but some of the land will rise as well. Quite a bit of Africa will be underwater. He says in some places where there used to be land, there may be some scattered islands, but he's just going to indicate large pieces of land. What you don't understand is that the surface of the Earth won't remain stable. There will be such stress upon the Earth that its surface will crumble in places like a hard piece of clay. Some pieces will be forced against the others. This will cause certain areas to be pushed higher while others will disappear underwater.

Nostradamus then pointed to the area around the great island of Madagascar and was confused over what to call it. The significance of this confusion wasn't apparent until I did my research.

B: He's pointing to Madagascar, but he's calling it Zanzibar. The area surrounding it will be raised from the ocean bed because of the shifting of nearby land.

When I looked in the encyclopedia later I wondered why he ignored Madagascar and focused in on Zanzibar, which is a much smaller island closer to the coast of Africa. I found that there had been trade with Zanzibar even before the Christian era, but Madagascar was unknown. It was discovered in 1500, but was left alone during Nostradamus' lifetime because fierce Arabs controlled the harbors. He was speaking from knowledge that was common in his time. The information couldn't have come from us because we focused on the larger land mass of Madagascar, and had no idea where Zanzibar was. It was an interesting remark that reaffirmed to me that we were truly in contact with him again.

B: He says this other portion (the left side of the continent) will be composed of many scattered islands. The part in between will be like a sheltered bay, because of the curve of the land and the islands. There will be nothing left in the upper part (the portion that is mostly desert now). It would be similar to the land shelf off present-day North America, which sits just under the water, eventually dropping off into deeper ocean. He says the Mid-earth Sea—what we call the "Mediterranean"—will be much larger than it is now. He wanted to show us Africa and Europe first to indicate this.

This was another unusual remark that turned out to be significant. All my life I have considered the word "Mediterranean" only as the name of a place that is difficult to spell. I never once thought of its meaning. After his remark it was clear that it was a word derived from Latin. He was correct, in Latin it means: *medius* and *terra,* or middle of the land. He was using the name that was familiar to him. The great man never ceased to surprise and educate me.

She then turned her attention to the map of Europe. I was concerned that it would be confusing to him because our map showed no distinction between land and water. Brenda remarked curtly, "He says he's an educated man. He knows maps." I remarked that these maps were made by a machine and she retorted, "He says you have machines for everything. He refused to be surprised any more." I laughed and then kept quiet as she studied the map.

When she had finished, I asked, "Is that all that's going to be left of England?"

B: He says, yes, only the mountains between England and Scotland will remain. And those mountains in Scotland will be just scattered islands. There may be a few small islands where Ireland currently sits, but they will be very small. (*She pointed to Iceland.*) He says Iceland will become larger because of all the volcanic eruptions. Some of the land will be pushed up, but with the earth shifting, the volcanoes of Iceland will erupt quite a bit and gradually build up land.

He then referred to the islands off the coast of Portugal. He indicated that land would be pushed up to form more islands in that area. The mountainous parts of Europe, especially the Alps, would form the new shoreline, while most of France and all of the low countries would be underwater. He saw a strange event happening in the vicinity of the North Sea and the northern countries. Due to the shifting of the ocean, there would be volcanic activity in mountains that were underwater, causing that area to rise upward, forcing the water of the North Sea to drain out. The new shoreline would run on this spine of mountains. In the area of Italy he said the ocean floor would not rise, but volcanic activity would create part of the new shoreline there. Scattered islands would be all that would remain of the country of Greece.

He then turned his attention to Asia and continued with his commentary.

B: He says cities such as St. Petersburg [Leningrad] will be underwater. Much of the northern part of Russia, known as Siberia, will be like a very large shallow sea. The contour of Russia will be reshaped due to the land being compressed. This is caused by the rising and sinking of pieces of land. India will be underwater up to the foothills of the Himalayas. This will be the new shoreline which continues up through the mountains of Nepal and Tibet, and angles across the northeast part of Russia. Most of China will be islands created from the present mountain tops. Maybe when the center part of Russia rises it will cause China to drop. The flatlands will be totally underwater, but he says the water will be shallow enough that if the Chinese people wanted to they could build dikes, pump the water out, and reclaim the land as they do in Holland. He says he knows that the lowlanders in Holland and Belgium have made their country grow quite a bit by building dikes and pumping the water out. The Chinese can make the land habitable again, if they want to do the work. He says the Japanese Islands will be smaller and shaped differently, but they will still be there. In time they will grow larger. The shifting will make Japan's volcanoes stay active for quite a long time, and new land will be formed this way. Japan will be more distant from any land that's above water, because so much of China, Korea and those areas have submerged. The Philippines will suffer a harsher fate. They will be completely submerged. New land could be created there from under-water volcanoes, but it would take a long time.

It was strange how nonchalantly and unemotionally Brenda pronounced the demise of these countries. Apparently the part of her that viewed this scene acted as an objective reporter. I suppose it would be extremely difficult to discuss an event of such traumatic proportions if the emotions were involved.

Nostradamus' description of Australia was interesting because he saw it as one the lucky continents. There wouldn't be much change.

B: He says Australia was an unknown continent in his lifetime. But when he's in touch with the higher spirit states, he's able to transcend the lack of knowledge of his own time period. He says after the shift takes place the cardinal directions will be different relative to the land, because the poles will be located differently. The ocean floor between Australia and New Zealand will shift some, and sailors will have to relearn the currents. Australia will suffer damage, but it will look basically the way it does today. Since everything on Earth will be positioned differently, it will also have a new location.

D: *Will it escape destruction?*

B: I did not say that! It will suffer destruction and damage from great storms that will sweep the Earth at that time. Where some land masses will be sent underwater or lands underwater will be lifted up during the shift, the shape of the continent of Australia will remain similar to what it is now.

D: *Since it won't break up, will there be safe places for the people to go?*

B: He says to stay away from the coasts and to stay out of the desert. Considering that most of the major cities are on the coast they will suffer much damage from tidal waves. The central part of the country, which is all desert, will experience fierce storms and flash floods. There will be climatic changes all over the world. The weather won't stay the same anywhere.

She then referred to the North American continent. As John had seen, much of it disappeared beneath the angry and churning seas, never to rise again in our time. Nostradamus also indicated that there would be several areas where the shallow water could be pumped off to create usable land. He saw the Bering Strait appearing as a land bridge once again. He said the area between the St. Lawrence Seaway, the Great Lakes and Hudson Bay would be washed out very quickly by the melting of the ice caps. It would be a couple of centuries later before additional islands would be created by the new polar caps reclaiming their ice and thus lowering the sea level. He said the world map would appear differently further in the future because he didn't see the polar caps reforming for several hundred years. It would be a very gradual thing. But then, what's a few hundred years in the history of our planet?

I asked about new land forming around the United States, and he said he didn't know I wanted him to indicate ocean changes too.

B: Certain areas of land that aren't very far beneath the surface of the water will be shoved upward. He sees a land mass that will rise up and incorporate quite a few of what is now known as the Caribbean Islands. He's not positive about the final shape of this land, but it will be a fair-sized island. He apologizes for making these outlines smooth since he's not a map man. He says a map drawer would put in every little nook and cranny.

He began speaking again after Brenda finished drawing on the map of South America.

B: He says the chain of mountains along the western side of South America will rise somewhat forming a slightly smaller continent with many islands around it; some of them will be of fairly good size. He says that particularly the jungles of Brazil and the Guianas, and most of the Amazon Basin, will be under water. The southern chain of islands near Tierra del Fuego will raise up and be part of the land. From there new islands will connect with Antarctica.

I asked again about new land rising in the oceans. He indicated there would be a chain of islands emerging northward from the Hawaiian Islands.

B: This will be several islands so close together that one could swim from one island to the next. It will form a natural barrier to the ocean currents, so that part of the ocean (the right side) will have its own pattern. He says the main areas of new land will be in the southern Pacific and Atlantic in the area of Antarctica. If you're looking for Atlantis, the only thing that comes close to that is the land mass in the Caribbean. There will be no large continents or segments rising for millions of years. In time ice caps will begin to form again at new locations, and the water level will lower. He says the maps we have drawn show the world with the ice melted. When the poles first shift, the Earth will wobble until things settle down. So he says it's difficult to determine exactly where the poles end up.

Now that we knew approximately how the shift would affect the land masses, I asked how it would affect the people.

B: He's showing me scenes of unimaginable horror. The water forms huge waves of unbelievable height that rise and travel across the land. They wipe out buildings and people in an instant. In another scene I see hordes of people fleeing enormous fires that are sweeping through a city. In addition to the natural disasters there will be weather catastrophes; storms such as have never occurred before in the history of humanity. Living will be very hard for those who survive. The lack of cleanliness will contribute to disease and food poisoning. When the shift happens, for the most part all present governments will fall. There will be much vigilantism and military law for many years as people begin recovering from the disaster. The countries as they are known now, will no longer exist. He says everything will be split into many small duchies and kingdoms, as he's calling them. Each group of people that are banded together for mutual cooperation will take the place of present-day governments. So many people will be killed from the changes and diseases that there won't be many people left. He says the people who remain will band together in small groups to help deal with these changes. He says to alleviate some of the effects of this disaster people should continue with new technology and space programs before this shift occurs. Of the various alternatives he can see, the one where there is the least long-term harm done is where people develop space stations which orbit the Earth before the shift. Because a primary problem would be finding electricity to power things, solar-powered stations would be able to beam down electricity which would speed up the rebuilding process. He says if all of the technology is limited to the Earth's surface, it's going to be almost completely wiped out. But if the government plans ahead by allowing man to move into space, then all will not be lost. There is the possibility that the "Others" will help us during the shift, but it depends on how we handle the situation. If we try to work together in the most positive way possible, they will come and help. If we react negatively, by detonating nuclear bombs and such because we think it's the end of the world, then they will stay away.

D: *Many people want to know where they will be safe, if there will be any such place on Earth.*

B: He says the appropriate expression in English is, "Head for the hills!" He says if you live in a mountainous area you will need to survive the earthquakes that will occur there. The people in the flatlands will be safer from the earthquakes, but when the ice caps start melting, the people in the hills will be safer. But this will be a drawn-out process. Over time people will become sensitive to inner warnings and won't be caught off guard. They will be more prepared because they will learn to rely on their psychic abilities and listen to their inner prompting. He says to watch for the order of events. Earthquakes always come first, earthquakes and erupting volcanoes go together, and they'll be happening off and on throughout the entire process. There will probably be as much destruction in Europe and Asia in the way of earthquakes as in the United States. However, these countries won't be flooded with as much water as the U.S. will be. Their land masses will be closer together and easier to rebuild.

During the weeks following this session I studied the rough maps that Brenda had sketched. We had received a great deal of information, and none of it appeared to contradict what John had seen; it just added more details and a different perspective. But the maps were not as complete as I had hoped. Brenda was correct, she was no artist, and the area Nostradamus had helped to fill in looked very crude. This would possibly give the artist Beverly more material to work with, so she could produce a more professional and detailed map.

Then an idea suddenly occurred to me. I wondered if it would be possible for Beverly to go into trance and see if Nostradamus could show her the same things John and Brenda had seen. If she saw it herself, maybe we could clarify the problem areas. I could give her the suggestion that she would remember what she saw so she could duplicate it upon awakening. Even though it wasn't the normal method for an artist to use, it might be the answer. With the information received from all three sources, surely we could produce an accurate map.

Beverly agreed that it would be an interesting experiment and she wanted to try it. There was no guarantee that it would work. Once again I would be groping in the dark to find a way to accomplish something that had never been done before. First, we would have to see if she were able to reach the sufficient trance level to obtain this type of information, and then we would have to find a way for her to contact Nostradamus before we could proceed. These were all probables. It's to Beverly's credit that the challenge didn't scare her off. She was willing to try the unusual if it would answer her questions and produce an accurate map. There was certainly nothing to lose, and much to gain if we were able to succeed. If I and my subjects had been afraid to try strange experiments, then we would have remained in our normal, mundane lives, and none of these books would have been written. We had to be willing to take that first step that leads into the world of the unknown, and to carefully examine what we found there.

There are no written rules or regulations, no plans or guidelines that a hypnotist can follow in experiments of this type. During my 13 years of working in the bizarre I have had to break new ground and invent my own guidelines. If a method is workable and repeatable I use it. I don't worry about the mechanics of it. Thus, over the years my unorthodox techniques have developed and have been proven time and time again.

We set up an appointment for the session. On the day we met we were not sure if anything at all would come forth. I suppose it should come as no surprise that Beverly turned out to be an excellent subject, capable of entering a deep trance level. It should come as no surprise because I seem to be drawn to these type of people, or they to me. Maybe sensitive artistic types, such as Beverly, are just naturally able to enter these states more readily. The creative urge seems to come from the same area of the brain that I work with. But entering the deep level of hypnosis was only the first step.

The procedure that had worked so well with Brenda and John was to first take them to the spirit state where they were not encumbered by the demands of a physical body. Then each had used their own unique methods to locate Nostradamus. Thus, I began by asking Beverly to go to a time and a place when she would not be physically involved with a lifetime. The initial surprise came before I had even finished giving her the instructions.

Before I had a chance to count her backward, she interrupted me. "There *is* no time. You can't go back to a time when there is no time." I asked her to explain what she meant. "When you say 'go back to a *time* when there's no physical involvement,' that's an impossibility because when there's no physic involvement, there is no time. There's just beingness."

The subconscious is very literal, and Beverly's mind would not accept the instructions. I have found that the wording of a question or suggestion is very important, and relates directly to the type of answer or result I will receive. So the problem now was how to correctly word the suggestion. Her own subconscious had given me the clue. I asked her to go to a state of "beingness" when she was not involved with a physical body. This wording was acceptable to Beverly's subconscious, and when I finished counting she emerged into a place that had the feeling of deep spacelessness.

She attempted to describe it. "It feels very big. There are probably other realms but I feel they are a distance apart. I know there are more levels that are still just me. It seems like what I'm feeling is the bigness of who I really am. Maybe I need to get past that or to go on to something else. You could get very wrapped up in this," she laughed. She was truly enjoying the feeling. "I can really see how confined we are in the physical. That confining hurts unless you get out because the physical body is *so gross.* I don't mean bad, I mean it's so thick. Yet it's easy to get out of that body and the part that comes out is so *light.* It goes right through what is thick and heavy. If it was the other way around, and thick and heavy was trying to come out of lightweight, it couldn't. But if lightweight or nothingness is trying to come out of heavy, it's easy, because nothing goes right through everything."

It was obvious she had journeyed to a state where she was detached from her present physical life. It's common for the spirit form to become disassociated and objective, but it also has access to knowledge not available to the physical or conscious mind.

I wondered if there were anyone around (perhaps a guide) that she could ask for instructions or directions on how to proceed with the experiment. She chuckled with delight, "We're going to play! I don't think I need anyone to help. I can probably bounce where you need me to. It's almost ecstasy!" She seemed very confident and happy, so I decided to take the plunge by asking if it were possible for her to look in on someone's life while they were living on Earth. She replied, "I think you just pop in. I can see whatever is me bouncing around in the universe. I don't know if I can make a connection or not, but I can try." Since she was willing to cooperate, I asked her to focus in on Nostradamus and try to locate him while he was alive in the 1500s in France.

Immediately she found herself in a room with a stone floor. There was bright sunlight streaming in a small window. It almost obliterated the bearded figure sitting at a table. She described him, "He has a lot of clothes on for it to be this warm. He's wearing britches, a shirt, and something like a cloak. I don't know why he has so much on. It must be spring. The walls are kind of damp and cold because they're stone, but the sun is pouring in."

She wasn't sure if he was the man we were seeking, but she began describing the feeling she was getting from him. "He writes papers a lot at that drawing table. I think he's old and wise and by himself. This room isn't a prison, but it has that feeling. It's enclosed, although I think he has the freedom to go in and out. But within it's pretty contained, like a lot of time is spent in there. Maybe like a prison of one's own making. I think it's because of dedication, too, not because he's forced to stay in there all the time. I think he's lonely and misunderstood. I wish there were even a dog or something. He's sort of hunched over the table, like he's weary."

She then made the discovery that she was invisible, and she knew he couldn't see her. We had again succeeded in locating the great man, but another problem presented itself. I knew we would have to get his attention if we were to proceed to where he could show her the same map he had shown to John. This became a problem, because he seemed to be totally oblivious to her presence. "Whatever is me is flowing around the room—not fast—but like the wind. Going around the room and observing him, and he's not aware that I'm here."

She thought of different ways to attract his attention: have something in the room fall, have the scent of flowers come in on the breeze and swirl around the room, have a butterfly enter through the open window, but nothing seemed to have any affect. He didn't move. He seemed to be frozen in time, while she was pure energy swirling around the room. Maybe that was what had occurred, she had entered another dimension at a point where time had stopped or didn't exist. She also sensed that Nostradamus didn't know he was frozen in time, so time was probably continuing normally for him. Perhaps our two dimensions weren't meshing and were still separated by an invisible impenetrable wall. Incredible as it sounds, that seemed to be the only explanation. If this were true, then contact would be most difficult if not impossible. But I had to keep making the attempt because the map was important to our project. How could we break through to that space where Nostradamus lived and functioned?

After several attempts it was obvious that it wasn't going to work. We were just not able to alert him to our presence. But this proved to be an important point. I wasn't controlling this, or I could have made the connection happen. Beverly also wasn't controlling it because she was desperately searching for a way to make him aware of her and was unsuccessful. It reemphasized the theory I had come to accept. All of this was in the hands of other entities and forces beyond our control.

The answer came in the form of a sudden inspiration, like the proverbial lightbulb going off in my head. Maybe we didn't need him! Nostradamus was absolutely essential for the interpretation of the quatrains, but maybe we didn't need him to give us further information about the map. True, he must have seen it in his mirror in order to show it to John, but maybe we could get it from the same source that he had. It was worth a try. If Beverly was able, in her spirit state, to locate him in the past, maybe she could move to a future state and look at the world herself. Maybe we didn't need Nostradamus as a mediator for this phase of the project. This could be the reason we weren't having any success in speaking with him. Maybe *seeing* the future world would be more accurate than looking at the map.

I decided to pursue this line of thinking. "Since it's so difficult to contact him, let's see if you can do it without his help. You may have more abilities than you realize because you're free and can see anything you want. I am interested in the world of the 20th century, the world of the future."

She replied, "I'm having trouble with that. 'Future' doesn't compute very well."

I knew it was going to be difficult to explain a concept such as time to a spirit who had no interest in the physical, because I had had this experience many times.

D: *I know time is difficult to understand. But when we're in a physical body we live in this physical world, on the planet Earth, which is a physical, solid mass. There is much concern about what's going to happen to our planet because it is our home. There has been talk that at some time in the future our Earth may move and shift, and this would cause the land masses to change their shapes. Can you see something about that for me?*

B: Well, it *is* going to shift. It *does* that periodically.

D: *When this shift occurs, can you see the way the world will look afterwards?*

The transition was smooth and natural. As though a button had been pushed, Nostradamus' room faded and she was in a place to view the future world. She immediately began to describe what she was seeing, and proceeded to give, not only a description, but the mechanics of how the entire Earth shift would operate. She became very animated and used a lot of hand motions.

B: Nothing will really look the same any more. I see a level of the Earth with Earth below it, and when the Earth shifts, only the top level moves northward and the level underneath doesn't. That causes areas to crack open. (*She proceeded to give an analogy.*) Try to see the United States on a table made out of hardpacked dirt that's a foot thick, and under that is more dirt that was joined together at one time. Now when the poles shift, this upper foot is going to move northwards, and it's not going to take the lower portion with it. It will separate.— Remember this is an analogy, I don't know how many *thousands* of feet deep it is.—Only the upper part moves and becomes disjointed from the bottom part. Then the upper foot of dirt is not substantial enough to hold together, so it will split and crack like parched earth. As it shifts northward it will disturb the waters which will cause further splitting, cracking, and flooding. The waters will move in from the north, and the seas above Canada and Alaska will flood the upper part of the North American continent, and then a *greater* part. Below it, the Great Lakes will flood downward. And on either side of the United States the upper parts of the Pacific and Atlantic Oceans will flood downward. All of this water will cover a great portion of the United States, which will break off and separate because of the cracks. By the time that flooding subsides, it's hit the southern oceans below the United States, and it starts all over again. So a great deal of water will seemingly move from the north downward.

D: *What will happen to the polar caps?*

B: They will melt, but the thicker areas will not break up as easily as the areas of land. The North pole is going to shift northwards, back about a quarter down on the other side, closer to Russia and Siberia. The South Pole will move upward, possibly into southern South America. If you could visualize the United States as it lies now, the continent will turn northward and slightly twist to the right.

Beverly saw the United States broken up into six or seven island-type masses. The largest portion was again reported to be in the middle of the country. The East and West Coasts were mostly inundated, and most of the upper area around the Great Lakes and all of the southern area was gone.

B: The higher mountainous areas, of course, will be exposed. If the water comes up to 8,000 feet on a 10,000-foot mountain range, then only those upper 2,000 feet would remain above water. There are other mountain ranges—like in the central U.S.—that are only 5,000 feet tall and would normally be under water. But other circumstances are at work, because the first foot of land we spoke of earlier will shift northward, leaving land underneath it, and these other mountain ranges would then be forced upward. Those that may be only 5,000 feet would be pushed up higher by the land mass underneath it, to an altitude of perhaps 10,000 feet. Then that area will also be 2,000 feet above the water level. Do you understand? Some low land will be pushed upward to where it sits as high as your tallest mountains.

Imagine the world being round like a ball. The North Pole is at the top, and when this plate of the United States shifts northwards, what's underneath shifts, too. But instead of following the curvature of the ball, it will push outward once it gets past the roundest point of the planet. Do you understand what I mean? It's going to start shifting northward and when it hits an area that confines it, it has no place to go. When that happens, it's going to come out away from the planet. That's what will happen to the area we call the Midwest. It will involve Arkansas and the states above it. Kansas and Nebraska, which we think of as plains states, are going to be pushed outward, too.

She had found the answer to one of our main questions concerning the map: Why would the central section remain above water even though it had a lower elevation? We would not be able to rely on our present elevations.

B: It will be caused by activity that's occurring very, very far away, making these lower lands in the Earth's subsurface rise. The pushing up of that land will not happen from directly under the United States. It will be happening from the shifts that are taking place across the whole planet.

Although all of this area will shift northward, climates will be different. Very cold climates, such as the northern portions of Canada and Alaska will become temperate, but it will take some time. It's almost as if this whole side of the world is going to be temperate. I don't think there will be any cold climates at all. When the South Pole moves northward, it will move into a tropical climate, so both poles will melt. And the new poles working from the inside out, would take many, many years in those positions to spread enough cold to freeze into poles like we have now.

Beverly then proceeded to relate the same information about the remaining portions that Brenda and John had given. Since it did not contradict, but was repetitious, I will not repeat it here. I will only include the additional information:

D: Will any large cities be left?

B: I don't know. Seattle. Denver. Cities will develop on the middle land mass. I don't see anything there *now* that we would call a major city, since St. Louis and Kansas City will be gone. The Midwest has smaller cities and a lot of undeveloped farm land.

D: Which cities in that area will have the most commerce or people?

B: One will be Harrison, Arkansas, or a city very close to it. There will be another city just south of it on the east side of that landmass that will become a big port and a trading center. It might even be—no, it's not as far south as Little Rock.

This mention of Harrison by both John and Beverly was a surprise because Harrison at this time (1989) is a small city whose main claim to fame is that it is the home of the tourist attraction "Dogpatch." The entire area is mountainous and sparsely populated.

B: Many of the small towns will enlarge, particularly on what will then be coastline because the remaining people will go to those areas to find work. Most of the transportation will be by water at that time because the United States will have broken up into (*counting*) ... probably four or five major sections, with several little island areas. They won't be lengthy trips by water, but ships or very large boats will be utilized to carry things from one land mass to another, like we now do by rail or truck. So there will be jobs along the coastline and people will gravitate toward those areas. They will be port cities, but none of them will ever again be as large as the cities you have now—like Los Angeles, New York, and Chicago. I think the populations will be more evenly spaced, and no one city will gain tremendous importance or size over others.

D: What about Antarctica?

B: It will shift north toward the equator, and a bit to the east, as will South America. This will move it into a more temperate climate. It won't break up as quickly as other land masses because much of what holds it together is ice. There will be major cracks in it, and eventually the land will separate because of the ice melting, but that won't happen for a while. It will be habitable and people will be able to go there. But it won't be worth living on because the ice will remain for a long time and nothing will grow there. The ice cap will not melt immediately, but it will crack.

Amazingly, Beverly's description of all the other continents matched John and Brenda's to a remarkable degree.

D: Will the climates of Europe and Asia change?

B: Yes, but not drastically. Some areas will become colder, but some will become more temperate. Russia will not be as cold as it was, but by far, the better weather will be in the western hemisphere.

D: *When we were looking at the eastern seaboard of the United States I forgot to ask about the capital, Washington, D.C.*

B: It will be gone.

D: *What will happen to the seat of government?*

B: It will relocate to the far northwest: Washington state, Oregon area. Government as you know it will not exist anymore. Means of communication will be so advanced by that time that, although *physical* things will be lost, the knowledge won't be lost. Paper work, computers, disks, and whatever, *may* be physically lost, but not lot of knowledge will be lost because it is so easily accessible at that time.

D: *What about the President and government officials?*

B: You will not have a President in the same way you do now. After the shift there will be more of a council or a board of directors. You may have that even before the axis shift, but if not, certainly afterwards. You won't be ruled by *a* President any longer. The sharing of knowledge and decision-making between a group of people of high integrity and knowledge will serve your needs better. I don't see anything like a House of Representatives or Senate at that time. Those groups are too *big* to be effective, and on the other hand, *one* President is too *small*. You will have settled in, or *will* then settle in to a council group of a few people that will help guide what goes on in the country.

It's important to realize that the only portion of this book Beverly read before this experiment was the chapter dealing with John's version of the Earth shift (Chapter 17). She had not seen or been told about his view of his future life, yet she was describing a very similar scenario concerning the functioning of our government.

D: *If this shift happens suddenly will the present government be able to escape from the capital?*

B: Many people escape, but I don't know about the current government authorities. Many people will know this is going to take place before it actually happens. It won't come as a thief in the night. You will have forewarning.

D: *How will we know?*

B: It will be almost common knowledge by that time. There will be psychic information that won't even be considered psychic by that time. It will be a "knowingness" that these things are going to occur and some preparations will be made. There may be jarrings ahead of time, and in some areas that's their only forewarning. Some people won't know, so it will come as a shock to them, but the more informed people *will* know that this is going to happen. They won't know *exactly* when, but there will be plans that can be thrown into action as soon as it starts, because preparations have been made ahead of time. While we talk about it as a possibility at this time, as it comes closer to happening the things we are talking about now will be accepted as truth and fact. They will not be doubted the way they are now.

D: *Maybe there will be more scientific facts to back it up.*

B: That may be true, but I think it's more likely that we'll listen to our inner selves. Our psychic abilities will become a part of us, just like our other senses: sight, taste, touch, smell, and hearing. It will be relied upon to provide accurate data, where it isn't today.

This was a comforting thought and gave me hope that portions of civilization would survive. The shift wouldn't occur so suddenly that everyone would be caught offguard. Preparations would be made and warnings would be heeded when the realization that something of a tremendous magnitude would soon occur and could not be prevented. This renewed my faith in a mankind that would not allow his entire civilization to perish. It would be, as Nostradamus had said, the end of civilization "as you know it," but it would not be the end of humanity. Drastic changes would occur but humankind is versatile enough to adapt their way of life to changes and go on. They wouldn't allow life to be totally destroyed if it was in their power to do anything about it.

D: *If we are going to continue space exploration, where would that be located?*

B: The space headquarters will be out of that same Washington-Oregon area. NASA and everything in Florida will be gone, so they'll move their headquarters.

That again was similar to what John had seen in his future life as the female space traveler.

B: At that point, national government won't concern itself with ruling its people as it does now, but it will be more closely associated with space ventures. That will be more the purpose of the government, rather than handing down laws for private citizens as they do now.

D: *You think the main focus will be on space?*

B: Right. Interplanetary travel, and communion with people from other planets will be more important. Elections won't be held in the same manner they are now where several parties fight each other. There will be something like a council that will have the support of all of the people and everyone will work in unison. The focus of the government won't be to control yourselves, but to move outward because your "selves" will be much more *under* control, independently or individually. You won't need the government to do it *for* you and *to* you any more.

D: *Do you think all of these drastic changes will be caused by this great shift?*

B: No, not *because* of it. I think they're coming regardless, because of the evolution of humanity. Humanity is moving more and more into a psychic and spiritual realm which will occur at about the same time the axis change takes place. They actually will be working in conjunction with each other. And when I say "at the same time," I don't mean within a year. I'm talking about within two or three decades. Psychic awareness gradually evolves more and more to where it is acceptable to operate this way. All of these changes have already begun, but within the next two to five years psychic awareness will become much more widely accepted. Right now you're into it, but it hasn't reached an acceptable point with the masses. During the 1990s, you'll take it for granted that that's the way life should be on the planet. That's why I don't think it will be such a drastic change by that time, because so many things that are just theories now will be so widely accepted by then that you will be aware and know about the axis change. You will anticipate it and be prepared to continue working through it.

D: *Then it won't be so drastic that everyone will be completely traumatized by it. It will be bad enough, but with no warning at all it would be terrible.*

B: Even in the late 1990s there will be people who still say, "Naw, that's not so." These are the same people who don't believe you can really send men to the moon nowadays.

D: *There are always those who doubt.*

B: Right. But the majority will have changed their thinking.

I had apparently covered the entire globe, so I prepared to bring her back to full consciousness. She interrupted me.

B: You have many games that you play to occupy yourself.

D: *Yes, I do.* (Laugh)

B: I don't mean you. I mean everyone. It really won't make any difference, but if this gives you pleasure, then that's fine.

D: *You said, "It really won't make any difference." Is that because a large number of people who now inhabit the Earth will be making transitions, and they won't be terribly concerned about where the land masses will be?*

B: Partly, but even more so than what you think. Yes, souls will be in a different level of consciousness. But it won't make much difference, or any difference, because there's a bigger level that we're not even discussing yet. I'm not being derogatory, but it *is* just a game.

Before she awakened, Beverly was given instructions that she would remember the shapes, and the dimensions of what she had seen, so she would be able to draw them later. I then brought her back to full consciousness and was once again amazed at the amount of information that can be uncovered when this special state of consciousness is tapped into.

We had tried to solicit Nostradamus' help but were unable to make him aware of our presence and our intent. But all the answers we were searching for were accessible in that other dimension. Maybe we located the same source Nostradamus used to obtain his information of future events. If this is true, then it's not a place known only to him, but one which is accessible to all who develop the ability and have the curiosity and desire to search.

We discussed this after she awakened. Beverly was astounded by the experience. She was grateful for the information that would help her on the production of the maps, but she was confused by the procedure that had produced it. She said it felt strange when the information came through because she knew she had absolutely no control over it. The only thing she could compare it to was the feeling that she was one big mouth and the information was coming out without any thought or action on her part. We laughed at this amusing visual metaphor.

When we were discussing the poles having shifted, melted, and not refrozen, she remarked that since the climate of the area would be tropical, it would take time to cool it down to where the area would freeze. She compared it to when you put water in the freezer to make ice cubes. It will happen in a short length of time. But if you were to place the ice cube tray in the refrigerator, it might freeze, but it would take a considerable length of time. This was a good analogy.

It took two sessions to obtain all the information necessary for the preparation of the maps. During the second session I showed her black-and-white maps and had her color out the missing parts of the world while in trance.

Beverly felt confident that she would be able to reproduce the maps accurately, according to what she had seen. It was an interesting project, but she quickly admitted that she hoped the condition of the world the map portrayed would never become a reality. She hoped in that respect that the maps would *not* be accurate.

And thus, the maps depicting the future world were created. It was truly fitting that they were created by this method since everything else related to this project was paranormal and unorthodox. It was once again evidence that forces other than our own were truly guiding our efforts in this.

When Beverly, Brenda's and John's versions are compared, they are not exactly carbon copies. I think this could be explained because of the difficulty of the project. Nostradamus also said that land masses would change and appear differently as the ice caps once again began to form. We have no way of knowing if John, Brenda and Beverly were looking at the Earth during the same stages of development. All versions still depict a world that chaos has forever changed. A planet composed more of water than of land. A world picture that I hope will never be seen by humans.

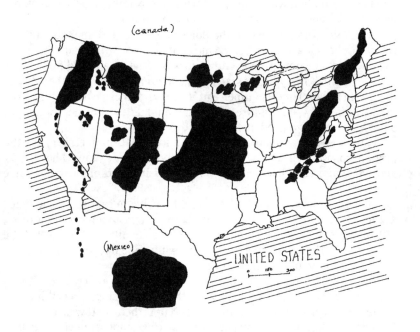

This map shows the North American continent after the Earth shift.
Striped lines are existing large water masses. White areas are existing
land. Black areas are remaining land that will be above water after the
Earth shift.

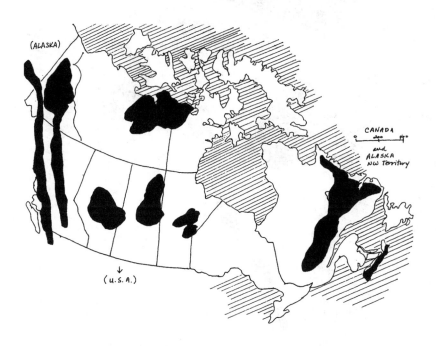

(ALASKA)

(U.S.A.)

CANADA
and
ALASKA
NW Territory

This map shows Canada and Alaska after the Earth shift. Striped lines are existing large water masses. White areas are existing land. Black areas are remaining land that will be above water after the Earth shift.

This map shows the South American continent after the Earth shift. Striped lines are existing large water masses. White areas are existing land. Black areas are remaining land that will be above water after the Earth shift.

This map shows the European continent after the Earth shift. Striped lines are existing large water masses. White areas are existing land. Black areas are remaining land that will be above water after the Earth shift.

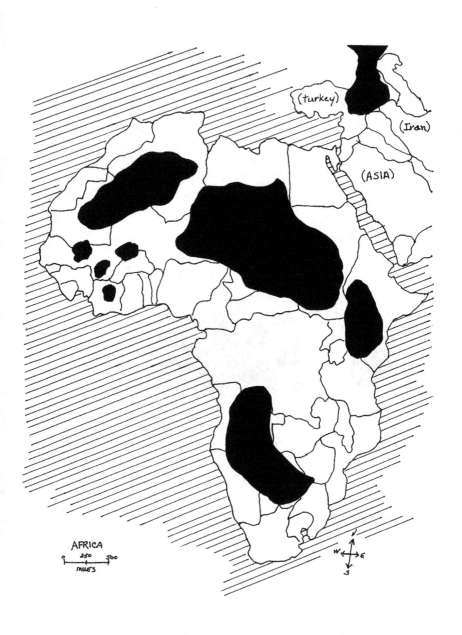

This map shows the African continent after the Earth shift. Striped lines are existing large water masses. White areas are existing land. Black areas are remaining land that will be above water after the Earth shift.

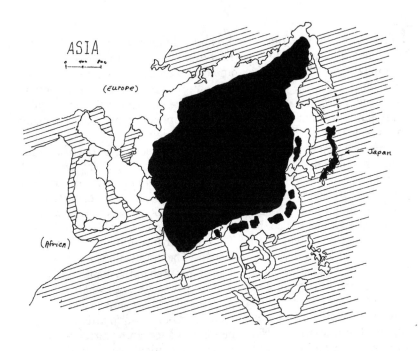

ASIA

(Europe)

(Africa)

← Japan

This map shows the Asian continent after the Earth shift. Striped lines are existing large water masses. White areas are existing land. Black areas are remaining land that will be above water after the Earth shift.

Chapter 29

ƒinding the Date of the Shift

NOW THAT WE HAD DISCOVERED approximately what the world would look like after the axis shift, the next thing would be to establish its date as closely as possible. To give something a date gives it more substance, more form and makes the possibility more likely. As long as it remains vague the consequences are less likely to take on that form and substance. Thus, it is with great reluctance that I attempted to supply a date for such an awesome event. How presumptuous of me!

In order to pursue this, I at least had to come to the conclusion that such a horrible thing was possible. In the beginning of my work with Elena this was one of the first topics Nostradamus brought up, and one prediction that gave me a great deal of difficulty. I had to come to terms with it within my own conscience before I could go on with the work he had assigned to me. Even though I had come to terms with it I still hoped in my heart that he was wrong. That the Earth would not shift and civilization as we knew it would not perish. The implications were too awesome in scope and almost impossible to comprehend. I wanted to believe that an alternate path could become the reality. A path where life could continue and not be disrupted by such horrifying consequences. Thus, the only way I could write about the condition of the world after a climactic axis shift and attempt to find the date of such an occurrence, was to approach it as an interesting story or a theoretical event. In this way I could be objective, and it did not touch me personally. My mind didn't have to wrestle with the terrible repercussions on the human race. Thus, I am not vouching for the validity of the map but I am only reporting the information that came forth.

It was the same problem when we tried to pinpoint the date of the shift by translating CENTURY VIII-49 in Chapter 17, "The Fate of the Anti-Christ and the World." In this case it had to be treated as a detective story because it became more complicated than previously thought. The astrological symbols in the quatrain seemed to be very explicit, so it appeared it would be rather simple for an astrologer to find the date. It read: "Saturn in Taurus, Jupiter in Aquarius, Mars in Sagittarius, the sixth of

February." Nostradamus said this referred to the date of the shift of the Earth which would occur after the year 2000, in the early part of the 21st century.

I was working on this chapter in the summer of 1989. John was now living in Florida and our only contact was by mail or telephone. We had clarified dates and exchanged information on several of the quatrains. John had difficulty finding a 2000 ephemeris, so he had to put off finding dates that Nostradamus said would occur after the year 2000. Finding the ephemeris turned out to be a major obstacle. For some reason the first printing was sold out everywhere, and he would have to wait until a second printing made a copy available.

When he finally obtained a copy, this quatrain was put off as it became increasingly difficult to decipher. John tried but he was hampered by having no more information than the translation of the quatrain as presented in Ms. Cheetham's book. He said that Saturn in Taurus was easy enough to find because Saturn was a slow moving planet, going into a sign only once every 28 years. Once that date was established the rest should fall into line. He was able to identify the year as 2029 because of the movement of Saturn, but the other signs refused to cooperate. He felt he had reached a dead end.

I couldn't understand how this could happen when the signs were so precise in the quatrain. But were they? On a hunch I decided to check other translations of the quatrains and to find the literal translation of the French. When I did this, I made an astounding discovery. Ms. Cheetham's translation was not accurate according to the literal French. "Saturn: au beuf joue en l'eau, Mars en fleiche" translates as: "Saturn in bull, Jupiter in water, Mars in arrow." I have a limited knowledge of astrology, but I thought this information might be enough to make a difference. In Ms. Cheetham's defense, she's not the only one who has translated the quatrain incorrectly. Several other books list it as "Jupiter in Aquarius," but she also refers to this lineup of signs as a conjunction which is incorrect. A conjunction occurs when two or more planets are no more than ten degrees apart. The planets in this quatrain are definitely not in conjunction because two of the signs are opposite.

It was becoming time-consuming, not to mention expensive, to keep calling John in Florida, so in the winter of 1989 I consulted with a woman friend who was expert in astrology. I knew this was going to get complicated and I felt that I should have someone with whom I could consult on a regular basis. She was also trained in metaphysics so I thought she would be able to apply intuitive insight to the reasoning required. Nostradamus had once told us that the "drawer" of horoscopes had to be willing to try the unusual, and to apply strange alternative meanings even if they didn't seem to fit the standard astrological methods. My friend was willing to help with this, but she wanted to remain anonymous. I agreed to protect her privacy, so I will refer to her as Mae.

When I showed her the original translation versus the literal French, the first thing she said was that many people who are not astrologers make this same mistake. They assume that because Aquarius is represented by a water-bearer and the glyph is wavy lines, that it is a water sign. But it isn't; it's an air sign and the wavy lines really represent the flow of energy, not water. The other signs were probably correct because, on the basis of astrological symbols, the bull could only mean Taurus and the arrow would most likely mean Sagittarius, the archer. So the first step would be to assume that Nostradamus meant that Jupiter was in a *water sign* and to track it from there. So Mae obtained a 2000 ephemeris, I gave her the data, and left her to the search. I continued working on the rest of this book while I anxiously awaited the call that said she had found the answer. I never doubted that she would find it, because I knew Nostradamus would not lead us into a blind corner and abandon us. It was simply a matter of trying to understand the complicated way his mind operated.

When she was ready I went to her house. As I sat on the couch and saw the papers spread out before her I had a moment of panic. The scribbling made no more sense to me than hieroglyphics, yet I would be required to understand these signs and symbols well enough to put them into common language that the layperson could comprehend. I sighed: that was one of the hassles of being a writer. I knew I would never remember the technical data or be able to decipher it from my notes. So I turned on my trusty tape recorder, my mainstay during these experiments. I kept nodding that I understood what she was saying, although I did not. I knew it was all being recorded so I could transcribe the information later and try to put it into understandable terms. Mae said I could probably do it better than she could anyway because of the very fact that I do not understand the technical words. I would have to put it in simpler terms through sheer necessity. The data is there and if professional astrologers want to refer to the dates given, they will be able to see the deeper implications.

As indicated earlier the simplest place to begin was to find out when Saturn would be in Taurus. Since it was such a slow-moving planet, it would only traverse through the positions once every 28 years. This gave us the year 2028 or 2029, and from there we could begin. The ephemeris indicated the other planets wouldn't move into their positions mentioned in the quatrain until late 2029. Mars moves into Sagittarius on the 24th of September and stays there until November 4th, so this narrowed down our time span. Mae estimated that the date of the shift would have to be between the 6th of September and the 4th of November, 2029. She also thought it was significant that Mars and Saturn were involved since these two planets together are often considered malefics, or indications of war or destruction. I thought that would aptly apply to this situation since this shift was supposed to occur at the height of the Anti-Christ's war.

Next, we needed to check the position of Jupiter during this time period. What water sign would it fall under? Mae thought the water sign of Scorpio would be most fitting because Scorpio is ruled both by Mars, the planet of war, and Pluto, the planet of transformation. She explained that Scorpio is the sign of death and rebirth and often correlates to *major* changes, upheavals, and destruction, in order to clear out the old and make room for the new. It could be symbolized by the Phœnix, the bird who is consumed and rises from its own ashes.

Because the quatrain specifically mentions the 6th of *February,* and all of this was zeroing in on September and October, we had another puzzle on our hands. Mae said this was the first thing she checked out. Mars and Jupiter were *both* in Libra all during February, but Libra had no correlation to the quatrain and was not associated with such drastic changes. Also the number six didn't seem to fit. Like a detective looking for clues, it was now obvious that Nostradamus was again using one of his tricks, and it was a very clever one at that. Only an inventive astrologer could hope to decipher these symbols and puzzles by deviating from any set rules. Mae would have to let intuition guide her. When we found the first astrologer to work on this project, Nostradamus told me he would have to be willing to try the unusual.

Mae finally came to the conclusion that February did not literally mean the month. Since the major part of February falls under the sign of Aquarius, which is ruled by Uranus, she decided that February actually referred to both that sign and the ruling planet. Uranus is the outer planet which relates to destruction in the form of *sudden* changes and unexpected things. It challenges rigid structure in life and brings newness and change. It is also the planet that rules the New Age. February, represented by the sign of Aquarius, could also correspond to the *Age* of Aquarius, in which all of these changes will supposedly occur.

She also examined the planet Pluto because it is the outer planet that relates to upheavals from the inside which bring things up out of the dark (earthquakes). Pluto is the cosmic "housecleaner" which rules endings and beginnings. It is the planet of transformation and the force which transforms the atomic structure of life so that various energies can regroup into their new forms. Pluto also rules mass consciousness. And Mae discovered Pluto is in the sign of Aquarius during the time period she had pinpointed!

After she made these connections, she examined both Uranus and Pluto to see how they would be affecting the Earth at that time. Whenever there are connections between Mars and Uranus, there are apt to be *major* sudden changes that wipe out a lot of the old patterns. And wherever Mars and Pluto are involved, internal things that have been brewing for a long time come to a head.

Mae would have to find the proper water sign for Jupiter, and also which aspects would indicate that something of this nature would occur. She explained, "When you're dealing with astrology, you can't take one thing out of context; you look at the overall picture. There are combinations of energies at work which indicate that things of a particular nature are apt to happen." She then began to see that some out-of-the-ordinary configurations were at work during the period of time she had chosen to zero in on.

She explained, "One of the first things I noticed was that during September all three of the outer planets and Saturn were retrograde. That's another indication of mass transformation, especially since the outer three represent cosmic forces which affect the whole of humanity. Periodically, these four planets are retrograde at the same time, and it usually indicates sweeping changes, particularly affecting the masses. In this case the Earth shift would certainly affect all of humanity, and the very ground of their existence."

The date she selected for this dubious honor was October 24, 2029. I will use her own words for the astrological positions at that time since it's difficult to explain them simply. It will be interesting to other astrologers although it may be confusing reading for the layperson.

"On the 24th the Sun moves into the sign Scorpio which is directly opposition Taurus, and the Moon is conjunct Saturn in Taurus (the sign mentioned in the quatrain). Mars is in Sagittarius (mentioned in the quatrain) and also exactly opposition Uranus in Gemini. As I mentioned, Uranus is the planet that corresponds to sudden destruction. (It was the planet she speculated was indicated by February in the quatrain.) Mars is also quincunx the conjunction of Saturn and the Moon. Quincunx is a very problematical aspect and often indicates something out-of-the-ordinary, or of a difficult and drastic nature. It's anything that doesn't fit into the familiar context of things. The planet Neptune is semi-square Saturn, and Mercury is also quincunx Saturn. Then Venus is exactly conjunct Mars, which is not the best of aspects for Venus. Venus is the planet of harmony, love and beauty, so its energy is almost opposite to that of Mars, the planet of war. At the time, the North Node is at the exact degree of the center point of our galaxy, and is also retrograde and conjunct Mars. So the North Node and Venus are both under the influence of Mars, and all three in opposition to Uranus. When major events such as this happen, the Sun usually is involved in an aspect of tension, since the Sun represents our source of life. And sure enough, the Sun is conjunct Jupiter in Scorpio and they are opposition the Moon and Saturn in Taurus, and also square Pluto in Aquarius. The conjunction of the Sun with Mercury also pulls it into these aspects. In other words, *all* the planets are lined up in what you might call aspects of tension.

"There is so much going on here. The three planets mentioned in the quatrain are in their proper signs, if we assume that 'Jupiter in water' means a water sign and that sign is Scorpio. Because there was no other time when Saturn was in Taurus, Mars was in Sagittarius and Jupiter was in one of the water signs, it would appear that Nostradamus knew this and so gave the clues in the manner he did. It was also very significant to me to note that the Sun is with Jupiter in Scorpio, the sign of death/rebirth and transformation and the moon is with Saturn in the opposite sign from Taurus. And Saturn in Taurus seems to be the focus or the fulcrum of this event. Remember, Saturn rules the physical and thus the Earth and all its forms and their crystallization.

"The other thing I find to be beyond coincidence—and I didn't even think about it until later when I was reviewing what I had come up with—is that two and four do add up to six (the 24th of October). I had already checked six as a date (from September through December) and also six degrees for the planets' positions, but there didn't seem to be many correlations.

"I also noticed that a couple of days later, on the 27th, the Moon is conjunct Uranus, the planet of the sudden and unexpected. And together, the Moon and Uranus are opposition Mars at that time. None of these combinations of aspects happen very often. As I worked on this I had strong intuitive impressions that this shift would happen over a period of time, and not all at once, although there could be an epicenter or time center to it. I feel that the *major* event will take place between the 6th (note the 6 again!) of September, which is when Saturn goes retrograde, and sometime in December. Interestingly enough, on the 5th of December there is a *solar eclipse* in Sagittarius, and it will be directly opposition Uranus at that time, and conjunct the North Node. Then on December 20th there is a *total lunar eclipse.* Eclipses mark turning points or beginnings and endings of cycles and are often triggers for other aspects. I saw that as pertinent because it falls on the heel of all of the rest.

"I see these things as more than coincidence. The fact that the four outermost planets and the North Node are retrograde, and the Sun, the Moon and all the planets are involved in aspects of tension on that particular day (the 24th of October), is just so out-of-the-ordinary that it really caught my attention."

Mae spoke of some less commonly used aspects which I will not discuss in depth because I believe they would be of interest only to astrologers. She then mentioned a new planet named Chiron. It was discovered about 12 years ago (1977). She said that astronomers call it an asteroid, but astrologers are working with it as a minor planet. (Could this be one of the new planets Nostradamus referred to in Chapter 12, "Nostradamus and Astrology"? It has been assigned rulership of Virgo by some authorities.) It orbits elliptically between Saturn and Uranus, actually orbiting *through* the orbit of Saturn, and is called the "bridge." This means it is considered to be a bridge between the physical, material (Saturn), and higher consciousness (the outer planets). It's also considered a maverick and a catalyst, and is frequently involved where events affect masses of *people,* particularly where consciousness change is involved. Mae thought it was significant that Chiron is in the sign of Taurus during this time period and in opposition to Jupiter and the Sun on October 24th. She also found that it was in some aspect with nearly every one of the planets during the designated time period.

The other less-used aspects, such as biquintile, novile, and septile, were present with Mars and other planets. She said that that many aspects don't happen frequently, especially in relation to the planet Mars, Uranus and Pluto. Without going into complicated details, she said these aspects represent realization, redemption, and divination in inner guidance. All of these together could represent events moving people into making contact with that which is eternal and out of attachment to the material. She said it was at such times of major upheaval that people come into realization. Mae found it significant that so many of the aspects involved had similar indications. In other words, they were not flowing, positive aspects, but nearly *all* were negative or points of tension which bring the necessity for change, and they relate to each other in that way.

When I mentioned that the translation of the quatrain referred to the Anti-Christ's death by a massive tidal wave, she immediately made the correlation again with the sign of Scorpio. She said it was the water sign which rules death and transformation, indicating that the old must die so the new can be born. Checking the chart of the Anti-Christ, she found that his Neptune (which rules the oceans) is in the sign of Scorpio and is the focus of a T-square with his Aquarian stellium (holding all his personal planets) and his Leo North Node. To compound that, his Pluto (the ruler of Scorpio) is in Scorpio's house, the eighth house of death! And to add to the significance of this Pluto, Neptune, and Scorpio involvement, the shift chart's Neptune is *exact* quincunx his natal Pluto in the eighth house!

As complicated as all of this appeared, it seemed obvious to me that Mae had found the date we were looking for through her careful calculations and detective work. I felt that her deductions would stand up to the scrutiny of other astrologers. This does not mean that I (or she) have accepted this as the date of the shift of the Earth and the cessation of civilization as we know it. But I believe that it's a remarkable deduction of the symbols and puzzles Nostradamus included in this significant quatrain. He certainly had no intention of making it easy to find. He said to me once, "I have dealt in mystery for too long. I cannot simply hand you the answers. Let me see the brilliance of *your* minds."

I feel we came to an accurate conclusion that the quatrain means: Saturn is in Taurus, Jupiter is in Scorpio and Mars is in Sagittarius. February refers to Aquarius and its ruling planet, Uranus, also to the Age of Aquarius, and six refers to the 24th. Thus the date is October 24, 2029.

I was fascinated by Mae's diligent astrological detective work and I think her date deserves merit, especially when compared to CENTURY III-96 which was translated in Chapter 22, "The Hidden Room." Nostradamus indicated it referred to a time in 2036 when political maneuvering and the shifting of loyalties was occurring as different factions fought among themselves. One group was still holding to the beliefs of the Anti-Christ even though he was no longer on the Earth. Since 2036 was only seven years after the Earth shift caused the cessation of hostilities in 2029, it would seem logical that small groups might still be having problems.

Mae was still unsure about her deductions. She decided to call Mark Lerner, the publisher of a monthly astrological magazine. She wanted his input on the quatrain because of his expertise and knowledge of ancient astrology. She thought he might be able to pinpoint something she had overlooked. I was always open to any insight that might help solve the puzzle. Mae talked to him on the phone and he agreed to look at the material. We sent him the quatrain and our literal translation as well as the traditional one. As an afterthought I included the charts of Ogmios and the Anti-Christ. The only information he was given was that we suspected this quatrain had to do with a possible pole shift. Without having any background of how the information was obtained, he was able to provide some interesting and amazing corroborations. These seemingly unrelated incidents continue to give me faith in the material presented to us by Nostradamus.

Mark mailed me a tape which outlined his conclusions, and prepared his own chart for the Anti-Christ. I was impressed that he listed the birthplace as Jerusalem, Israel. He said later that he had simply picked that place at random. He did not have access to our information that the Anti-Christ's parents had been killed in the Israeli War, and that he was taken from that area to be raised by his uncle. Mark said when he randomly chose the birthtime 5:25 A.M. he noticed that this placed Neptune exactly at mid-heaven at the top of the chart. He remarked, "This indicates a Pied Piper figure. If somebody were going to be a spiritual guide for the Aquarian Age, it might very well be somebody with Neptune directly above at the top of the chart. This is someone who would mesmerize millions of people. This person was born just before sunrise with Capricorn as the ascendant. Capricorn is symbolically similar to the Devil card in the Tarot, and is ruled by Saturn."

He was immediately struck by interesting connections between the horoscopes of Ogmios and the Anti-Christ. "Good old Ogmios, whoever he is ... it's interesting that the north and south nodes in his chart are the *reverse* of the nodes for the Anti-Christ. The nodes have been used for thousands of years. They are not planets, but relate to the orbits of the moon and the Earth and how they link up with the Sun. They are a very fateful and destiny-oriented part of a chart. All the planets are basically going around the zodiac in the normal way, but the nodes go *backwards,* and every nine years the nodes will reverse themselves. They represent the past and old karma, and there is a great range of potential karma between these two figures. Basically, there are nine years and a few months between the birth and the cycles of these two people and they are *linked* through the nodes. Somehow they definitely seem to be twins or paralleling each other. In other words, Ogmios was born first, then nine plus years later this other figure was born with the nodes in the reverse position. One way of looking at this is to say that Ogmios has the Anti-

Christ's number, or at least he has a look-in to this person's personality and world, and the reverse is also true to some extent. It's as if these two people, or energies or whatever they are, are playing out a cosmic game here or on a higher level. They obviously have a connection, almost as though they were two parts of the same energy. In order to fulfill God's will or God's law you have to have good guys and bad guys. We wouldn't have any decent movie without the two opposites, and hopefully good always wins out over bad. At any rate, Ogmios is sort of the forerunner to the Anti-Christ, or at least coming in before him. It's also interesting that this Ogmios figure has several planets in Libra, which (like Aquarius) is an air sign. Therefore, both of these two figures are operating on the *mental* and *spiritual* levels. There is a lot of airiness going on, which could symbolize a battle in the air, missiles, planes, communications, computers, and things like that. Ogmios has Sun and Neptune together, and Neptune is a Christ-like energy. Also Jupiter in Ogmios' chart is a direct square or right angle to the Anti-Christ's.

"In 1993 the whole planet will experience a very rare conjunction of Uranus and Neptune in Capricorn. The last time this happened was 171 years ago at the death of Napoleon. This Ogmios figure will have his mid-life crisis hit in 1993. That's when this person sort of comes of age, or needs to go through a major revolution in consciousness. On the other hand, the Anti-Christ's chart will be triggered in the *latter* part of the 1990s. There will definitely be an awakening factor for the Anti-Christ at that time. Uranus and Neptune will be in his birthsign, Aquarius, in the late 1990s, and Jupiter will be there in 1996–1997. The Anti-Christ mid-life crisis will strike in 2002 because Uranus will be opposing its own position in the birthchart in the spring and summer of that year. Ogmios is experiencing all this nine years before the Anti-Christ. Maybe he needed to come in earlier so he would have extra time to do whatever he needs to do."

It is amazing that Mark could pinpoint the similarities between these two figures when he did not know the information behind the two charts. He considered them to be twins, opposites, or mirror images of each other. He even compared the energy to the Jesus/Judas, hero/villain roles.

Mark then studied the wording of the quatrain and attempted to locate the signs in the ephemeris. He soon came to the same conclusion as John and Mae: it couldn't be done. He agreed that the literal translation probably inferred Jupiter had to be in a water sign, but he did not agree with Mae's conclusion (October 24, 2029) because February 6 was not involved in the solution. He said her date was definitely a possibility according to one level of looking at the quatrain and it could be significant. But he thought that, because Nostradamus seldom gives exact dates, he would not have included February 6 unless it was important. He thought that in order to be true to the quatrain he should look for that date first in the ephemerides, and then see if the other signs lined up. He had the same problem; it wasn't working out, *until* he located February 6, 2002. The following is his solution, based on his logic and his knowledge of ancient astrology:

"On that February 6 Saturn is nearing a station. That happens twice a year for outer planets when the planet appears, from the Earth's point of view, to be almost stationary. It's a powerful time when the planetary energies are strengthening for good or for ill. On this date Saturn is virtually not moving. Where is it? It's in the sign Gemini. You could consider this to be the wrong position, because when Saturn is in the sign of Gemini it's definitely not in Taurus, as mentioned in the quatrain. *However,* the tropical western zodiac that we are using is connected in a different manner to the so-called sidereal or constellational zodiac of the actual star groups. On that date when you have Saturn in Gemini, the stars of the Taurus constellation are *behind* Gemini. The *key* star of the Taurus constellation is Aldebaran, a tremendous giant sun. The ancient Persians had four main stars that lit up the four corners of their sky. One was Aldebaran or the 'right eye of the bull.' I believe Nostradamus was familiar with this type of astrology. If we're saying that Nostradamus was thinking more constellationally than he was sign-wise, he could be talking about the constellation of the bull, not the sign. I think if he said 'Saturn in bull,' he was actually thinking of Saturn being in conjunction with Aldebaran, the eye of the bull. It is also important that Nostradamus begins the quatrain with Saturn. It is obvious that something must be going on with that planet. If you want to make a connection with the Anti-Christ, he is a Satan/Saturn-type figure, and if there was going to be some kind of dire calamity, Saturn would have to be a weighty influence. Referring to the other signs, Jupiter is in the water sign of Cancer on that date, but Mars is in Aries; it has nothing to do with arrow. Looking at it constellationally Mars in the sign of Aries is connected to the stars of the constellation Pisces, the sign of the fish. That is the only part that does not fit. But the signs indicate something, with a strong lineup of Earth, Sun, Saturn and Aldebaran, the great star from thousands of years ago that represents the eye of the bull.

"Another thing that is happening at that time is that Mercury, the planet of communication and movement, is nearing a station. In fact, two days after February 6th, both Mercury and Saturn will be motionless in the sky from the Earth's point of view. There are Aquarian energies with Venus, Uranus, Neptune, the Sun, the Moon, and the nodes all in Aquarius. I bring this up because our good friend, the Anti-Christ, has a stellium in Aquarius in his birth chart, so he has a lot of Aquarian energy. It would seem there has to be some kind of connection.

"Let's notice some other remarkable points. The first nuclear chain reaction occurred on December 2, 1942 in Chicago. Oddly enough, 59-plus years later in 2002 Saturn is in the same position in Gemini (the eye of the bull). This date would be the return of that cycle. Oddly enough, when this energy was released in 1942 Jupiter was also in the water sign of Cancer, because when 59 years go by from one event to the next Jupiter and Saturn will return to the same positions. It's the *only* time they do that simultaneously. So we are seeing a cosmic return of the release of nuclear energy in February 2002. There's a link between these two dates and the harnessing of the atom. This is just a link, a date, it doesn't prove anything. It doesn't mean there will be a pole shift or a giant conflagration or anything else on that date. It doesn't have to refer to a war, the actual detonation of a nuclear weapon, or even a nuclear accident. Who knows? It could refer to a resolution of the nuclear problem. The signs definitely refer to something nuclear but it doesn't necessarily have to be bad; it could indicate a positive event. It could very well be that work such as this will illuminate the possibilities and avoid negative occurrences."

Mark then mentioned something that had totally escaped my attention. We had been so intent on locating the signs and placing them in the proper positions that we hadn't noticed February 6 is the only one or two days off from the Anti-Christ's *birthday.* Was Nostradamus slyly trying to sneak this into a quatrain in the same manner he had planted the birth stellium in CENTURY VI-35 in Chapter 12? Mark felt there was a strong connection. He said the Anti-Christ would be 40 years old in 2002, and this was a Biblical cycle as well as a symbolic pregnancy cycle. The sun and other planets are returning to the same positions as the day he was born. Mark commented, "The Sun is returning right in the heart of this person's life. There is also a Moon/Pluto conjunction in Sagittarius on that day. We know that Pluto is a planet of extremes, so there is the possibility of something extreme happening, whether it is a pole shift, a nuclear event, a lot of psychic and emotional turbulence or whatever. Mars will be making what we call an "inconjunct" or quincunx, exactly *five* signs away from the Anti-Christ's Neptune on that particular day. This is a stimulation where someone could go off course or be placed in an extremely awkward situation that would be very difficult for them. It's a powerful time when something could go wrong.

"Another interesting point is the position of Mars, considered a planet of war and strife. On February 6, 2002, it will be squaring the Sun in the United States' chart, so there is tension there. Jupiter on that day will be in the water sign of Cancer and is returning to its home position in the United States' chart, where it was in 1776 when the United States was born. There is definitely a lot of energizing of the United States' chart. Even the Saturn position in Gemini is on the horizon of the United States' chart. In 1776 Uranus was in Gemini, so on February 6, 2002, Saturn will be crossing the United States' Uranus. Uranus rules uranium and revolutionary events, as well as nuclear-related activity, radiation *etc.*

"I want to go on record and say that I, Mark Lerner, am not predicting atomic war, a pole shift, or anything similar. I'm just researching this for your benefit. I'm trying to find a logical date based on the quatrain and astrology, and to decipher things that *could* connect to this particular thing. I *am* saying that if you were looking for something and you wanted to find it in this quatrain, there is a lot to find. I can see the links. There is a lot of synchronicity with the Anti-Christ turning 40, his birthday, and the connections back to 1942 and the release of atomic energy with an exact Saturn and Jupiter return to that time. So it looks like a rather unusual and eventful period, but I am not predicting anything."

Mark Lerner did not realize how extremely helpful he had been. How could he possibly know the implications of his analysis? He knew nothing of the content of the other predictions and astrological references that Nostradamus had already revealed to us. It is amazing that while he was working blind his remarks were very accurate. He was unaware of the many layers the great master could combine into one quatrain when his whims suited him. It now appeared to me that the quatrains that referred to the most important events had the most complicated structure. CENTURY VI-35 in Chapter 12 is another case in point; its layers had to be peeled off like an onion. There still may be more information in these quatrains that is waiting for another investigator to find.

It is my assumption that both dates (2002 and 2029) could be accurate. Nostradamus was giving us the Anti-Christ's birthdate. He was also giving us the time and the conditions under which he would come to full power, when he could begin using nuclear destruction. This is similar to CENTURY VI-35 in Chapter 12 which refers to the Anti-Christ using nuclear weapons for the first time at the beginning of 1998. Could it become more pronounced by 2002 when he is creating havoc for the entire world? Could it refer to a major nuclear accident caused by human error or by the shifting of the Earth's plates, and that the Anti-Christ would take advantage of this? Or could it be, as Mark Lerner suggests, the resolution of the nuclear problem in peaceful ways? Either way, the similarities and implications are remarkable. It also appears that the United States will be heavily involved in the event in 2002.

There are many layers and many possibilities. It would appear that the date Mark found would not necessarily refer to a pole shift but to something nuclear, and this is why it involved only part of the symbols mentioned in the quatrain. The date that Mae found could refer to the actual pole shift and thus involved all the symbols. Her solution didn't have to incorporate the exact date of February 6 because that date had other meanings. When we are exposed to this type of convoluted maneuvering it creates a reverent respect for the wonderfully complex mind of Nostradamus. And we may have only uncovered the tip of the iceberg. I wonder if Nostradamus himself fully understood what he was incorporating into these deceivingly simple four-line poems. He believed he did not truly compose them, that they occurred through automatic writing and were literally written by an unseen hand. Maybe he was right. Maybe no one on Earth had the mind capable of coordinating so much into so few words. This could be the reason the quatrains have never truly been deciphered until now. The gate was not ready to be opened.

I telephoned Mark to tell him my conclusions and he agreed they were possibilities.

I asked him if it made any difference that John's chart for the Anti-Christ was for the 4th and his was for the 5th of February, 1962. He said there was a total solar eclipse on the 5th. In India and other places in the world astrologers were predicting the end of the world, especially relating it to the seven planets in Aquarius. There were two very powerful eclipses that year, in February and August, that energized Aquarius and Leo, which are the signs of the new age of the upcoming 2000-year cycle. Nostradamus had said that eclipses would have something to do with the Anti-Christ, but he never clarified what he meant. Mark said that the one on February 5th was one of the most powerful eclipses that has ever happened, at least in recent memory. He said people don't realize that 1962 was an amazing year. It was the year of the Cuban missile crisis, and also the founding of Findhorn, Scotland, as a training center for enlightenment; important positive and negative events.

I told him that his date of 2002 was important because Nostradamus had referred several times that the reign of the Anti-Christ would last less than the revolution of Saturn (27 years). Remarkably Mark's date (2002) and Mae's date (2029) were exactly 27 years apart. Before Mark made his deductions we didn't have a date to start counting from.

He was astounded when I told him that we were in contact with Nostradamus while he was still alive in the 1500s. But when I told him that Nostradamus saw his visions in a black obsidian mirror he was startled. He exclaimed, "Are you ready for this? On Christmas Day a friend gave me a piece of pure black obsidian. I'm looking at it now because it's sitting right here on my computer." He described it as a sphere about the size of a softball. It was amazing to him that after he received the unusual object Mae called him to ask about working on Nostradamus material. He had had a fascination with Nostradamus—not just the quatrains, but the man—for a long time and had written about him in his magazine. Now it appeared that there was definitely a connection. These synchronicities have occurred repeatedly while working on this assignment. Little clues or affirmations were constantly appearing to let those involved know in subtle ways that these connections were meant to happen. They would appear as coincidences to anyone who was not involved in the project. But to the rest of us they were simply silent reminders that we were on the right track in fulfilling our karmic destinies.

Mae made this statement as a finale to all the research and astrological calculations:

"I believe that Nostradamus may have worded this quatrain (and most likely many others) in such a way as to include the timing of more than one possible or probable outcome. Since outcomes always depend on which choices are made and which path is taken, he covered several 'probable' dates which depend on the path taken and choices made by Earth's inhabitants. There are no 'set-in-concrete' outcomes dictated by astrological configurations, only certain energy patterns which exist, and we always have the choice of how we use them. Certain patterns may already have been set in motion, but like a hand of cards dealt us, we're the ones to decide how to play it. We can play it smart, or we can give it away."

In researching Nostradamus, I found an old French proverb that applies here:

Qui vivra verra.

"He who lives to see will know."

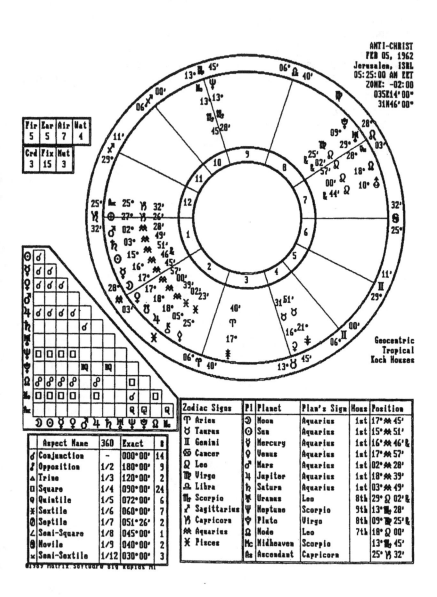

Fir	Ear	Air	Wat
5	5	7	4

Crd	Fix	Mut
3	15	3

ANTI-CHRIST
FEB 05, 1962
Jerusalem, ISRL
05:25:00 AM EET
ZONE: -02:00
035E14'00"
31N46'00"

Geocentric
Tropical
Koch Houses

	☉	☿	♀	♂	♃	♄	♅	♆	♇	☊	
☉	♂										
☿	♂	♂									
♀	♂	♂	♂								
♂	♂	♂	♂	♂							
♃	♂	♂	♂	♂	♂						
♄					♂						
♅											
♆	□	□	□	□							
♇					⅗						
☊	⚹	⚹	⚹	⚹		⚹		□			
							⚹	□		♂	□
	☉	☿	♀	♂	♃	♄	♅	♆	♇	☊	

Aspect Name		360	Exact	#
♂	Conjunction	–	000°00'	14
☍	Opposition	1/2	180°00'	9
△	Trine	1/3	120°00'	2
□	Square	1/4	090°00'	24
Q	Quintile	1/5	072°00'	6
⚹	Sextile	1/6	060°00'	7
⊙	Septile	1/7	051°26'	2
∠	Semi-Square	1/8	045°00'	1
⊕	Novile	1/9	040°00'	2
⚼	Semi-Sextile	1/12	030°00'	3

©1987 Matrix Software Big Rapids MI

Zodiac Signs		Pl	Planet	Plan's Sign	Hous	Position
♈	Aries	☽	Moon	Aquarius	1st	17° ♒ 45'
♉	Taurus	☉	Sun	Aquarius	1st	15° ♒ 51'
♊	Gemini	☿	Mercury	Aquarius	1st	16° ♒ 46' ℞
♋	Cancer	♀	Venus	Aquarius	1st	17° ♒ 57'
♌	Leo	♂	Mars	Aquarius	1st	02° ♒ 28'
♍	Virgo	♃	Jupiter	Aquarius	1st	18° ♒ 39'
♎	Libra	♄	Saturn	Aquarius	1st	03° ♒ 49'
♏	Scorpio	♅	Uranus	Leo	8th	29° ♌ 02' ℞
♐	Sagittarius	♆	Neptune	Scorpio	9th	13° ♏ 28'
♑	Capricorn	♇	Pluto	Virgo	8th	09° ♍ 25' ℞
♒	Aquarius	☊	Node	Leo	7th	18° ♌ 00'
♓	Pisces	Mc	Midheaven	Scorpio		13° ♏ 45'
		As	Ascendant	Capricorn		25° ♑ 32'

This is the horoscope for the Anti-Christ's date of birth, February 5, 1962.

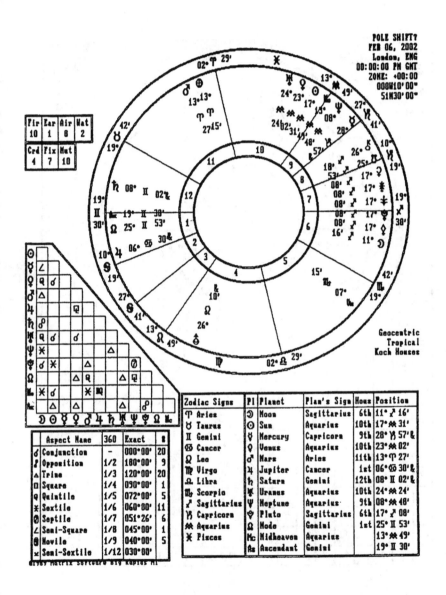

POLE SHIFT?
FEB 06, 2002
London, ENG
00:00:00 PM GMT
ZONE: +00:00
000W10'00"
51N30'00"

Fir	Ear	Air	Wat
10	1	8	2

Crd	Fix	Mut
4	7	10

Geocentric
Tropical
Koch Houses

Zodiac Signs		Pl	Planet	Plan's Sign	Hous	Position
♈	Aries	☽	Moon	Sagittarius	6th	11° ♐ 16'
♉	Taurus	☉	Sun	Aquarius	10th	17° ♒ 31'
♊	Gemini	☿	Mercury	Capricorn	9th	28° ♑ 57' ℞
♋	Cancer	♀	Venus	Aquarius	10th	23° ♒ 02'
♌	Leo	♂	Mars	Aries	11th	13° ♈ 27'
♍	Virgo	♃	Jupiter	Cancer	1st	06° ♋ 30' ℞
♎	Libra	♄	Saturn	Gemini	12th	08° ♊ 02' ℞
♏	Scorpio	♅	Uranus	Aquarius	10th	24° ♒ 24'
♐	Sagittarius	♆	Neptune	Aquarius	9th	08° ♒ 48'
♑	Capricorn	♇	Pluto	Sagittarius	6th	17° ♐ 08'
♒	Aquarius	☊	Node	Gemini	1st	25° ♊ 53'
♓	Pisces	Mc	Midheaven	Aquarius		13° ♒ 49'
		As	Ascendant	Gemini		19° ♊ 30'

Aspect Name	360	Exact	%
♂ Conjunction	-	000°00'	20
☍ Opposition	1/2	180°00'	9
△ Trine	1/3	120°00'	20
□ Square	1/4	090°00'	1
Q Quintile	1/5	072°00'	5
⚹ Sextile	1/6	060°00'	11
⊙ Septile	1/7	051°26'	6
∠ Semi-Square	1/8	045°00'	1
⊕ Novile	1/9	040°00'	5
⚺ Semi-Sextile	1/12	030°00'	

© by Matrix Software BIG Rapids MI

This is the horoscope for a possible date of the Earth shift, February 6, 2002.

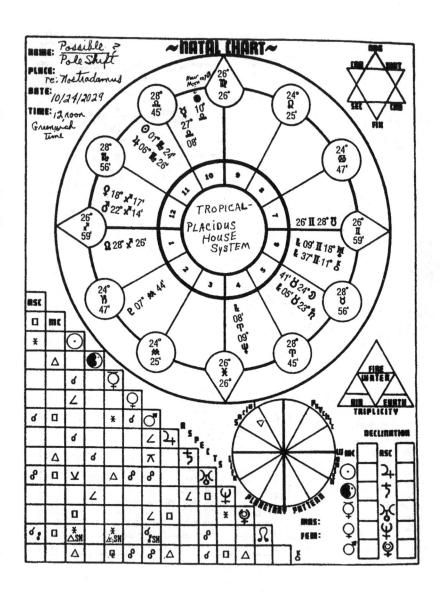

This is the horoscope for a possible date of the Earth shift, October 24, 2029.

Chapter 30

𝕽esearch into
𝕹ostradamus' 𝕷ife

𝕬FTER WORKING ON THIS PROJECT for over two years, I felt the information I had gathered would not be contaminated by doing research into Nostradamus' life. Since I had become so personally acquainted with him, I felt I knew him better than any modern researcher could hope to. I was curious to see if there might be any parallels between what we had found out about him, and what the biographers reported. I had deliberately held off looking for confirmation until the end of 1988 when the first volume was in the process of being published. Personally I didn't feel that I needed any corroborating evidence because I knew we had been in touch with the great man. There was no doubt in my mind about that. The bulk of information that had come forth was evidence enough to sustain my faith in his reality and his immortality. But for the sake of the books and for any skeptics, I felt I should try to research his life.

I began to search through Library of Congress catalogs and the University of Arkansas ordered books on Nostradamus for me through interlibrary loan. Some of these were difficult to obtain, and some were rare, with only one copy available in the United States. In a few cases I was only able to receive a photocopy because the original was too fragile to be loaned out. All of this gave me more respect for the facts I uncovered, because the average person would not have gone to these lengths to obtain obscure and forgotten books unless they were as interested in research as I am.

There was a surge of books on Nostradamus written in the early 1940s, probably due to the beginning of the Second World War and people's renewed interest in prophecy as a hope for the future, which at that time looked very dim indeed.

As there must always be a balance, there were also a few books written by debunkers. People can seldom agree on anything, especially a personage as controversial as Nostradamus. The skeptics thought that he was not a prophet but merely a shrewd businessman. One suggested that he was a wino and made up the quatrains while hallucinating in a drunken stupor. One author believed that Nostradamus was a charlatan who used vague wording and astrological symbols to try to fool people, especially royalty. That author then went 180 degrees in the opposite direction to try to prove that all of the quatrains refer to contemporary events in Nostradamus' lifetime. He stated that they were cleverly disguised puzzles that the people of Nostradamus' day could have been able to figure out and apply to events in their time. That entire book was devoted to showing the connection between the quatrains, royalty, and countries in Europe during the 1500s. Sometimes the explanations became very laborious as the author attempted to avoid any reference to the future, or anything out of the realm of a shrewd businessman or charlatan. He was one writer I found that painted an unfavorable picture of Nostradamus. He believed that much of the story of Nostradamus is legend, with little basis on fact.

I thought I would find answers to all of my questions once I started reading about Nostradamus. This was not the case. All the modern authors repeated the same story, and the little innuendoes about the man's life, as though they copied the information from each other. I was more interested in their sources. One I was able to track down contained information not mentioned in the more modern books. This was Edgar Leoni's book, *Nostradamus: Life and Literature.* The author had done exhaustive research into every aspect of the life and works of Nostradamus and uncovered sources not mentioned by any other writer. He admitted that the prophet's personal life was not very exciting, and his enduring fame has come from his quatrains and their eternal puzzle. Much confusion exists concerning a number of biographical details. It's impossible to find out the exact truth because of the discrepancies caused by the loss or destruction of old documents which would provide the proof.

All of the authors expressed the same intense disappointment I had felt when I began studying the quatrains. They had expected to be challenged, but then became resigned to the impossibility of ever making any sense out of the puzzles. In James Laver's book, *Nostradamus,* he remarked after tediously examining a convoluted quatrain, "At this point it is likely that the impatient reader will fling the book away in disgust. What indeed is all this juggling with names, these Greek words turned inside out, these anagrams that mean two things at once? Do they not rather destroy than reinforce any possible belief in the prophetic powers of the Provencial Jew who apparently knew so much yet would not take the trouble to express himself clearly? ... I had expected a certain obscurity but the reality was worse than I had feared. ... These four-line stanzas of crabbed French verse, obeying neither prosody nor syntax, arranged in no intelligible order and bristling not only with words in half a dozen foreign languages but with initials, anagrams and made-up names—how can there be a hope of finding any meaning in such a publication at all?

And if there were, would it be worth the trouble? ... A great danger awaits anyone who sets out to interpret the quatrains of Nostradamus. He becomes so completely engrossed in the fascinating crossword puzzle of the text, in the Sherlock Holmes pursuit of clues and cryptograms that in the end he is liable to become the victim of his own ingenuity, and to see connections and meanings where none can reasonably be supposed to exist. All the commentators have succumbed in some measure to this tendency."

It was reported that Jean de Roux, a curé who in 1710 attempted to place the interpretation of Nostradamus on a scientific basis, came to the same conclusion. His first impression, like that of everybody else, was one of disappointment, and he concluded that further study of the Prophet would be a waste of time. But apparently, like all of us who have been involved with the great man, he had been bitten by the bug of curiosity. He spent the rest of his life searching for an understanding of the quatrains.

Maybe our ignorance was to our advantage. No one involved with our experiment had done any studying at all. I read the quatrain for the first time when I opened the book and read aloud to the entranced subject. Even after I read it I was not enlightened, the puzzles were too obscure. I was just a puppet reciting verse which made no sense to any of us. I made numerous errors in pronunciation, and my naïvete about the subject matter often tried Nostradamus' patience. He became my stern schoolmaster, determined to further my horrible lack of education (in his eyes). Maybe we were chosen for this task because we weren't hampered by the complete immersion into the puzzles that plagued the other translators. I respect them for their perseverance and patience, but this dedication may have kept them from trying unusual interpretations, and possible crazy explanations. They had become such experts that their focus had narrowed, and strange and new possibilities had been closed off for them.

On the other hand, we were certainly approaching this with an open mind. Our minds were so open they were empty. We were open to any explanation that came from Nostradamus because we didn't know what the others had deduced through their own intellect. Maybe, when he first approached me through his student, Dyonisus, he was looking for unfettered and innocent minds so he could transfer the true definitions of his visions. If we were unwittingly a part of the relaying of the visions to him, it may also have been part of this naïvete. We were chosen to do our job without any conscious efforts on our part. When it became complicated and we tried to understand our role in all of this, we were told to not question because it was beyond our comprehension anyhow. This was probably why we were chosen. We weren't supposed to use our intellect, our human deductive powers, or our skill at unraveling puzzles. We had seen that these were more than puzzles invented by a human being, they had come from other realms and were beyond the understanding of mere mortals. The answers had to come from other dimensions which none of us, including Nostradamus himself, could understand. We were supposed to trust and allow the information to flow. We couldn't doubt it or question it because we had nothing to compare it with. As I began my research, I had renewed respect for whatever force was behind all of this, and while I found numerous similarities to our story, I found no contradictions.

There have been many amusing stories attributed to Nostradamus' life, but it's now believed that a lot of these are fictionalized accounts. He was, after all, a very secretive man, even in his own lifetime. He was a man who gave out little information concerning himself, and guarded well the secrets of others. Even after Nostradamus' death, his son, César, was careful to reveal nothing his father would not have approved of, and thus he added little to the story. There seemed to be a protective shroud which still conceals the man. In the final analysis, we may have had access to more of the details of Nostradamus' life, and have been able to show a truer picture of his personality than any of the biographers who have attempted to understand the man in the 400 years since his death.

In Leoni's book there was a physical description of Nostradamus which he attributed to the earliest biographer, Jean Chavigny. These are the exact words of the 16th century student and disciple of Nostradamus:

"He was a little under medium height, of robust body, nimble and vigorous. He had a large and open forehead, a straight and even nose, gray eyes which were generally pleasant but which blazed when he was angry and a visage both severe and smiling, such that along with his severity a great humanity could be seen; his cheeks were ruddy, even in his old age, his beard was long and thick, his health good and hearty (except in his old age) and all his senses acute and complete. His mind was good and lively, understanding easily what he wanted to; his judgment was subtle, his memory quite remarkable. By nature he was taciturn, thinking much and saying little, though speaking very well in the proper time and place; for the rest, vigilant, prompt and impetuous, prone to anger, patient in labor. He slept only four to five hours. He praised and loved freedom of speech and showed himself joyous and facetious, as well as biting, in his joking."

Leoni said there are three portraits of Nostradamus in existence. The most famous one, done by his son César on copper, is in the Bibliothèque Méjanes in Aix; a copy hangs by the prophet's tomb in Salon. The second is in the Library of Grasse and the third is in the Museon Arlaten at Arles. These all seem to agree with Chavigny's description.

The similarity between this description and the ones supplied by all the subjects involved in this experiment is too close to be questioned. All the features match. John remarked that he was a short man, coming only to his shoulder. Even the personality appears to be the same. There can be no doubt left in my mind that they were all seeing the same man, and that man was the authentic master himself. Coincidence cannot even be considered, the odds rule that out entirely.

The following is a compilation of the various biographical information contained in the books, along with comparison to what we discovered. For more thorough research it is suggested that the bibliography be consulted. Some of these books are difficult to obtain, but may be located through interlibrary loans at cooperating universities and libraries.

Michel de Notredame was said to have been born on December 14, 1503, by the old Julian calendar (December 23 by the Gregorian calendar), but he told us that this is possibly incorrect. He came from a Jewish family, but in his part of France all Jews were forced to convert to the Catholic faith and be baptized. Young Michel was raised by his grandfather, and it is widely suspected that he was taught the forbidden mysteries of the Kabbalah along with his other studies. In those days medicine was intertwined with astrology and magic.

At a very early age he entered the University of Avignon. He was far ahead of the other students, especially in matters relating to the stars and other natural phenomena, which were under the heading of philosophy in those days. He shared many of his heretical views with his fellow students: that the Earth was round like a ball, and that the planets and the Earth revolved around the sun. He was ahead of the scientific belief of the time, nearly a century later Galileo would be persecuted for such opinions.

He had an excellent memory and an absolute passion for learning. It was said that on many occasions he confounded his instructors, particularly in the subject of philosophy. He needed only to read a chapter once in order to repeat it with exact accuracy. This is remarkable because in those days a short sentence was composed of about 25 lines of print, punctuation was scanty, and paragraphs were few and far between. This was a time when all educational emphasis was on memory. Such ability made an impression on his teachers and was enough to give young Michel a top rating as a scholar.

He was sent to Montpellier to become a physician. In those days one studied physical sciences, physiology and anatomy by delving into Aristotle. One learned natural history by studying Pliny and Theophrastus, and acquired knowledge of medical science by reading Hippocrates, Galen, Avicenna, and others. This explained why Nostradamus was so impatient with my lack of knowledge of the ancient Greeks. They had been the absolute mainstay in the background of his education.

After completing the courses, he also taught. He had scarcely become qualified as a doctor when an outbreak of plague hit the city. Plague did not always mean the notorious "Black Plague" but was a term given to anything contagious, and could refer to such diseases as influenza, measles, chickenpox, diphtheria or whooping cough. But in those days of antiquated medical knowledge these deadly diseases spread like wildfire. While other physicians fled the diseased city, he stayed to fight the plague, and had extraordinary success although no one could understand why. It was and still is a matter of much speculation. He seemed to use unorthodox methods during all the time he practiced his trade. These methods were never understood or repeatable by his colleagues. One of his early biographers claimed he had a mysterious powder which he used to purify the air. Could it have been a type of disinfectant? It was said that he constantly experimented with various mysterious combinations of medicines. Because of his unauthorized and secret remedies, he was disliked by his fellow physicians. It was bad enough for him to use unorthodox methods, but to be able to perform cures with them was inexcusable. A particular bone of contention was Nostradamus' refusal to bleed the patient, a popular form of treatment that was used to treat everything. Nostradamus believed this weakened the patient.

After the plague, it became difficult for him to return to teaching. He found it restrictive to continue teaching traditional medicine when he had had such success with his own methods. He left the university and began to wander.

Eventually he settled in Agen where he married and had two children. It was said that he was so happy he probably would have spent the rest of his days there, and possibly the quatrains would never have been written. But fate stepped in in the form of the dreaded plague, and his wife and children died in spite of all he could do. I feel we were in possession of a bit of information from our work that the biographers didn't have. According to Dyonisus, Nostradamus had been away treating others when his family fell ill, and when he returned it was too late to help them. His enemies said that their deaths were payment for his vanity and pretentiousness.

Nostradamus' entire world was destroyed by their deaths and he became a wanderer once more. During the latter part of the 1530s and into the 1540s he traveled extensively for eight years.

He journeyed outside of France, but no one has ever been sure of all the places he visited. There are few surviving written accounts. It has been speculated that he consulted various groups of learned men: alchemists, astrologers, philosophers, and men who practiced medicine but also dabbled in magic. A vast amount of knowledge of science and philosophy, which had never received the sanction of the Church, was believed to have been passed on through secret societies. The scientists who worked within these secret groups were men who were unwilling to be bound by the narrow theological dogma. Maybe it was during this period of his life that Nostradamus made the journey to Malta to confer with the Arabs living there. (This journey was mentioned in Chapter 20.) He told us it was during his younger days, but he didn't want to discuss it because presumably it would cause him trouble if it ever became known. It's believed that during this period of his life his gift of prophecy began to manifest itself. He tried to keep this ability hidden, but it became more and more difficult because it was often spontaneous.

Several more outbreaks of plague kept him occupied during his wanderings about France. He also had to contend with rival doctors who openly accused him of practicing magic, and labeled his a sorcerer. In the time period in which Nostradamus lived astrologers were held in high esteem, but witches were not tolerated and were done away with by various means, especially burning at the stake. The accusations against him did not cause much trouble because the populace was too grateful for his cures to worry about how he was able to accomplish them.

In 1547 at the age of 44 he became tired of wandering and decided to settle in Salon. He tried marriage again, this time to a widow. Salon was not large enough to inundate him with patients, and it is believed he may have had students during this time. The biographers mentioned only Jean Chavigny as a student. They say almost everything that is known about the great master has come from him since he wrote about Nostradamus after his death. He is mentioned as a student and disciple, and they think he may have encouraged Nostradamus to write the prophecies and later, to present them to the world. Other biographers disagree. They think Chavigny may have given himself more importance than he deserves because he's not even mentioned in Nostradamus' will. I am inclined to agree. I think this could have been the time period when Dyonisus and the others lived with Nostradamus and studied under him. Dyonisus said that there were between 25 and 30 students who trained with him over the years. According to Dyonisus, Chavigny did not come along until later. He said that during the last ten years of his life Nostradamus began to write and became more of a recluse. Thus he didn't teach at that time in his life. Apparently Chavigny remained with him after the others had gone off on their own pursuits.

The fact that no other students are mentioned in the biographies would explain Dyonisus' secrecy and hesitancy to speak about Nostradamus when we first contacted him. It would also explain why Nostradamus did not attach the importance to Chavigny that he believed he had. I think Chavigny overestimated his own role with the master and his importance existed in his own mind. Out of all his students, why should Nostradamus single out Chavigny simply because he was the last?

Several biographers disagree on the number of children Nostradamus had and their sexes. The dates of their births are not known. Chavigny says there were six children, three boys and three girls. Garencières says there were three sons and one daughter. Dyonisus said he had three, but this could have been the number of children Nostradamus had at the time Dyonisus was studying with the master. The oldest was reported to be César, who painted the portrait of his father and was also a writer. In Nostradamus' writings there is a famous letter supposedly written to his son when he was a baby in 1555. Nostradamus was married in 1547. Did he wait eight years to have his first child and then have six altogether? He would have been in his fifties by that time. This bothered me because it didn't match with our story. John saw Nostradamus as he was preparing to celebrate the birth of his first son. He had difficulty making out the date on the horoscope Nostradamus was preparing because the numerals were written differently, but he thought it might be either 1551, 1557, or 1541, 1547. I began to wonder whether César was indeed his first born, or if there had been another before him. This was wild speculation until I found the following quote in Leoni's book: "Nostradamus left behind six children, three boys and three girls. ... In addition to these three sons (César, André and Charles), mention must be made of a fictitious son, referred to usually as Michel the younger. He is said to have made an unsuccessful effort to follow in his father's footsteps, and to him are attributed various odds and ends of occult literature."

Leoni says there are several references to this older son, who was later killed by a soldier, but it's debated whether he existed or not. Jaubert, the first biographer after Chavigny (1656), wrote that Michel was the eldest son and César was the second. Could this have been the baby boy that Nostradamus was so happy about? Or am I only trying to justify the information we obtained? Maybe no one will ever know for sure. Of the other sons, César was the only one who married, but he had no children. The three daughters married and there may be living descendants of Nostradamus from them.

While in Salon, Nostradamus also began to write. He was the first person to publish an almanac forecasting the weather when his small book was published in 1550. He wrote these almanacs regularly for several years.

He had been working on the quatrains for several years, and the first edition of the *Centuries* was published in 1555. Chavigny says that Nostradamus struggled within himself for quite a while trying to decide whether or not to publish them. Finally his desire to be useful to the public overcame his fear of ridicule or persecution. The Catholic authorities censored all literature and had to consent before anything could be printed. They gave permission after being assured that there was nothing in the quatrains that would be contrary to their religion. His first book contained only three complete centuries and 53 quatrains of the fourth century. They became an instant success, which was difficult to understand since none of the predictions had yet been fulfilled and they were considered impenetrable enigmas. Maybe their popularity rested upon the people's fascination with puzzles, but it made Nostradamus a celebrity, plunging him into notoriety. In the preface of that publication he explained the reason for his deliberate obscurity. He had purposely concealed the meanings of his prophecies so they would not be deciphered too soon and get him into trouble. He said he could easily have dated all of the quatrains, but it would have offended the people in power and would have brought down the accusation that he was somehow in league with the devil. This fits in with what he told us. He knew he was in constant danger of persecution and accusation of being a sorcerer.

In his day a man's fate often rested on the displeasure of the Church.

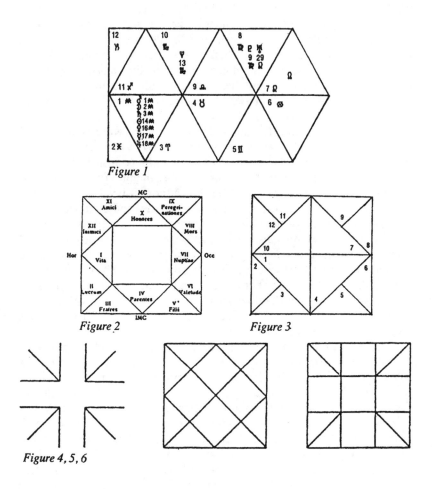

Figure 1.

Figure 2.   *Figure 3.*

Figure 4, 5, 6

Figure 1.   Horoscope design that Nostradamus used for the Anti-Christ. John reproduced it upon awakening from trance, and determined that it referred to February 4, 1962.

Figure 2.   A common horoscope design that was used in the 1500s and which was known to have been used by Nostradamus.

Figure 3.   Horoscope design that Nostradamus used for his newborn son which John reproduced upon awakening.

Figures 4, 5, 6.   Common geometric designs used for horoscopes which date from ancient Roman, Islamic and Byzantine times.

Discourteous statements, written or spoken, about royalty were considered insults and were severely dealt with. Understanding the circumstances Nostradamus was living under it's easy to see why he felt the need to couch his prophecies in symbolism and double-entendres. It's amazing that he even wrote them at all. He must have felt a tremendous need to pass them down to future generations considering the danger he was risking by writing them down and then daring to publish them. He allowed people to think of them as puzzles, hoping that others in the future would decipher their deeper meaning.

It was also true that he came to the attention of King Henry II and Catherine de' Medici. Catherine had an interest in the occult that was almost a mania. She was surrounded from childhood by astrologers and others involved in strange practices, possibly magic. In 1556 Nostradamus was asked to come to Paris. He had a short visit with the King and then went to see Catherine. One of the things she requested was that he cast the horoscopes of her children. Quote from James Laver: "If we believe in Nostradamus at all we must believe that he knew all about them. ... For the moment his problem was not to see but to conceal, to pronounce a true oracle without offending the Queen. She was known to have ambitions for her sons both outside and inside France. He contented himself with telling her that they should all be kings." This is almost precisely what Nostradamus himself told us about the visit. He said it was like walking a tightrope over a firepit.

There is a mention in Mr. Laver's book of an incident involving Catherine de' Medici which sounded very familiar, because Nostradamus told us about it. But in his book the incident was supposed to have occurred with another astrologer, Cosmo Ruggieri, who was one of Catherine's favorites and supposedly a scoundrel. The incident was a famous seance, known as the Consultation of the Magic Mirror, which was conducted at her chateau. Many magicians used mirrors in their rituals, especially in Italy, thus she was familiar with the practice. One of her biographers reported the seance in detail. A ceremony was performed which invoked the angel Anael, and the Queen saw, in the glass, the images of her sons. The similarity between this account and what Nostradamus told us is too striking to be coincidence. Does this mean that it was Nostradamus and not Ruggieri who showed the Queen her sons and told her of their futures? Could the facts have become muddled over the years, or did court intrigue or some other reason cause the event to be credited to the Queen's favorite astrologer? In André Lamont's book, *Nostradamus Sees All,* he also mentions this seance and attributes it to Nostradamus. These were the first accounts I had found of a magic mirror and it gave me cold chills to realize that one had actually existed. Later, I found a picture of Nostradamus showing Catherine de' Medici the images of her sons in a mirror. It looks like a traditional mirror, but this could have been the artist's rendition. It is amazing correlation that a mirror is even mentioned in connection with Nostradamus' predictions. I also wondered who was the angel Anæl who had been invoked?

After Nostradamus' visit with royalty, his fame became widespread, as did the lies and absurd stories which began to circulate about him. A crop of imitators arose who published forgeries under his name intending to discredit him, and many were jealous of him. As his health began to deteriorate, these petty annoyances began to make him bitter. It's no wonder he didn't want to reveal personal details of his life to us. Nostradamus tried to forget the insults as he prepared his second, larger edition of the *Centuries* for publication. The preface, dedicated to the King, was as difficult to read and as obscure as the quatrains. It's supposed to be a series of elaborate calculations based on Biblical chronology. Some writers have said that this is another one of Nostradamus' puzzles and tricks, and that hidden within the preface is a code to the interpretation and order of the quatrains. They claim he gave the key to the code to King Henry II and Catherine de' Medici. Other writers think this is only wild speculation.

In his commentaries (among them his letter to his son, César), Nostradamus speaks of conversing with angels and demons. He said he saw glowing spirits or shimmering apparitions. John saw himself as a glowing figure. Nostradamus also wrote that he heard a voice coming from the limbo that helped with the prophecies. What better description of the special meeting place? It was certainly a limbo, a place without form and substance. All of my subjects who were involved in this project said that he could hear me but could not see me. Was it my voice or the voices of the others that he heard coming from the gray mist? Nostradamus believed that if a prophet was truly inspired by God that he would be sent a divine mentor, *i.e.*, angel, demon, genius, or whatever was needed, in order to supply the knowledge he was seeking. I wonder which category we fell into? I hope it was on the side of the angels, because we never intended the great man any harm. We feel we were called into duty by his persistent search to understand his visions.

In 1564 King Charles IX, his mother, Catherine de' Medici, and a huge entourage came by Salon to see Nostradamus. She still hoped for positive predictions in regard to her sons, but he was unable to supply it. Nostradamus was now an old man and so ill that he couldn't edit the new edition of the *Centuries* he was preparing. He was well aware that he would have to wrap up these loose ends before he died.

His health began to fail after 60 due to severe attacks of gout which developed into arthritis. In Charles Ward's book, *Oracles of Nostradamus*, the author says a man's 63rd year—or climacteric, as it was called—was a very important milestone in his life in ancient times. It was believed that something dramatic might happen in that year of life because it was considered to be extreme old age. If a man could surpass that critical year he would live for a long time afterward. It sounds like superstition, but they based the belief upon the lives of famous people.

The crippling effects of gout and arthritis made it increasingly difficult for Nostradamus to get around. Because of the forced inactivity he began to suffer from dropsy and knew that he did not have long to live. Dropsy is defined as an abnormal accumulation of fluid in cavities and tissues of the body. It's an obsolete term for modern-day edema. He wrote his last will and testament and gave instructions for his burial. He said he didn't wish, even after death, to be trodden under foot by the people of Salon, so he asked to be buried upright in the wall of the Church of the Cordeliers. He sent for a priest to hear his confession and have the last rites administered. He then told Chavigny that he would not see him alive in the morning. True to his last prediction he died during the night, although as a doctor he undoubtedly knew from his own symptoms that he was dying. The dropsy (edema) had become so severe he had difficulty breathing, and instead of sleeping in his bed he slept sitting upright on a bench at the foot of the bed. Essentially, he died of suffocation. It was the equivalent of drowning in his own fluids. Dyonisus correctly identified the cause of Nostradamus' death, although he didn't know the name for the affliction.

Nostradamus died on July 2, 1566, the year of his climacteric. The next day he was carried to the church to be buried within the wall as he had instructed. His life had been so mysterious that a rumor began to circulate among the people of Salon that he was not really dead, but had had himself put into a magic cabinet in order to finish his prophecies. They would put their ears to the wall of the tomb and thought they could hear him moving around inside. Many believed that he had been buried with the manuscript key of his predictions and the missing 48 quatrains of CENTURY VII, but no one was brave enough to open the tomb.

During the French Revolution, the Church of the Cordeliers was destroyed. His remains were later removed to the Church of St. Laurent, and in 1813 a new plaque was placed on the crypt. But no manuscript was ever discovered.

When he died, Nostradamus left nearly five million paper francs and a sizable fortune in personal property. This was in addition to his gifts to the Church of Cordeliers and to needy friends. His will, published in Edgar Leoni's book, spelled out all the specific bequests, the amounts of money to be given to his wife and his children after their marriage, and also the disposal of certain pieces of furniture. The executors were instructed to gather all of his books, letters, and papers and not to sort or catalog them, but to tie them in parcels and baskets and lock them in a room in the house. Later, they would be given to one of his sons when he was old enough to study and understand them. He left the brass astrolabe (which John had seen) to his son César, along with a large gold ring.

I found an unusual notation in the will which may have some bearing on the story we uncovered. Nostradamus had counted all of his money and prepared a careful listing of it. The executors of the will were instructed to verify it, and place the coins in three coffers or chests located in the house. Then they would take possession of the keys to the chests.

Strangely, he left two walnut coffers which were located in his study to his daughter Madeline, "together with the clothes, rings and jewels that she will find in the said coffers, without anyone being permitted to see or look at that which will be therein." She didn't have to wait until she became of age, as the other bequests read, she was to take possession of the chests immediately upon his death. It seemed odd that on the one hand he had the executors carefully count the money and then take possession of the keys, while on the other hand no one was allowed to see what was inside of *these* chests. Could one of them be the chest that John had seen in the study? The one which Nostradamus told us contained ancient treasures and Roman antiques and coins he had found in his earlier days? Or did one of them contain the magic mirror and other items of magic paraphernalia? When we had asked about the chest he had told us it was none of our business. Thus he remained secretive even to the grave, allowing no one but his family to look in his precious chest or to catalog his personal papers.

Nostradamus' student, Jean Chavigny, said he devoted 28 years of his life (after Nostradamus' death) to editing the *Centuries* with notes. He said he collected twelve books of the *Centuries*, of which volumes VII, XI, and XII are imperfect. The *Presages* were collected by Aimes and reduced into twelve books in prose. In Nostradamus' preface he said these would explain more clearly the locations, times and conditions of the disasters in his prophecies. The few *Presages* that are now in print contain only 143 quatrains in verse, so we must suppose that those written in prose have perished. Could this be another reason why Nostradamus wanted to interpret his quatrains in prose form in our time, because his originals did not survive?

In Rolfe Boswell's book, *Nostradamus Speaks,* he described an unusual method of astrology which Nostradamus used. "Nostradamus called his chart the *Grand Romain* (The Great Roman). An oblong figure resembling a coffin and representing the 'Sepulcher of the Great Roman' is formed by drawing lines from the vowels of the Latin words *Floram Patere.* These two six-letter words are placed around the twelve lines of the zodiac. By using this formula to support his knowledge of judicial astrology, Nostradamus is supposed to have worked out his calculations and prophecies." Could this have been the geometric design that John saw him use for the Anti-Christ's horoscope? None of the astrologers I consulted have been able to identify the design for the "Great Roman." Maybe someone somewhere has the answer.

In Leoni's book there was a drawing of a horoscope that Nostradamus actually had made. It's the only known example of his method that has survived. When I first saw it in the book I was startled because when I compared it to John's drawing of Nostradamus' horoscope for his newborn son, they looked remarkably similar. John said he had never seen horoscopes made in this way, and Nostradamus had told us they (the two examples given in this book) were methods used by the ancients. They didn't use the horoscope wheel which is so common today.

In a letter to his eldest son, César, he writes that he burned some ancient occult manuscripts after digesting their contents thoroughly. Boswell says that old biographers are of the opinion that these may have been ancient texts possibly taken from Egypt and Babylonia after the captivities, and handed down to Nostradamus from his Jewish ancestors. This is considered possible because when the Romans destroyed the Temple at Jerusalem they found that the holiest documents had vanished. But of course, Nostradamus could have come across some of these forbidden manuscripts in his travels. He did say that the book he compiled of astrological data contained information dating from the ancient Egyptian and Babylonian times.

In Leoni's book he said that until the 19th century a person had to have an enormous amount of learning, including mastery of several languages, classical and medieval geography, and mythology, to even try to understand the prophecies. In essence, the reader was required to have the same knowledge as Nostradamus. But in the last 100 years many reference books have been written which have simplified this task.

Interestingly enough, a few of the authors I covered during my research mentioned the Hadrian quatrains (see Chapter 8). One correctly identified the anagram "Hadrie" as referring to the Emperor Hadrian, but he didn't go far enough with his imagination. He thought Nostradamus was paying a compliment to Henri of Navarre, implying that he possessed the virtues of the Emperor Hadrian. Erika Cheetham didn't make the connection between Hadrie and Hadrian. She said it was an anagram for King Henri, as did many other translators.

Some authors also correctly understood that Nostradamus gave his characters names associated with Greek mythology in some cases. One made these associations because in his home country of England, school children were still taught these subjects, but he didn't apply the idea broadly enough, as Nostradamus had intended. He mostly applied his interpretations to events that had already taken place. Thus, it was easier for him to recognize the association of the names.

Laver interpreted a quatrain (CENTURY IX-89) that contained the name of Ogmios. While he correctly identified him as the Celtic Hercules, he thought the name referred to France, because an image of the god appeared on the Republican five-franc pieces in 1792 and 1848. In all of our interpretations Ogmios referred to the leader of the underground, the nemesis of the Anti-Christ. Laver's interpretation would partially fit because Nostradamus did say that Ogmios would be from France. We haven't interpreted this quatrain yet, but since it mentions the Arabs, I think we're safe in assuming that it also relates to our central character. Of course, Nostradamus has often chided me in the past for jumping to conclusions and offering assumptions, but he also told us to use our own intellect once he has supplied the clues.

Many of the books about Nostradamus written at the beginning of World War II insinuated that most of the quatrains dealt with the past, mainly the French Revolution. The authors thought that few of the quatrains referred to the war that was presently waging, except those that contained the anagram "Hister" for Hitler. Most of the writers made only a small effort to predict the future, as though they would rather connect the details of the quatrains to events in history they were familiar with and could verify. Many of the ones they thought belonged in the past were quatrains we discovered belonged to the time of the Anti-Christ. They presented a very good case, but it has been established that Nostradamus often referred to many events in one quatrain, especially when there were similarities. So we are probably all correct. Nostradamus was simply more complex than the translators gave him credit for. They tried to put him into a little box and limit his abilities, but when he contacted us 400 years in the future, he showed that he refused to stay confined to that box.

I found no mention that Nostradamus ever published the book of philosophy he was working on, unless it was *Paraphase of Galen*, a philosophic discourse published in 1557. Of course, it was mentioned in his will that he left quantities of papers which were to be given to his sons, but no inventory was made of them. Some later editions of his *Centuries* contained quatrains that were not found in the earlier ones, and they may have come from these papers.

Many forged quatrains were added to Nostradamus' *Centuries* in the ensuing years. Some have been recognized as fakes because they didn't follow his unique style. An interpreter in 1709 said, "His prophecies have this in common with thunder that they only burst out and make a noise when they are accomplished." Yes, many of them can be understood only in hindsight.

From that time to this many serious researchers have tried to examine, analyze, and explain the mysterious physician. They have always come away shaking their heads in amazement. The man will forever remain an enigma in history. We may have come closer than anyone else to finally understanding Nostradamus the man, and appreciating the genius of Nostradamus the prophet.

Garencières said that while he was attending school in France in 1618, it was the custom to give the student Nostradamus' book of prophecies as their first book to read after the primer. The teachers thought the crabbed and obsolete words would give the scholars some idea of the old French language. Thus, the book was published from year to year like an almanac. This is probably one of the reasons it has survived. Garencières was Nostradamus' first translator, and he admitted that some of the words were meaningless to him. He thought the *Centuries* were difficult to fathom except in their original French, and even this presented many difficulties. He apologized for translating the quatrains into what he called "clumsy English." He said people had been driven mad trying to understand them. He wrote, "For these reasons (dear Reader) I would not have thee entangle thyself in the pretensions of knowing future things."

The question of Nostradamus' mirror remained an enigma until I discovered it in several books. In those days mirrors were usually polished metal. The writers described this as the type of mirror that was common among magicians. But a mirror made of obsidian would have been an extreme rarity. Had mirrors ever been made of this material?

This puzzled me until, while researching material for another one of my books, I found a mention of just such a mirror. I was reading a book on archæological discoveries in the Holy Land, and I found that a farmer operating a tractor in the fields of western Galilee had turned up a group of outstanding artifacts, one of which was a large obsidian mirror. The archæologists dated it at 4500 B.C.E., thus it was extremely old. The mirror was described as a unique example of highly advanced stone technology, because obsidian is a hard and extremely brittle volcanic glass. Only an experienced master could produce such a large oval disk, regular in shape and thickness, with a handle on the back carved from the same block of obsidian. The face of the mirror was smooth and polished to a high gloss. The experts said that the effort and skill invested in its production must have been immense. It's considered to be the finest, largest, and most ornate obsidian mirror ever found. Obsidian is a rare material found in areas of recent volcanic activity, and it occurs only in a few areas in the Near East. The discovery of this mirror in Isræl indicated that it was probably an article that had been traded, as it couldn't have been native to the area. With the introduction of metal technology the older stone technology waned in popularity.

I think it's logical to assume that if one such mirror existed, others did also, even though they were extremely rare and old. This would explain why Nostradamus protected it in a velvet bag and was so secretive about it. He told us that some of these ancient artifacts still existed in Europe during his day, and were considered very valuable, even if the owners didn't know of their special magical properties.

Laver knew Nostradamus used astrology, but that didn't account for the names and other details that riddled his quatrains. Thus he believed that these visions were not the work of the conscious mind. Leoni thought Nostradamus may have used self hypnosis, and Laver came to the conclusion that Nostradamus received his visions while in trance. He also thought that Nostradamus was able to enter this state of trance by practicing magic. He didn't mean this in a negative way because he thought it was conducted by means of ritual, and he noted that religion also uses rituals. He said it was only a tool, a means to an end which helped Nostradamus to concentrate and separate his conscious from his subconscious. I have always wondered if there were any such thing as *real* magic. We all would like to believe in fairy tales. I know something definitely happened while working with Nostradamus, but what was it? In Chapter 23, "Nostradamus' First Contact," we entered Nostradamus' study after he had made an invocation. He seemed to be as surprised to see us as we were to be there. Whatever method he used it must have been extremely powerful. It succeeded in drawing us there, and it also was able to expel us when he wanted us to leave. When Nostradamus began his chant John was pulled back into the Tapestry Room. He said if he had tried to remain, he knew he would have been zapped with the feeling of electricity. So I believe Nostradamus had discovered *real* magic, because it worked. Since we will never know *how* he made it work, this may remain one of the mysteries that will forever surround the man.

Laver thinks that all Nostradamus had to do was remember enough of his visions to make notes when he awakened, or that he may have used automatic writing. He wrote, "I find it impossible to avoid the conviction that Nostradamus *could* sometimes foresee the future and foresee it with an astonishing particularity of detail. Most of the commentators, of course, go much further than this. They believe that the whole scroll of future history was, by a privilege accorded to no other mortal man, unrolled before his eyes, and that the admitted obscurity of his message is deliberate. This is to take the authorship of the *Centuries* from Nostradamus and to give it to the Deity Himself."

Liberté LeVert made a comment at the end of his book, *The Prophecies and Enigmas of Nostradamus,* that sparked a startling thought. I suppose I had read the same thing in the other books, but it only now hit me with a great force.

He reiterated that Nostradamus' quatrains were not published in one book in the beginning. There were three separate continuing versions. The first appearance of the *Centuries* was published in 1555 and contained only the quatrains from I-1 to IV-53. The second group of quatrains, IV-54 through VII-40 or VII-42, was published next but the date is in dispute. Mr. LeVert says it was published in 1557. The date of the first publication for the third group, the complete CENTURIES VIII, IX, and X, is also uncertain. Mr. LeVert thinks it was actually printed in 1558 and not after Nostradamus' death as the other biographers claim. Chavigny claimed that he was the one who edited and compiled the quatrains after Nostradamus' death, but many of the biographers doubt many of his claims.

The part that struck me was the comment, "Why this Bonhomme (1555) edition ended with IV-53 we do not know, but there are two major possibilities. Many of the almanacs and prognostications (written by Nostradamus) gave one reading per month, and there may have been some feeling that the 353 of Bonhomme plus twelve more for the months gave readings for a year. If this was the case, though, the schema was not developed or explained, and it is more likely that the printer stopped setting type when he reached a signature break."

It was this constant referral to the first book of quatrains ending in the middle of the Fourth Century that kept bothering me. It sounded familiar, and something in my subconscious was stirring. Then suddenly, I rushed to get my tattered and bookmarked copy of the quatrains which had been with me through this entire adventure. When I opened it to the place we had stopped working with John, I froze. I was totally stunned. We had stopped at the exact same place that Nostradamus' first edition had stopped!

When I first began to work with Brenda, I picked more than a hundred quatrains at random out of the book. These were the ones that caught my attention for various reasons. Then I developed a more systematic pattern and began at the front of the book and proceeded through the quatrains and centuries in order, omitting the ones already covered. I carefully checked them off and initialed who had translated them, Brenda or John.

My work with Brenda began in July 1986 (after the initiator, Elena, had moved to Alaska) and continued for six months, becoming sporadic around the beginning of 1987. During that short time we succeeded in covering over 400 quatrains. When she could no longer work on this project John came into the picture and we interpreted over 100 of the quatrains in the six weeks from April to May of 1987, before he moved to Florida. The last quatrain covered by John was CENTURY IV-35. During the summer of 1987 I was able to have a few sessions with Brenda, but she was experiencing psychic burn-out and wanted to stop the sessions. Every appointment after that was canceled for one reason or another. This brought us up to CENTURY IV-65, the last to be interpreted in this book. The utterly amazing thing is that this brings us to the exact number that LeVert thought were intended for Nostradamus' first book of quatrains: 353 plus 12.

This, to me, was mind-boggling. I could only hold Ms. Cheetham's book and stare at the numbers. I had experienced the same feeling when I first realized that I might be helping Nostradamus to write these quatrains. How, by any stretch of the imagination, could this be coincidence? Why did we stop in the middle of the Fourth Century at the exact same place that Nostradamus stopped his first edition? Was he faced with the same problem that I was? Just as my source of communication was cut off, was his also? Just as I decided to go ahead and assemble the quatrains that I had and try for publication, did he decide the same thing, to go ahead with what he had? The implications were beyond my mind's capacity to comprehend. It only gave me a headache and made the room spin. This is probably why the guardian kept insisting that I merely do the work and not ask questions.

I had enjoyed these meetings with Nostradamus and deeply regretted that we parted with the job half done. There were still roughly 450 quatrains that had not been deciphered, but I could now see the faint glimmer of a light on the distant horizon. If we were so closely tied with the great master that we were influencing the writing and publishing of his quatrains, then there was hope. If he published almost 1000 quatrains, that meant that my job wasn't finished. Either I was to continue to be involved with him, or the remainder came from someone else. Maybe it was destined that I would find another subject and regain contact with the great man. Only the future would hold the answers to this enigma. My discovery of this similarity (both of us stopping in the middle of the Fourth Century) only served to emphasize that I and the other players in this strange scenario were mere pawns being manipulated by higher powers in the invisible dimensions. Since the project seemed to be for the good of all humanity, I knew I would follow wherever it led. I had made my commitment at the beginning and I knew I could not renege it now.

Laver quotes from Carl G. Jung, the famous psychologist, referring to the Collective Unconscious: "The unconscious is anything but a capsulated personal system; it is the wide world, and objectively as open as the world ... a boundless expanse full of unprecedented certainty, with apparently no inside and no outside, no above and no below, no here and no there, no mine and no thine, no good and no bad. It is the world of water, where everything living floats in suspension; where the kingdom of the sympathetic system, of the soul of everything living begins, where I am inseparably this and that, and this and that are I; where I experience the other person in myself, and the other, as myself, experiences me." (*The Integration of the Personality.*)

Quote from Laver: "In this World-Soul or Collective Unconscious there is certainly all the Past, and if there is anything in Nostradamus ... there is all the Future also, and both Future and Past are but one Eternal Present. The mind grows dizzy at the edge of this abyss. We cling to our pathetic individualities and would have them continue for ever, not knowing that the phrase has no meaning and that the Ego is not the essential part of ourselves. We are already absorbed into the fullness of God, and even if this absorption were still to come it would not be annihilation, for the Ocean into which we are absorbed is not an Ocean of Matter but an Ocean of Mind. But Mind is a unity and to be part of it is to be all of it. Physically we are animals, but psychically and spiritually we are trees, or rather we are One Tree and its name is the Banyan Tree. We are members one of another and Time is merely one of our dimensions."

Was this concept what the guardian of the tapestry had hinted at when he told us we were like children in kindergarten asking college questions? He said we were not yet ready to try to understand what was behind this whole project. Maybe James Laver came very close to comprehending the workings of this mechanism, even though he wrote these words over 40 years before we were launched into our adventure.

In his book Laver refers to CENTURY VIII-99: "Through the powers of three temporal kings, the sacred seat will be put in another place, where the substance of the body and the spirit will be restored and received as the true seat." He acknowledged that it referred to the Papacy, but could not see how the prophecy could come to pass since it was unlikely that the seat of the Vatican would be moved away from Rome. But I wonder if the translation of the three temporary kings might refer to the last three popes. It has been predicted that they will be the last of the Papacy before the destruction of Rome by the Anti-Christ. (See Chapter 15, "The Last Three Popes," and Chapter 16, "The Ravage of the Church," in Volume One.)

When these predictions concerning the destruction of the church first came forth, I was horrified. How dare I write something that would be considered so radical, controversial, and even heretical? I'm a Christian and a former Sunday school teacher who has no wish to see harm befall any religious institution. I tried to argue with Nostradamus that these predictions were merely wish-fulfillment on his part because he was under such persecution by the Inquisition. He admitted that he did have such feelings, but insisted he was accurately reporting what he saw in his magic mirror. With much misgivings, I combined the various quatrains which related to the church into two chapters of the first volume. I decided that I must report what was given to me and not censor or change anything simply because it made me uncomfortable. If I hadn't made that decision, I probably wouldn't have written these two volumes at all, because *all* of their future contents certainly disturbed me.

But then in my research I came across a remarkable discovery which greatly reduced the burden of guilt I was feeling. I found that we were not the first to predict the destruction of the Catholic Church. A man who lived over 800 years ago, and 400 years before Nostradamus, also saw the same vision.

The Irish St. Malachi was a bishop who lived from 1094 to 1148. In 1139 he went to Rome, and while there he had a remarkable prophetic vision. He saw all the popes that would sit in Saint Peter's Chair. He didn't identify them by name, but rather by the most striking events of their reign or by their coat-of-arms. He wrote the list down, mostly referring to each one by a two-word Latin motto, and deposited his predictions in the archives of the Vatican. Malachi died on his way home and his prophecies lay forgotten in the archives until they were rediscovered at the end of the 16th century. They were first published in 1554 at Venice. Did Nostradamus have access to the predictions of Malachi? It's possible but not probable as communications were not as widespread as they are today. Also, the priest's prophecies didn't really become known until after Nostradamus' death when they were published again in 1595.

According to Malachi's list there are only three more popes remaining. Interpreters in the past thought he meant that when the time of the last pope was reached, the end of the world would occur, or possibly the Second Coming of Christ. The remainder of Malachi's list are: (1) Flors Florum: Pope Paul VI, who died in 1978 after a 15-year reign. Pope Paul VI carried a fleur-de-lis on his coat of arms. (2) De Medietate Lunæ: Pope

John Paul I, who only served as pope for one month before dying of a heart attack. Even if one does not know Latin, this phrase can be easily seen to connote "from the half moon," or "moon to moon," and that's exactly how long that poor pope lasted. (3) De Labore Solis: the present Pope John Paul II, because he came up from the earth of the common people. He took the name John Paul in honor of his fallen predecessor. (4) De Gloria Olivæ: the one who will have a short reign before our last pope, the tool of the Anti-Christ, comes upon the scene.

Instead of giving the last pope a two-word motto, Malachi assigned him a whole sentence. The way it's worded it sounded as though he was inferring that this would be the pope at the end of the world. "In persecutione extrema sanctæ Romanæ Ecclesiæ sedebit Petrus Romanus qui pascet oves in multis tribulationibus; quibus transactis, civitas septicollis diruetur, et Judex tremendus judicabit populum." Translation: "During the final persecution of the Holy Roman Church, there will sit upon the throne Peter the Roman, who will pasture his flock in the midst of many tribulations; with these passed, the city of the seven hills will be destroyed; and the Great Judge will then judge the peoples." It is said that the name "Peter" is more than just the name of a person; it indicates a last epoch in contrast to that of Peter the Apostle who began it.

Laver predicted that according to the average reign of most of the popes, the time period of the last pope would bring us to the end of the 20th century. The only difference between our predictions is that we don't see it as the end of the world, or the Second Coming. We were told by Nostradamus that the destruction of Rome and the dissolution of the church would follow the havoc created by the betrayal of the last pope as the tool of the Anti-Christ. I found an old saying about Rome that seems to fit: "While stands the Colosseum, Rome shall stand, when falls the Colosseum, Rome shall fall, and when Rome, falls the world."

Nostradamus' *Centuries* were condemned by Pope Pius VI in 1781, and have occasionally been the center of ecclesiastical controversy ever since. The Vatican forbade the book because it was "found to contain a prophecy of the abolition of the papal authority." So apparently, even within the confines of the Papacy, they saw something within the quatrains which related to the future of the church.

With the aid of the interlibrary loan program, I came across the book, *After Nostradamus,* by A. Voldben, which was translated from the Italian. In this book the author traces the prophecies of not only Nostradamus, but many seers down through the ages to the present Jeane Dixon. It was amazing that the gist of their prophecies followed the same pattern as ours. Mr. Voldben said that a few of these prophets had dared to put dates on the coming events. He said this was always hazardous and presumptuous because the events of the cosmos do not conform to our petty Earth calendar, and many of the dates have come and gone without the event occurring. He said it was more important that they had agreed upon the same *sequence* of events, and not the dates. Thus, it may be that our dates are also not accurate, even with Nostradamus supplying the astrological references. Did all of these prophets, Nostradamus included, dip into a common thought pool or find a common thread? Whether or not what they saw will become reality, it can't be denied that somehow they were all seeing the same things and interpreting them within their own distinct vocabulary and concept structure.

This brings us to the most modern of the prophets, Jeane Dixon. When several books mentioned her predictions of the Anti-Christ, I knew I would have to read her book. Again, the similarity is something I cannot totally fathom. It's as though we were both reading from the same script. In *My Life and Prophecies* she discusses many of the concepts that have been presented in this book, including the last pope and trouble in the Catholic Church. Dixon said that one of our most influential national institutions was being used as a cover-up for chemical and bacteriological warfare experiments. She saw these experiments being conducted on the Indian and Russian borders and foresaw germ warfare in the future.

She also could see the infamous "Cabal" of which I was hesitant to write. She calls it the "government within a government" and says they are financed by a well-oiled political "machine." They control our elections and numerous social and economic factors that we are unaware of. She also saw that a member of this "machine" lives in New York City. Quote: "The social and religious chaos generated by this political machine throughout the United States will prepare the nation for the coming of the prophet of the Anti-Christ. This political unit of the East will be the tool of the serpent in delivering the masses to him."

This brings us to her most powerful prediction and, to me, the most shaking: Her knowledge of the coming Anti-Christ, even to his exact birthdate. She says there is no doubt in her mind that the prophet of the Anti-Christ and the Anti-Christ himself are actual identifiable persons, and not ideologies or governments.

On *February 5, 1962* Jean Dixon had a powerful vision that was filled with symbolism. From these symbols Ms. Dixon deduced that the person who will be known as the Anti-Christ was born that day. She saw that his life would parallel the life of Christ to a remarkable degree, even though he was to be the mirror image or exact opposite of Him. She saw that he was no longer in the country where he had been born but had been taken to another Middle Eastern country, possibly a densely populated area of the United Arab Republic. She didn't know the reason for the move, but felt there were forces working around him that protect him. She said an event of tremendous importance would happen to him around the age of 11 that would make him aware of his satanic mission and purpose in life. Quote: "He will then expand his influence, and those around him will finally form a small nucleus of dedicated followers when he reaches the age of 19. He will work quietly with them until he is 29 or 30 years old, when the forcefulness and impact of his presence in the world will begin to bear his forbidden fruit." She saw that he would have the backing of a powerful "machine" that would advance his cause beyond anything ever thought possible.

Her remarks about the prophet or forerunner of the false Christ sound similar to John's impressions of the evil Imam. She thinks he is the one referred to in the Bible in the book of Revelation 13.11–15:

"And I saw another beast coming up out of the earth, and it had two horns like those of a lamb, but it spoke as does a dragon. And it exercised all the authority of the former beast in its sight; and it made the earth and the inhabitants therein to worship the first beast. ... And it did great signs, so as even to make fire come down from heaven upon earth in the sight of mankind. And it leads astray the inhabitants of the earth, by reason of the signs which it was permitted to do in the sight of the beast, telling the inhabitants of the earth to make an image to the beast ... and to cause that whoever should not worship the image of the beast should be killed."

Quote from Dixon: "His domain will be the intellectual seduction of mankind. It means a mixture of political, philosophical, and religious ideology that will throw the populations of the world into a deep crisis of faith in God. ... As official forerunner, one of his (the prophet's) first duties and responsibilities in readying the world for the advent of his 'master' is to manipulate the available propaganda machines. With teaching and propaganda the prophet will cause people not merely to accept the Anti-Christ but rather to desire him with positive enthusiasm, to create the conditions of his coming and to participate actively in organizing the frightful and terrifying despotism of his World Empire.

"Secondly, there will be 'miracles,' the signs and wonders that will 'lead astray the inhabitants of the earth.' His most convincing sign will be the conquest of the powers of nature, of which the 'fire from heaven' is the ultimate symbol. These will not be supernatural or preternatural events, but rather the prodigies of science and human achievements, but interpreted in such a way as to lead men away from God and toward the worship of the Anti-Christ."

Note the similarity between this fire from heaven and Nostradamus' prediction that Rome would be destroyed by some type of force or fire coming down from the sky. He was never able to clarify whether this would be caused by an extremely unusual natural event or something man-made. It astonished him so much that he could not define it.

"The prophet will communicate to men through his world propaganda machine the supreme ambitions of human science. He will announce that science is able to penetrate all of the secrets of nature, to domesticate all of the forces of nature, especially those of life, indeed of human life itself! He will profess that men will be able to live as they please, so long as they please, and to die as and when they please—and all without suffering— if they will only follow him."

This all sounds very much like the scene we were shown of the evil Imam and the group of backers in the estate on the banks of the Nile.

These are all supposed to be preparations accomplished before the Anti-Christ enters the public scene. Ms. Dixon says that from his first appearance he will completely mesmerize the youth of the world. Around the time he is 30 years old, as a result of the tremendous propaganda efforts by the prophet of the Anti-Christ, "the youth will have become extremely vulnerable to the coming of the man. I see that the youth of the world will accept him and will work closely with him in placing the world into his eager hands. ... When the 'man' has reached the age reserved for the outset of his mission, no one will be able to hold the children back, for to capture the youth and, through them, the world, the little boy was born." She says that through our far-advanced communications network the entire world will be exposed to this new "spiritual" ruler even though his headquarters will be in the Holy Land.

Ms. Dixon states: "The Anti-Christ will be a phenomenon of the political order. He is not simply a religious 'heretic' whom the world at large could safely ignore. No! He will hold earthly power in his hands and use it as his instrument. All the tyrants of history are mere children in comparison with him. This means first of all that he will be a military figure beyond anything the world has ever previously seen. He will conquer the whole earth and hold it in complete mastery with the most modern weapons. He will rule his new World Empire with the utmost of military might and glory. Furthermore, the Bible prophecies make it intelligible that the World Empire of the Anti-Christ will be a totalitarian state in the most extreme meaning of the word. He will exercise power over the entire world and each person intensively, controlling even his thoughts. There will be no 'neighboring state,' and the whole world will become an island within the universe. War as it has been known will fade away, and the Anti-Christ will announce himself as the 'prince of peace.' ... But I foresee something deeper in the coming godless social order of the Anti-Christ, something more than mere political system, something that reaches into the fallen condition of human nature. He will establish and lead a strange and fundamentally anti-human 'religion' of atheism and anti-religion. ... So there is more involved here than the mere political authority of a World Empire. I see two definite characteristics distinguishing the Anti-Christ: dominion over men with a rod of iron and seduction of their minds by a false ideology and propaganda. He will present himself to all mankind as the supreme ruler who stills and quells all warfare on Earth, as the teacher of man's new modernized approach to life that leaves the Christian heritage behind as outmoded, and as the 'redeemer' of all men from their old fears, guilt complexes, and mistreatment of each other. He will be the exact opposite of Christ. He will be His adversary and at the same time appear to be His imitator. ... He will seem to be a religious figure, offering to men a strangely twisted fulfillment of their spiritual desires. ... He will receive the worship of many people, as if he, in his own person, were actually God."

She quotes Cardinal Newman's comments on the Anti-Christ: "He promises you civil liberty; he promises you equality; he promises you trade and wealth; he promises you a remission of taxes; he promises you reform. This is the way in which he conceals from you the kind of work to which he is putting you; he tempts you to rail against your rulers and superiors; he does so himself, and induces you to imitate him or he promises you illumination. He offers you knowledge of science, philosophy and enlargement of mind. He scoffs at times gone by; he scoffs at every institution that reveres them."

We can only stand in awe that our predictions are the same as a prophet who lived 800 years ago, as well as a modern seer. It adds validation to what Nostradamus revealed to us. With evidence this overwhelming, there can only be one conclusion. We really were in touch with the great master. He was correctly passing on to us what his visions revealed to him, even though in the beginning we were ready to dismiss it as an absolute absurdity. Once again, I wondered if we were locked into this future that Nostradamus saw in his mirror, or now that we are forewarned, can we follow an alternate time line that branches off from the main nexus of the Anti-Christ? Can we succeed in lessening the monster's impact now that we have been given enough clues? Will we recognize him when he first begins his devious plans? Nostradamus said his main concern was that we not be caught off guard, that we have some hay behind us to land on. But will the world listen and take our hopes for humanity to safe harbor when the monster rears his ugly head?

The Anti-Christ, the Imam, and their backers have all laid their plans well. They have the patience to wait generations to carry out their plan to turn the world into a state of absolute anarchy, so they can control it under absolute power according to their whims. They have laid their plans almost too well, but they didn't foresee the one factor that might prove their undoing. How could they possibly know that the instrument of their destruction would be an old man who sat in his study staring for hours on end at a black polished mirror? What possible threat could a man be who had died 400 years ago? No one anticipated the power and love that one man felt as he sat mesmerized watching the unfolding of events of unspeakable horror. Because he lived in a time when revealing such things could have cost him his life, he was fully justified in keeping the terrible visions to himself. But he could not. He felt, as I do, that the information was revealed for a reason. And that reason was to try to save humanity. He found a way to break through the barriers of time and space to reveal to us the most carefully guarded secrets in the world. No one counted on the abilities of a true genius and an undisputable magician and prophet: Nostradamus.

Let us reassure him that his warnings have not been in vain, nor have they come too late. Let us promise him that now that we know the truth, we will do everything in our power to accomplish what he wished, to save humankind and our beloved Earth. His mission has been accomplished. The rest is up to us.

Through the veil of time and the mists of past, present and future (which all seemed to be blended together in his eyes) he has offered us his hand to give us hope and salvation. A hope, an answer from the grave ... yet *not* from the grave, because in this misty other dimension the great master lives forever, and is forever concerned with humanity.

THE END OF VOLUME TWO.

Bibliography

BOSWELL, ROLFE, *Nostradamus Speaks,* New York, 1943.
CANTWELL, JR. M.D., ALAN, "AIDS and the Doctors of Death," *Wildfire Magazine,* Volume 4, No. 1, 1989.
CHEETHAM, ERIKA, *Further Prophecies of Nostradamus,* New York, 1985.
———, *The Prophecies of Nostradamus,* New York, 1975.
Collier's Encyclopedia and Yearbooks.
DIXON, JEANE, *My Life and Prophecies,* New York, 1969.
FORMAN, HENRY JAMES, *The Story of Prophecy,* New York, 1940.
HOWE, ELLIC, *Nostradamus and the Nazis,* London, 1965.
HUGHES, THOMAS PATRICK, *A Dictionary of Islam,* Delhi, 1973.
LAMONT, ANDRÉ, *Nostradamus Sees All,* Philadelphia, 1942.
LAVER, JAMES, *Nostradamus,* London, 1942.
LEONI, EDGAR, *Nostradamus: Life and Literature,* New York, 1961.
LE VERT, LIBERTÉ E., *The Prophecies and Enigmas of Nostradamus,* New Jersey, 1979.
LINDSAY, JACK, *Origins of Astrology,* London, 1971.
PATTERSON, FRANCINE, "Conversation with a Gorilla," *National Geographic,* October 1978.
ROBERTS, HENRY C., *The Complete Prophecies of Nostradamus,* New York, 1982.
VOLDBEN, A., *After Nostradamus,* New Jersey, 1974.
WARD, CHARLES, *Oracles of Nostradamus,* New York, 1940.
WOOLF, H. I., *Nostradamus,* London, 1944.

Index

A complete index and quatrain index for all three volumes of Conversations with Nostradamus *will appear at the end of Volume Three.*

Quatrain Index

About the Author

$\mathcal{D}$OLORES CANNON was born in 1931 in St. Louis, Missouri. She was educated and lived in Missouri until her marriage in 1951 to a career Navy man. She spent the next 20 years traveling all over the world as a typical Navy wife and raised her family.

In 1968 she had her first exposure to reincarnation via regressive hypnosis when her husband, an amateur hypnotist, stumbled across the past life of a woman he was working with who had a weight problem. At that time the "past life" subject was unorthodox and very few people were experimenting in the field. It sparked her interest, but had to be put aside as the demands of family life took precedence.

Photo by Richard Quick.

In 1970 her husband was discharged as a disabled veteran, and they retired to the hills of Arkansas. She then started her writing career and began selling her articles to various magazines and newspapers. When her children began lives of their own, her interest in regressive hypnosis and reincarnation was reawakened. She studied the various hypnosis methods and thus developed her own unique technique which enabled her to gain the most efficient release of information from her subjects. Since 1979 she has regressed and cataloged information gained from hundreds of volunteers. She calls herself a regressionist and a psychic researcher who records "lost" knowledge. The *Conversations with Nostradamus* trilogy are her first published books. *Jesus and the Essenes* has been published by Gateway Books in England. She has written eight other books (to be published) about her most interesting cases.

Dolores Cannon has four children and twelve grandchildren who demand that she be solidly balanced between the "real" world of her family and the "unseen" world of her work. If you wish to correspond with Dolores Cannon about her work, you may write to her at the following address. Please enclose a self-addressed stamped envelope for her reply.   Dolores Cannon, P.O. Box 754
Huntsville, AR 72740-0754